Paths to Excellence
and the Soviet School

John Dunstan

Lecturer in Soviet Education
Centre for Russian and East European Studies
and Faculty of Education, University of Birmingham

NFER Publishing Company

To Liz
my fiercest and dearest critic

Published by the NFER Publishing Company Ltd.,
Darville House, 2 Oxford Road East,
Windsor, Berks. SL4 1DF
Registered Office: The Mere, Upton Park, Slough, Berks. SL1 2DQ
First published 1978
© John Dunstan, 1977
ISBN 0 85633 150 3

Printed in Great Britain by
Staples Printers, Love Lane, Rochester, Kent.
Typeset by Cameographics Ltd., 33 Boulton Road, Reading, Berks.
Distributed in the USA by Humanities Press Inc.,
Atlantic Highlands, New Jersey 07716, USA.

CONTENTS

Contents   7

Preface

This book is a product of research carried out under the auspices of the Division of Education, University of Sheffield, and completed at the Centre for Russian and East European Studies (CREES), University of Birmingham. I wish to thank first of all Professor W.H.G. Armytage, Head of the Division, who supervised the work, and Professor R.W. Davies, Director of the Centre, who gave it his blessing; I am grateful to both for their help and constant encouragement. My thanks go also to Mr R.T. Pullin, University of Sheffield, for his careful scrutiny of part of the text. Drafts of several chapters were presented to the CREES Soviet Education Seminar and I benefited greatly from the comments of members, notably the late Geoffrey Barker, ever generous with his time and sagacity. Mr Jack Miller, editor of *Soviet Studies*, published by the University of Glasgow, merits acknowledgement of his friendly and constructive criticism of a section of the book; and since part of chapter 1 and most of chapter 6 appeared as an article in that journal I should like to take this opportunity of thanking him and his colleagues for agreeing to its reappearance.

Comments and materials on sports education in the USSR were kindly made available to me by Dr J.W. Riordan, University of Bradford, and Mr Alan Bell, Director of the National Documentation Centre for Sport, Physical Education and Recreation, which is located on the Birmingham campus. Some fascinating material on various aspects of provision for high-ability children which had yet to reach the bibliographies was supplied by Dr Marianna Butenschön of Hamburg. Mr Bryan Woodriff, Kingston Polytechnic, allowed me to read his unpublished work on foreign language teaching in the Soviet Union, and other material was furnished by the Society for Cultural Relations with the USSR, London. Documentation on mathematics and physics education was

provided by Mr George Avis, University of Bradford, Mr Tony
Fitzgerald, University of Birmingham, and Mr F.R. Watson,
University of Keele, and I am endebted to the last-named also for
access to the unpublished report of a study visit and to the British
Council for permission to use it. For similar reasons I am grateful to
Dr Brian Holmes, Institute of Education, University of London; the
Institute Library holds a valuable series of reports of the comparative
education tours to the USSR organized by the Universities of
London, Reading and Oxford over a number of years. For
consultations on mathematics teaching, learning and terminology I
should like to thank Dr Michael Cross, Mr Fitzgerald, Dr Tony
Gardiner and Ms Sue Rhodes.

Finally, I wish to record my thanks to the University of
Birmingham for sponsoring a research visit to the USSR which
enabled me to study fundamental documents not available in the
West and to make contact with educational institutions, and for
assisting me to visit libraries in West Germany for further data
collection. In this respect I am particularly endebted to Professor Dr
Oskar Anweiler and Herr Friedrich Kuebart, Institut für Pädagogik,
Ruhr-Universität, Bochum, for their interest and hospitality.

February 1978   N.J.D.

Introduction

The aim of this book on Soviet secondary education is to shed light on certain aspects of it which in the West are little known but nevertheless the object of intense curiosity, to dispel some common misunderstandings about it, and thus to make available something of the Soviet experience at a time of great change in secondary education in many parts of the Western world.[1] It focusses on high-ability children, shows why they have come to receive special attention, examines how they are provided for, and discusses the problems of differentiation and selection which many of these forms of provision entail.

Excellence of one kind or another is a matter of great interest to almost everybody. The heroes of the sports ground, the concert hall, the test circuit all have their admirers and their partisans. Other heroes, such as those of the research laboratory, are more likely to remain unsung. In either event, the performance which has earned them their reputation is the outcome of much investment of time and energy by themselves and others. In many cases it began at school, and the level of performance must so often be related to the quality and the degree of the attention paid to overt and covert talent in those formative years.

Yet excellence is not something vouchsafed only to a favoured few; if it seems to be such, there is cause for concern. Human potential is immeasurable and ought to be given every opportunity to manifest itself and every stimulus to develop. It is, moreover, many-sided. It is not something to be encouraged in one field of worthy endeavour and ignored in another. If it is a sin to bury one's own talent, it is a greater sin to bury someone else's. The school has a duty to foster all the positive endowments of all the children within its charge, and not only the individual but the whole society will be the beneficiary. There is a utilitarian argument here which perhaps merits wider attention.

Of course, all this is easier said than done. There are immense difficulties, firstly with regard to the feasibility of provision of manpower and resources, and secondly with respect to the nature of that provision and its social implications; children are variously endowed and differentiation sooner or later raises the problem of selection and the spectre of privilege. At times the prevailing ethos may be more concerned to lay the ghost than to raise it. That too is difficult enough. But at other times the climate may favour differentiation despite all the complexities which accompany it. At others again, the mood will be one of compromise and a quest for balance.

       *   *   *   *   *   *   *   *   *   *

It is a commonplace that secondary education in the USSR is organized on a comprehensive basis, yet the country also possesses special schools for clever children. This true but incomplete picture fascinates Western observers of all political persuasions. Epithets like 'realist' and 'elitist' fly thick as leaves on the autumn wind. Their comments are not infrequently based on little evidence and less understanding. However, they seem to feel that the Soviet experience has some bearing on the situation close at hand, either as something to be imitated or as something to be shunned; and given this feeling it is surely important to know more about what really happens, more about the chain of issues and alternatives and solutions linked to the dilemma of enabling the high-ability child to achieve his or her potential while simultaneously seeking the good of the greatest number. These things the present book seeks to illustrate and to appraise.

Two misconceptions about Soviet education, one partial and one complete, merit a brief mention here. It is sometimes said that the Soviet school has been moving away from uniformity. The situation, however, is not as clear-cut as this. There has certainly been a noticeable movement towards diversification over the 1960s, but more recently the process seems to have greatly slowed down and altered its nature. In the course of this study we shall chart these developments and try to account for the change.

There is a further notion that Soviet education along with other institutions is an enormous juggernaut lumbering relentlessly upon its way, directed single-mindedly from above and entirely unresponsive to voices from below. A growing body of research has shown that this 'totalitarian' model is untenable. Soviet education does not exclude differences of view or groupings of those who advance them. Prior to decision-taking, expressions of opinion are frequently invited and considered, and even after the decisions have been reached the defeated interests are not necessarily silenced. To be sure, education is not the most sensitive of areas, and here as elsewhere criticism must not touch the fundamentals of the system. With this reservation, dissentient voices may be raised again not only in the event of a change in policy but also because they persist and have powerful backing. Attitudes and behaviour may sometimes impede or modify the implementation of a programme, while strong disagreement may result in compromise. The following pages will provide further evidence on these points also.

＊　＊　＊　＊　＊　＊　＊　＊　＊　＊

The structure of the book is as follows. It traces and discusses, successively, the formative forces, origins, development, present state and prospects of a number of institutions. Firstly, the standard 'unified' school is broadly examined with particular regard to the question of differentiation and to cognitive aspects of the curriculum. Next, attention is turned to variations on the prototype in the pursuit of excellence in a diversity of fields: schools for the arts, sports schools, language schools, mathematics and physics boarding schools, and other mass schools with a special profile. Then the study explores strategies for encouraging special talent beside or within the formal curriculum of the ordinary school: beside it in the shape of optional studies, and within it by means of the 'differentiated approach' or by experimental structures. Finally, new and changing forms of traditional extra-curricular means of nurturing gifts are considered. A concluding chapter draws the foregoing into an overall pattern, and a brief selection of illustrative materials is provided as appendices.

A few comments on data may be made. A feature of the book is that it is based primarily on a wide range of Soviet sources, the vast majority of which are not available in translation. (This is less true of chapter 3, for which little such material could be found.) Ranging from official documents to news flashes, from research papers to popular articles, they constitute, despite difficulties of interpretation, the most important repository of ideas and information. The sources have been partly supplemented by drawing on the work of Western scholars, and here it is appropriate to mention the major contribution to research on Soviet education made in recent years by West Germany. Eye-witness accounts by visitors have been used, including the author's own impressions; the danger of subjectivity must be faced, but on the other hand such reports can be highly perceptive and sometimes they bring more formal materials to life.

The persons of this drama are a motley gathering: scientists from the academician to the local physics teacher, educators from the President of the USSR Academy of Pedagogical Sciences to the boarding-school tutor, politicians, administrators, industrial workers, ambitious parents, and clever children. Although the last-mentioned are the central characters, our glimpses of them are tantalisingly few; and this, though unavoidable, is regretted. So one of their representatives who does not appear elsewhere shall be singled out here as he delights the assembled children and scientists at the end of the Novosibirsk Maths and Physics Summer School with his particular version of an official plan fulfilment report: 'Altogether we have slept 60,000 hours, drunk 9,000 litres of water, and eaten 23,000 breakfasts, dinners and suppers, *i.e.* 15 tons of various foodstuffs'.[2] This lack of deference to the sacred cows of bureaucracy is curiously encouraging. And having listened to him, we now have our own plan to fulfil.

Notes

1 In view of the interest which the topic has attracted in the West, there is a surprising absence of detailed treatment of it in English. The first stage of the debate is summarized with terse discernment by Nicholas De Witt, *Education and Professional Employment in the USSR* (Washington, DC, 1961), 18-19, and discussed by Richard V. Rapacz, 'Polytechnical Education and the New Soviet School Reforms', in George Z.F. Bereday and Jaan Pennar (eds.), *The Politics of Soviet Education* (New York, 1960), 36-44. The subject was reviewed by John J. Figueroa, 'Selection and Differentiation in Soviet Schools', in Edmund J. King (ed.), *Communist Education* (London, 1963), 124-152. The only reasonably up-to-date brief study of the whole problem, written from a critically sympathetic standpoint, is Joan Simon, 'Differentiation of Secondary Education in the USSR', *Forum for the Discussion of New Trends in Education,* vol. 11, no. 3 (Summer 1969), 87-90. There is a largely factual account of means to develop individual aptitudes in the IIEP report 'Observations of the IIEP Mission to the USSR', in *Educational Planning in the USSR*·(Paris, 1968), 247-252, based on a study tour of 1965 but still interesting and useful. Of several articles published in German, among the most important are: Detlef Glowka, 'Das sowjetische Schulwesen am Beginn einer neuen Etappe?', *Neue Sammlung,* vol. 7, no. 3 (May-June 1967), 203-222, a lucid and comprehensive analysis; Wolfgang Mitter, 'Einheitlichkeit und Differenzierung als Problem der sowjetischen Schulreform', in Oskar Anweiler (ed.), *Bildungsreformen in Osteuropa* (Stuttgart, 1969), 108-140, up to the time of its appearance the most complete treatment of the present topic; and, from the GDR, W. Kienitz and H. Brauer,·'Das neue System des Wahlunterrichts in der sowjetischen Mittelschule', *Vergleichende Pädagogik,* vol. 3 (1967), 377-

383, useful as a candid inside view of what has become a distinctive feature of the contemporary curriculum. On the other hand, the full-length work by Kienitz and others, *Einheitlichkeit und Differenzierung im Bildungswesen* (Berlin [East], 1971), while offering a convenient juxtaposition of data, appears to be inhibited by its comparative framework from a searching examination of the problems which confront specialized schools in the USSR. Glowka discusses the question of differentiation in its social context in his valuable study *Schulreform und Gesellschaft in der Sowjetunion 1958-1968* (Stuttgart, 1970); here he concentrates more on policy development and implementation than on the structural and functional characteristics and problems of the resultant institutional forms. The Soviet curriculum reform against the background of the revolution in science and technology is most fully presented in Gerda Achinger, *Die Schulreform in der UdSSR* (Munich, 1973. A recent examination of the senior stage of secondary education in the USSR and Eastern Europe. Wolfgang Milter and Leonid Novikov, *Sekunderabschlüsse mit Hochschulreïfe im internationalen Vergleïch* (Weinheim and Basel, 1976), which was received only when this book was in proof, also includes a section (181-202) on the main problems of differentation in the Soviet School, this is sound, but adds nothing of substance to our own findings.

2   A.A. Bers and B.A. Frolov, *Olimpiada — pervyi shag v nauku* (M., 1964), 29.

Chapter 1

The Soviet School:
The First Fifty Years

Differentiation in the Early Soviet School

If differentiation is defined as modification into special forms for special functions, Soviet education at the post-primary stage has always been differentiated to a greater or lesser extent; indeed, from 1926 to 1934 this was partly true of the primary level as well. Throughout the Soviet period, educational policy has moved hither and thither in the area between the poles of a common course for all children for as long as reasonable, on the one hand, and vocational training from as early an age as feasible, on the other. The school has followed with a greater or lesser degree of alacrity depending on the pace of policy change and the practical circumstances.[1]

Theoretically, the Soviet school was least differentiated at its inception. The so-called unified labour school of 1918 had the lofty but, given the situation of chaos, civil war and lack of resources, quite unrealistic goal of five years' primary (from 8-plus) and four years' secondary schooling for all. The school was free, compulsory, coeducational and secular. It was pervaded with the humanistic views on education of Lunacharsky, Commissar for Education, and of Lenin's wife Krupskaya, to some degree reminiscent of the young Marx's vision of the future society in which the free all-round development of the individual is assured as he works at a variety of tasks ('to hunt in the morning...') and his interests are identified with the community's. The utilitarian tradition of Russian education, Tolstoyan ideas of free upbringing and Western European and American reform pedagogy blended well with this. Great importance was attached also to the child's relationship with his social environment, but his own creative development was vital and a number of skills were to be taught as part of general schooling. Among many others, these included modelling, woodwork and metalwork, while agriculture had a central role to play in rural education.

Lenin may well have preferred the more concrete formulation of the older Marx, for whom education should be intellectual, physical and technical; Marx defined the latter component (*polytechnische Ausbildung*) as the general scientific principles of all processes of production, and at the same time an initiation into the practical use of the basic tools of all trades.[2] Lenin added the concepts of hard work and conscious discipline; in 1920 he called for a 'polytechnical horizon' and consented only reluctantly to a reduction in the length of the unified labour school course for the sake of earlier vocational training.

Progressive educationists, however, were not of one mind. Oskar Anweiler and Sheila Fitzpatrick have each drawn attention to the controversy on various matters between the 'orthodox progressives' of the Petrograd Collegium of Narkompros (the People's Commissariat of Education) and the 'leftists' of Moscow.[3] The Petrograders sought a triple division of the two senior classes into arts, engineering, and mathematics and science courses, while for the Muscovites this infringed the principle of the unified school. Lunacharsky, himself a moderate though with sympathies for the Petrograd line, compromised by making such arrangements optional, depending on local circumstances.[4] That the state needed specialists and that young people had different inclinations and gifts was even affirmed in the document 'Basic Principles of the Unified Labour School' accompanying the decree of 16 October 1918, and it went on: 'Therefore from a certain age, about 14, a division into a number of tracks or groupings is permitted in the school, but in such a way that many basic subjects remain common to all pupils'.[5] This would be the recipe for producing, not the blinkered specialist nor the superficial know-all, but the educated person. It was not to be forgotten in the 1960s when the issue again became topical.[6]

Opposition to attempts by Narkompros to turn certain vocational and technical schools surviving from the tsarist era into general schools, or occasionally technical *vuzy* (institutions of higher education), was spearheaded by the trades unions. Pressing needs of the national economy soon brought about the emergence of a new line, with the proponents of the unified labour school increasingly on the defensive, being under attack also from the Ukrainian Narkompros. Glavprofobr (the Chief Committee on Vocational and Technical Education) was set up in January 1920, with responsibility for vocational and technical training at all levels and considerable independence from the rest of Narkompros, thus symbolising the point of departure from the principle of the unified school. Thus, although in September 1920 Lunacharsky said that the unified school was a school common to all in the sense of the rights of admission and the rights which it gave on completion, but at the same time it could be diversified and they had recommended that the senior classes of the secondary stage should be divided into two or three branches so that young people could select a specialism in accordance with their inclinations, it was another kind of differentiation — by type of school — that was more characteristic of the decade.[7]

During the period of the New Economic Policy (NEP) the Soviet school acquired a highly diversified structure which it is beyond the scope of this historical outline to sketch in more than the barest detail.[8] A new statute on the unified labour school was issued in December 1923, changing the primary stage to four years and the full secondary one to five (with a middle course of three years and a senior one of two). Meanwhile full primary education for all remained a pipe dream. Nevertheless, in addition to the unified labour school, schools for peasant youth (*shkoly krest'yanskoi molodezhi*, ShKM) were set up in 1923 to produce a rural intelligentsia. Originally they covered only forms 5 to 7 (*i.e.* from 12-plus), but in 1927 it was decided that within three years they should become the standard seven-year school for rural areas, thus including the primary level. In 1926 seven-year industrial schools (*fabrichno-zavodskie semiletki*, FZS) with 8-plus entry were established.[9] These innovations provide the earliest and most extreme Soviet examples of economic necessity causing drastic modifications to the principle of the unified school to the extent of vertical *ab initio* differentiation.

The optional horizontal differentiation within forms 8 and 9 of the unified labour school took on a new and compulsory format in 1924, when pupils had to choose one of three vocational courses, catering mainly for primary-school teachers; for civil servants; and for workers in commerce, industry and agriculture, and occupying up to a third of their time. The aim was to produce manpower for the local economy and to relieve pressure on entry to higher education where the workers' faculties (*rabfaki*) enjoyed priority, but these courses had a chequered history.[10] According to figures for December 1926, white-collar employees' children were over-represented in RSFSR schools possessing both the middle and senior courses (34 per cent of enrolment but 12.3 per cent of the working population), and those of industrial workers were slightly under-represented in such schools

(13.6 per cent of enrolment compared to 17 per cent of the working population, which was predominantly agricultural at this time).[11] In contrast to that of white-collar employees' children, the proportion of working-class children decreased as they proceeded from one form to the next; rural children were greatly under-represented in the senior classes, and in the cities senior secondary education, though available, remained alien to workers and their children.[12] The old Russian gymnasium was new in name only, and remained academic, apolitical and effectively middle-class; few of its pupils could be admitted to *vuzy* because of the class basis of selection, but their parents did their best to secure them the maximum possible secondary education.[13]

The year 1928 marked the start of a new era in Soviet history which demonstrated strikingly the effects of rapid economic development on social mobility. After the inauguration of the First Five-Year Plan, industrialization transformed an economically backward country into a great power within a remarkably short space of time and despite the intervention of the Second World War in 1941. The rapid rate of growth generated an enormous demand for skilled and highly skilled workers, in both the physical and intellectual senses. Between 1926 and 1937 the total of workers and employees more than doubled, while that of the intelligentsia increased 3.8 times (within this category the scientific intelligentsia increased 5.9 times and engineers and architects 7.9).[14]

Correspondingly, the period of the Five-Year Plans brought attempts to turn the senior classes of the unified labour school into vocational or secondary technical schools, but mainly by the Komsomol leadership who objected to its social composition. These were resisted by Lunacharsky, but after he was replaced by A.S. Bubnov in 1929 Narkompros itself took a sharp turn towards vocationalism. In 1930 the unified labour school in the traditional form was in effect abolished and replaced by a system of job-oriented education for all children from the age of eleven, either in the greatly enhanced FZSs in the industrial cities, schools for collective farm youth *(shkoly kolkhoznoi molodezhi,* with the old initials ShKM) in the country, or seven-year community schools *(shkoly kommunal'noi semiletki,* ShKS) in rural towns. The two senior classes were now converted into additional secondary technical schools.[15] For the relatively short time that these arrangements remained in force the Soviet school was diversified more thoroughly than ever before, albeit on an essentially geographical basis, in accordance with the demands of local production and for the sake of economic development. From the centre of the educational stage — at least in theory — the child himself had over the 1920s been pushed into the wings, where he was to remain for decades.

The Problem of Giftedness

The question of excellence and how to cater for it within the unified labour school framework had received very little attention during the first Soviet decade. This was not due to some ideological taboo, but to practical circumstances. Theoretically, in the enterprising and relatively free educational atmosphere of the 1920s, all sorts of exciting experiments might have been tried out. Lunacharsky himself had paved the way in the 1918 declaration on the unified labour school. Stressing the importance of the individual in socialist culture, while pointing out that this individual would bring his endowments to full flowering only in the harmonious and solidary society of his peers, Lunacharsky maintained that socialist upbringing enabled the individual to pride himself on the development of all his abilities in order to serve the whole collective. From this he concluded: 'The aim here is to avoid impeding the development (*izbezhat' zaderzhki v razvitii*) of especially gifted natures'.[16] Of course, this is not the same as to say that 'especially gifted natures' should be actively developed, but it is implicit, since it may be impossible to avoid impeding their development without giving them particular attention. Hence it was that in 1920 a decree of the government set up a special fund for the support of youthful gifts,[17] and schools for outstanding artistic talent founded before the revolution continued to receive encouragement.

However, Lunacharsky went on to say something else. 'But if this aim is honourable and in no way to be disdained', he continued, 'another is much more important — to reduce if possible the number of the backward'. It was a question of priorities. In the situation of widespread illiteracy among both children and adults the notion of devoting time and money to the exceptionally able must have seemed irrelevant to the idealistic builders of the new society for whom literacy was the mortar that would bind the stones together. It was essential for the maximum assimilation of political teaching and for the acquisition of labour skills. But the campaign against illiteracy was hampered by the chaos and privations of the early years; during NEP cultural questions were given low priority in the face of economic constraints, funds for education were transferred to local budgets and thus the campaign received a further though temporary setback; and the census of December 1926 told its own dreary story. While 68.9 per cent of the population aged between 16 and 34 were literate, only 64.5 per cent of those between 12 and 15 and 47.1 per cent of eight- to eleven-year-olds were so classified; in other words, illiteracy was increasing from below,[18] and it took the cultural drive of the Five-Year Plan era to solve the greater part of the problem. Given this and many other difficulties besetting mass education, it is not in the least surprising that little was heard about the needs of gifted children.

On the other hand, this was also a time when educationists assiduously studied and enthusiastically advocated the adaptation of leading trends in progressive Western pedagogical thought. Conservative teachers, material circumstances and more important priorities might well retard or prevent their implementation, but the foreign books and journals and the ideas they contained steadily came in. Some of these ideas related to special education for intellectually gifted children. Josef Petzoldt's earlier notions of educating the gifted to form a leadership elite were rejected on political, moral and pedagogical grounds, but American enrichment programmes, with a system of accelerated groups according to IQ or special classes working to extended syllabuses, met with the approval of certain Soviet educationists. The most eminent of these was P.P. Blonsky, who is associated with the science (or pseudo-science, depending on one's position) of pedology. It may be interesting to look at Blonsky's views on the education of intellectually gifted children against the pedological background.

Blonsky himself defined pedology as the study of the growth, behaviour and constitution of the child throughout his various stages. A mixture of anatomy, physiology and psychology, pedology was said to relate to pedagogy as botany to gardening.[19] In turn it was regarded as an application of psychology. But the pedological umbrella sheltered a wide diversity of attitudes. On the basic question of the determinants of human development, Blonsky set great store by the biological or hereditary factor, implying the essential spontaneity of mental growth, while for Zalkind and others the social environment was of primary importance, and in Soviet conditions environmental change was held to increase the ability to be educated.[20] Neither party, however, denied the existence of the other factor. Indeed, Blonsky's views on the education of the gifted show that he was not averse to structuring the school environment in the interests of the 'intellectually superior child' as well as those of other children.

In an article for the second volume of the *Pedagogical Encyclopedia*, published in 1928, Blonsky, speaking of general giftedness, defined gifted children as those with an IQ of 110 or above; this represented some 20 per cent of the child population. Children with a high IQ, he claimed, tended to be either top pupils or the natural leaders of their class, and often their teachers' favourites, but to keep them in this position for years on end was the surest way to breed arrogance. Thus it was precisely the ordinary system of education that nurtured a school aristocracy. But if such children were brought together with their intellectual equals, they lost their arrogance along with their superiority. Furthermore, in customary conditions very able children were under-extended and this led to laziness and failure to realize their potential. Blonsky contested the notion that 'talent will always show itself' and maintained that highly intelligent children needed to be treated very delicately, like the sensitive plant, and the ordinary school could scarcely manage this. As for average children, when outstanding ones were withdrawn and they were left in a homogeneous group they became more lively, forthcoming and active. The objections to special provision that Blonsky had previously enumerated — that separation would breed intellectual arrogance and contempt, that education would degenerate into forced instruction, that the mass of children would be deprived of models and stimuli and thus be impeded in their development, and that their teachers would likewise be less inspired — were for him outweighed by the arguments in favour. He had less to say about the organizational aspects of special teaching, but listed three possibilities when discussing the American experience: teaching the gifted in the same groups as other children; in special groups in the same school; and in special schools. He ruled out the first as it was only feasible in schools with very considerable individualization of teaching, and in practice this did not apply to the mass school; and the German experience suggested that the third solution involved a certain amount of wastage. Although Blonsky did not specifically express his preference for the second method — special groups in the mass school — this seems to have been the way that his thoughts were tending.[21]

Reading these lines one marvels at how open educational debate could be in the Soviet Union of the 1920s, and simultaneously at how familiar the arguments remain in the Anglo-Saxon world. Thirty years later and more, some of them were to crop up again in the USSR. In comparison with later developments, however, there are two notable omissions from Blonsky's review: national need as an argument for special teaching within the school framework, and egalitarian principle as an argument against it. The absence of the former is explained by the fact that in 1928 Soviet pedagogy was not yet being systematically and exclusively geared in theory and in practice to the furtherance of the country's economic and political development. As has been seen, various moves had been made in this direction by reorganizing the school system, but the 'two-factor theory' remained supreme and leading educational thought was even now predominantly child-centred. On the second point, the lack of any discussion as to how specialized provision — not limited by Blonsky to pupils over a certain age — would accord with the principles of the unified labour school does not signify that he was oblivious to the problem, for in fact he went on to advocate a form of positive discrimination in order to avoid what he termed unfavourable class composition in groups of children of a high IQ. The children of workers and the poorest peasants might receive preferential treatment at the time of admission, since a child with an IQ of 110 in adverse life conditions was no less gifted than one with an IQ of 125 in excellent conditions. Interested in genetic considerations as Blonsky was, it cannot be maintained that he was blind to the effects of the social milieu. Similarly, his failure to consider the possibility of *collective* arrogance arising in the special groups is more apparent than real, for an awareness of this is hinted at in his recommendation that the children should be re-grouped each year so that the groups would not become preoccupied with their collective selves (*zamknutye*).[22]

Developments in the Stalin Era

By 1930 pedagogy had become so fraught with controversy that, in a situation demanding stability, reaction could not be long delayed. There was talk of the school becoming absorbed into the factory or farm and withering away as a separate institution. Moreover, neglect of academic studies, particularly of the sciences, boded ill for socialist construction. So, following Bubnov's condemnation of the 'leftist deviationists', among whom V.N. Shul'gin played the enforced role of chief scapegoat, the Central Committee intervened with the famous decree 'On the Primary and Secondary School' of 5 September 1931. This heralded a series of measures reinstating formal instruction, discipline and achievement, of which little had been heard since the revolution despite Lenin's views on hard work and discipline of oneself. Concurrently there were changes of emphasis in psychological theory. By the end of the 1920s biological or genetic factors in child development had in the main been eclipsed by social or environmental ones; but during the early 1930s these too came to be regarded as inappropriately passive in their implications and by 1936 ceded to the 'third factor', purposive upbringing.[23]

The 1936 decree 'On Pedological Perversions in the System of the Narkomprosy' dealt the death blow to the pedologists and incidentally harbingered the end of any lingering thoughts of special teaching for gifted children distinct from the common curriculum. In 1931 the party had bidden the Commissariats of Education to realize the principle of one-man management in the schools and to increase teachers' responsibility for the quality of school work. However, the pedologists were strong there, the education authorities were said to be sympathetic to them, and they must have had friends at court, otherwise it is incredible that they continued to flourish and even after their journal *Pedologiya* was closed down together with *Psikhologiya* at the end of 1932 they survived until 1936. Then, however, the party decisively intervened, upbraiding the Narkomprosy for entrusting the pedologists with major functions in the leadership of the schools and the upbringing of the pupils (*e.g.* admissions, organization of the routine timetable, determination of the reasons for under-achievement and behavioural defects, and removal of problem children to special schools), thus demeaning the role of the teaching staff. This had been exacerbated by their having their own professional organization and a certain supervisory role *vis-à-vis* the teachers; pedagogy had been relegated to the background. They had applied their objectionable theories — in particular, 'the "law" of the fatalistic conditionality of children's destiny by biological and social factors, the influence of heredity and some sort of unchangeable environment', which was 'in flagrant contradiction to Marxism and the whole practice of socialist construction which successfully re-educates people in the spirit of socialism and liquidates the survivals of capitalism in the economic structure and the consciousness of the people' — by means of pseudo-scientific tests and questionnaires. This was all due to the indiscriminate transplanting of bourgeois ideas, which, in order to preserve the status quo, aimed 'to prove special giftedness and the special rights of the exploiting classes and "superior races" to exist, and, on the other hand, the inexorable physical and intellectual fate of the labouring classes and "inferior races"'.[24] The decree proceeded to restore pedagogy (by which it meant teaching plus purposeful upbringing) to its full rights, and to outlaw pedology and all its works.

Probably because of this decree, pedology is generally associated with intelligence testing and little else. This was certainly part of it, but it should be said that a number of pedologists looked askance at psychometry. Apart fom the divisive effect of pedological activities on the management of the school, involvement in psychometry was nevertheless a major reason for the downfall of the movement. Not only were many of its practitioners ill-trained, but also their findings might be unacceptable to the regime,[25] and they do seem to have had a cavalier attitude about assigning backward or rebellious children to special schools, where things went from bad to worse because of lack of direction and poor quality staff. Blonsky was one of those who favoured tests, and his support of selected groups for the gifted had no future; the 1936 decree linked the two by implication and by banning the former proscribed the latter also, on ideological grounds which were simply not open to debate. If anyone had any doubts about this, they were dispelled the following spring, when the Council of People's Commissars of the RSFSR abolished Narkompros's so-called model schools, mainly because they had retained selection according to intellectual giftedness. The Council said it regarded this as 'an attempt on the part of certain leading workers of Narkompros to smuggle pedological perversions, condemned by the Party, into the school'.[26] The warning was clear.

Stabilization brought standardization of the curriculum, syllabuses and textbooks. Physical work was gradually eliminated, the epithet 'polytechnical' being dropped in favour of 'general-education'. With a common course of study up to completion of the primary stage, or to FZU (14-plus), secondary technical school (15-plus) or *vuz* (18-plus) entry level, the system formally established in 1934 possessed a uniformity such as it had never had before; in contrast with the early Soviet period, socio-economic conditions no longer so drastically impeded the translation of policy into practice. On the other hand, the actual school of the Stalin era was of a very different character from the official school of 1918: system-centred instead of child-centred, emphasizing received knowledge instead of a spirit of enquiry, and displaying a quite un-Marxist lack of interest in physical work. For a child to pursue his particular bent, extracurricular means had to be sought. However, the stress on academic work and achievement was advantageous to children from intellectual homes, especially at the senior stage, admission to higher education becoming dependent on examination in 1935.

At the same time, the celebrated official uniformity[27] of Stalinist education should not lead one to a superficial assumption that the schooling received had begun to be qualitatively and quantitatively similar for all; apart from the general cultural lag in rural areas, where in the late 1930s some 70 per cent of school-children lived, large numbers of them left school on or soon after completing the primary stage. In 1937/38 70.2 per cent of all pupils were in the first four years (urban 59.9 per cent, rural 74.5 per cent), and in 1940/41 the primary stage still accounted for 61.5 per cent (urban 43.5 per cent, with the next four forms already approximating to this proportion, but rural 66.8 per cent). As for the two top forms, in 1937/38 these covered 1.5 per cent of pupils (urban 3.5 per cent, rural 0.7 per cent), and by the eve of the war they were catering for 3.4 per cent (urban 6.7 per cent, rural 1.9 per cent).[28] Thus in some respects the urban-rural gap was widening. Moreover, the chance of preparation for *vuz* entry was limited to a small (and, though growing, about to be checked) and mainly urban minority. Despite earlier attempts to proletarianise the universities, the results of which peaked in 1933 when workers represented over half of all students, the tendency of the upper strata to hold a stake in higher education disproportionate to their size in the total population was confirmed in 1938 when the white-collar groups comprised 17 per cent of the population but 47 per cent of the student body,[29] outstripping the category of workers. No countrywide figures have since been published, but the situation of 1938 adumbrated that of thirty years later (see the following chapter). The school system was not as entrenched as is generally believed, for by 1939 plans were afoot to differentiate the senior curriculum on a vocational basis, with agricultural, industrial and technological, transport and pedagogical branches.[30] But World War II intervened.

The war, or the threat of it, brought many changes. Although the Soviet Union did not enter hostilities until the German invasion of 22 June 1941, much of the legislation of 1940 can be attributed at least in part to the darkening international scene. 'Labour reserve schools' were established to provide vocational training for up to a million 14-year-olds, mostly conscripted, to remedy the shortage of skilled workers, which was itself due to the expansion of the senior (general and 'specialized', *i.e.* technical) and middle sectors of secondary education. Fees were introduced in higher and secondary specialized education and in the top three forms of the general school; this was ostensibly because of the workers' increasing prosperity, but its disincentive function was evident, and the principle of free schooling remained thus infringed until 1956. It is not difficult to see the implications of these two decrees for educational opportunity. A second principle temporarily went the way of the first in 1943 when coeducation was abolished because of the alleged difficulties it was creating — the decree referred in general terms to school discipline, physical development, military training and preparation for work — but single-sex education was never completely achieved and was discontinued in 1954. On the other hand, the principle of compulsory schooling was extended by advancing the age of entry to seven; this may also be regarded as an attempt to counter the deprivations of war. The years 1943 and 1944 saw too the expansion of military and naval schools. But in general, apart from these changes, the old arrangements remained until the time of Khrushchev. Meanwhile the period of post-war reconstruction and subsequent growth brought opportunities for the replenishment of the ravaged labour force. Social mobility thus received a general boost, until the economic slowdown of the late 1950s tended to restrict its functioning to the lower levels with the continuing shift of population to the towns.

The Khrushchev Reform

Khrushchev's well-known polytechnical reform was introduced, after a period of experimentation, by a decree of 25 December 1958 in an attempt to inject labour training into the secondary general school, thus increasing the supply of young skilled manpower and enhancing the role of physical work in upbringing — or so it was hoped. Over the 1950s, and especially since 1955, the output of school leavers with full secondary education had come greatly to exceed the number that could secure *vuz* entry, yet these young people had set their sights on higher education and were reluctant to consider alternatives, some of them evincing an un-Soviet attitude to manual labour. Simultaneously the reduced birthrate of the war years was beginning to affect the workforce.[31] In 1955 a modest amount of handicrafts and practical work had been restored to the curriculum after an absence of some 20 years. This was in accordance with a decision of the XIX Party Congress (1952) to prepare for universal polytechnical training in the general school. The timetable envisaged manual work for forms 1 to 4, activities in the school's workshops and on its garden plot for forms 5 to 7, and practicals in mechanical and electrical engineering and agriculture for forms 8 to 10. The following year it was reported that specialized production classes had been set up experimentally in schools in a number of republics. The Ukraine had over 300 such classes.[32] This was a curtain-raiser to the Khrushchev reform: in 1958 the cardinal Marxist principle of *polytechnische Ausbildung* as one of the three essential components of education was reasserted with a vengeance. The compulsory period of general education was increased from seven to eight years and the weekly load of labour training and manual work at least doubled, from two hours in form 1 to five in form 8, but in the three senior forms (an eleventh year being added) it could rise to as many as twelve, *i.e.* one third of the total programme. Up to 80 per cent of *vuz* entrants had to meet a prior requirement of at least two years' full-time work experience. Vocational and technical education was to be expanded, as were part-time and evening courses, both technical and general. Differentiation in full-time general education was now by type of training as between schools, since they were not uniformly equipped and might develop their own specialisms.

In the event, this legislation raised more problems than it solved. The reform was rushed into without due preparation and provision of staff, textbooks and training facilities; the young people were overloaded and yet the level of training was often superficial; it was inadequately geared to the requirements of the economy; and academics became alarmed at the deterioration in the quality of *vuz* candidates. In 1964, therefore, the senior school course was shortened to two years, its curriculum was cut back in hours, those devoted to physical work being reduced almost to the 1955 level, and the proportion of *vuz* entrants from production was henceforth to be exactly correlated with the proportion of candidates in that category. A subsequent decree of March 1966 went still further by making specific vocational training in the secondary general school optional, depending on whether it was in a position to provide it. Physical work remained on the timetable, but tended to be done on the premises of the school.

By the late 1950s there were thus several and varied precedents for departing from the principle of the single secondary general school with the common curriculum, particularly, but not only, with respect to the senior forms. A very important point, however, is that, with the possible exception of the Narkompros model schools on which research is needed, the criterion for implementing such a departure had never yet, as far as can be traced, been explicitly that of superior *intellectual* ability. True, certain special schools for the highly talented were already in existence, providing for youngsters with exceptional *artistic* ability, but the two fields of talent were not considered, by some at least, as analogous, since artistic gifts unquestionably demanded very specialized treatment from a tender age.[33] Schools teaching a number of subjects in a foreign language had been set up experimentally as from 1948 (and were to undergo considerable expansion in and after 1961); these also involved children of primary age, but, partly for that reason, were not regarded as catering for exceptionally gifted pupils. Then as now, however, they were in great demand and could therefore pick the most promising six- or seven-year-olds, so that the average level of intelligence was likely to be somewhat higher than in ordinary schools. Khrushchev's proposals for reform sparked off a lively debate on specialized education for highly talented children, and during the 1960s it continued, was greatly broadened and found concrete expression in new institutional forms and also in curriculum innovation affecting ordinary schools. Before examining these departures from the norm and changes within it, it is logical to look more closely at the norm itself, and it is to the Soviet mass school of the past decade, its structure, content and problems, that we now turn.

Notes

1   For a short history of Soviet education to 1954, see Luigi Volpicelli, *L'évolution de la pédagogie soviétique* (Neuchâtel, 1954). An excellent detailed account of the first fifteen years of the Soviet school is Oskar

Anweiler, *Geschichte der Schule und Pädagogik in Russland vom Ende des Zarenreiches bis zum Beginn der Stalin-Ära* (Berlin [West], 1964), to which I am much indebted. For the early period see also Sheila Fitzpatrick, *The Commissariat of Enlightenment* (Cambridge, 1970).

2   *Instructions to Delegates* . . . (1866); German text in Marx/Engels, *Über Erziehung und Bildung* (Berlin [East], 1971), 164.

3   Anweiler, *op. cit.*, 113-117; Fitzpatrick, *op. cit.*, 29-30.

4   Anweiler, *op. cit.*, 119; N.K. Goncharov, 'O vvedenii furkatsii v starshikh klassakh srednei shkoly', *Sovetskaya pedagogika* (hereafter *Sov. ped.*), 1958, no. 6, 19-21.

5   'Osnovnye printsipy edinoi trudovoi shkoly', *A.V. Lunacharskii o narodnom obrazovanii* (M., 1958), 524.

6   For example, A. Arsen'ev, 'Uroki po interesam', *Trud*, 16 March 1967.

7   Goncharov, *op. cit.*, 20.

8   The school system of the RSFSR is meant here; in the Ukraine it was *considerably more streamlined. (For RSFSR, see Glossary.)*

9   For full details of these, and of alternatives for senior pupils, *e.g.* industrial apprentice schools (FZU), see Anweiler, *op. cit.*, 199-205.

10   *Ibid.*, 206-207, 366-367. Attached to several *vuzy* and existing from 1919 until 1941, the function of the *rabfaki* was to prepare people lacking secondary education for higher education, thus proletarianising the *vuzy*.

11   Anweiler, 'Educational Policy and Social Structure in the Soviet Union', in Boris Meissner (ed.), *Social Change in the Soviet Union* (Notre Dame and London, 1972), 179 (quoting *Narodnoe prosveshchenie*, 1928, no. 12, 72 *et seq.*). Anweiler also gives data on the changing social composition of higher educational establishments.

12   *Ibid.*, 180-181. Evidence for the poor regard in which education was held by many lower social groups, especially the peasantry, is adduced by David Lane, 'The Impact of Revolution: The Case of Selection of Students for Higher Education in Soviet Russia', *Sociology*, vol. 7 (1973), 241-252.

13   Anweiler, *loc. cit.*, (1972); Sheila Fitzpatrick, 'Cultural Revolution in Russia 1928-1932', *Journal of Contemporary History*, vol. 9, no. 1 (January 1974), 42-43.

14   Alex Inkeles, 'Social Stratification and Mobility in the Soviet Union', in Reinhard Bendix and Seymour Martin Lipset (eds.), *Class, Status and Power* (London, 2nd edn., 1967), 518 (reprinted from *American Sociological Review*, 1950).

15   Anweiler, *op. cit.*, (1964), 369-370.

16   'Osnovnye printsipy . . .' (see note 5 above), 531. In a recent edition of this document there is a curious misprint, so that the text reads 'to avoid impeding and developing *(izbezhat' zaderzhki i razvitiya)* especially gifted natures' *(Narodnoe obrazovanie v SSSR. Obshcheobrazovatel'naya shkola. Sbornik dokumentov 1917-1973 gg.* (M., 1974), 138). But anyone inclined to see an egalitarian hand at work here should reflect that within its context the 1974 wording is

nonsense.

17 N.S. Leites, *Umstvennye sposobnosti i vozrast* (M., 1971), 134.

18 N.K. Krupskaya, 'Znat' osobennosti kazhdogo raiona', *Pedagogicheskie sochineniya,* vol. 8 (M., 1960), 289-298. (Written in 1928).

19 Levy Rahmani, *Soviet Psychology: Philosophical, Theoretical and Experimental Issues* (New York, 1973), 31.

20 *Ibid.,* 31-32.

21 P. Blonsky, 'Vospitanie odarennykh detei', *Pedagogicheskaya entsiklopediya,* vol. 2 (M., 1928), cols. 423-428.

22 *Ibid.,* cols. 426-427.

23 Raymond A. Bauer, *The New Man in Soviet Psychology* (New York, 1952), 80-86, 123-127.

24 There are various editions of the text of this decree. A recent one is in *Narodnoe obrazovanie vs SSSR* . . (see note 16 above), 173-175.

25 For examples see Bauer, *op. cit.,* 108-114.

26 *Narodnoe obrazovanie vs SSSR* . . ., 175-176.

27 The comprehensive history of Soviet education in the Stalin era remains to be written; a close study might reveal greater pressures towards diversity than conventionally supposed.

28 Derived from *Narodnoe obrazovanie, nauka i kul'tura v SSSR* (M., 1971) 78-79.

29 Inkeles, *op. cit.,* 525-526. Another source (Yu. S. Borisov, 'Izmenenie sotsial'nogo sostava uchaschikhsya vo vysshikh i srednikh spetsial'nykh zavedeniyakh (1917-1940 gg.)', in *Kul'turnaya revolyutsiya vs SSSR 1917-1965 gg.* (M., 1967), 138) gives the figure of 42.2 for 1 January 1938 (workers 33.9 per cent). I owe this reference to Mr. P. H. Kneen.

30 Goncharov, *op. cit.,* 21.

31 The reality was more complex than this necessarily brief summary suggests. Of several accounts of the reform's causes, features and effects, a good recent one is David W. Carey, 'Developments in Soviet Education', in *Soviet Economic Prospects for the Seventies* (Washington, D.C., 1973), 603-606.

32 'K novomu pod'' emu narodnogo obrazovaniya', *Uchitel'skaya gazeta* (hereafter *Uch. gaz.*), 11 February 1956; G. Pinchuk, 'Vospitaem obrazovannuyu, trudolyubivuyu molodezh'', *ibid.,* 24 March 1956.

33 For example, Academician M. Lavrent'ev, 'Nuzhny li spetsial'nye shkoly dlya "osobo odarennykh"?', *Pravda,* 25 November 1958; B. Zibel', 'V chem prav tov. Vasilenko', *Trud,* 13 December 1958.

Chapter 2

The Secondary General School Today

Structure of the Education System

Being concerned with general and not technical education, this study concentrates on the secondary general-education school, as it is called, and on variations on the theme. At first, however, this school must be placed within the overall educational framework of the country.[1] The first stage is pre-school education; nurseries cater for children aged between six months and three years and nursery schools for those from three to seven years. The two categories are increasingly combined in the same establishment. In the early 1970s 15 per cent of children in the younger age-group could be accommodated, and 32 per cent overall. In some large cities the provision of nursery schools, available for some 80 per cent of the children, is said to meet public requirements, but elsewhere, although there is an ongoing campaign to develop these facilities, demand continues to outstrip supply.[2]

The secondary general-education school (*srednyaya obshcheobrazovatel'naya shkola*) is the common compulsory school from the age of seven-plus, with (in 1976) a primary stage of three years, a middle one of five and a senior of two. It may be that the whole ten-year course can be followed in the same school, but there are also separate primary schools and eight-year schools combining the first two stages. After their eighth school year, nearly two-thirds of pupils proceed to form 9, especially if they aspire to higher education. The remainder enter one of three levels of technical education: (1) specialized secondary schools (*srednie spetsial'nye uchebnye zavedeniya*), with three or four-year courses, training medium specialists, some of these schools (*uchilishcha*) being for semi-professional fields such as nursing and primary teaching, and others (*tekhnikumy*) for highly-skilled jobs in such areas as engineering and commerce (the reader must be warned against confusing such establishments with those 'special schools' which are in most cases *general* schools with a bias towards languages or some other subject and to which much of this book is devoted; yet another use of the term 'special schools', referring to institutions for the mentally or physically handicapped, will be familiar but does not concern us here); (2) secondary vocational schools (*srednie professional'no-tekhnicheskie uchilishcha, srednie* PTU), a fairly recent (1969) and rapidly expanding innovation training skilled workers with a full secondary education, also with three- or four-year courses; and (3) vocational schools (PTU), with courses of six months to three years, training skilled workers who are supposed simultaneously and if necessary subsequently to attend schools for working youth (*shkoly rabochei molodezhi,* ShRM) or schools for rural youth (*shkoly sel'skoi molodezhi,* both officially known since 1958 as evening (shift) schools, so as to complete their ten-year secondary education. Some form 8 leavers enter employment, but are not legally supposed to do so until they have reached the age of 16. A full ten years of secondary education for all, considered to be of cardinal importance both as an ideological goal and because it makes workers more adaptable, efficient and innovatory, was 86 per cent achieved by one or other of the four paths mentioned above in 1975, and the figure should rise to 95-97 per cent by 1980. Ordinary PTUs are gradually to be converted into secondary PTUs, catering by then for 21-23 per cent of eighth-form leavers.[3] The proportion of entrants to the ninth form is to remain about the same, but demand for higher education much exceeds the supply of places, and a number of ten-year school leavers enter specialized secondary or vocational schools for shorter periods. In 1975, 12.5 per cent of them enrolled in the former and 13 per cent in the latter.

Admission to higher education is competitive. Overall, only about 23 per cent of applicants to the USSR's network of higher educational institutions (*vysshie uchebnye zavedeniya, vuzy*) — numbering over 800, including some 60 universities — make the grade, though this bald statement conceals a good deal of variation: certain *vuzy* are much more sought after than others because of their prestige or location, and some subjects are regarded as softer options. At the University of Erevan in Armenia, for example, the competition in arts and social science subjects is far keener than in mathematics and physics, for which good candidates are in short supply;[4] but the pressure to read mathematics and physics at Moscow State University is intense. Statistics on higher education enrolments require caution since they may include evening and correspondence students also; thus in 1970 total student numbers exceeded 4.5 million, of whom just under half were full-time.[5] Entry to evening and correspondence courses is said to be less exacting, and the present trend is to increase the proportion of full-time students in order to raise the effectiveness of higher education, but the part-time programmes themselves are rigorous enough. Full-time courses mostly last for an arduous five years, with continuous assessment and half-yearly examinations to keep students up to the mark. Higher education remains the key factor in social advancement, and several Soviet studies have shown that the children of specialists and white-collar employees are over-represented at *vuzy* in relation to the share of these groups in the population; in the late 1960s they formed less than a quarter of the population but between about 47 and 65 per cent of students at various universities and groups of *vuzy*; and their proportion of entrants exceeded that of applicants.[6] Students from working-class backgrounds, however, outnumber the others in higher technical education. It is unlikely that higher education will be significantly expanded; all the signs are that attempts will increasingly be made to sell to senior pupils the notion of alternatives to the *vuz*.

As there is no overall shortage of adequately qualified *vuz* candidates, a paradoxical move to increase their numbers can be interpreted only in ideological terms. A decree of 1969 provided for the establishment of 'preparatory faculties' at certain *vuzy*, to give a second chance in the form of courses of eight months (full-time) or ten months (part-time) to people who had completed their secondary schooling without reaching a sufficiently high standard for admission to higher education, namely young workers and collective farmers with at least one year's on-the-job experience and demobilised servicemen. Success in the examinations at the end of the preparatory course guaranteed entry to the first undergraduate year proper. Known popularly as *rabfaki* by analogy with their predecessors of the 1920s and 1930s, in 1970/71 such courses were offered by 498 *vuzy*, with 62,000 students and a pass rate of 87 per cent.[7] This presumably refers to the total taking the examinations, since it is rumoured that up to half of the original entrants drop out; but if the rumour is correct it suggests that standards are high and that this path to the *vuz* is no easy option. It appears to be an attempt to reduce social inequality in higher education by augmenting working-class representation on a respectable academic basis.

Organizational Aspects of the General School

In 1975/76 the Soviet Union had 149,486 secondary general schools, against 174,645 five years earlier. It is necessary to remember that in Soviet usage secondary education includes the primary stage. The decrease in the total is explained by the amalgamation of primary and to a lesser extent of eight-year schools in favour of ten-year schools, which accounted for over one school in three, compared to one in four in 1970/71.[8] Each school has its catchment area (*raion obsluzhivaniya*) and all children living within this have to attend it, with certain exceptions. The basic unit for planning a catchment area is the microdistrict (*mikroraion*), which is strictly defined as the territory allocated to a school of any type (primary, eight-year or secondary) for teaching children in the first three forms.[9] Thus the number of microdistricts in a given area equals the number of general schools there, insofar as they all provide a primary course. The catchment area for eight-year and secondary schools may cover several microdistricts, especially in country areas, but in towns such catchment areas and microdistricts may well coincide and thus have in effect the same meaning, which is reflected in popular usage of the term *mikroraion*. Children who do not attend the local school include such categories as the handicapped, for whom there are special schools; children from needy or single-parent homes who have been admitted to a boarding school; those whose parents have moved to another part of the city but do not wish their children to change schools, at least not in the middle of the year; and those who have secured entry to one of the rather small minority of schools specializing in the arts, sport, languages or certain other academic subjects — of which more later. One account puts the number of commuter children in a city school class as high as nine, and claims that it is pretty typical.[10]

The child comes into school, perhaps as early as eight o'clock, six days a week for a 35-week school year, slightly longer in the case of the three most senior forms to allow for examinations and/or production practice. According to the 1970 regulations it may be up to a week longer in ten-year schools where the language of instruction is not Russian. In the first four years the school day consists of four 45-minute lesson periods; in forms 5 to 8, five; and in the top two forms, five or six. In the RSFSR's schools for non-Russian national groups and the other Union republics this may be increased by two or three periods a week.[11] Such lengthening of the week and year allows a modest degree of flexibility for the inclusion of the native language, literature, history and possibly geography of the non-Russian republic or national group, while the three Baltic republics have the tradition of an eleven-year course.

Table 2.1 collates the curricula (in the narrow sense) effective in the RSFSR and the Ukraine in the late 1960s. Totalling the periods or teaching hours per week suggests that, if the regulations in force earlier were the same as those which applied in 1970, the increase in the weekly workload did not have to be taken too literally, *i.e.* that it could be averaged over the whole ten-year course. Totalling the hours per subject horizontally facilitates a rough-and-ready comparison of subjects between the republics. If one takes language and literature, possibly the most sensitive area, it appears that the time spent by Ukrainian children on their native language and literature is 86.6 per cent of that spent by young Russians on theirs, but the literature accounts for only a minor part of the difference. The extent of divergences in the history and geography syllabuses is not, however, revealed. As in Russian schools, the amount of time the Ukrainians spend on a foreign language is not quite a third of that employed on their own, but in addition they spend on Russian language and literature a period equivalent to two-thirds of the time devoted to their own; the importance attached to Russian as a potentially unifying *lingua franca* and culture-bearer is never far to seek. It is no surprise that the subjects adversely affected by this extra load are not those of major ideological or scientific importance — in fact the Ukrainians manage to cram in *more* history, mathematics, physics and chemistry. Table 2.2 presents the standard (RSFSR) curriculum of more recent date. The amount of homework laid down

Notes to Table 2.1

1   The RSFSR curriculum from a source specifically mentioning the 1968/69 school year was not available to the author, but the one reproduced here was effective in 1967 and remained so throughout the decade, except that options were built up to the given level in stages.
2   The layout of the Ukrainian curriculum has been altered to facilitate comparison.
3   Entitled 'History of the USSR and the Ukrainian SSR' in the Ukrainian curriculum.
4   Entitled 'Natural Science' in the Ukrainian curriculum.

Sources
RSFSR curriculum: M.A. Prokof'ev (ed.), *Narodnoe obrazovanie v SSSR 1917-1967* (M., 1967), 91; N.P. Kuzin *et al., Education in the USSR* (M., 1972), 38.
Ukrainian curriculum: V.I. Chepelev (ed.), *Public Education in the Ukrainian S.S.R.* (Kiev, 1970), 72.

TABLE 2.1 Standard RSFSR School Curriculum[1] and Curriculum in Ukrainian Schools Teaching Through the Medium of Ukrainian,[2] 1968/69

Periods per week per form

Subject	1 R	1 U	2 R	2 U	3 R	3 U	4 R	4 U	5 R	5 U	6 R	6 U	7 R	7 U	8 R	8 U	9 R	9 U	10 R	10 U	TOTALS R	TOTALS U
Russian Language	12	–	10	–	10	5/4	6	5	6	3/4	3	3	3	2	2	2 2/0	2	–	–	–	53	24
Russian Literature							2	–	2	2	2	2	2	2	3	3	4	–	4	4	18	17
Mathematics	6	6	6	6	6	6	6	6	6	6	6	6	6	6	5	5	6	6	5	6	58	59
History[3]							2	2	2	2	2	2	2	3/2	3	3	4	4	3	3	18	18.5
Social Studies																			2	2	2	2
Nature Study[4]			2	2	2	2	2	2													6	6
Geography									2	2	2	2	2	2	3	3	2	2	–	–	11	11
Biology									2	2	2	2	2	2	2 0/2	2 0/2	2 0/2	2	2	2	11	11
Physics											2	2	2	2	3	3	4	4	5	5	16	17
Astronomy																			1	1	1	1
Technical Drawing											1	1	1	1	1	1	–	–			3	3
Chemistry													2	2	2	2	3	3	3	3	10	11
Foreign Language									4	3	3	3/2	3	3 2/3	2	2	2	2	2	2	16	14
Art	1	1	1	1	1	1	1	1	1	1	1	1	–	1							6	6
Music and Singing	1	1	1	1	1	1	1	1	1	1	1	1	1	1							7	7
Physical Education	2	2	2	2	2	2	2	2	2	2	2	2	2	2	2	2	2	2	2	2	20	20
Labour Training	2	2	2	2	2	2	2	2	2	2	2	2	2	2	2	2	2	2	2	2	20	20
Ukrainian Language		12		8		7/8		6		4/3		3/4		2		3		4		4	–	44.5
Ukrainian Literature										2		2		2		3		4		4	–	17
Civil Defence																				1	–	1
Total periods per week for compulsory subjects	24	24	24	24	24	24	24	27	30	32	30	33	30	33	30	36	30	36	30	36	276	305
Options																					18	11

increases gradually from maxima of one hour in the first year for the seven-year-olds, to two hours for the third year (9-plus!) and four hours for the top three forms. One's impression is that the maximum tends to be the norm.

At most schools, lessons finish in the early afternoon. Over 20 per cent of the pupils in forms 1 to 8 are, however, at extended-day schools or are accommodated in extended-day groups; the latter implies a combination of ages. This means that they stay on for meals, games, supervised homework and activities — when the schools are run on orthodox lines — and then go home in the early evening. There is a good deal of variation in both the quantity and the quality of such provision, but the idea is approved by authorities and parents alike, for the schools possess many of the advantages of boarding education without its drawbacks. Little or no capital expenditure is incurred in buildings and furniture for dormitory accommodation, running costs per pupil are only about twice as much as at ordinary day schools (compared to at least ten times as much at boarding schools), and the children can still be under close institutional control for most of the working day, while parents pay no fees (except for meals in some cases) and are not only able to go to work without worrying about their offspring roaming the streets unattended out of school hours but also they can spend time with them and be responsible for them for part of every day. A school visited by the writer in 1974 operated a morning extended-day group for children due to attend the second shift. Figures on multi-shift operation by schools, due to shortage of facilities, are seldom seen, especially global ones, but in 1965/66 30 per cent of pupils were said to be on the second (afternoon) shift and one per cent on a third in the evening.[12] Again, there seems to be much regional variation: in the 1974/75 school year the second shift was attended by 20 per cent of pupils in the Mordovian Autonomous Republic (RSFSR) and under 20 per cent in Moldavia, whereas in 1975/76 in Azerbaidzhan 72 per cent of schools were reported to be working double shifts.[13] In small rural schools, arrival and departure times may be staggered so that older and younger children can be taught separately for at least part of the day.

Aims and Functions of the General School

For the aims of the secondary general school reference may best be made to the 'Legislative Principles of the USSR and the Union Republics on Public Education', a sort of educational constitution and thus carrying enormous weight, published in 1973.[14] Of the five paragraphs in the relevant section, three concern moral rather than intellectual aims and will be considered shortly. The other two, which

TABLE 2.2 Standard Curriculum in Primary, Eight-year and Secondary Schools, RSFSR, 1972/73

Subject	Periods per week per form									
	1	2	3	4	5	6	7	8	9	10
Russian Language	12	11	10	6	6	4	3	2	-	1
Literature	-	-	-	2	2	2	2	3	4	3
Mathematics	6	6	6	6	6	6	6	5	6	6
History	-	-	-	2	2	2	2	3	4	3
Social Studies	-	-	-	-	-	-	-	-	-	2
Nature Study	-	1	2	2	-	-	-	-	-	-
Geography	-	-	-	-	2	3	2	2	2	-
Biology	-	-	-	-	2	2	2	2	1	2
Physics	-	-	-	-	-	2	2	3	4	5
Astronomy	-	-	-	-	-	-	-	-	-	1
Technical Drawing	-	-	-	-	-	-	-	1	2	-
Chemistry	-	-	-	-	-	-	2	2	3	3
Foreign Language	-	-	-	-	4	3	3	2	2	2
Art	1	1	1	1	1	1	-	-	-	-
Music and Singing	1	1	1	1	1	1	1	-	-	-
Physical Education	2	2	2	2	2	2	2	2	2	2
Labour Training	2	2	2	2	2	2	2	2	2	2
Elementary Military Training	-	-	-	-	-	-	-	-	2	2
Total periods per week for compulsory subjects	24	24	24	24	30	30	30	30	32	34
Options	-	-	-	-	-	-	2	3	4	4

Note   A new course entitled 'Principles of the Soviet State and Law' was introduced into the form 8 timetable in September 1975.

Source   *Sbornik prikazov i instruktsii Ministerstva prosveshcheniya RSFSR,* 1972, no. 11, 2.

clearly contain moral implications also, are these:

> Effecting the general secondary education of children and young people appropriate to the contemporary requirements of the social and scientific and technological process; equipping pupils with a deep and firm knowledge of the principles of academic subjects (*nauki*); and inculcating a desire for the constant improvement of their knowledge and an ability independently to widen and apply it . . . .
> Preparing pupils for vigorous labour and public work and the conscious choice of an occupation.

In a nutshell, it is the school's task to transmit up-to-date knowledge and simultaneously instil a purposeful attitude to the process of receiving it, both now and for the future. For its continuing power and increasing prosperity in a time of rapid technological change the Soviet state needs citizens with a high level of general education backing their subsequent training and increasing their efficiency and adaptability on the job; it is also necessary for them to be oriented in the most appropriate way towards that training and that job.

There is nothing in the document about presenting the pupils with alternative approaches, nor is it to be expected. Lenin's much-quoted dictum that a school outside politics is hypocrisy and a lie is borne out in the frequent attribution to the Soviet school of the function of a political tool (among many others) for the building of communism, and the single-minded exemplification of this function in official pronouncements and through the media suggests that it is as characteristic of the cognitive domain of educational objectives as of the more obvious affective domain. Indeed, the Minister of Education has said so: 'The school is an ideological organization. It is impossible to separate its cognitive functions from its upbringing functions — they are two of a kind'.[15] For the Marxist concept of knowledge includes its political application. What is a truism for the student of the Soviet Union is a trial for the student of comparative education: in the USSR truth is relative to the overall task of communist construction, the party determines in breadth and depth how that task shall best be carried out, and is deemed to be the only possible exponent of events and ideas. Facts, theories, trends and criteria are selected and discarded, highlighted or ignored, according to their serviceability. This is certainly not to imply that it happens nowhere else; but the general goal-directedness of much of Soviet life renders it particularly salient. Later it will be necessary to review certain of the impediments to the school's performance of the political function. The existence of obstacles, however, does not prevent the drawing of a generalized picture of the Soviet school in its more formal aspects.

Formality, to change the meaning slightly, is indeed the keynote. Impressions of rather bare classrooms, the blackboard perhaps the sole form of study aid other than the textbook; serious, docile children sitting in rows, keeping their elbows firmly on their desks when raising their hands to answer or ask a question, getting to their feet when called upon; the teacher standing dominant at the front, the lesson proceeding on a set pattern — these recur. To claim that such an atmosphere is universal would be rash; officialdom in any country is unlikely to take a visiting foreign delegation or send an exchange teacher to a poor school in a deprived area, and visitors may have an inhibiting effect on pupils and teachers alike. But whatever one's reactions to the picture one sees, one can normally be fairly sure that it is officially approved, and thus it may be taken as a model. It should be added that the spread of special subject rooms with appropriate equipment (see below) demands some adjustment of the generalized view, and that beneath the formal surface a friendly and relaxed relationship can often be detected. But the children are there to learn, and it is the teacher's responsibility to see that they do so. He, or more likely she, has a plan to fulfil: she is obliged to base her work on a detailed official syllabus stipulating the number of hours to be devoted to each topic (for a summarized example, see Appendix A), and each year she is supposed to improve on the achievement-rate of her pupils.

To calculate this she questions the children on their homework from time to time and awards a mark on a five-point scale with '5' as excellent and '3' as satisfactory. She notes this in that characteristically Soviet institution, the pupil's personal record book (*dnevnik*), in which he enters each day's lessons and the homework set and teachers also write comments, messages and requests to parents, who have to see and sign the book once a week. The record book seems to epitomise official norms of system and control, extended, moreover, through the school to the home. At the end of the school year, pupils with unsatisfactory marks in one or two subjects are given remedial holiday work, and if this applies to three subjects or more they are kept down. If the same thing happens a year later, the staff meeting, with the agreement of the district education office, is empowered to expel them and their future is then decided by youth agencies. Conversely, pupils who combine excellent results with exemplary behaviour and take an active part in the school's activities are awarded honours.

This emphasis on hard work and achievement is set in a context of mixed-ability grouping. With rare exceptions, and then usually for experimental purposes, there is no streaming or setting in what is known as the mass school (to see the 3-4 per cent who repeat a given year as the victims of a form of this is to move a very long way from the traditional English concept). This is because streaming is considered to represent unjustifiable, fatalistic discrimination. In the case of a two-form entry or larger school, pupils are divided throughout their school career, except for optional subjects, on the basis of alphabetical order of surname. The absence of streaming, while demonstrating a rejection of the notion of predetermined intelligence, does not signify, however, that all children are universally regarded as being of equal potential, as is sometimes supposed. In the words of the psychologist N.S. Leites:

A person's abilities are not given from birth in a finished form. There is no doubt that all abilities, including general ones, develop in the process of the interaction of the child with the surrounding world, under the influence of teaching and upbringing in the widest sense of these words. It is no less certain that, even in relatively uniform conditions of life and activity, the mental characteristics of children are not uniform and develop to a differing degree.[16]

But it is nevertheless true that the notion of potential is of central importance, and the educator's approach to it is fundamentally different from that of his Western colleague. If the general line in the West is that the child's stage of development inhibits the learning process and the teacher must adapt to it, the Soviet view, following Vygotsky, is that the teacher can and should accelerate development.[17] She should not pitch her teaching at the child's present level, setting him work which is relatively easy for him, but at the level he can reach by his own efforts *together with her assistance,* giving him tasks which really extend him but do not sap his independence. In this way there should be compensation for adverse environmental influences. Striking such a delicate balance systematically in a class of up to 40 children, already, perhaps, at varying levels of intellectual development and from different backgrounds, presents obvious problems. But it follows from this that there must be an identifiable minimum standard that anyone not mentally deficient can achieve, given purposeful teaching and a ready response, and that there must be a mechanism to evaluate performance. Hence the preoccupation with marks. A conspicuous form of continuous assessment fits the general pattern so well that examinations might be thought superfluous, and indeed, except for the important school-leaving examinations at the end of the eighth and tenth years, not all republics hold them, and even then perhaps only in one or two subjects.

A number of studies indicate a link between children's intellectual attainment and family circumstances. Zyubin has shown that the children of white-collar workers figure more frequently among top pupils than those of skilled or unskilled workers.[18] Zemtsov in his study of parents and pupils in Bashkiria finds that the children of parents with higher education are more likely to be graded excellent or good than those of parents of other educational levels, and the probability of excellence steadily decreases as one moves down the seven-point educational scale; the reverse is true of satisfactory achievement, but variation in unsatisfactory achievement is fluctuating and slight. Thus, in the case of children of parents with higher education, 51 per cent were graded excellent and good, 47.1 per cent satisfactory, and 1.9 per cent unsatisfactory; with those whose parents had received four years of schooling only, the respective figures were 18, 77.5 and 2.7, with 1.8 per cent nil response.[19] Vasil'eva's findings from two contrasting districts of Leningrad in 1967/68 support this and also show that, with minor exceptions, the higher the family's position on the social scale, the greater the likelihood of more rooms, a separate flat, a private library, and a workplace for the pupil. This is no surprise but it is refreshing to see it spelt out. It says something, however, for the effectiveness of Soviet education that, even in the bottom manual worker category, 44 per cent of families occupying only one room possessed a collection of books and 56 per cent provided a workplace for their child, while 88 per cent of those with two rooms or more had a place for the child to work in.[20]

Although, in contrast, character education in the Soviet secondary general school and affective aspects of the curriculum are not a major focus of this study, the importance attached in the USSR to that area of teaching and learning can hardly be exaggerated; a brief consideration is therefore indispensable. The Russian term is *vospitanie* — character education, moral education or upbringing. The Legislative Principles[21] show that excellence is not to be understood and pursued in intellectual terms alone:

> Forming a Marxist-Leninist world-outlook in the younger generation, instilling socialist internationalism, Soviet patriotism and a readiness to defend the socialist motherland.
>
> Inculcating high moral qualities in pupils, in the spirit of the requirements of the moral code of the builder of communism.
>
> Ensuring the harmonious all-round development of the pupils and of their culture; improving their health, aesthetic and physical education.

Ideology is thus meant to provide a powerful dynamic in the process of shaping Soviet man, and it operates not only through the formal curriculum — in which the most senior pupils follow a one-year course in Marxism and civics designated social studies, a course for eighth-formers in civics and law was introduced in 1975, and the teaching of other subjects is expected to evince a Marxist-Leninist approach and draw on Marxism-Leninism for explanation and illustration — but through the whole of school life, inside and outside the classroom, in the formation of attitudes, beliefs and values within the context of the collective or peer-group.

One of the essentials of communist morality is Lenin's

fundamental notion of conscious discipline, which means self-discipline without the somewhat negative connotation possibly conveyed by that term. Conscious discipline is internalized but purposeful obedience and leads to a high standard of personal behaviour. For example, the child is taught to work hard not just because it is necessary and good in itself but because one owes it to one's fellows; such service is honourable, and so anti-social behaviour ranging from dropping litter to vandalism is slated because it shows a lack of respect for the labour of others. Work is a matter for joy, so that it must never be imposed as a punishment. The following story is reported from a reader for eight-year-olds:[22]

> Three children are discussing the coming of communism. The first says he would like to fall asleep and wake up when communism has arrived. The second claims that it would be much more exciting to watch it happening. But the third declares: 'I should like to build it with my own hands'.

However, the hero does not mean 'all by myself'. The collective is implicit, and the child learns that the collective is more important and wiser than he is and that he must accept its decisions even when they are opposed to his own wishes, and seek its welfare at whatever cost. This is the nub of patriotic education: service to that wider collective entrusted by history with the leadership of the builders of communism, service extending if necessary to the ultimate sacrifice of self. But the collective is also responsible for its members.

The children's collective, it is believed, is the indispensable context for the attainment of the Marxist goal of the 'all-round development of the individual'. In the interaction between teacher or leader and youngsters, the notion of *vospitanie* runs like a scarlet thread stitching together the entire patchwork quilt of the process of education. We recall Marx's insistence on the combination of intellectual, technical and physical education. The Marxist-Leninist world-view is inculcated through the teaching of atheism and materialism, especially in physics and history lessons and Pioneer pep-talks. Belief in a higher supernatural power is superfluous, given a charismatic human surrogate of the eminence of Lenin, presented as the archetypal father-figure who deserves thanksgiving for the blessings of life; the sublime pattern for the youth of today, revered as a dedicated, fearless hero, yet a kind man who loved children; and even now the source of inspiration. Technical education synthesizes mental and physical labour, and the moral significance of work has already been cited. Certain labour skills, *e.g.* motor cycling, may form part of military training. Physical education calls for effort, perseverance, and very often teamwork; a display of outstanding physical prowess promotes loyalty to the collective, patriotic pride and international prestige. At all levels physical fitness presupposes a reasonably disciplined regimen, and so the pupils' health is specifically included among the aims of the school. These also feature aesthetic education, for perceptiveness to the beautiful in nature and in man's attitudes and attainments, resulting in a heightened awareness of moral values which is ultimately internalized in one's own behaviour, is to be another characteristic of the New Soviet Person. In common with the rest of the educational programme, it is believed that the child's aesthetic development, both in appreciation and in creativity, can be systematically encouraged by sustained encounter with appropriate forms of artistic expression — those considered the best, from before the October Revolution and since — with the inevitable corollary that certain forms are ruled out. Red is beautiful — in Russian the two words are cognates. Music, dance and drama are valued also for the opportunities they present for collective enterprise, and the arts as a whole are regarded as a powerful means of political education.

Moral education is faced with a number of present and future problems. Despite a strenuous propaganda campaign, upbringing in the family does not always support the aims of the school. A large number of single-parent families, associated with a rather high if fairly stable divorce rate (2.7 per 1,000 population in 1968 and 1973), and high female employment (86 per cent of all women of working age), meaning that the majority of children not covered by pre-school and extended-day facilities are looked after while at home by grandmothers or grandmother substitutes, together form the basis of what is known as the 'feminisation' of upbringing, which the school does little to counteract since not only are most pupil leaders girls but also the teaching profession is about 70 per cent female. What happens as early as the primary stage? The Pioneer Brigade Council sends leaders into the Octobrist groups. There are few lads among them. The neatly-dressed girls 'read the little ones fairy stories, organize ring dances with singing, and play blind man's buff. The little boys are bored. They want to play soldiers, argue about planes, or knock a hockey puck around, but the leaders make them jump over a skipping rope'.[23] Young and older children need a father figure to balance the female influence, but young men generally regard teaching as a woman's job. A further problem is exemplified by the Soviet census of 1970 which showed that single-child families predominated among families with children (urban: 51.4 per cent; rural: 35.8 per cent).[24] It had been calculated that merely to renew the population families should average 2.2 to 2.5 children, not only to avoid the economic problems of an ageing population but also because of the danger of an only child growing up to be an egoist.[25]

The state's commitment to the systematic raising of material standards brings with it the risk of fostering a consumer ethic in strident disharmony with the qualities of the New Soviet Person; this will inevitably present a continuing challenge to the upbringer. Critics of the Soviet system assert a lack of congruence between the protected environment of the child and the wider world beyond the school. Already during adolescence other collectives may exert their influence, and the fact that such socializing agents may be outside direct official control has important consequences for the upbringing programme. According to research at Kursk Pedagogical Institute, up to 86 per cent of young teenagers spend their free time in these 'spontaneous groups'.[26] Boys are particularly attracted to them. Some are harmless, they meet a need and their solidarity is enviable; others, however, can lead to hooliganism and rebellion against the school's rules and values such as diligence and achievement.[27]

Problems of School Reorganization

As a bridge to a closer study of how the Soviet school has responded to demands on it for the provision of facilities for specialized academic education we turn now to a survey of the major problems besetting school reorganization and cognitive aspects of the curriculum in secondary general education. Secondary reorganization in the Soviet context does not mean the recasting of several types of school in a common mould but the amalgamation or abolition of small and inefficient schools which do not offer a full ten-year course, the expansion of ten-year schools, and the supplying of alternative means of general education — listed at the start of this chapter — at the senior stage (forms 9 and 10). The realization of full secondary education for all is regarded not only as an essential precondition for the all-round development of the individual and maximum effectiveness of the workforce in the era of the scientific and technological revolution, but also as a highly significant factor in attaining the systemic goal of eliminating the gap between town and country. A major indicator of Soviet educational achievement is the increase in complete secondary day schools: from 31,909 in 1965/66 to 44,226 in 1970/71, 49,863 in 1974/75, covering three pupils in four, and 51,466 in 1975/76.[28] Children at very small schools run a disproportionate risk of being disadvantaged for lack of facilities and good teachers; several age-groups may have to be coped with at the same time, considerably taxing the teacher. It is policy to close or amalgamate 'dwarf' schools not only for pedagogical but also economic reasons: per-pupil costs in small primary schools are at least two or three times as high as in the primary classes of an average secondary school.[29]

Small schools are, of course, characteristic of rural areas, which accounted for 94.6 per cent of all primary schools in 1970/71, with an average enrolment of 27, compared to 106 in urban primary schools,[30] and amalgamation fits in with the policy of building consolidated settlements to serve as models for the transformation of the countryside and the improvement of everyday conditions. In 1970, for instance, Orel Region contained 4,500 communities on 412 collective farms and state farms; it was planned to reconstruct 800 villages so that each farm would have about two settlements with all amenities, instead of the existing nine or ten.[31] These facilities include secondary schools, without which much-needed specialists are likely to move from the farms to the towns. The proportion of country children, who represent half of the USSR's total young schoolgoing population of 45 million, in full secondary (compared to other) schools has increased from 40.1 per cent in 1965/66 to 62.3 per cent in 1974/75.[32] Despite this advance, access to the senior forms remains much easier for urban children. In the USSR as a whole, the ratio of urban 8-year schools to complete secondary schools was roughly 1:1 in 1965/66 and 1:2 in 1970/71; that for rural areas was 3:1 in 1965/66 and 2:1 in 1970/71. The proportion of senior pupils to all pupils is about half as large in urban areas as in rural.[33]

Reducing the number of schools aggravates other problems characteristic of rural areas, given a vast country with a harsh climate and poor local communications during much of the year. In order to maintain regular attendance, the provision of transport and particularly of boarding facilities attached to the schools is essential. The latter especially is the theme of an ongoing campaign, and at the end of the Ninth Five-Year Plan period (1971-1975) it was announced that over 1.4 million children, or about 39 per cent of those in need of hostel places, were so catered for.[34] However, standards vary widely: to cite two contrasting examples, in 1975/76 the exemplary Orenburg Region provided accommodation for 25,000 children, or over 80 per cent of those needing it, over 16,000 received free meals, and over 85 per cent of the hostel staff had had specialized pedagogical training. In 1974, on the other hand, it was reported that the far from exemplary Abkhazian Autonomous Republic in Georgia accommodated under 9 per cent of those in need, apparently because very few of the hostels offered full meals.[35] Where there are delays in the provision of adequate hostels and catering, it seems to be due not to lack of finance but rather to want of persistence in applying it by local agencies.

A further problem is the shortage of teachers in many rural areas.

Newly-trained teachers are assigned to specific posts like other graduates, but rural jobs tend to be unpopular because of the urban-rural gap in living standards, fears of isolation and loneliness, and the known difficulties of work in small schools. The process of planning and allocation seems to be inefficient, but it can hardly be otherwise when there is widespread evasion of rural assignments. The resulting shortfall means that certain teachers find themselves teaching subjects for which they were not trained as part (occasionally the whole) of their workload, and that some subjects are taught for fewer hours or not at all.[36] Attempts have been made to rectify this by offering pay incentives for rural posts, by easing entry requirements to pedagogical *vuzy* for rural candidates, and by encouraging collective farms to award scholarships to their young people on condition that they return home to teach; but since they are liable to arrive at the *vuz* less well-prepared in any case, such arrangements may do little to maintain standards. Clearly the teacher shortage and the likelihood that teachers are overworked is apt to create learning problems and impair pupil performance.

Problems of Intellectual Education

The highly achievement-oriented ethos of the Soviet school was touched upon earlier. While there is much in this that is commendable, it also has its negative side. From time to time, *vuz* authorities complain that the quality of student applicants gives the lie to their level of attainment as stated in the leaving certificates issued by the schools.[37] The teacher bears the main responsibility for the progress of her charges, and the need to produce evidence of ever-better results for her head to transmit to the local education office sometimes leads her to cook the books, a symptom of the affliction known as 'percentomania'.[38] This is reduced to the absurd in a brilliant sketch in which a harassed schoolmaster implores a blasé ninth-former to give him grounds to upgrade him from '2' to '3', the crucial question being how to spell the Russian word for 'cow'; from its sound there are two ways in which this might be spelt, and the lad gets a second chance.[39] But the cavalier attitude of Ven'ya Gusev (Benny Blockhead) and his like to their studies is far less a cause of complaint and concern that that pupils are overloaded with work because of the requirements of the programme. An APN survey in the mid-sixties revealed that 50 per cent of pupils spent an excessive amount of time on homework, 15 per cent of 12-year-olds doing 3.5 to 4 hours and 7 per cent 4.5 to 6 hours,[40] and the comparative heaviness of official norms (then two hours for this age-group, now 2.5) has already been noted. These findings were not substantiated by a later investigation, which concluded that on the average the time spent by senior pupils on homework was well below the official maxima, and the problem was to teach them to plan their input rationally over the week.[41] Where it occurs, however, overloading lowers interest in study, and when combined with poor learning techniques it is a major cause of 'repeating' (*vtorogodnichestvo*), the necessary consequence of a minimum standard supported by sanctions.

The practice of repeating has received much frank discussion in recent years. Although some would like to abolish it, most regard it as a necessary evil to be gradually eliminated by improved teaching and environmental conditions. Its fiercest critics argue that it is not justified by its results; following a ministerial statement (in 1968) that the eight-year school was completed (on time) by some 80 per cent of young people, the other side of the coin was exposed: 20 per cent of pupils entering form 1 nevertheless failed to complete, the repeater's new teachers needed at least a term to discover his weak points, he had the illusion of knowing everything already, was separated from his friends and dropped out. It might be preferable to move up those with unsatisfactory marks, since experiment had shown this to be justified, and issue differentiated leaving certificates.[42] The latter suggestion, ideologically unacceptable since a second-rate education for a minority must not receive formal legitimation, was castigated by the editor of the teachers' newspaper.[43] An all-Union average of 82 per cent completing the eight-year course on time was quoted in 1970 by a Ukrainian writer who pointed out with obvious pride that in his republic the figure was 95 per cent.[44] Since then a marked reduction in repeating has taken place, with a due completion figure of 93.4 per cent for the period of the Ninth Five-Year Plan,[45] although there is no knowing to what extent teachers may have had to compromise with their consciences.

Repeaters and dropouts (*vybyvshie*)[46] have been the subject of study by sociologists and others. Professor V.A. Zhamin, the Soviet Union's leading economist of education, points out that there are economic objections to repeating: it introduces an irrational element into school planning and financing, it delays entry to the workforce, and those who drop out enter production with a level of education not up to its requirements.[47] Although unwillingness to learn is the predominant cause of repeating (37.5 per cent of cases in a Lenin State Pedagogical Institute (Moscow) survey of schools in various districts of the RSFSR, Lithuania and Moldavia in 1967/68, and 22 per cent (14 per cent with a negative attitude and 8 per cent with a low level of willpower, to whom might be loosely linked 18 per cent with inadequate habits of work, a category not listed in the three-republic survey) in a Rostov Region study reported in 1972), particularly common in the middle school years and one to be eradicated primarily by obvious pedagogical means, there are contributory causes. In Zhamin's view, the operation of a second shift prevents the rational organization of work and leisure and is prejudicial to health. Poor health or physical handicap accounted for over 12 per cent of repeating in the three-republic study and 9 per cent in the Rostov one, while mental backwardness was attributed to 22.7 per cent in the former and 27 per cent (termed 'weak development of thinking') in the latter.[48] Zhamin considers that the need of these children for additional attention may cause a lowering of interest on the part of normal children; he calls for regular medical checks, followed by treatment and where necessary transfer to special schools for the handicapped.[49] In the Rostov survey the negative influence of family and peers accounted for 13 per cent of repeating, and with this may perhaps be equated 'absence not connected with illness', 12.7 per cent in the other study, since the family is not mentioned there, although there is doubtless overlap with 'unfavourable living and material conditions', at 9.8 per cent.[50] There is unfortunately no perfect match of categories between the two surveys, and in some instances repeating must be due to a combination of causes, but they nevertheless tend to reinforce each other.

Another investigation reveals a high correlation between poor performance and an unfavourable home background. An analysis of 6,979 records (a 15 per cent sample) of underachieving (*neuspevayushchie*) pupils (repeaters and dropouts) in five Bashkir towns during the period 1967 to 1969 found that one in three came from 'incomplete' families — *i.e.* families not including both natural mother and natural father — and two in three stepchildren left school early.[51] A Leningrad study showed that achievement was 6 to 7 per cent higher in complete families than in incomplete ones, and that poor home conditions had a particularly bad effect on boys,[52] whom the Bashkir survey had found to outnumber girls among repeaters by three to one. Underachievers were four times as numerous among children whose parents were unduly fond of alcohol. Deviant behaviour was noted in every second underachiever, being usually more frequent in dropouts than in repeaters.[53] Zhamin cites their limited outlook and interests as a cause of this.[54] Thus Soviet experience illustrates the axiom that the unintended effects of upbringing and environment upon learning need to be reckoned with in order that the planned ones may be more effectively achieved.

The dropout problem is particularly conspicuous at two levels: prior to completion of the eighth form, with which we have been mainly concerned, and during the ninth, when certain new factors apply. Rates for the RSFSR in the school year 1968/69 were as follows: forms 1 to 10, 3.2 per cent; forms 1 to 8, 2.4 per cent; forms 9 and 10, 10.9 per cent.[55] A later (1974) report from the Moldavian Ministry of Education cited the not unfamiliar cause of inadequate hostel accommodation, but quoted poor knowledge as the main reason for dropping out at this stage; it was particularly common among pupils from rural areas, who accounted for over 70 per cent of form 9 dropouts and repeaters. The actual position was difficult to gauge as some school directors, evidently students of Gogol, included 'dead souls' in their returns of pupil enrolments, or alternatively understated the number of form 9 entrants at the start of the year as a sort of reserve. The directors themselves were to blame for some of the dropping out because they brought pressure to bear on pupils to enter form 9 and refused to issue the necessary leaving certificates to those who wanted to transfer after form 8 to technical schools.[56] It is worry about fulfilling the plan that induces heads to resort to such measures, and further examples could be quoted. But the vocational technical schools have their own plans to fulfil, and tackle the task aggressively by despatching representatives known popularly as 'recruiting-sergeants' (*verbovshchiki*) who visit the pupils' hostels and homes to drum up students.[57] The dropout problem is, therefore, due in part to systemic factors which the surveys do not reveal: the agents of the planned economy devise their expedients as they endeavour to cope with the human element. This said, it ought to be stressed that the significance of repeating and dropping out should not be magnified into a general indictment of Soviet education; the former at least could be abolished forthwith if the authorities saw fit, but it is retained with its various consequences as the price of commitment to a universal minimum standard of achievement, and it is decreasing.

Systemic factors are presumably ineluctable. However, if the best way to deal with shortcomings is to remove their causes, there is much that can be done: rationalization of the school network, better residential and transport facilities, more efficient teacher supply, improved diagnostic services and remedial action, more effective work with parents, more energetic activation of the public... Much of this is indeed being done. It may be necessary, however, to penetrate beneath the causes to their own causes. In general, it is beyond the scope of this section to speculate, for example, on the dichotomy of the real and the ideal evidenced in the reluctance of young men and women to go east; and it is well outside the writer's field to delve into such matters as the politics of local construction and finance. But since a major factor in underachievement is overloading, it behoves us to look in general terms at teaching methods and syllabuses and in fact the whole question of curriculum reform.

Curriculum Reform

Curriculum reform is the counterpart of universal tén-year schooling. The latter is to provide the broadening of education demanded by the revolution in science and technology, while the former seeks to secure the necessary depth.[58] In 1961 science was promised the new and enhanced status of a driving productive force. Automation is expected to herald the development of a new, broad job profile bridging the gap between mental and physical labour; with increasing scope for logical thought, ingenuity and initiative, the creative aspects of labour will gradually supersede the mechanical.[59] Towards the end of the Khrushchev era scientists were more and more voicing their concern that the school was lagging further and further behind in what was required of it: attempts had been made to update syllabuses by hotch-potch alteration, mainly by addition, they were heavily descriptive and rigidly self-contained, and pupils were taught to learn things parrot-fashion rather than to think them out for themselves. The reduction of the 11-year secondary course to ten years was to heighten the urgency of reform. Such was the situation confronting the 500-strong Commission set up to determine the content of the secondary curriculum in October 1964.[60]

The Commission sought to carry out its brief by generalizing new concepts, establishing focal ideas for each subject, organizing syllabuses on a linear plan and coordinating the treatment of themes where possible to provide inter-subject links. The primary and middle stages were now to be seen as parts of a larger whole. Experiment had convinced psychologists that rationalization of the primary syllabuses would allow that stage to be reduced from four years to three, while careful selection of content would accelerate the development of the children's cognitive abilities by making increased demands on them. This would also, as it were, give back a year to post-primary education, enabling the senior stage to be partially disburdened. Overloading remained a salient issue: specialists were reluctant to see their subjects take the cuts, and the theoretical level of the course had to be raised while its accessibility was safeguarded.[61] To develop the intellectual qualities necessary in the age of the information explosion, the methodological keynote was to be a 'creative atmosphere' with a 'differentiated approach' to individuals and groups, learning together through interaction and problem-solving. I. Szianawski, the Polish educationist, sees this new emphasis on group teaching and group activities as profoundly important: teacher and textbook have their *unique* position no more and the class is no longer the sole social category.[62] It sounds rather like a return to the discovery methods of the 1920s, but in practice this can scarcely be so — the teacher is still very definitely in charge.

What has been the effect of the Commission's recommendations on the practice of the school, since the publication, after countrywide discussion of its earlier proposals, of its third and final report, backed up by legislation, in November 1966? New syllabuses began to be introduced from September 1967, the three-year primary course was instituted in 1969/70, new textbooks began to be produced, tests (*kontrol'nye raboty*) are carried out in schools for subsequent analysis and improvements to syllabuses, and advanced teacher education and research is going forward.[63] In the continuing evaluation process, the teacher now acquires an enhanced role, and the school becomes an active partner in determining the final content of education.[64] For more efficient teaching and use of study aids, special subject rooms (*kabinety*) are being introduced apace; by 1975 some 62 per cent of schools (urban 81 per cent, rural 47 per cent) had eight or more of these.[65] But problems remain, some of them due to the specifics of the reform, others to wider issues.

The new syllabuses had been tried out in experimental schools; but these enjoy favourable conditions and specially qualified staff, and neither the conditions nor the results were necessarily matched in ordinary schools. Initially the primary course proved to be too theoretical and difficult, and senior science courses devoted too little attention to the application of theory; this was to be corrected, as was lack of coordination between syllabuses and textbooks, the latter sometimes remaining overloaded.[66] Implementation of the reform must inevitably be hampered by recurrent problems such as the teacher shortage and hold-ups in the supply and distribution of textbooks and equipment. There must also be many teachers habituated to full-frontal instruction who are reluctant to change their ways or who are insufficiently resilient or skilful to make a success of an extraordinarily demanding type of teaching. The system of regular in-service training and assessment, once in five years, the latter leading in extreme cases to dismissal for inefficiency, is helping to solve this problem, but in some areas the shortage of teachers must mitigate the effects of sanctions.

The ultimate problem posed by various western commentators is that a rigidly prescribed framework for thought and action seems to be intrinsically incompatible with the development of independent judgment, and especially with the encouragement of divergent thinking and what Liam Hudson calls the gifts of intellectual sprightliness and flexibility, the prerequisites of scientific and technological advance.[67] Against this the USSR can point to its achievements in these spheres. The suggestion is prompted that it has come so far mainly by the power of the convergent thinker, the dedicated, logical but probably conventional researcher who thrives under a rigid belief system. So far — and how much further if real breakthroughs depend on the interplay of *both* types of reasoning? This side of the curriculum, however, is in general less hidebound by ideological constraints. A more open question is how well the other side will fit the Soviet citizen for living in the golden future time when his reach has ceased to exceed his grasp.

Curriculum Differentiation: An Overview

We now turn to a closer study of the various forms of curriculum differentiation at the secondary school stage, confining our attention to the general schools. The Russians are insistent that teaching should be a means of levelling up, so that no child should be permanently disadvantaged by unfavourable home circumstances, and they are unlikely to accept that existing damage due to such causes may be irremediable. With high but not impossible expectations of them, the average are also drawn ahead. But what, it may be asked, of children of well above average ability, who are disadvantaged in another way, maybe frustrated and difficult if prevented from rising to the heights of which they are capable, maybe content to coast along, but in either case a loss to the state and society? Traditionally it is said that they gain intellectually as well as socially by helping their less able comrades in the same class, and the special stimulus they require is received in extracurricular activities; but not everyone agrees that these are adequate, although some new forms have been developed. Before consideration of the subject of provision for outstanding intellectual ability, however, *special schools for the artistically gifted* and *special sports schools* are to be examined. This will be followed by a survey of *special foreign language schools,* which pre-date other schools with an academic bias and are sufficiently idiosyncratic to warrant their treatment as a separate category.

Discussion of differentiation has centred on three main issues and found expression in corresponding innovations in Soviet educational practice. Firstly, are special schools for young people with salient intellectual gifts desirable? The fierce debate of this question in 1958 has proceeded continuously if somewhat mutedly since then, with the result that since 1963 a very small number of such institutions have been established, *boarding schools specializing particularly in mathematics and physics.* Secondly, how can specialized education be provided for the *mass* of intelligent young people, in accordance both with their own interests and abilities and with the broad requirements of the economy? Here two main solutions have been proposed, rendered authoritative by the Curriculum Commission and implemented: *schools with a special profile* (or subject-bias); these are highly diversified, ranging from experimental schools with specialized alternative groups of courses at the senior stage to schools merely providing special classes in a given subject; and *optional studies,* to be taken in addition to the basic curriculum; the important difference between this concept and that of special-profile schools is that options are envisaged in *all* schools with pupils in form 7 (13-plus) and above. It is worth noting, again in respect of intellectual ability, that the above catalogue broadly reflects that chronological sequence of the more intense debates and also a passage from more extreme measures to compromise solutions. Thirdly, there has been a new interest in the question of individual abilities and the nature of giftedness; this has accompanied a miscellany of experiments in *differentiation within the class* and even between parallel classes, although the extent of the latter should not be exaggerated. To these approaches should be added the traditional one: *special-interest clubs and extracurricular activities* such as *olympiads,* a solution which has continued to be put forward at intervals throughout the debate as the only orthodox means of fostering talents, but also one open to innovation. The whole area of special provision in the school's quest for excellence is sensitive and controversial; but the nettle has had to be grasped, as later chapters will show.

Notes

1   For more detailed accounts of the Soviet education system, see Nigel Grant, *Soviet Education* (Harmondsworth, 3rd edn., 1972), lively and reliable; Seymour M. Rosen, *Education and Modernization in the USSR* (Reading, Mass., 1971); J.J. Tomiak, *The Soviet Union* (Newton Abbot, 1972); and, for a Soviet description, N.P. Kuzin *et al. Education in the USSR* (M., 1972).

2   Ekkehard Eichberg, *Vorschulerziehung in der Sowjetunion* (Düsseldorf, 1974), 13-15.

3   M.A. Prokof'ev, 'XXV s"ezd KPSS i zadachi sovetskoi shkoly', *Uch. gaz.,* 3 April 1976.

4   B. Mkrtchyan, 'Kto stanet fizikom', *Izvestiya,* 28 August 1970.

5   *Narodnoe obrazovanie, nauka i kul'tura v SSSR* (hereafter *NONK*) (M., 1971), 152.

6   George Avis, 'The Sociology of Soviet Higher Education: a Review of Recent Empirical Research', in Bohdan Harasymiw (ed.), *Education and the Mass Media in the Soviet Union and Eastern Europe* (New York, 1976), 43-44.

7   S.S. Gal'tsov and S.I. Tyul'panov, 'Podgotovitel'nye otdeleniya,

komplektovanie i metodika', *Vestnik vysshei shkoly,* 1971, no. 3, 81;
V.P. Elyutin, 'Spetsialisty zavtrashnego dnya', *Literaturnaya gazeta,*
24 May 1972. For these references I am endebted to Ms Ann Simpson.

8   *NONK,* (M., 1977), 26.

9   V.A. Zhamin, *Optimizatsiya razmeshcheniya seti
       obshcheobrazovatel'nykh shkol* (M., 1975), 15.

10   A. Levina, 'Shkol'niki v chas pik', *Komsomol'skaya pravda,* 24
       November 1974. I owe this reference to Dr. Marianna Butenschön.

11   The basic document is *Ustav srednei obshcheobrazovatel'noi shkoly*
       (M., 1971), approved 8 September 1970 and reprinted in *Narodnoe
       obrazovanie v SSSR. Obshcheobrazovatel'naya shkola. Sbornik
       dokumentov 1917-1973 gg.* (M., 1974), 228-235.

12   M. Kaser, 'Salient Features in the History of State Boarding Schools',
       Annuaire de l'URSS 1968 (Paris, 1969), 135 (note).

13   For Mordovian ASSR, 'V Sovete Ministrov RSFSR', *Uch. gaz.,* 16
       January 1975; for Moldavia, V. Cheban, 'Rodina stanovitsya bogache
       ı sil'nee', *ibid.,* 7 January 1975; for Azerbaidzhan, 'V Tsentral'nom
       komitete profsoyuza', *ibid.,* 7 October 1975.

14   'Osnovy zakonodatel'stva Soyuza SSR i soyuznykh respublik o
       narodnom obrazovanii', *Pravda,* 21 July 1973; reprinted in *Narodnoe
       obrazovanie v SSR . . .* (see note 11 above), 93-104, at 97. The
       order of the paragraphs has been altered here for convenience.

15   M. Prokof'ev, 'Segodnya i zavtra nashei shkoly', *Pravda,* 12
       December 1966.

16   N.S. Leites, *Umstvennye sposobnosti i vozrast* (M., 1971), 3-4.

17   L.S. Vygotsky, 'Learning and Mental Development at School Age', in
       Brian and Joan Simon (eds.), *Educational Psychology in the USSR*
       (London, 1963), 21-34, at 28-31, 33. For the application of this
       to primary curriculum reform in the 1960s, see the editorial
       introduction in *ibid.,* 11-12.

18   L.M. Zyubin, 'Psikhologicheskii aspekt problemy perevospitaniya
       pedagogicheski zapushchennykh detei i nesovershennoletnykh
       pravonarushitelei', *Voprosy psikhologii,* 1969, no. 3, 139.

19   L.G. Zemtsov, 'Nekotorye sotsial'nye aspekty vseobshchego srednego
       obrazovaniya', in R.G. Gurova (ed.), *Sotsiologicheskie problemy
       obrazovaniya i vospitaniya* (M., 1973), 13.

20   E.K. Vasil'eva, *Sotsial'no-professional'nyi uroven' gorodskoi
       molodezhi* (L., 1973), 21, 23.

21   See note 14 above. The founding father of the classical theory of
       Soviet upbringing is A.S. Makarenko (1888-1935).

22   For this example I have to thank Dr. Felicity O'Dell.

23   V. Bazhenov, '"Nemuzhskaya" professiya', *Uch. gaz.,* 4 October 1975.

24   *Itogi Vsesoyuznoi perepisi naseleniya 1970 goda,* vol. VII (M., 1974),
       250-251.

25   D. Valentei and G. Kiseleva, 'Sem'ya, deti, obshchestvo', *Pravda,* 5
       October 1969.

26   L. Korotun *et al.,* 'K idealam kommunisticheskoi nravstvennosti',
       Uch. gaz., 15 November 1969.

27   N.I. Kortyshkov, 'Ikh nel'zya ne zamechat", *ibid.,* 18 January 1973.
28   *NONK,* (1977), *loc. cit.*
29   K. Nozhko, 'Effektivno ispol'zovat' resursy', *Uch. gaz.,* 31, July 1975.
30   *NONK,* 46.
31   S. Semin, 'Puti preodoleniya razlichii mezhdu gorodom i derevnei', *Pravda,* 23 October 1970.
32   *NONK,* 47; Usanov, 'Rubezhi 1975 goda', *Uch. gaz.,* 18 January 1975.
33   *NONK,* 46.
34   Usanov, 'Uverennyl shag vpered', *Uch. gaz.,* 14 February 1976.
35   For Orenburg, V. Kyrkalov and V. Tsypursky, 'Vtoroi dom shkol'nika', *Uch. gaz.,* 7 February 1976; for Abkhazia, S. Tarkhanova, 'Strannyi paradoks', *ibid.,* 24 August 1974.
36   For example, in 1975 it was reported that 221 schools in Chita Region, south-eastern Siberia, lacked any foreign language teaching (V. Galkina, 'Postupaet "vnekonkursnik" ', *ibid.,* 21 August 1975).
37   For an authoritative comment see V. Elyutin, 'Konkurs, student, professiya', *Pravda,* 19 July 1969.
38   One of the many references is T. Tamarin, 'Zalozhniki pedagogiki', *Izvestiya,* 6 February 1969.
39   M. Kazovsky, "Karova", *Uch. gaz.,* 9 December 1972.
40   M.V. Antropova and A.A. Markosyan, 'O rezhime dnya i nagruzke uchashchikhsya', *Sov. ped.,* 1966, no. 10, 42. For a parental *cri de coeur* see V. Mekhtieva, 'Professiyu — ne po podskazke!', *Literaturnaya gazeta,* 8 March 1972.
41   A.Ya. Zhurkina, 'Izuchenie byudzheta vremeni starsheklassnikov', in Gurova, *op. cit.,* 95, 98-99.
42   M. Prokof'ev, 'Proveryaetsya zhizn'yu', *Pravda,* 12 March 1968; T. Tamarin, 'Byt' ili ne byt' vtorogodnichestvu?', *Izvestiya,* 4 June 1968; *id., loc. cit.* (1969).
43   'Zalozhniki prozhekterstva', *Uch. gaz.,* 11 February 1969; also in K. Kovalevsky, 'Ministerstvo proveryaet, izuchaet, rekomenduet', *ibid.,* 27 February 1969. Certificates must show at least the official minimum of attainment.
44   V.I. Chepelev (ed.), *Public Education in the Ukrainian SSR* (Kiev, 1970), 67.
45   Usanov, *loc. cit.* (1976).
46   The term 'dropouts' is preferable to the alternative 'early leavers' as the latter suggests that the pupils are under age when they leave. The correct leaving age is 15, but Moscow data of 1968 have shown that 61.5 per cent of *vybyvshie* from eight-year education are aged from 16 to 18 (Zhamin, *op. cit.,* 47).
47   *Ibid.,* 36, 39.
48   Collated from *ibid.,* 40-42, 45.
49   *Ibid.,* 46-47.
50   *Ibid.,* 40-42. Other causes not mentioned above in the text were 'lack of hostels and extended-day groups', 4.1 per cent (the three republics) and 'big gaps in knowledge', 11 per cent (Rostov Region).

51 V.D. Popov, 'Nekotorye sotsiolo-pedagogicheskie problemy vtorogodnichestva i otseva', in Gurova, *op. cit.*, 25-28. Zhamin (*op. cit.*, 44) refers somewhat obliquely to the negative influence of 'irregular family relationships'.

52 Vasil'eva, *op. cit.*, 27.

53 Popov, *op. cit.*, 28, 30, 35.

54 Zhamin, *op. cit.*, 48.

55 Popov, *op. cit.*, 22.

56 'Polozhenie ostaetsya trevozhnym', *Uch. gaz.*, 19 February 1974.

57 O. Railyanu, 'Vremya ne zhdet', *ibid.*, 11 February 1969.

58 Gerda Achinger, *Die Schulreform in der UdSSR* (Munich, 1973), 44.

59 *Ibid.*, 30-35.

60 For a useful introduction to the work of the Commission, see Detlef Glowka, 'Das sowjetische Schulwesen am Beginn einer neuen Etappe?', *Neue Sammlung*, vol. 7, no. 3 (May-June, 1967), 209-213; for a more detailed analysis, *id.*, 'Das Verhältnis zwischen Wissenschaft und Curriculumreform in der UdSSR', *Bildung und Erziehung*, vol. 24, no. 5 (Sept.-Oct. 1971), 474-484; and for a study of this in relation to the concept of the scientific and technological revolution in Soviet theory, see Achinger, *op. cit.* The reform and its more recent progress are surveyed in John Dunstan, 'Curriculum Change and the Soviet School', *Journal of Curriculum Studies*, vol. 9, no. 2 (November 1977), 111-123.

61 Glowka, *op. cit.* (1971), 477; Achinger, *op. cit.*, 74-82; Dunstan, *op. cit.*, 114-116.

62 Ignacy Szianiawski, 'Die vierte Schulreform in der UdSSR', *Bildung und Erziehung*, vol. 22, no. 4 (July-Aug. 1969), 262-263; Achinger, *op. cit.*, 92-93.

63 For details see *ibid.*, 104-112; and for later developments, Dunstan, *op. cit.*, 118-119.

64 Glowka, *op. cit.* (1971), 481 ('final' at any given stage — change is taken for granted).

65 Usanov, *loc. cit.* (1976).

66 Achinger, *op. cit.*, 106-109; Dunstan, *loc. cit.* and 120.

67 Liam Hudson, *Contrary Imaginations* (Harmondsworth, 1967), 59 *et seq.*

Chapter 3
Special Schools for the Arts

Aesthetic Education: Mass and Specialized
In the Soviet view, aesthetic education is an important component of
the process of upbringing and the well-rounded development of the
personality. It has several functions: it helps to widen the child's
outlook, make him more perceptive, inculcate a moral sense along
with such values as compassion and love of the motherland, foster
comradely relationships and encourage creativity. Like so many
other ingredients of the mixture that is Soviet life, art has a political
purpose. It is a tool for the building of communism. As such it has to
be used in certain ways, and there are others in which its use is
impermissible or inadvisable, though the limits are easier and more
difficult to define according to the nature of its forms. Nevertheless,
there is still much scope for developing the creative impulse.

For members of the general public who want themselves to dance,
act, sing, make music or follow some other aesthetic pursuit, there
exists a wide network of clubs, mostly under the auspices of the
Ministry of Culture, collective farms or trade unions. For the
younger generation there are similar clubs, and here the name of the
Ministry of Education must be added, as it is responsible for facilities
at Pioneer Houses and Palaces (these and the extent of their
availability are to be considered in general terms in a later chapter),
as well as extracurricular activities in general schools. These clubs or
circles have been described by various writers on Soviet education;[1]
our forbearing to dwell on them now must not be taken to imply any
underestimation of their enormous role in artistic training, often at a
high level, but they are concerned with the mass of young people,
talented and less talented, whereas our purpose is to consider special

provision for the more talented and the very talented indeed. By the same token we note, but will not otherwise tarry over at present, the part-time schools, mostly for music but some for fine arts, which children attend out of school hours, sometimes in the morning (where a second school shift still operates) but usually starting at 4 o'clock.[2] Bereday's team reported that 30 to 40 per cent of a given form might attend such schools for six to eight hours a week. The timetable of ordinary full-time day schools includes one art lesson a week for the first six years, and forms 1 to 7 have a weekly period of music and singing.

Special schools for children and young people gifted in the arts have a long history, in some cases going back to the tsarist era. The oldest is probably the Vaganova (Kirov) Ballet School in Leningrad, dating from 1738. They are not part of the system of general secondary education, since they count as 'specialized secondary educational institutions' training medium specialists and in this instance come under the authority of the Ministry of Culture. The argument for their existence runs along the following lines: under communism the cultural level of the people is to be raised as high as possible; therefore the artistic abilities springing from the people's natural endowments are to be brought to full flowering; therefore, too, the individual whose endowments form the basis of outstanding abilities must be actively assisted to develop and perfect such abilities for the benefit of the whole people; he or she must be provided with the best possible environment and surrounded with the appropriate formative influences; in most cases this process must start in childhood for maximum effectiveness; for such children, ordinary schools do not provide sufficiently intensive teaching in the arts; therefore special schools are essential. To provide equality of opportunity for artistically gifted children from more remote areas, an adequate number of such schools must have boarding accommodation, and they should follow suitably imaginative recruitment procedures.

Special schools for the arts are of various types. Their specialisms, in order of frequency, are music, fine arts and ballet. There are also a few schools combining some of these specialisms. (We are omitting here secondary colleges of music (*uchilishcha,* 242 with over 105,000 students in 1973[3]), drama schools (8 with 1,200 students in 1968[4]), colleges of fine arts, and other specialized secondary establishments of a semi-artistic kind such as those training theatre technicians, since they recruit at 15-plus or after and may thus be regarded as *normal* 'specialized secondary educational institutions'; circus schools will have their turn later.)

Special Schools: Development since 1958

Statistics on the schools are not published systematically, and random references, as is so often the case, tend to be erratic. The figures for ballet schools are the most consistent, with 16 in 1958 and 18 by the end of the 1960s.[5] Full-time secondary schools specializing in fine art numbered five in 1958 and about 50 in the late 1960s, in association with institutes of fine arts.[6] The position with music schools is much more obscure. However, it can at least be said that the USSR's full-time secondary schools for those with outstanding gifts in music appear to have increased from five in the late 1950s to about a dozen in the early 1960s, 19 by 1963, 24 by 1966 and 36 by 1973.[7] The number of young musicians in these schools also doubled (from about 7,000 to 14,000) between 1963 and 1973,[8] but the overall proportion of children in the above types of school cannot be satisfactorily calculated for lack of data. It can, however, be concluded that by the late 1960s there were about 90 special schools for highly gifted children in the USSR, or roughly 0.2 per cent of all day secondary general schools,[9] and since then their number has increased by over a dozen. Such schools are so few that they can be expected to be much in demand and consequently highly selective.

Certain authorities have also alluded to 7-year or 8-year schools with extended music teaching, *i.e.* ordinary schools specializing in music. Here the figures quoted are over 1,200 in the early 1960s, rising to some 3,500 by 1966.[10] Finding it impossible to substantiate these figures — or indeed to glean any further generalized information about such schools — from elsewhere, the present writer is of the opinion that they have somehow become confused with those for part-time music schools. An American investigator, writing in 1963 on the basis of an earlier visit, reported specifically that there were 1,800 part-time 7-year music schools and 100 similar schools for art.[11] One of the standard Soviet handbooks on educational statistics records an increase in the Ministry of Culture's 'children's music and art schools' from 1,756 with 316,300 pupils in 1960/61 to 4,504 with 760,000 pupils in 1970/71.[12] The category is not defined but the table is sandwiched between one on out-of-school establishments for children and another about children at Pioneer camps. This piece of circumstantial evidence suggesting that the figures refer to extracurricular facilities is reinforced by a survey of education in the RSFSR which specifically classifies 'children's art and music schools' as out-of-school establishments.[13] Other official sources cite 'primary music schools', rising from 1,900 with 330,000 pupils in 1963 to 7,000 with over a million in 1973;[14] this seems to be an alternative term for the same part-time institutions. When these data are tabulated in accordance with their respective years and designations, a steady growth pattern emerges which heightens the impression that schools which some have believed to possess a music profile are in reality part-time establishments in the majority of cases.

TABLE 3.1 Part-Time Schools for the Arts

Date	'Children's music and art schools'	'7-year music schools'	'Primary music schools'	'Schools with extended music teaching' (*sic* 1966)
Early 1960s(?)				1,200
1960/61	1,756			
1963 or earlier		1,800		
1963			1,900	
1966				3,500
1968/69	3,826			
1970/71	4,504			
1973			7,000	

Note   The first column is broadly comparable with the others since the art schools form a small minority, about 100 being reported in 1963.

Sources See notes to the text, 10-12, 14; figures for 1968/69 cited by Glowka, *Schulreform und Gesellschaft in der Sowjetunion 1958-1968*, footnote to 24, from *Zhenshchiny i deti v SSSR* (M., 1969), 138.

We say 'in the majority of cases' because, given the Soviet education system's capacity for experiment, the existence of ordinary schools with a music profile is certainly not to be ruled out. A rare documented instance is the 8-year boarding school at Ioshkar-Ola in the Mari Autonomous Republic, which provides early training for national cadres of musicians and artists and whose leavers proceed to one of the institutions offering a four-year course of secondary vocational training in art or music. Among boarding schools with a music profile, the total number of which is not known, this school is evidently a showpiece.[15] Tartu in Estonia has 13 secondary schools, six of which have a miscellany of special profiles; three of these specialize in music along with another profile.[16] Other unusual combinations, to be found in Moscow, are an ordinary school with a distinct drama profile in the form of specialized options,[17] and a German language school with special classes in painting and art appreciation.[18] What now follows, however, concerns the few arts schools for the outstandingly gifted which incorporate a senior course.

Selection: Policy and Procedures

At what age do the schools recruit their pupils, and how exactly do they go about it? Special music schools admit children at the age of seven to the first form. The two choir schools also take 8-year-olds. At the ballet schools, practice varies; the commonest age of entry is 10, after three years of primary education, but the Bolshoi Ballet School takes young people at 13 or 14 if they are to specialize in folk dancing or the dances of the Soviet republics.[19] The special full-time art schools for children are said to recruit their pupils at the age of eleven into form 5,[20] since talent of this kind is thought not to become evident until such an age.[21] From Estonia, however, comes a report of an 11-year school which has an art stream filled competitively from the outset, progression to the specialist senior course being dependent on further examination.[22]

In 1960 George Bereday wrote that with their superior locations, reputations and comforts ('silk aprons instead of cotton ones') parents who valued the benefits of differential education were bound to fix their sights on special schools, even if their children's talent was not much above average.[23] Human nature being what it is, Bereday's claim would be difficult to refute; in any case, as will be seen later, there is evidence of parental aspirations from other areas of secondary education. The same author also comments that these schools do not canvass the total age-group, but merely select the most suitable applicants, though these no doubt include children discovered and encouraged by their teachers.[24] Yet apart from the mind-boggling problems which would have been involved in attempts by five music schools (as they then were) to cover more than 4 million seven-year-olds, such a picture is less than fair — although it is supplemented in another volume under Bereday's editorship. The catchment area of the Central Music School in Moscow is countrywide and it recruits through the national and local media. Also, there is specific provision for musically gifted children who have no parents to push them forward.[25] Thus the Koku Music School at Kishinev, the Moldavian capital, which also has a ballet section, includes a quota of 15 orphans among its annual intake,[26] and special children's homes or boarding schools sometimes refer pupils to the Central Music School.[27] Two of these institutions are in Tashkent and Leningrad. Every March a number of teachers from the Leningrad establishment visit the ordinary children's homes and boarding schools in 18 surrounding regions and pick out about 200 potential entrants; in June they come to the school for tests and 30 are selected. Not all are orphans or from poor homes — a minority are simply from places without adequate musical facilities, and their parents contribute to their maintenance,[28] doubtless in accordance with the standard scale of fees for residential education, as was envisaged in 1958.[29] These are income-related and may be waived in cases of need.

Such talent-scouting is not unusual. The same procedure is followed by the staff of the Solomiya Krushel'nitskaya Music School at Lvov in the Ukraine;[30] and teachers from the Alma-Ata Conservatoire sometimes travel to remote parts of Kazakhstan to spot the musically gifted children of nomadic tribesmen for training at the special music boarding school at Alma-Ata.[31] Speaking generally of special music schools, Miriam Morton, whose book *The Arts and the Soviet Child* (1972) is to be commended as the standard and indispensable account of its subject, estimates that about 10 per cent of the pupils are from remote rural areas or distant towns without a conservatoire,[32] so that it is quite normal for these schools to be residential, either in full or in part. Their equivalents for the fine arts also have boarding accommodation.[33]

At all types of schools for the artistically gifted there are likely to be children whose gifts were first noticed during their activities at Pioneer Palaces and so on, where the tuition is by experts.[34] But, as well as spotting talent in dancing clubs at ordinary schools,[35] the famous Vaganova Ballet School in Leningrad sends its scouts over the whole country. This school and the Bolshoi Ballet School aim to take five children from each of the other fourteen Soviet republics for later replenishment of the ballet companies in these republics or the staffs of ballet schools there.[36] Thus, although in 1959 and 1960 it was variously reported that the Leningrad school recruited from one half to two thirds of its annual 60-pupil intake from the city itself,[37] its celebrated reputation enables the remainder to be highly diversified, and this must be equally true of the Bolshoi Ballet School, of whose 518 pupils in 1969, 39, or 7.5 per cent, were from foreign countries.[38]

Elizabeth Moos has described the entrance examinations at the Leningrad schools. They comprise three parts — physical fitness and strength, musical ability, and dance. The physical examination is naturally of fundamental importance, and is conducted by a team of specially-trained anatomists, doctors and dancers. The anatomists assess the child's physique for actual and prospective extensibility, flexibility and so forth.[39] Anyone ignorant of ballet may well be surprised to learn what tremendous resilience is required of the performers; to gauge the child's capacity and potential for this is the responsibility of the doctors and dancers. Only those who reach the necessary physical standards are allowed to proceed to the next stage. Physical attractiveness and superior intelligence have been said to be other important criteria.[40]

The special music schools also test their young candidates for health as well as for musical aptitude: rhythm, memory and sensitivity. Before a panel of five or six people, including the head of music, the person in overall charge of other subjects and the head tutor, a teacher asks each child to sing a song, play a short piece, repeat individual notes and phrases and identify single notes and the number in a chord.[41] At the Riga Music School in 1967 the tests took two days, but instrumental ability was not required; instead the child was asked to demonstrate his proficiency as he chose, in singing or dancing.[42] At the Moscow Art School in the late 1950s the examination continued for ten days.[43]

The ratio of successful candidates to applicants to the music schools varies, but is said to be about one in five or six.[44] At Kishinev in 1968 90 out of 500 made the grade. Sometimes the competition appears to be less stiff; the following year the proportion was 70 out of 200,[45] and at Riga in 1966 it was 30 out of 80.[46] The varying number of places in a given year doubtless depends on long-term planning considerations. A problem here, however, which makes comparisons difficult, is the definition of 'applicant'. It is not always possible to distinguish between the number of *original* applicants and the number permitted to take the entrance tests; it should not be assumed that they necessarily coincide, for the latter may also be geared to planning requirements or depend on available facilities. One writer states specifically that in 1958 the Central Music School in Moscow accepted only 40 out of 250 children admitted to the entrance examination.[47] With a prestigious school such as this, it seems highly likely that a good many more expressed interest. This was certainly true of Moscow's special art school in 1958; of 1,500 initial applicants 250, or one in six, were called for examination and 50 were chosen[48] — one in five of the examinees and one in thirty of the original applicants. This matter of definition may account for the remarkable inconsistency in two sets of data on the Vaganova Ballet School in Leningrad from the late 1950s: both agree that the school selects 60 pupils each year, but the number of applicants is variously stated to be about 600 and 2,000.[49] It seems likely that the figure of 600 represents a rather lengthy shortlist, and that one in 33 of the initial applicants and one in ten of those examined satisfied the requirements. According to an account of the Bolshoi School published in 1963, 75 candidates were chosen from 1,200 examinees.[50] The overriding impression is that entry is very competitive indeed.

All the special secondary schools for the artistically gifted are coeducational except for the two choir schools in Moscow and Leningrad which are for boys only.[51] In 1958, while boys predominated at the Moscow Art School in the ratio of seven to three, which was said to be traditional, they were outnumbered by girls at the Tashkent music boarding school (about two to three), and at the Vaganova Ballet School there were twice as many girls as boys.[52] At the latter school the proportion, as might be expected, was said to depend on the job situation,[53] but this probably remains fairly constant, because the same sex ratio was reported more recently. The ratio at the music school also appears typical.[54]

Social Composition

With schools operating a highly selective admissions policy the social composition of the student body is bound to be a matter of curiosity. The criterion is said to be giftedness, but, as mentioned above, Western commentators have speculated about the extent to which ambitious parents use the schools essentially as a differentiated and therefore superior channel of education. That they try to do so is evident from occasional Soviet remarks, and this attitude is condemned, but how far do they succeed? As far as we know, there have been no sophisticated analyses of the social composition of these schools, but it is possible to collate a handful of random references.

At the Vaganova Ballet School the children are predominantly from working class homes (60 per cent — say 65 per cent if children from abroad are excluded from the calculations). This was conceded in two essentially critical works on the Soviet school on the basis of a visit in the 1958/59 academic year, and corroborated in a friendly but not blinkered account published in 1972.[55] In 1960 it was claimed that the reason for this was that rank-and-file ballet dancers are not unusually well paid.[56] One cannot rule out this consideration; but if it were all that important one would still have to explain the presence of a very substantial number of children from non-working class families. It should also be remembered that ballet dancers do not have to be famous to enjoy popular esteem in the USSR, and that in artistic professions job satisfaction counts for a great deal. The prestige of the vocation must appeal to parents, especially if their children so obviously enjoy what they are doing.

Let us formulate a hypothesis — ingenuous, some may think — about the social composition of the Vaganova School: that it is so inundated with applications that it can generally afford to be rigidly selective in whom it accepts, operating strictly on the basis of outstanding promise; that gifts for the dance are evenly distributed across the population; and that therefore the proportional intake of workers' children should approximate to the proportion of workers in the population (USSR: 1959, 80.5 per cent; 1970, 72.7 per cent[57]). It is assumed that by 'working class' our American sources (and presumably their Soviet ones) meant 'engaged mainly in physical work'; the population statistics are used in this sense. We find, on reference to reality, that there is not an exact match, but the gap is not wide and it is narrowing, not because of any apparent variation in the admissions policy of the school but because of demographic change. The 8 per cent additional representation of non-working class children may be due to greater awareness on the part of their parents. But the social composition of Leningrad itself is another explanatory factor; it has been noted that the school takes 50 to 66 per cent of its pupils from the city, and non-working class families are of course more heavily represented there than in the country as a whole. However, if 'working class' is used in its strict official sense, *i.e.* industrial manual workers and state farm peasants, in the local context it was already *over*-represented at the school in 1959 when this group comprised 57.9 per cent of the population of Leningrad and its subordinated settlements.[58]

The slenderness of the remaining evidence makes generalization impossible. Some of it suggests that the social composition of the Vaganova School in broad terms (backgrounds of involvement in primarily physical or mental work) may not be so very different from that of the average special school for the arts, but that the individual cases from which the mean is computed may range quite widely. In 1975 the vice-chairman of the Executive Committee of the Novosibirsk City Soviet stated:

> Of the 690 students admitted in 1974 to the theatrical, choreographic, musicians', and cultural-educational schools of Novosibirsk, 484 are of worker and collective farmer background. Over 70 per cent of the pupils of the city's music schools are also the children of workers.[59]

One cannot be absolutely sure what kind of schools the writer has in mind, and one notes with curiosity his apparent distinction between musicians' schools (which may refer to 15-plus entry) and music schools (which may or may not be part-time). But they are certainly mentioned in the context of selective education for the gifted and in both cases the working class component exceeds 70 per cent. At the Kishinev special music school in 1969 a mere 20 per cent of the pupils came from professional backgrounds.[60]

On the other hand, a Belorussian study is said to have shown that two-thirds of the students in music schools (again, the term is not defined) in Minsk and five regions in that republic were from the intelligentsia,[61] and at the special music school in Alma-Ata nearly 90 per cent of the pupils occupy this category.[62] If the raw material could be found it might be instructive to make a comparative study of overall provision for special education for gifted young people in Kazakhstan and Moldavia. It might be feasible to ascertain whether, given that there are many more working-class children at the Kishinev school, this is due to greater equality of opportunity resulting from more generous provision of special schooling; or, if the facilities are fewer, whether it reflects a specific admissions policy. Certainly no evidence has yet come to light of any kind of *class-based* quota system in this sector of education.

Organizational Aspects

That special schools of this kind tend to be smallish, averaging 300 to 400 pupils, is not remarkable, but the Uspensky Music School at Tashkent has as many as 600,[63] and it comes as a surprise to learn that the Bolshoi Ballet School had no fewer than 518 young people on its books in 1969,[64] about twice as many as the average ballet school.[65] They all lead a very full and busy life, since the schools provide an ample, if somewhat reduced, programme of general education in addition to intensive training in their specialism.

At the music schools all children take courses in piano, theory, solfeggio, harmony, counterpoint, music literature, analysis and orchestration. The specialisms include chamber music class (for pianists and others), orchestra class, piano accompaniment, instrument teaching method, conducting, rhythmics and others.[66] As may be imagined, the ballet schools devote most time and attention to classical dance (unless pupils are specializing in national dance, in which case it is reduced by about half), but the curriculum also covers historical Russian and folk dance, *pas de deux,* ballet and theatre history, makeup, acting techniques and other subjects.[67] At art schools, the special subjects in order of importance are drawing, which accounts for nearly half of the specialized programme, painting and sculpture, composition, modelling (for the 11- and 12-year olds) and history of art (for the 15- and 16-year olds).[68] Music schools, if the one at Tashkent is typical, provide their pupils with facilities for the other arts, and ballet schools bring art history and music firmly into the curriculum,[69] but schools for the fine arts seem to reciprocate not nearly so generously.

The workload of special music school pupils is compared with that of children at ordinary schools in the following table; the figures represent hours over the total 11-year course which applied during the early 1960s, since later comparable data are not to hand. At that period pupils at music schools devoted nearly half as much time again to their overall work programme as children at ordinary schools. Classes in general subjects consist of not more than 20 to 25

TABLE 3.2 Total (Eleven-Year) Course Hours, Special Music Schools and Ordinary Schools, c.1963

	Music School (stringed instruments specialism)[1]	Ordinary School (urban, RSFSR)
General subjects	7,514	9,908
Specialism[1]	3,062	–
Labour training	–	2,671
Practice (estimate[2])	6,760	–
Total	17,336	12,579
Options (maximum)	1,160[3]	226

Notes Homework in general subjects is extra

1   Piano specialism is 442 hours less
2   The figure for practice is included because without it the absence of labour training in the music school gives the false impression that the load is lighter there. It is based on the statement by a music school director that the hours spent on music in the first three forms are about two a day; in forms 4 to 6, three; and in the other forms 'more than three' — say four (Madison, *op. cit.,* 247). If anything, this errs on the modest side (cp. *CET, 1967, loc. cit*). Incidentally it corresponds fairly closely to the situation at an English choir school of our acquaintance. On the assumption that practice has to be a daily habit, the above hours were multiplied by seven, from this the weekly course hours for the specialism were deducted for the applicable number of school weeks, and the remainder was designated as practice. It was also assumed that practice would continue at the same rate during the holidays. It is not clear from the sources whether practice hours can be identified in length of time with class hours (*viz.* 45-minute teaching periods).
3   The figure of 1,160 assumes that each of the options on offer can be taken by the same child; thus it may be much smaller.

Sources *Music school:* Bryce, *op. cit.,* pp. 62, 66. *Ordinary school:* conflated from 'The Curriculum for the Eight-Year and Secondary Schools of the RSFSR', *Soviet Education,* vol II, no. 3 (January 1960), 30-31 (translated from *Narodnoe obrazovanie,* 1959, no. 11)

pupils,[70] somewhat fewer than in ordinary schools and probably with the aim of teaching more intensively to counterbalance the reduced number of hours. At Riga in 1967 such classes comprised only 10 to 12 children; thus, it was claimed, there was little need for homework.[71] The music teaching varies from individual tuition to groups usually not exceeding a dozen. Like the music schools, those for ballet demand a substantial input of practice, with two hours a day for the 10-plus beginners and four or five by the time they have reached the age of 13.[72]

Such a school, then, is no place for debutantes and dilettantes; discipline and dedication are what it requires. Although the over-14s have an incentive for good progress and conduct in the form of a monthly allowance,[73] in general the pupils' work has to be its own reward. The heavy demands on their time leave them little opportunity for the sport and other leisure activities which figure in the lives of ordinary Soviet children. Indeed, the pupils at the Vaganova Ballet School are apparently not allowed to take part in sport[74] — although fencing and, necessarily, gymnastics have their place in the timetable — and, incredible as it sounds, it is reported that Pioneer circles do not function at the Central Music School.[75] These are the leading institutions of their kind and so ought not to be taken as typical, but such points do bring home, albeit with exaggeration, the tempo of life in special schools for the arts.

One consequence of this and of other factors is that there has to be provision for transfer from the schools. Thorough though the selection procedures are, they are not foolproof, and if the child's aptitudes do not come up to expectations, transfer to an ordinary school is likely at some stage.[76] Maybe his talents prove to be no match for the demands made upon him, maybe the pace is too rigorous, or maybe later physical development rules out a career in ballet. At the Moscow Art School as many as one in six were said to drop out and return to an ordinary school.[77] At the Riga Music School about 18 per cent were weeded out at the end of the first year.[78] The rate of eventual success at special music schools has been quoted as about 50 per cent of entrants.[79] But the transfer can work both ways; able older children are sometimes accepted from mass schools.[80] Exceptionally gifted children from the less well-endowed ballet schools may also be transferred to Moscow or Leningrad.[81]

There are two careers open to artistically gifted young people who wish to make a living by their art: performer or teacher. Those who finish the ballet schools may combine the two: the best join the Bolshoi or Kirov ballets and the next best other companies, but the professional life of a ballet dancer in the USSR is short; retirement at 35 is usual, and the ballerina, who is perhaps already teaching part-time, may then move to a full-time teaching post.[82] In art, the 17-year-olds go on to higher education, usually at the institute of fine arts to which the school is attached, though some enter film or theatre institutes. The USSR has 50 institutes of fine arts and these train teachers as well as artists.[83] At the Moscow Art School the less proficient transfer at 14 or 15 to a secondary college of art,[84] and presumably this happens elsewhere.

At the special music schools too some children, no doubt the less outstanding ones, leave at 15 to enter secondary colleges of music, and ultimately in all probability teaching, though higher education is also accessible by this route. Of those who stay on to complete the senior forms, some apparently go straight into teaching or professional work, but the normal course is to embark upon higher music education.[85] Many gain places at conservatoires — the proportions quoted for different schools range from one-third to 100 per cent,[86] but this does seem to be the path of the great majority — eventually to become performers or composers, while others enter music institutes. The country has 150 such institutes for the training of music teachers.[87] Pupils from the choir schools join male voice choirs, the most prestigious of which is the Glinka State Academic Choir, or become choirmasters.

Questionings: 1958 and After

Thus it is that a small and carefully selected number of gifted Soviet children and young people undergo a rigorous programme of education and training in institutions designed to produce, or to lay a sound basis for producing, the country's top leaders — performers and teachers — in various fields of the arts. It may be thought that against a background of much ideologically-based approbation, respect and practical support for the performing arts and the fine arts on the part of the authorities — always assuming, of course, that the message conveyed is for the good of the cause — the need for highly specialized provision from an early age in order to achieve this goal is sufficient legitimation for the departure from the principle of the unified labour school. After all, the proportion of children selected is so tiny that it scarcely represents a serious inroad into the comprehensive system. And yet not everyone is happy about it. From time to time a bubble of disquiet comes to the surface and breaks. This should not be exaggerated, but it happens; and this raises the question why, and what attitudes lie beneath.

It is not surprising to learn that the only time in recent years when bubbles came in a string was during the period when Khrushchev turned the world of education upside-down. The reforms of the later 1950s constituted an attempt to return to what Khrushchev saw as first principles: a reassertion of the state's primary role in the upbringing of children, a reaffirmation of physical labour as a primary component of education, and a re-emphasis of respect for such labour as an essential goal of the socialization of young people. In Soviet terms these aims were beyond reproach; it was Khrushchev's distinctly utopian methods that proved to be at fault. He created much controversy. Interest groups were galvanized into action. To some extent they succeeded in modifying what were later branded his hare-brained schemes, but the resulting chaos was still considerable.

Special schools were one of the issues debated in the fairly free atmosphere of those later 1950s (symbolized simply but effectively in the film *The Clear Sky* when a scene of shocked reaction to a radio announcement of the death of Stalin cuts to one of the ice on a mighty river rapidly breaking up in the sunshine of a glorious spring day . . .). William K. Medlin learned from discussions with Soviet educational officials that ever since 1956 certain groups had insisted on the provision of such schools for children with artistic and intellectual gifts, whereas what he mysteriously termed 'another social stratum' had favoured a more egalitarian system.[88] Unfortunately he says no more about these intriguing conversations. We turn therefore to the evidence, such as it is, of published statements about schools for the artistically gifted; the much fuller data on those for the intellectually gifted will be examined in later chapters.

The first point to stress is that at this time special schools for the arts were a going concern; outwardly at least they were approved by the authorities and they did not come under official public attack. In a conference paper published in April 1957, the eminent educationist N.K. Goncharov envisaged the wide development, over the next 15 to 20 years, of such secondary schools, with entry either at 7-plus or at 11-plus depending on the arts specialism.[89] In the summer of 1958 E.I. Afanasenko, the RSFSR Minister of Education, referred to them in matter-of-fact terms: providing general secondary education and simultaneously ensuring the development of the children's natural gifts, they were evidently a necessity. Judging from the context of his remarks, the Minister seemed to be citing them as a precedent for setting up special schools for gifted young scientists.[90] As we shall see, the latter category formed the centre of interest of the ensuing debate. In his Memorandum of 21 September to the Central Committee, Khrushchev advocated both types of school in the same breath,[91] but in the Theses of the Central Committee and the Council of Ministers issued on 16 November the special arts schools received individual attention: 'it is desirable to retain schools for children showing superior abilities in music, choreography and the fine arts'. They should have boarding facilities and 'give their pupils a general secondary education, work training and special training in some field of art. On completing their studies at these schools, pupils can go direct to appropriate higher educational establishments'.[92]

Does the use of 'retain' suggest that the retention of the schools had been queried, thus independently confirming Medlin's report? And at what level? What did Khrushchev the equaliser really think about them? Answers to such questions can only be speculative. But it seems clear that the retention of their hitherto existing curricular structure had been challenged. A few days before publication of the Theses, I. Beloded, Minister of Education of the Ukraine, had commented briefly that the schools were unobjectionable but their pupils must not be mollycoddled and seniors must take part in socially useful work;[93] the Theses stipulated the inclusion of labour training. Cosseting these children and cocooning them away from life was to be a not uncommon criticism of these schools. Perhaps Beloded's statement represents an authoritative compromise: they shall continue, but they must be modified and their shortcomings rectified, and the remedy is a good and regular dose of physical work.

Nevertheless, the debate continued for a short while. Some outright opposition was expressed, if not at a high level, but most contributors came out in support of the schools, qualifying it with critical comments and suggestions as to how the dose was best administered. A. Sharipov, the Kazakh Minister of Education, however, expressed his support without qualification, though he did not extend it to science schools.[94] With obvious concern about attitude formation, N. Levitov, an educationist, felt that music, art and ballet schools should not advertise themselves as establishments for the specially gifted: 'observations show that in these schools success increases in arithmetical, and the superciliousness of the children in geometrical, progression'.[95] Meanwhile a technical inspector of wagons at a coking and chemical plant had referred, equally forcefully and much more colourfully, to dodgers in special schools growing up like hothouse plants, 'fearing physical work as the devil fears incense'. Everyone ought to go to work after form 8 and take part in the factory's cultural activities, and it should be for the workers' collective to decide later if, for instance, a young man with a good voice should go on with his musical studies.[96] A teacher thought that compulsory factory work would put a brake on the young artist's development,[97] but two university students argued that such experience would enhance the quality of his art.[98] Reviewing letters received, the teachers' newspaper *Uchitel'skaya gazeta* said that there was general agreement that special schools for the artistically gifted should be kept, but some also favoured the two years' industrial experience before higher education that had been proposed for pupils from the mass schools, and all considered compulsory labour training in the schools to be essential.[99]

What form did this labour training take? A visitor to the Tashkent Music School reported that it possessed a well-equipped workshop where the pupils went through the whole process of making records, from the raw materials to the finished recorded product, for which the sale was countrywide. The older ones also helped with the cotton harvest.[100] There seems some doubt, however, as to whether production training developed very much in these schools, since the practical artistic work itself came to be regarded as labour activity, some kinds of manual work might be hazardous,[101] and in any case the partial retreat from polytechnism in the mid-sixties must have withdrawn the pressure for it.

In the opinion of one director, artistic children are often difficult to bring up because they are naturally temperamental and self-centred; she found summer farm work to be a good antidote for this.[102] Some have a tendency to be interested in nothing but their specialisms;[103] this must be fought as it contradicts the fundamental principle of all-round development. As one writer puts it: 'Yes, these children are naturally gifted (*talantlivy ot prirody*), but what a lot of effort and inspiration are required from teachers and tutors for the school to produce people who not only can make music and draw but also love labour, value comradeship and acknowledge their responsibility to society'.[104] The residential arrangements at many of the schools doubtless offer various opportunities for self-help and serving the school community. Cultural isolation may be avoided and socially useful activities pursued by having the children go out to give public performances and help in music clubs at other schools.

Since the debates of 1958 special schools for the artistically gifted have been very little in the public eye; occasionally the education press reports the opening of a new one and that is virtually all. Judgments on them, whether for or against, seem to have been equally sparse. In 1967 the eminent sociologist M.N. Rutkevich in a famous article referred approvingly to them (and other special schools), in the form of boarding schools for gifted children from remote areas, as a means of achieving full, factual equality.[105] Five years later Academician Kapitsa justified them in other familiar terms: their specialisms are little taught in ordinary schools, training from an early age is necessary, and such schools are few.[106]

On the other hand, V.N. Stoletov, President of the USSR Academy of Pedagogical Sciences, has gone on record as being implacably opposed to the notion of special schools for gifted children, on the grounds that talents cannot be reliably prognosticated. 'The little boy who today charmingly strums on the guitar or mandoline or is quite good at drawing the bow', he says, 'is not bound to be a future virtuoso, wildly applauded by demanding concertgoers.' Well-rounded personality development in such schools he believes to be impossible. Stoletov is thinking mainly of mathematics and science schools, and his remarks will be reconsidered later in the context of their date (February 1973), but they are worthy of mention now as he specifically includes a reference to 'musical culture', and by extension special schools for the arts do not secure the dispensation that was customary in 1958.[107]

It seems that special full-time schools for artistically gifted children have come to stay. It is argued that they are the most effective means of providing intensive teaching in the formative years in order to produce cadres of certain kinds. They are openly selective, with highly competitive entry on the basis of merit, and boarding arrangements ensure that deserving children are not disadvantaged by distance. In other words, they are a classic example of the meritocratic interpretation of the principle of equality of opportunity. The training is rigorous, but those who survive the long apprenticeship earn a certificate of admission to a respected profession and a successful career. Despite their strongly entrenched position, however, in words at least these schools are not unassailable. There are some individuals who resent what they see as privilege and special treatment, and others fear that such conditions may breed egotism and arrogance, even though teachers and tutors are on their guard. Thus, against a framework of limited differentiation in the interests of quality, there are occasional signs of an egalitarian position which we shall notice again.

Notes

1   For example, Deana Levin, *Leisure and Pleasure of Soviet Children* (London, 1966); Miriam Morton, *The Arts and the Soviet Child* (New York and London, 1972).

2   George Z.F. Bereday *et al.*, *The Changing Soviet School* (Boston, 1960), 365; Levin, *op. cit.*, 77-80.

3   *Bol'shaya sovetskaya entsiklopediya*, vol. 17 (M., 1974), 96.

4   K.A. Gaevskaya, article in *Pedagogicheskaya entsiklopediya*, vol. 4 (M., 1968), col. 439.

5   Bereday *et. al.*, *op. cit.*, 370; Morton, *op. cit.*, 315-316.

6   Bereday *et al.*, *op. cit.*, 367; Morton, *op. cit.*, 278. The figure of 50 is also quoted in Nigel Grant, *Soviet Education* (London, 1964), 91, and Harold J. Noah, *Financing Soviet Schools* (New York, 1966), 34.

7   Bereday *et al.*, *op. cit.*, 365; Noah, *loc. cit.*; Grant, *op. cit.*, 107; Mayo Bryce, *Fine Arts Education in the Soviet Union* (Washington, D.C.: G.P.O., 1963), 29; Detlef Glowka, *Schulreform und Gesellschaft in der Sowjetunion 1958-1968* (Stuttgart, 1970), 24; *Bol'shaya sovetskaya entsiklopediya*, *loc. cit.*

8   A.A. Nikolaev, article in *Pedagogicheskaya entsiklopediya*, vol. 2 (M., 1965), col. 890; *Bol'shaya sovetskaya entsiklopediya, loc. cit.*

9   This calculation may encounter objections in that these schools are not usually classified as general but as specialized (*i.e.* technical) secondary schools. However, as the latter do not as a rule admit children under 15, the comparison seems justified, and is certainly more useful.

10   Grant, *loc. cit.;* Glowka, *loc. cit.*
11   Bryce, *op. cit.,* 19, 28.
12   *NONK,* 148.
13   M.P. Kashin and E.M. Chekharin (eds.), *Narodnoe obrazovanie v RSFSR* (M., 1970), 137.
14   See note 8 above.
15   *Uchitel'skaya gazeta,* 23 January 1971; Lev Gurov, 'Shkola, gde rozhdayutsya muzy', *Kul'tura i zhizn',* 1972, no. 4, 26-27. For further details of medium-level musical training see Nikolaev, *op. cit.,* cols. 890-891, and Gaevskaya, *op. cit.,* cols. 438-439.
16   A. Owen and F.R. Watson, *Report to the British Council on a Visit to the USSR* (unpublished duplicated typescript, 1973), 12.
17   N.G. Kort (interviewed by G. Simanovich), 'Teatral'nyi klass', *Sovetskaya kul'tura,* 26 July 1974. This and the next reference were supplied by Dr Marianna Butenschön.
18   'Besuch in der Moskauer Schule Nr. 50', *Sowjetunion heute,* 1 May 1972.
19   Gaevskaya, *op. cit.,* col. 439.
20   Bryce, *op. cit.,* 22.
21   Universities of London, Reading and Oxford, *Comparative Education Tour to the USSR,* Easter 1967, 25. (Duplicated typescript at Institute of Education Library, University of London; hereafter *CET, 1967.)*
22   Levin, *op. cit.,* 28.
23   George Z.F. Bereday, 'Class Tensions in Soviet Education', in George Z.F. Bereday and Jaan Pennar (eds.), *The Politics of Soviet Education* (New York, 1960), 75-76.
24   Bereday, *op. cit.,* 75.
25   Bereday *et al., The Changing Soviet School,* 365-366.
26   Morton, *op. cit.,* 142.
27   Bereday, *et al., op. cit.,* 366-367.
28   Bernice Q. Madison, *Social Welfare in the Soviet Union* (Stanford, 1968), 246-247. For a detailed account of the Tashkent school see Elizabeth Moos, *Soviet Education Today and Tomorrow* (New York, no date [?1959]), 46-48.
29   *Bringing Soviet Schools still Closer to Life,* Soviet Booklet No. 44 (London, 1958), 11.
30   Vladimir Popov, 'Dom, polnyi muzyki,' *Uch. gaz.,* 29 October 1974.
31   Morton, *op. cit.,* 140.
32   *Ibid.,* 139.
33   For a short account of the Leningrad Art School, which takes pupils from all over the USSR, see N. Soya, 'Khudozhestvennaya shkola-internat', *Sem'ya i shkola,* 1958, no. 3, 33.
34   Levin, *op. cit.,* 76.
35   Grant, *loc. cit.*
36   Morton, *op. cit.,* 307, 314; Bryce, *op. cit.,* 34.
37   Moos, *op. cit.,* 49; Bereday *et al., op. cit.,* 370.
38   Morton, *op. cit.,* 307.

39 Moos, *loc. cit.*
40 Bryce, *loc. cit.*
41 Morton, *op. cit.,* 140.
42 *CET, 1967,* 67.
43 Bereday *et al., op. cit.,* 368.
44 Glowka, *loc. cit.*
45 Morton, *op. cit.,* 142.
46 *CET, 1967, loc. cit.*
47 John T. Figueroa, 'Selection and Differentiation in Soviet Schools', in Edmund J. King (ed.), *Communist Education* (London, 1963), 130.
48 Bereday *et al, loc. cit.* Bryce, *op. cit.,* 22, gives an annual intake of 50 from about 200 examinees.
49 Moos, *loc. cit.* (600); Bereday *et al., op. cit.,* 370 (2000).
50 Bryce, *op. cit.,* 34-35.
51 Gaevskaya, *op. cit.,* col. 439.
52 Moos, *loc. cit.;* Bereday *et al., op. cit.,* 367, 370.
53 Moos, *loc. cit.*
54 Morton, *op. cit.,* 140, 314.
55 Bereday, *loc. cit.; id. et al.,* 370; Morton, *op. cit.,* 314.
56 Bereday, *loc. cit.*
57 *Itogi Vsesoyuznoi perepisi naseleniya 1970 goda,* vol. VI (M., 1973), 6-7.
58 *Itogi Vsesoyuznoi perepisi naseleniya 1959 goda RSFSR* (M., 1963), 152.
59 Leonid F. Kolesnikov, 'Selective Schools in Russia: How the System Works,' *The Times,* 20 September 1975 (letter).
60 Morton, *op. cit.,* 140.
61 K. Buslov *et al., Struktura sovetskoi intelligentsii* (Minsk, 1970), 110, cited in Zev Katz, *Patterns of Social Mobility in the USSR* (Cambridge, Mass., 1973), 85.
62 Morton, *loc. cit.*
63 *Uch. gaz.,* 3 February 1970.
64 Morton, *op. cit.,* 307. For a brief illustrated description of the Bolshoi Ballet School, see B. Lavrenyuk, 'Shkola Bol'shogo Baleta', *Sovetskaya zhenshchina,* 1972, no. 1, 29-31.
65 Deduced from Gaevskaya, *loc. cit.*
66 Nikolaev, *op. cit.,* col. 891.
67 Bryce, *op. cit.,* 53-54; Lavrenyuk, *op. cit.,* 29.
68 Bryce, *op. cit.,* 48.
69 Moos, *op. cit.,* 47-50.
70 Morton, *op. cit.,* 141.
71 *CET, 1967, loc. cit.*
72 Moos, *op. cit.,* 49.
73 Morton, *op. cit.,* 139.
74 Moos, *loc. cit.*
75 Figueroa, *loc. cit.* In 1955 the Pioneers and Komsomol at the Leningrad Music School were described as 'much more passive than at other schools' (I. Dzerzhinsky, 'Let us Talk about our Union', *Current*

Digest of the Soviet Press, vol. VIII (1956), no. 12, 35 (from *Sovetskaya muzyka,* 1955, no. 10).

76   J.J. Tomiak, *The Soviet Union* (Newton Abbot, 1972), 82.
77   Bereday *et al., op. cit.,* 368, 370.
78   *CET, 1967, loc. cit.* In 1966 the figure was said to be about five (*CET, 1966,* 29).
79   Glowka, *loc. cit.*
80   Bereday, *et al., op. cit.,* 370; *CET, 1967, loc. cit.*
81   Morton, *op. cit.,* 316.
82   *Ibid.,* 312; Moos, *op. cit.,* 50-51.
83   Morton, *op. cit.,* 278, 283.
84   Pearl Greenberg, 'Art Education in Russia', *School Arts,* vol. 57, no. 10 (June 1958), 12.
85   Moos, *op. cit.,* 47; Madison, *op. cit.,* 247.
86   *Ibid;* Grant, *op. cit.,* 107; *CET, 1967, loc. cit.*
87   Morton, *op. cit.,* 165.
88   William K. Medlin, 'Education', in Allen Kassof (ed.), *Prospects for Soviet Society* (London, 1968), 262.
89   N.K. Goncharov, 'O perspektivnom plane razvitiya narodnogo obrazovaniya v SSSR na blizhaishie 15-20 let', *Sov. ped.,* 1957, no. 4, 21.
90   E.I. Afanasenko, 'Voprosy perestroiki shkoly', *Uch. gaz.,* 14 August 1958.
91   *Pravda,* 21 September 1958.
92   *Bringing Soviet Schools . . .* (see note 29 above), *loc. cit.*
93   I. Beloded, 'Goryachaya podderzhka obshchestvennosti', *Uch. gaz.,* 13 November 1958.
94   A. Sharipov, 'The Main Thing is to Prepare the Youth for Productive Labour', *Soviet Education,* vol. 1, no. 4 (February 1959), 33 (translated from *Sov. Ped.,* 1958, no. 12).
95   N. Levitov, 'Razvivat' sposobnosti vsekh detei', *Uch. gaz.,* 20 December 1958. For a comment on the dangers of arrogance in young musicians, see Dzerzhinsky, *loc. cit.*
96   V. Vasilenko, 'Kto opredelit odarennost' detei?', *Trud,* 22 November 1958. For a similar view, see Olga Tomson, 'Talanty ne zateryayutsya', *ibid.,* 8 December 1958.
97   B. Zibel', 'V chem prav tov. Vasilenko', *ibid.,* 13 December 1958.
98   'Nuzhny li shkoly dlya odarennykh detei', *Uch. gaz.,* 5 December 1958.
99   *Ibid.*
100 Moos, *loc. cit.*
101 Grant, *op. cit.,* 91; Noah, *loc. cit.*
102 Madison, *loc. cit.*
103 N. Nezhinsky, 'Kvalifikatsii bortsa i cheloveka', *Izvestiya,* 11 May 1963, referring to certain music schools.
104 Gurov, *op. cit.,* 27.
105 M.N. Rutkevich, 'Sotsial'nye istochniki vosproizvodstva sovetskoi intelligentsii', *Voprosy filosofii,* 1967, no. 6, 18.

106   'Obmen mneniyami s akademikom P.L. Kapitsei', *ibid.,* 1972, no. 9,
       129.
107   V.N. Stoletov, 'Posovetuemsya, tovarishchi!' , *Uch. gaz.,* 15 February
       1973.

Chapter 4

Sports and Circus Schools

Physical Education and the Soviet Child

Karl Marx regarded physical training as an essential component of education and indispensable for the all-round development of the individual, and Lenin himself was a vigorous devotee of physical fitness. Yet physical education took several years to consolidate its position in the Soviet school curriculum. It was faced with powerful competitors for resources in chronically short supply: teachers, equipment and facilities. The goal of staffing schools with properly qualified PE teachers remains partly unachieved to this day, and games have never figured in the timetable. Thus, while some schools do provide efficient PE instruction and extracurricular activities, others are more limited in what they can offer.

However, it would be quite wrong to conclude from this that sports education in the Soviet Union is considered to be a trivial matter. What has happened is that the main responsibility for it has been entrusted to out-of-school agencies. Sports 'sections', each catering for a number of sports, are provided not only by schools but also under the auspices of the Pioneer organization, trade union or other adult sports clubs, and these are intended for the mass of children. Developments of this kind can in most cases be traced back to the 1930s, a period of stabilization and purposeful construction yet also of increasing vigilance in view of the growing might of Nazi Germany, a period when diligence, self-discipline and teamwork, characteristic features of sport, steadily established themselves among the civic virtues. In 1934 a system of graduated standards under the slogan 'Be Ready for Labour and Defence' was instituted; it survives today in a much modified form as a mass-participation fitness programme, known as GTO from its Russian initials,[1] and is complemented by a system of rankings and titles indicating special proficiency.

Children's sports schools functioning after school hours were opened, 300 of them by 1939. These were designed for children aged 10 to 16 of above average athletic promise which could be fulfilled only by intensive coaching. After 1948, when the party decided to take steps to boost the USSR's performance in the international sporting arena, they grew more rapidly, rising to 2,772 in 1967 with 838,700 members, and 4,938 in 1975 with 1,633,132 youngsters enrolled.[2] In 1966, in order to begin such training at the earliest possible date in those sports that required it, such as swimming, as well as to prolong it for the purpose of achieving maximum proficiency, the age range was broadened from 7 to 18 and the schools became known as 'Children's and Young People's Sports Schools' *(detsko-yunosheskie sportivnye shkoly* or D YuS Sh.[3] They have the twin functions of producing high-calibre athletes and training future leaders of physical education and sports clubs. Applicants have to pass a strict medical examination and have good marks for school work and conduct, although sometimes a 'difficult' child is admitted in the hope that the special training will act as a corrective; there is a strong element of moral education in it. More recently the DYuSSHs have specialized in up to four sports.[4] The training increases in duration as the young people grow older and can rise to as much as fifteen hours a week.

Mass Schools with a Sports Profile

No more will be said here about the DYuSSHs as detailed accounts of them are available[5] and this book is concerned essentially with special provision within the general school framework. Full-time schools with a sports profile, however, are also to be found in the USSR and are rather less known. They originated in Georgia in 1946, when a secondary school which also gave a specialization in association football, taught by well-known coaches, was opened in Tiflis. This later became a boarding school.[6]

More recently, special classes in swimming — significantly, a sport in which the USSR's performance at international level has not been conspicuously good — have been tried out experimentally at certain general day schools in Leningrad, Minsk, Estonia and Moldavia. The children have swimming sessions in the early morning, start and finish the normal school programme later in the day than elsewhere, and swim again in the early evening. The great advantage of such an arrangement seems to be that it avoids the acute dropout problem said to be characteristic of the DYuSSHs, and the children do better at their studies.[7] In the Lenin Hills district of Moscow, the noted DYuSSh specializing in swimming cooperates on a similar basis with a nearby general school.[8] The splitting-up of the training into two distinct daily periods is obviously more effective than a single long evening session, twice a week at least, which has to compete with a substantial load of homework.

Sports Boarding Schools: Aims, Development and Modus Operandi

If the sports sections are designed to fulfil a mass role and the DYuSShs to develop the athletic potential of children and young people of superior ability, sports boarding schools operate on a still higher plane. They are meant to produce stars — and stars able to shine in an international setting. In the summer of 1971 the sports columnist of the teachers' newspaper, who had consistently advocated these schools, commented enthusiastically on the (1970) decision by the Ministry of Education and the Committee for Physical Culture and Sport of the USSR Council of Ministers to open a countrywide network of them. At the moment, he said, sports education was unnecessarily centralized; the new measure would attract highly-qualified staff to remoter parts of the country and improve the selection of highly gifted children. Significantly, he had just been discussing the need to groom young talent for the Olympics.[9] If, as it is believed, only under communism is physical perfection to be attained, it befits the Soviet vanguard to prove its capacity for leadership — not only to its followers but also to the uncommitted. And again we have an example of residential education advocated as facilitating the growth of excellence and providing due opportunities for the meritorious but geographically disadvantaged. To achieve optimum results the boarding schools display special features: rigorous training from a suitably early age, expert coaching, strict medical care, a particularly nourishing diet, and usually superior facilities.

The credit for the idea of putting special sports schools on a residential basis is given by Soviet sources to the East Germans, who were reported to have about 40 of them in 1970.[10] The first such Soviet school was opened in Tashkent, the capital of Uzbekistan, in 1962. Others followed; the Ukraine's first such school, specializing in volleyball, basketball, football, tennis, gymnastics, light athletics, swimming and fencing was opened in Kiev in the 1966/67 academic year, purportedly in consequence of the important decree of the Central Committee and the USSR Council of Ministers dated 11 August 1966 and entitled 'On Measures for the Further Development of Physical Culture and Sport'.[11] In June 1969 they were said to number about 30; they were to be found in almost all the republics, with the notable exception of the RSFSR, which was still dragging its feet sixteen months later.[12] In 1970 dissatisfaction with the Soviet team's performance in the World Cup led to a call for development of football boarding schools,[13] and a further decree provided the legal basis for expansion.[14] By February 1971 sports boarding schools apparently numbered 18, with another 24 planned.[15] Had some closed, or were the figures wrong? Certainly the ensuing school year saw new ones in the Pervomaisky District of Moscow, Alma-Ata, Rostov-on-Don, and probably elsewhere.[16] By 1976, now in every republic, they apparently totalled some 25 for the whole USSR; by 1977/78 there were 27 of them.[17] While some specialize in a number of sports, typically four, others do not: in 1972 five had a football specialism, six volleyball, and 21 gymnastics.[18]

Children are mostly admitted to these schools at the age of 11 or 12 (to forms 6 or 7), though this may take place earlier depending on the sport, and conversely some may be accepted later. They continue until they have received a full secondary education, completing form 10.[19] It must be admitted that data on recruitment are scarce and the instances from which one tries to generalize are a good deal fewer than one would like. As a rule, children who have done well in Republican school games are invited to apply to the schools, or they may be recommended by their sports coach or teacher.[20] At Rostov-on-Don in 1971, the teachers themselves went talent-spotting all over the region — a practice derived from the experience of other specialized schools.[21] The schools may also advertise. When the Znamensky Brothers Athletics Boarding School in Moscow did this in May 1973 for their first intake, 900 letters poured in from all over the country;[22] and at School No. 62 in Leningrad, a city where every year 6,000 second- and third-formers are taught to swim in their PE lessons under the direction of the special school's instructors, there were a thousand applicants for the swimming specialism alone.[23] The documents required of applicants to the Pervomaisky District School in Moscow in 1971 were: parents' written permission, health certificate, testimonials from former secondary school and DYuSSh, athletics ranking certificate (a third (adult) ranking is required), and school report.[24] The overriding importance of general secondary education is in no way belittled; hence there is interest in academic results so far achieved, and poor marks may lead to rejection, or to acceptance conditional on improvement.[25]

The applicants, perhaps after an initial winnowing — leaving three in ten of the original would-be swimming champions who applied to the Leningrad school, these 300 being selected on the basis of their previous performance[26] — take a series of aptitude and medical tests lasting ten days. Twelve-year-olds of exceptional physical stature, *i.e.*

girls over 170 cm (5 ft 7 in) tall and boys over 180 cm (5 ft 11 in), were exempted from the tests at the Znamensky Brothers School.[27] The selection process may consist of several stages; to follow through the Leningrad example, half of the 300 swimmers were taken to special summer camps, and after a further test 30 were finally accepted as pupils. According to the director of the school, the situation was the same in other sports. In 1975 the total enrolment there was 570, planned to increase to 670, and boys comprised 65 per cent of the roll.[28] No data are available on the social composition of these schools, except for one in Latvia where the children of workers comprised 51.4 per cent, collective farmers 19.1 per cent, and white collar workers 18.9 per cent.[29] We shall refer to this again.

The sports boarding schools resemble other specialized residential schools insofar as they follow the standard curriculum fairly closely, in order to achieve a not inferior level of secondary education, but are heavily weighted in their specialism. Thus 12-year-old gymnasts at the Tallinn school in Estonia in 1970 spent 25 periods a week on subjects other than PE and related activities[30] — three periods fewer than in the standard Soviet timetable, but possibly six periods less than the Estonian norm because of the national language component — and eight periods on gymnastics, two on swimming and two on PE. If the experience of other specialized schools is anything to go by, it would be argued that the organization and atmosphere of these schools achieved 'intensification of the learning process', enabling more work to be concentrated in less time. By form 10 the young people's weekly workload was almost doubled for sport (23 periods, including 19 of gymnastics), and about the same time was spent on other subjects. Practice varies from one school to another; the weekly periods devoted to sport at the Tashkent school in 1968 rose from six for the 11-year-olds to 14 for the 18-year-olds.[30]

The special requirements of sports boarding schools in terms of facilities may, however, create a need to operate differently from other such specialized schools. Although the two schools just mentioned possessed good amenities, this is certainly not the case everywhere, and so other facilities in the area have to be utilized. Thus, every day after third period, children sally forth from the Alma-Ata school to various stadiums, the local swimming bath or the riding school.[32] In some cases the schools are deliberately sited near to existing facilities,[33] but in others the use of external resources is evidently regarded as a stopgap measure until their own accommodation has been constructed.[34] One point where they differ markedly from other specialized boarding schools is that of diet, mentioned above; its particularly nutritive character meant that the daily per-pupil expenditure on food at the Tashkent school in 1968 was one rouble 64 kopecks, almost double that at mass boarding schools (84 kopecks).[35]

Another possible difference is suggested by school No. 62 in Leningrad. Although it is called a boarding school, in fact more than half of the pupils (300 out of 570) live at home.[36] It is not known how typical this is of sports boarding schools, though we have met it in connection with schools for the arts. The arrangement has pros and cons. Authorities on boarding schools feel that there is a danger that such schools can become self-centred and cut off, which runs counter to the communist collective ethos, and an admixture of day pupils, though not to this extent, is thought to be a healthy means of keeping the school in touch with the world outside; but it is unusual. On the other hand, while his boarders and day-pupils are equally committed, the director of the Leningrad school considers that the latter find it more difficult to adjust.[37]

Sports Boarding Schools: Problems and Prospects

In the course of their short life the sports boarding schools have certainly encountered their fair share of problems. It is possible to identify certain groups most likely to express concern: teachers in the schools, educationists and ideologists, and parents. By the nature of their work it is the teachers who are most likely to feel frustrated by the internal problems of the schools. Such flaws as the absence of stop-watches and general shortage of equipment at Rostov-on-Don in 1973[38] or waste of time in moving between lessons and sports activities[39] may seem ludicrous or petty to the observer, but to the practitioner they are serious and exasperating. A high dropout rate is unsatisfactory to teachers and educationists alike; it suggests either that the selection policy and procedures are wrong or that the curriculum is badly designed, or both, and is a poor return not only on the teachers' input of labour but also on the state's investment. At the Leningrad school, 120 (one in four) pupils dropped out during the first year of operation and returned to ordinary schools, but the situation has steadily improved: in the second year it was down to 80, and in the third year this figure was halved.[40]

Although defenders of the schools play down the possibility of overloading and claim that the two sides of the children's activities are mutually supportive,[41] others doubt this and fear that their academic work will suffer or that their experience will be restricted because of the demands of sport.[42] While 83.2 per cent of pupils at the Latvian school were said to have a heightened capacity for mental work thanks to the beneficial influence of sport and PE upon the organism, in the first half of the 1968/69 school year over 10 per cent of all teaching time was lost; the reporters clearly felt it necessary to stress that this was seldom due to the intrusion of sports meetings (1.2 per cent) but mainly to pupils' returning late from trips home. Illness and injury, however, were a fairly frequent cause, morbidity being increased by a lack of suitable winter clothing.[43]

There is some difference of opinion as to whether the schools have a beneficial influence on mass sport. Originally it was claimed that they would help it by dispersing highly-trained sports coaches through the length and breadth of the land. This, however, implies much greater expansion and wider distribution of the schools than has actually taken place. Their critics assert that they are distracting attention (and, presumably, funds) away from mass sport without achieving the expected results. The Sports Committee of Georgia has been accused of limiting its interest to such schools and other special groups and teams.[44] From here it is but a short step to censure of the schools on grounds of privilege and the possible furtherance of an unfitting life-style.[45]

There are ideological objections also to sport as a career, not in the sense of teaching it but of being a professional who makes a living from his performance — in fact the latter eventuality is officially impossible in the Soviet Union and even Olympic champions will have trained in some other capacity as well. This explains the concern felt by some people that the intensive special teaching will produce professional sportsmen,[46] and also accounts for the extraordinary content of the curriculum of the Tallinn Sports Boarding School, which is reported to include specialist subjects like the psychology of sport, physiology, history of physical education and educational philosophy.[47] The present author has never come across this sort of thing at the secondary school level, unless it be in the form of the education option tried out in certain schools. It seems to have an obvious career orientation function, but in the direction of PE teaching. This is a perfectly honest vocation, but because of the unmistakeably clear line that sport is secondary to one's career the schools may find themselves in something of a cleft stick, and thus seem to have little compunction in saying, for example, that of 103 leavers only 37 went on to physical culture and sports institutes.[48] Their situation is paradoxical: they are criticized for not turning out enough top sportsmen, and at the same time they are castigated for devoting too much attention to sport.

Parental attitudes also play a part here. Perhaps it is an indication of the success of the ideologues in glorifying physical work while simultaneously decrying sport as a career that in general parents are alleged not to take sport particularly seriously nor to regard the schools as very desirable. They would much rather be able to say that their Sasha was at an English school.[49] Soviet parents do not normally relish the prospect of handing over their children to a residential institution even though they will return home at weekends, and, except in cases of need, boarding schools have to offer something really attractive, such as training for a prestigious career in the performing arts or in a scientific field, in order to persuade them to do so. If sports schools were truly sought after, white-collar workers' children would assuredly form a greater part of the pupil body than the 18.9 per cent quoted above in respect of the Latvian school. At this school a survey showed that 77.8 per cent of the pupils had taken up sport and PE 'because they saw in them a means of promoting all-round development' (which, being interpreted, presumably signifies 'because of enjoyment'), while only 10.8 per cent had acted upon the advice of their teachers and a mere 6.2 per cent had been guided by parents and coaches, revealing a regrettable lack of purposeful orientation.[50] There may also be reluctance or resentment on the part of DYuSSh coaches at having to hand over their pupils to a new boarding school.[51]

The overall picture is not easy to assess. School No. 62 in Leningrad, though rather ill-supplied until it gets its new premises, is reported by foreign visitors to have a most congenial atmosphere; despite press comment about attitudes to sports schools, its director says that it is very popular among parents; and with the evidence of hundreds of applications, neither the impressions nor the claim can be questioned.[52] A leading sportsman has praised the schools for their superior training: as a rule the young people are more self-disciplined and serious in their attitudes to both sport and study.[53] On the other hand, in February 1971 it was stated that because of opposition, including that of parents, the sports boarding school at Minsk was on the brink of closing for lack of pupils, and others were in a similar position.[54] At the Latvian school in 1969, up to a third of the pupils were of necessity non-sports specialists.[55] The popularity of the schools appears to vary considerably from one to another, and their development has not kept pace with the plans of 1971.

This is likely to be due to both practical and ideological considerations. Judging from the experience of ordinary boarding schools, one cannot rule out questions of cost to the state, although no objections on this score have been noticed.[56] Officially the sports boarding schools have a most important role in training champions to display to the world the physical excellence of Soviet man and woman. Yet not everyone feels that they are delivering the goods, while at the same time by no means everyone wants to let them have the raw materials, in the form of promising youngsters, from which the goods have to be produced. There is doubt about their *modus operandi* and confusion about their career orientation function.

They have also been exposed to the egalitarian objections which have been increasingly levelled at specialized schools in recent years. In sum, they present more of a conundrum than any other type of specialized provision for talented young people in this age-group.

Such reflections prompt another look at the special sports classes mentioned earlier, for this may well be the direction in which the specialized sports education of the future lies. As will be seen, there are precedents and parallels in other areas. The Soviet Ministry of Education and the All-Union Committee on Sport have given special swimming classes official backing and the Moldavians have taken up the idea with particular alacrity. In addition to the eight swimming classes already in existence, Moldavia plans to introduce a further twenty, for acrobatics, light athletics, volleyball and basketball. A report of this development rather labours the point that the children do not live in a school boarding house and are not cut off from home.[57] It is not difficult to imagine a future situation in which a handful of highly efficient sports boarding schools, acceptable because they are at once successful and too few to represent in most people's eyes an infringement of the comprehensive principle, are complemented by a much wider network of specialized sports classes catering for the above average together with many of the well above average.

While preparing this book for the printer, many months after the foregoing paragraph was initially drafted, the writer came upon an interview with S.P. Pavlov, Chairman of the USSR Council of Ministers Committee for Physical Culture and Sport. In this he mentioned that in 1977/78 there were 1000 specialized classes in various kinds of sport working on the extended-day timetable (which usually means after lesson time but under staff supervision), and the task had been set of establishing no fewer than 50,000 (*sic!*) classes with a sports profile by 1980. This was evidently to be a joint enterprise of the education authorities, trades unions, Komsomol and physical culture organizations.[58] The target is as awe-inspiring as the discovery in oneself of the gift of prophecy.

The Moscow Circus School

It is a moot point whether the Moscow Circus and Variety School should rank among schools for the artistically gifted or those for the athletically gifted; it embraces both categories, but is essentially in a class by itself. It will be reviewed here because it is only its Department of Physical Education and Acrobatics which recruits children. It also has a Department of Clowning and Spoken Genres which admits young people with eight or ten years of secondary school behind them, as does, by implication, its Department of

Variety.[59]

The school was founded in 1927 and was said in a recent account to have some 400 pupils. There are 50 applications for every place, and with this sort of selection dropping-out is reported to be negligible.[60] The younger ones are enrolled at the age of eleven into form 5 for a seven-year course, about half of the timetable consisting of circus training and the remainder comprising standard school subjects,[61] as the school also provides a full secondary education. Teenagers with eight years of schooling are admitted to four-year courses.[62] On completing the school, over 90 per cent of the children are destined for the state circuses;[63] at the end of 1970 the USSR had 49 permanent circuses, 15 travelling circuses and 20 'other circus enterprises'.[64]

Notes

1   James Riordan, *Sport in Soviet Society* (Cambridge, 1977), 144, 219. Dr. Riordan has been most helpful in supplying some of the material used for this chapter and in discussing various points.

2   *Ibid.,* 146, 337, 341. According to S.P. Pavlov, however, (interviewed by I. Tarabrin), 'Glavnyi rekord — zdorov'e', *Uch. gaz.,* 9 February 1978, there were 3,235 such schools in 1977/78 and a further 300 planned for opening by 1980.

3   Riordan, *op. cit.,* 337.

4   Miriam Morton, *The Making of Champions* (New York, 1974), 26-29.

5   Deana Levin, *Leisure and Pleasure of Soviet Children* (London, 1966), 67-75; Morton, *op. cit.* Written for young people, Morton's book has a general chapter on sports schools and then focuses successively on schools for classical wrestling, acrobatics, artistic gymnastics, swimming, chess and football (soccer).

6   'Pervaya v strane', *Uch. gaz.,* 6 July 1971.

7   I. Tarabrin, 'Ne radi rekordov', *Uch. gaz.,* 19 April 1975.

8   Morton, *op. cit.,* 63-64.

9   Tarabrin, 'Itogi i perspektivi', *Uch. gaz.,* 31 July 1971. See also *id.,* 'O kubkakh, lodkakh, plavanii i prestizhe', *ibid.,* 1 October 1970. In this respect the scheme has borne fruit: in 1976 the Leningrad Sports Boarding School trounced all comers in the swimming event of the Spartakiad (the all-Union school games), yet this was only its second team, as its top eight swimmers were competing at the Montreal Olympics (*id.,* 'Uspekh plovtsov Leningrada', *ibid.,* 10 July 1976).

10   Tarabrin, *loc. cit.* (1970); P. Gutiontov and A. Rigin, ' "Orel" i "reshka" zolotoi medali', *Moskovskii komsomolets,* 26 February 1971 (I owe this reference to Dr. Riordan).

11   O.A. Zavadskaya, *Razvitie obshcheobrazovatel'noi shkoly Ukrainy v period stroitel'stva kommunizma (1958-1968 gg.)* (Kiev, 1968), 217. They are not, however, specifically mentioned in an official exposition of the decree (*Spravochnik partiinogo rabotnika,* issue no. 7 (M., 1967), 255-260).

12   Tarabrin, 'Spartakiada yunykh', *Uch. gaz.,* 7 June 1969; *id., loc. cit.*
      (1970). In 1970 four were mentioned in Uzbekistan (Riordan, *Sport
      and Physical Education in the Soviet Union* (London, 1975), 18), and
      in 1973 there were three in Kazakhstan (*Kazakhstanskaya pravda,* 18
      March 1973, abstracted by CARC in *ABSEES,* vol. IV, no. 1 (July
      1973), 77).
13   S. Sal'nikov, 'Meksikanskoe posleslovie', *Pravda,* 6 July 1970. (For
      this and the next reference I have to thank Dr. Riordan).
14   'Soobrazheniya osvedomlennogo cheloveka', *Moskovskii
      komsomolets,* 26 February 1971; Tarabrin, *loc. cit.* (1971).
15   'Soobrazheniya . . .' The inconsistency in the figures cannot be
      explained. The source appears to be authoritative, so it is unlikely that
      they represent 'guesstimates' resulting from the non-availability of
      official statistics. Possibly fears of closures (see below) were in fact
      already justified.
16   *Sovetskii sport,* 17 September 1971, abstracted in *ABSEES,* vol. II,
      no. 3 (January 1972); 'Uroki zdorov'ya', *Uch. gaz.,* 2 October 1971;
      Sovetskii sport, 25 September 1973, abstracted in *ABSEES,* vol. V,
      no. 1 (January 1974), 75. In 1973 they numbered over 20 (*Sovetskii
      sport,* 20 December 1973).
17   Riordan, 'The Problems of Soviet Sports Specialization', *Morning
      Star,* 15 January 1976; Yu. Ivanov, 'Dostizheniya i zadachi sovetskoi
      shkoly', *Vospitanie shkol'nikov,* 1976, no. 2, 4.
18   Riordan, *loc. cit.* (1975).
19   *Ibid.*
20   *Ibid.;* Sports Council for Northern Ireland, *Physical Education and
      Sport in the Soviet Union: Report of a Study Tour . . .* (Belfast, 1975),
      16. (Hereafter SCNI).
21   *Sovetskii sport,* 25 September 1973.
22   *Ibid.,* 5 May 1973; cited in Riordan, *op. cit.* (1977), 344.
23   Sports Council (Olive W. Newson), *USSR Physical Education and
      Sport Study Tour . . .* (London, 1975), 25; Tarabrin, *loc. cit.* (1976).
24   *Sovetskii sport,* 17 September 1971; see also Riordan, *op. cit.* (1975 —
      see note 12 above), 19-20. On the other hand, a Latvian school does
      not employ sporting attainment as a criterion for selection, and has
      been criticized in consequence (Yu. I. Berdichevsky and V.E.
      Mefodovsky, 'Poka edinstvennaya', *Fizicheskaya kul'tura v shkole,*
      1969, no. 7, 15-16).
25   Riordan, *op. cit.* (1975), 19.
26   SCNI, *loc. cit.* At the Znamensky Brothers School in 1973, 150 were
      shortlisted from the original 900.
27   *Sovetskii sport,* 5 May 1973; Riordan, *op. cit.* (1977), 345.
28   SCNI, *loc. cit.;* Sports Council, *op. cit.,* 24-25.
29   Berdichevsky and Mefodovsky, *op. cit.,* 15.
30   Riordan, *op. cit.* (1975), 18-19.
31   *Id., op. cit.* (1977), 343.
32   'Uroki . . .' (see note 16 above).
33   Morton, *op. cit.,* 96.

34 Sports Council, *loc. cit.*
35 Riordan, *op. cit.* (1977), 344, citing *Fizkul'tura i sport,* 1968, no. 7, 6.
36 Sports Council, *op. cit.,* 24.
37 *Ibid.,* 25.
38 *Sovetskii sport,* 25 September 1973; compare Berdichevsky and Mefodovsky, *loc. cit.*
39 Riordan, *op. cit.* (1975), 21.
40 Sports Council, *loc. cit.*
41 A. Grinevsky, 'Prazdnik sportivnoi yunosti', *Uch. gaz.,* 29 July 1969; Riordan, *op. cit.* (1975), 19.
42 *Ibid.,* 21; *id., loc. cit.* (1976).
43 Berdichevsky and Mefodovsky, *op. cit.,* 15, 16.
44 *Sovetskii sport,* 12 January 1973, abstracted in *ABSEES,* vol. III, no. 4 (April 1973), 76.
45 Riordan, *loc. cit.* (1976).
46 'Soobrazheniya . . .' (see note 14 above).
47 Riordan, *op. cit.* (1975), 19; *id., loc. cit.* (1977).
48 SCNI, *op. cit.,* 17.
49 'Soobrazheniya . . .'
50 Berdichevsky and Mefodovsky, *op. cit.,* 15.
51 'Soobrazheniya . . .'; *Sovetskii sport,* 21 October 1972.
52 Sports Council, *op. cit.,* 25-26.
53 Grinevsky, *loc. cit.*
54 'Soobrazheniya . . .'
55 Berdichevsky and Mefodovsky, *loc. cit.*
56 At the Latvian school, however, it was alleged that parents were put off through having to pay for teaching (*ibid.,* 15, 16). Since instruction is free in the USSR, either this is a deviation from the norm, or, more likely, the commentators are confusing instruction with maintenance.
57 Tarabrin, *loc. cit.* (1975).
58 Pavlov, *loc. cit.* (see note 2 above).
59 K.A. Gaevskaya, in *Pedagogicheskaya entsiklopediya,* vol. 4 (M., 1968), col. 439. No details of the latter are given; Mayo Bryce, *Fine Arts Education in the Soviet Union* (Washington, D.C., 1963) did not mention it in his description of the school.
60 Russell Miller, 'From Russia with Laughs', *Radio Times,* 21 December 1974 — 3 January 1975, 108. Gaevskaya (*loc. cit.*) quotes a figure of about 500 pupils for 1968.
61 Miller, *loc. cit.* See also Bryce, *op. cit.,* 41.
62 Gaevskaya, *loc. cit.*
63 Miller, *loc. cit.*
64 *NONK,* 342.

Chapter 5
Foreign Language Schools

Early Experiments
The foreign language schools are something of an anomaly within
the secondary general-education framework. They represent one of
the earliest divergences from the educational uniformity generally
associated with the Stalin era and they provide the sole example of
differentiation for other than artistic purposes involving children of
primary school age. As early as 1940 the Council of People's
Commissars approved a plan to introduce foreign language teaching
two school-years earlier than hitherto at 30 secondary schools in
Moscow and 20 in Leningrad. This was to be from form 3, entry to
which at that time was at 10-plus. Being for a mere two periods a
week[1], it cannot have had very satisfactory results.

After the Second World War there was an upsurge of interest in
foreign languages in school; new syllabuses were devised and further
experiments conducted at the primary level. This had been heralded
by an important lecture to the Academy of Sciences by Academician
L.V. Shcherba, the phonetician, shortly before his death in 1944.
Deploring the shortage of cadres for the diplomatic service and
commerce and indeed the overall lack of people able to communicate
with foreigners, he made various proposals to overcome this,
including 'the creation of special general-education schools where
the foreign language begins in the second year of study with the
maximum number of hours and a specially prepared methodology . .
. . a "foreign atmosphere" should be created and the geography and
history of the country and its civilization generally should be taught
in the foreign language'.[2] In a work published posthumously he saw
these as boarding schools whose everyday life should be permeated

by the language.[3] The early start was necessary since as children develop mentally their interests increasingly outpace the content and method of elementary foreign language instruction.[4] In 1948 the Council of Ministers of the RSFSR approved arrangements for secondary boys' schools[5] teaching a number of subjects in a foreign language. This appears to have been a pilot scheme whereby experimental schools were opened in Moscow and Leningrad[6], and which was expanded by various *prikazy* of the Ministry of Education during the 1950s.[7] A number of Uzbek schools began teaching various oriental languages on a similar basis in 1957, and special extended language syllabuses were also introduced into some Ukrainian schools, where the foreign-language medium teaching covered literature, geography of foreign countries, biology and modern history.[8]

Dissatisfaction with the efficacity of language teaching was aired in 1958 during the debate on the proposed polytechnical reforms. The Theses of the CPSU Central Committee and the USSR Council of Ministers, published on 16 November, said: 'The study of foreign languages must be fundamentally improved at all schools throughout the country; the network of schools in which a number of subjects are taught in foreign languages should be expanded'.[9] An *Izvestiya* follow-up, calling for language teaching from the first form and indeed in nursery school — some groups of pre-school children were already being taught a foreign language on parental initiative — stated that the special language schools were immensely popular but very hard to get into; the Ministry ought to open enough to meet the demand, and in other cities besides the two main ones.[10] Another writer wanted to see such a school in every city district.[11] One outcome of the 1958 legislation was that additional schools were opened in various parts of the Russian Republic.[12]

Aims and Development

However, it was the decree of the USSR Council of Ministers of 27 May 1961, 'On Improving the Study of Foreign Languages',[13] which set a rapid pace of development for the 1960s. The preamble noted the increasing importance of a knowledge of languages by specialists in all fields, in view of the country's expanding international contacts, and called for radical improvements in language teaching at all levels, with especial regard to colloquial skills and translation of foreign texts without dictionaries. Among its many provisions, the decree enjoined the opening of not less than 700 additional foreign language schools by 1965 (the existing number was not stated); the transition of boarding schools possessing suitably qualified teachers to this type of instruction, as from the 1961/62 school year; the organization of special training of teachers of the usual school subjects for work in special schools, also from 1961/62, the Ministry of Higher and Specialized Secondary Education (MVSSO) being empowered to lengthen courses by one year for this purpose if necessary; and the introduction of foreign language groups in nursery schools and primary classes, at the request and expense of parents.[14]

The purpose of the special schools, then, is not merely to produce young linguists to become older linguists, but rather to supply linguistically proficient young people who will be trained for jobs in various branches of the economy. In 1963 the RSFSR Ministry of Education recommended production training in eleven specialisms, mostly in the fields of communications and office work; but also nursery school upbringers (provided for by the decree of 1961), librarians, junior sales assistants and tailors.[15] A commentator mentioned also laboratory technicians for new chemical plant, programmers, Pioneer leaders and international sleeping car attendants.[16] During the Khrushchev era, individual schools developed distinctive production specialisms. At present, too, pupils' future career patterns still depend to some extent on the location of the schools; while the aim of the four language schools in Voronezh, an important engineering centre, was stated in 1972 to be to train potential engineers and scientists for whom the language would be a valuable tool,[17] the function of those in Moscow and Leningrad is sometimes said to be the production of budding recruits for the diplomatic service, the mass media, and publishing. Thus Boarding School No. 23 in Moscow, which specializes in Hindi and Urdu, has links with various publishing houses, Sovinformburo, TASS etc.[18]

However, the range may be considerably more diverse than first meets the eye. When the career-choices of 260 leavers from four 'English' schools (two each in Moscow and Leningrad) in 1968 were analyzed, it emerged that 26.5 per cent entered *vuzy* training teachers, translators etc., and 8.1 per cent went direct into employment where English was an important requirement, *e.g.* as librarians or translators. Thus just over one-third made a career in English. 39.2 per cent went on to scientific and technological *vuzy,* where special arrangements were available for them to keep their English up. 11.9 per cent were admitted to the senior forms of technical schools, at which level the language is not provided, and 14.2 per cent went into employment where English was not essential for them.[19] For nearly three-quarters of the leavers, therefore, involvement with the language was already built into their career patterns, but for the remainder it would depend on personal initiative.

We have a detailed account of the procedure whereby these schools were originally set up and administered in the RSFSR, and presumably this was broadly the same in the other republics. The republic's Ministry of Education initially set a target of 300 schools to be opened by 1965: 35 in Moscow, 24 in Leningrad and varying numbers in the other areas, from eight in Moscow Region and the Tatar ASSR to one in the Kalmyk ASSR and the Tuva Autonomous Region, with a median of about three.[20] They were formally opened by the Ministry on the application of the executive committees of territorial, regional and Moscow and Leningrad municipal soviets (councils) or of the Councils of Ministers of autonomous republics.[21] It is likely that the process was accelerated where there were strong local interests. The author was informed in a private communication that the first such school in Moscow was set up in the western suburb of Fili where there are motor and aviation works and a ball-bearings factory, powerful enterprises employing nearly all the residents, and where the local Party people would have factory connections. According to the 1961 regulations the language schools were administered and financed on a district basis in Moscow, like the mass schools, but directly by the autonomous republic Ministries of Education or by the territorial or regional education authorities elsewhere (and by the city authority in Leningrad), unlike ordinary schools, although the regional soviets and parallel organs were empowered to transfer these responsibilities to the district education authorities.[22] These measures were evidently intended to facilitate more centralized control and coordination where there was major scope for development.

Statistics on the language schools are sparse and sometimes contradictory, but the target set in 1961, of 700 more schools by 1965, was not reached. The existing number was not mentioned in the legislation, but Noah speaks of a goal of 1,200,[23] which suggests a starting figure of 500; in view of the experimental nature of the schools, however, this seems excessive. For 1962/63 Noah quotes a total of about 400, which casts further doubt on the notional starting figure, unless the number actually dwindled; but this possibility is unlikely, since another writer presents a picture of extensive development since 1961.[24] Glowka cites a figure of 500 for 1962/63 in the RSFSR, Ukraine and Belorussia,[25] whereas during that school year Goncharov quoted a total of about 700 such schools for the whole country.[26] Shortly afterwards complaints were voiced, in the RSFSR at least, that a number of regional education authorities were underrating these schools, which had been opened only in 34 areas (*territorii*); there were none at all in the Moscow and Leningrad regions (as distinct from the cities).[27]

In the mid-sixties a report by the International Institute of Educational Planning numbers the schools at 500, although the 1965 total should have been double that, according to information supplied to a delegation of British educationists in the spring of 1964.[28] The discrepancies may be partly accounted for, though not altogether clarified, by reference to a report in *Uchitel'skaya gazeta* of 25 April 1963, which states somewhat ambiguously that about 700 additional specialized language schools will be open by 1965, and over 500 already exist. The question is whether the target included or excluded the 500. Whichever the case, it was not reached: early in 1970 a responsible Soviet source gives the total (representing 1.4 per cent of complete secondary day schools) as more than 600,[29] *i.e.* still short of the *increase* planned for the period to 1965, let alone whatever overall total was envisaged by that date. The countrywide growth curve is thus seen to have risen sharply immediately after 1961 and to have largely levelled off since the middle of the decade.

In the two largest cities the schools seem to have increased at a steadier rate.[30] In the 1968/69 school year they catered for an estimated 7 per cent of complete secondary school pupils in Leningrad, and in both the 1970/71 school year in Moscow and in the following year in Leningrad they comprised 9.3 per cent of complete secondary schools.[31] No further data are available for the Union republics, except that in 1962 Kazakhstan had four such schools and Armenia five;[32] the Ukraine had 210 in 1964/65,[33] which must have been nearly half the total for the whole USSR; and in 1968/69 there were 266 in the RSFSR, with 138,900 pupils,[34] representing 1.3 per cent of the total of complete secondary schools and 0.95 per cent of the pupils in them.[35] Thus young Leningraders' chances of entering such schools were seven times greater than those of children in the republic as a whole. In 1966 the RSFSR Minister of Education had complained that in 36 areas the language school development plan was underfulfilled and in 24 not a single school had been set up.[36] (There are 73 administrative areas in the RSFSR).

As for the distribution of the four main language specialisms, the Moscow figures for the school years commencing in 1964 and 1970 respectively are: English, 24 and 46; French, 9 and 14; German, 4 and 15; and Spanish, 1 and 2.[37] The 'Hindi/Urdu' school was mentioned above, and two 'Chinese' schools were reported by Mrs. Simon in 1967/68. In that year the language profiles in Leningrad were: English 20, French 5, German 5, Spanish 1, Italian 1, Hindi 1, and Chinese 1.[38] The proportion of 'English' schools to the total of language schools in both Moscow and Leningrad is likely to approximate to the achieved national norm (USSR 1966/67 'over 60 per cent',[39] Moscow 1970/71 59.7 per cent, Leningrad 1967/68 58.8

per cent) and so the overall distribution for the two leading cities may be presumed to be normative. The situation has evidently changed since 1961 when the decree of 27 May made it clear that German was over-represented in the school curriculum at large, probably because of the availability of indigenous German speakers; there has certainly been a marked growth of English schools since 1963/64, when the figures were English 40 per cent, French 25 per cent, German 25 per cent and other languages 10 per cent.[40]

The overall proportions are, of course, fixed by the Ministry of Education. As no complaints have been noticed since 1966, the assumption may be ventured that the desired pattern has been more or less achieved. If this is so, and if the distribution of pupils by languages approximates to that of schools, a recent statement by the Minister that in 1976/77 there would be 46,000 pupils at French-medium schools[41] enables us to hazard an up-to-date estimate of the total number and percentage of pupils at language schools. If French schools comprise about 15 per cent of all such schools (*cp.* Moscow and Leningrad above), and we assume that pupils at them are in the same proportion, we arrive at a figure in excess of 306,000, or 0.9 per cent of pupils at complete secondary schools and 0.7 per cent of pupils at all day general-education schools.[42] If, on the other hand, the distribution of language-school pupils by languages approximates to that planned for pupils at mass schools (see note 40), *i.e.* 20 per cent taking French, the total is reduced to 270,000, or 0.8 and 0.6 per cent respectively of the above mass-school enrolments.

Another development, though rather different, concerns intensive study of Russian language and literature in the schools of individual Union republics. Such teaching was introduced into form 9 of eighteen Azerbaidzhani schools in 1972/73. Extension to forms 7 to 10 in 230 schools was planned for 1973/74, but administrative delays were reported.[43] In 1970/71, there were 1,287 complete secondary schools in Azerbaidzhan, so the programme was evidently of significant dimensions. Since 1973 Russian has been introduced into the first forms of Georgia's general schools, and a number of schools there have a special Russian language profile. At a boarding school at Zugdidi, for example, history, geography and physical education are taught in Russian from form 5 onwards. The main aim is to begin to train potential teachers of the language at an early stage, thus increasing and improving the supply.[44] In November 1975 the USSR Ministry of Education instructed the republic ministries to increase the number of schools and classes with this specialism.[45] Such arrangements, their functions and effects certainly merit enquiry, but at present too little is known about them to include them in our further considerations; in any case, the framework of this study may not be that most appropriate for the purpose, since questions of cultural hegemony seem likely to loom large.

Selectivity and Status

As we have seen, in 1969/70 the language schools amounted to only about 1.4 per cent of the total number of complete secondary day schools, and on the basis of certain assumptions we have estimated that in 1976/77 0.6-0.7 per cent of all Soviet pupils in day general-education schools, or roughly 1 in 150, were at special language schools. There is no evidence that their popularity has abated. This immediately prompts questions about admissions procedures and the sort of children enrolled. Mention has already been made of the possibility of preparation in nursery schools and the primary classes of ordinary schools, against payment. In Riga in 1967, such a preparatory class was held on two evenings a week for six months.[46] Anweiler sees this as an example of the state taking cognizance of a section of Soviet society's 'need for prestige', and an infringement of the principle of free education.[47] How far can this view be extended?

There is little doubt that these schools became prestigious institutions. Equally, there is little reason to suppose that this state of affairs was connived at by the authorities, rather the reverse. It appears that their social complexion developed spontaneously, that this has been recognized and that it is the cause of active concern. Although selection is nowadays denied, what might be termed 'selection by promise' certainly used to operate and seems to do so still, though perhaps in a milder form. A hilarious feuilleton of 1965 casts considerable light upon procedures. An 'English' school is opened in the district. The writer wants to send her son there and is told the best, the most able will be selected — the 7-year-olds must take entrance tests. The only people to give information to the worried parents are the assistants in the school corridors. (In England it could well be the caretaker). "They'll test their general development and imagination. Teach them poems and songs, give them little puzzles, show them pictures — let them be imaginative." Although the family overdo it, Serezha gets into the first form. After five days his mother is summoned to the school and is told of his terrible behaviour, namely fidgeting in class and running in the corridors during playtime, though there had been no complaints about him at nursery school. ' "Ours is a special school, don't forget that," the teacher went on sternly. "If he doesn't learn to behave properly, he'll have to go to an ordinary one." But he gets into the second form, begins English, and then the pressure really is on . . .[48]

Yet when a 'Spanish' school opened in a new suburb of Moscow — although the residents had petitioned for an English one — things appear to have been done with maximum haste and minimum formality. Although the RSFSR regulations of 1961 provided for an admissions committee consisting of the school director, an education office representative, and the school doctor,[49] there was no committee, nor indeed anywhere for such a body to sit; so all applicants were admitted to the first forms while there were places, and those with good or excellent marks, or even with satisfactory marks, to the other forms. Now, however, it is a very different story. Every spring, a Soviet journalist tells us, the commotion around such a school is like that around Moscow State University. 'Smartly turned-out children go before an incomprehensible and consequently still more terrifying committee, whose job it is to find out their aptitude for foreign languages by listening to their poems and hearing them describe little pictures. True, in a few years' time the shy little boy may prove to be a polyglot, and the forthcoming little girl to be not really so gifted after all. But at present she is the one who is enrolled in the "school teaching a number of subjects". In Moscow more and more such schools are opening, but will languages perhaps soon begin to be taught well and in good time everywhere, thus eliminating anxiety in children and adults?'[50]

Other reports, especially more recent ones, are conflicting: according to some the schools are obliged to take all local children wishing to enter and there are no special tests,[51] but Anthony Potts, who taught in such a school for a year and attended an interview, says that the first-form teacher was present and the seven-year-old boy had to answer various questions and repeat some English words; there was selection by ability, though not by influence.[52] All agree, however, that the child must be free of ill-health and speech defects, and a doctor and speech therapist were in active attendance at the interview just mentioned. According to the regulations of 1961, admission to forms 3 to 5 of new schools was explicitly on criteria of merit: 'the best in attainment and behaviour'.[53]

In 1969 Joan Simon indicated that while residents in one district of Moscow might have access to a language school, residents of another might not,[54] but expansion continued and not long after this there was said to be at least one such school for every district of the capital.[55] In 1974 Moscow had 29 districts and over 80 language schools. The headmistress of an ordinary school in Timiryazevsky District informed the writer that, with 50 mass schools and therefore 50 microdistricts, this district was very large; some districts might have only ten. Thus the language school's catchment area, which is determined by the local education authority concerned, is not identifiable with the microdistrict of the mass school. It is claimed that the social composition of the school reflects that of its catchment area: thus at an 'English' school in the 'science city' of Akademgorodok most of the pupils are the children of scientists and white-collar workers while those of manual workers constitute a mere 5 per cent, whereas at a 'French' school in the industrial part of Novosibirsk, manual workers' children comprise nearly half.[56] However, when a pupil's family moves to another district he continues to attend his old language school, and in Leningrad about 15-20 per cent of all pupils come into this category.[57] Also, there are arrangements for children to enter language schools in neighbouring districts when vacancies exist there but not in their own.[58]

But what if there are no vacancies? What if there are no schools? Glowka in 1967 quoted Soviet educational politicians as saying there were attempts to adapt supply to demand and thus to avoid the need for selection; they adduced this to refute the idea that the schools were special.[59] However, in such a huge country, where in rural areas efforts are still being concentrated on bringing the provision of *ordinary* schools up to urban standards, it is not in the least surprising that language schools have not been established with the same alacrity as in the major cities. It has been shown that in 1968/69 the Leningrad child's likelihood of securing admission to a language school was seven times greater than that of the *average* RSFSR child. There do exist some boarding schools specializing in a foreign language, but unlike the debate on mathematics and science education there has been little talk of tapping vast reserves of linguistic talent hidden in the depths of the country. In the continuing absence of evidence that supply is now perfectly matched to demand, it must be concluded that frequently children who would otherwise have entered a language school are unable to do so. With six special-profile schools of all types out of 13 secondary schools, Tartu, like the whole Estonian Republic, is unusually well endowed; thus at an English-language school in Tallinn in 1973 the suggested ratio of candidates to entrants, 2:1,[60] may be quite untypically high by Soviet standards.

The expression 'special school' has caught on, but the education authorities dislike it.[61] It appears to bear a social cachet which gives them qualms. In 1966 the rector of the country's leading pedagogical institute of foreign languages expressed her concern that some of the language schools were beginning to resemble *lycées* for the children of the well-to-do, with competitive entry, and she called for an enquiry into this.[62] In 1960 David Burg, generalizing from the instance of the school in the Moscow suburb of Sokolniki, had claimed that these schools were cloaked in secrecy because they were attended by 'the scions of the Soviet aristocracy'.[63] In the absence of knowledge of their number, this claim was exaggerated and with their continued development it has become steadily more implausible. Nevertheless, they are much sought after. This fact is expressed in somewhat dramatic terms in a short story by Yurii Trifonov:

> Natashka became a schoolgirl. The special English school in Utinyi Lane, object of desire and envy, gauge of parents' love and *their readiness to go to any lengths.* A different microdistrict! It was almost unthinkable. And it would have been too much for anyone but Lena. Because she got her teeth into what she wanted like a bulldog.[64]

Lena is, of course, the mother, the classic decision-taker in matters of childrearing in Russia, and she it is who shoulders the concomitant burden (with her own mother's assistance) of getting the child to and from school in another locality. She is not affluent, but she would call herself an intellectual.

A Soviet commentator has remarked that 'a new district without its special school is considered somehow sub-standard (*nepolnotsennym*)'[65]. A good knowledge of a foreign language has long been one of the hallmarks of the cultured individual in Russia. Besides that, a role is surely played here by the old truism that some parents are more ambitious than others and, whether in the hope of securing their children better jobs or in anticipation of improved chances of foreign travel, will always seek out what they believe to be the best ways of educating them. Even if they have scruples about this, the home background may confer advantages which will stand the young candidate in good stead for the (admittedly mild) selection procedures: not every child receives the same degree of encouragement to read and to draw, not every child has anglophile or French-speaking parents concerned to broaden his horizons, not every child begins to acquire the elaborated speech code which will impress his interviewer. And although the staff of the English department of the above-mentioned pedagogical institute have disclaimed marked preference for pupils of language schools,[66] the fact that 65.7 per cent of the sample of language-school leavers of 1968 entered *vuzy*,[67] compared with some 25 per cent of young people graduating from all the USSR's complete day secondary schools,[68] speaks for itself. At certain other language schools a *vuz* admission rate of 80–82 per cent is reported.[69] But to regard this as a deliberate piece of social engineering to cater for elitist aspirations is considerably less reasonable than to interpret it as the inadvertent outcome of a policy orientated on the pragmatic goal of providing the labour market with young people specially skilled in a foreign language, which nevertheless furnished a rare opportunity of 'working the system'.

A curious piece of evidence of the popularity of these schools, and also of the use of the institution to subsidise, as it were, the indigenous culture, comes from the pen of Roy Medvedev. Speaking of the spread of the Russian language in the schools of national minorities, he remarks that even in Kiev only a few Ukrainian schools have been preserved, and that in order to safeguard their number it was decided to convert them into schools teaching a number of subjects in English.[70] Thus, by meeting the social demand for foreign language schools, the position of the local language was indirectly entrenched.

Internal Organization

We turn now to a consideration of the internal organizational aspects of the language schools. The language teaching is the responsibility of a special deputy head, who, like the head, the teachers of and through the language, and the librarian, is paid at 15 per cent above the normal rates.[71] The foreign language is introduced at least three years earlier than in ordinary schools, in the second form (8-plus) or even before. According to the original arrangements for the RSFSR (1961/62), weekly language periods numbered four for forms 2 to 4, six for forms 5 to 7, seven for form 8, six for forms 9 and 10, and seven for form 11; these included one period a week for foreign literature (forms 8 to 11) and one for technical translation (forms 9 to 11).[72] To this should perhaps be added one period for options in forms 9 and 10 (two periods of language options for the three senior forms were introduced in 1964). In 1961 foreign language instruction in the mass schools began in form 5, with four periods a week, remaining at three thereafter (but two in the ninth and tenth forms of *urban* schools).[73] The eleventh school year was abolished with effect from 1966/67, except in some Union republics.

The 1972/73 edition of the curriculum for the RSFSR (see Table 5.1) gives the number of language periods per week as three for forms 2 to 4, six for forms 5 to 8, including two for foreign literature in form 8, and eight for forms 9 and 10, including two for foreign literature and a further two for technical translation or typing, the two latter counting as labour training. (The pupils of an 'English' school in Belgorod do practical language work in local enterprises).[74] In ordinary schools, the periods for the foreign language in 1972/73 were nil in forms 2 to 4, four in form 5, three in forms 6 and 7, and two in forms 8 to 10.[75] Thus, without taking into account periods for other subjects which may be taught in the foreign language (see below), the language instruction over the whole school course in 1961/62 was over two and a half times as much as in mass schools, and in 1972/73 was just over three times as much.

Normally only one foreign language is studied, but the 'French' school in Riga visited in 1967 provided not only French from form 1 and Russian or Latvian (reflecting the practice of schools in the national republics) from form 2, but also optional German or English from form 5 (11-plus).[76] The teacher-pupil ratios are more favourable to language learning as such classes are divided into groups of eight to fourteen,[77] with a norm of ten. (In *ordinary* schools, under the decree of 1961, classes of over 25 pupils may be divided into two groups for language work, but this reportedly depends on the teacher's discretion, dedication and staff availability.[78]). Special standard textbooks and aids are used and teaching is by the so-called 'conscious-practical' method, a compromise approach which certainly does not disregard grammatical theory but emphasizes oral work, largely without recourse to the native tongue. The present writer as well as many other visitors can testify to the fluency and purity of accent which even pupils in the middle forms display.

Otherwise the curriculum is the same as in ordinary schools, but, as already noted, to some extent subjects may be taught through the foreign language medium. Here too classes may be divided into groups of ten 'if necessary'. An experimental Moscow school visited apparently in the late 1950s was reported to be conducting *all* its senior teaching in English,[79] but no other such instances have been noticed. The 1961 regulations for the RSFSR list subjects as regional geography (form 6), economic geography of foreign countries (form 10), modern and contemporary history and electrical and mechanical engineering (forms 9 to 11). This meant an additional two hours per week language involvement in form 6, four in form 9, seven in form 10 and six in form 11.[80] In practice a transitional curriculum operated for a few years at the senior stage, but this made very little difference, as can be seen from the following table (5.2), which compares the arrangements actually in effect in 1962/63 with the situation ten years later. However, over this period there have been a number of experiments and other minor changes, so that the pattern is not uniform and the 1972/73 version must be regarded as approximate only. Since the dethronement of production training, electrical and mechanical engineering have presumably ceased to be taught in the senior forms, as the 1972/73 curriculum makes it evident that for these forms labour training means technical translation or typing. The notes to the 1972/73 curriculum also mention technical drawing

TABLE 5.1 Curriculum in Foreign Language Schools, RSFSR, 1972/73

Subject   Periods per week per form

	1	2	3	4	5	6	7	8	9	10
Russian Language	12	11	10	6	5	4	3	2	-	1
Russian Literature	-	-	-	2	2	2	2	3	4	3
Mathematics	6	6	6	6	6	6	6	5	6	6
History	-	-	-	2	2	2	2	3	4	3
Social Studies	-	-	-	-	-	-	-	-	-	2
Nature Study	-	-	2	-	-	-	-	-	-	-
Geography	-	-	-	-	2	3	2	2	2	-
Biology	-	-	-	-	2	2	2	2	1	2
Physics	-	-	-	-	-	2	2	3	4	5
Astronomy	-	-	-	-	-	-	-	-	-	1
Technical Drawing	-	-	-	-	-	-	1	2	-	-
Chemistry	-	-	-	-	-	-	2	2	3	3
Foreign Language	-	3	3	3	6	6	6	4	4	4
Foreign Literature[1]	-	-	-	-	-	-	-	2	2	2
Art	1	1	1	1	1	1	-	-	-	-
Music and Singing	1	1	1	1	1	1	1	-	-	-
Physical Education	2	2	2	2	2	2	2	2	2	2
Labour Training[2]	2	2	2	2	2	2	2	2	2	2
Elementary Military Training	-	-	-	-	-	-	-	-	2	2
Total periods per week	24	26	25	27	31	33	33	34	36	38

Notes (from original)
1 In the foreign language.
2 In forms 9 and 10: technical translation or typing in the foreign language.

In foreign language lessons with forms 2 to 10, and also if necessary in subjects taught in the foreign language, including technical drawing and typing with forms 9 and 10, the class is divided into three groups (10 pupils each).

Source *Sbornik prikazov i instruktsii Ministerstva prosveshcheniya RSFSR*, 1972, no. 11, 4-5.

as a subject taught in the foreign language, so this is allowed for in the table, although it is rarely cited in visitors' comments. In 1964 and 1965 there were reports that in certain secondary schools physics and mathematics were also to be taught in English, French or German,[81] but although specialized teacher training exists it is by no means clear how widely this measure has been applied to language schools. The IIEP report speaks of mathematics from form 4 and chemistry (not physics) from form 8[82]; at about the same time a school in Latvia was recorded as having taught biology through a foreign language for a while, but the practice has been discontinued because the vocabulary had proved to be too specialized.[83] In 1973 a special English school in Tallinn boasted a senior course in Estonian studies taught through the foreign tongue.[84]

TABLE 5.2 Foreign Language (FL) and Other Teaching in Special Language Schools and Ordinary Schools, RSFSR
(Periods per week and percentage of total periods per week)

Forms	1962/63 Language Schools — FL teaching, literature, translation and typing ppw	%	Other subjects through FL[1] ppw	%	Total FL practice ppw	%	Other teaching ppw	%	1962/63 Ordinary Schools — FL teaching ppw	%	Other teaching ppw	%	1972/73 Language Schools — FL teaching, literature, translation and typing ppw	%	Other subjects through FL[2] ppw	%	Total FL practice ppw	%	Other teaching ppw	%	1972/73 Ordinary Schools — FL teaching ppw	%	Other teaching[3] ppw	%
1	–	–	–	–	–	–	24	100	–	–	24	100	–	–	–	–	–	–	24	100	–	–	24	100
2	4	14	–	–	4	14	24	86	–	–	24	100	3	11.5	–	–	3	11.5	23	88.5	–	–	24	100
3	4	14	–	–	4	14	24	86	–	–	26	100	3	12	–	–	3	12	22	88	–	–	24	100
4	4	13	–	–	4	13	26	87	–	–	29	100	3	11	–	–	3	11	24	89	–	–	24	100
5	6	18	–	–	6	18	28	82	4	12	29	88	6	19	–	–	6	19	25	81	4	13	26	87
6	6	17	2	6	8	23	27	77	3	9	31	91	6	18	3	9	9	27	24	73	3	10	27	90
7	6	17	–	–	6	17	29	83	3	9	31	91	6	17.5	1	3	7	21	26	79	3	10	27	90
8	7	19	–	–	7	19	29	81	3	9	31	91	8	22	–	–	8	23.5	26	76.5	2	7	28	93
9	6	16	5	13	11	29	27[4]	71	2/3[5]	6/8	34/33	94/92	8	21	6	17	14	39	22	61	2	6	30	94
10[6]	6	16	7	18	13	34	25[4]	66	2/3[5]	6/8	34/33	94/92	8	21	3	8	11	29	27	71	2	6	32	94
11[7]	6	16	5	13	11	29	27	71	3	8	33	92	–	–	–	–	–	–	–	–	–	–	–	–

Notes

[1] Geography (forms 6 and 10), and history, electrical and mechanical engineering (forms 9 to 11). (Assumed to apply from previous year).

[2] Geography (forms 6 and 9), history (forms 9 and 10), and technical drawing (forms 7 and 8). However, this is not uniform — see text.

[3] Excluding options.

[4] Includes a period of options, which may have been devoted to FL.

[5] Two in urban schools, three in rural.

[6] Variant for form 10 in the surviving schools without production training is here omitted.

[7] Form 11 discontinued with effect from 1966/67 (but see note 91).

Sources 'The Curriculum for the Eight-year and Secondary Schools of the RSFSR', *Soviet Education*, vol. II, no. 3 (January 1960), 30-31 (translated from *Narodnoe obrazovanie*, 1959, no. 11); *Sbornik prikazov . . .*, 1962, no. 28, 22; *ibid.*, 1972, no. 11, 2-5.

Problems and Prospects

This brings us to the first of certain problems which these schools have encountered. The original scheme of employing the foreign language as a medium for the teaching of other subjects has come increasingly under fire and some schools are said to have abandoned it since about 1968. Bryan Woodriff was informed in 1971 that there was a shortage of people who could teach through the foreign language. Those who had framed the 1961 decree had anticipated this and provided for appropriate teacher training. By the end of the decade five pedagogical institutes in the RSFSR (the Lenin Pedagogical Institute and the Krupskaya Regional Pedagogical Institute in Moscow, the Herzen Pedagogical Institute in Leningrad, and others in Chelyabinsk and Yaroslavl') were offering courses entitled 'Physics in a Foreign Language', four gave similar courses in mathematics and three in chemistry, and the Lenin Institute also catered in this way for history, geography, biology and sketching and technical drawing.[85] But, with no statistical data to hand, it is impossible to gauge the extent to which the shortage of suitable staff, including modern linguists, which the Curriculum Commission had stated to be inhibiting the development of these schools,[86] had been reduced over the ten-year period.

There were also problems with textbooks and teaching aids. Woodriff reported that the standard textbooks had been translated into the requisite foreign-languages without regard to pupils' linguistic abilities. A teacher in 'Special School' No. 6, Moscow, felt that the time allotted to economic geography in form 9 was not enough to achieve 'a sufficiently deep knowledge' (to quote the syllabus) of the subject unless there was a flexible approach, and so she published her own English-language handbook on British economic geography to supplement the standard textbook on the economic geography of foreign countries and on the same methodological principles.[87] Now, however, catalogues include a fair range of textbooks and other aids for these schools.

It is possible that there is another reason for the partial abandonment of teaching other subjects through the foreign language. Already in 1966 Bernhard Schiff had raised the question of how the pupils' foreign language performance affected the scope and content of the subjects taught through it.[88] In less favourable conditions the latter might well be determined by the former. For the present, however, the handpicked children could generally be expected to be good at their language. But there is another aspect of the problem. The author well remembers one summer receiving an agonized plea from a Soviet teacher of English who had suddenly been told that from 1 September he would be teaching mathematics through the medium of the language — he had no idea how to explain mathematical procedures in English and desperately needed some textbooks. Afterwards, and despite import restrictions, it was pleasing to hear that the parcel of textbooks had crossed Siberia and arrived in the faraway Amur Region, battered but otherwise intact, just in time. One can only speculate to what extent linguists may themselves have had to play the part of geographer, historian and so on. But it is surely significant that none of the specialisms such as 'History in a Foreign Language' were listed at the RSFSR's top pedagogical institute specializing in foreign languages; the teachers of history and the other subjects were clearly meant to be qualified first and foremost in those disciplines. Where they were in short supply and other arrangements had to be made, it is obvious that the children might acquire no more than a superficial knowledge of such subjects, and this would have been an infringement of the principle of a well-rounded general education. Indeed, even when a subject such as mathematics or physics is taught in a foreign language by a mathematician or physicist, it seems likely that, however able the pupil is, his performance will be less than it would be without the partial obstacle of the language; achievement in mathematics and science is in any circumstances a high priority, and talent is a national asset to be appropriately cultivated.[89]

A further major problem is symptomatic of special schools for the gifted — the danger of overloading, creating psychological pressures and mental and physical strain. It is not for nothing that interviewees undergo a medical examination, and that the originally restricted number of hours allocated to physical education was soon restored to the conventional level. A team of medical workers in Leningrad investigated morbidity in five language schools, using four ordinary schools as a control group. In both types of school morbidity decreased from form 1 upwards, but its decrease was less marked in the language schools, where the rate was higher throughout, with an average of 66.5 cases per 100 pupils compared to 56.9 cases in the mass schools, and most pronounced in form 10 (70.9 as opposed to 32.8). Individuals at language schools tended to be absent for slightly longer periods. They were also ill somewhat more often, though not significantly so except for children ill three times or more (11.8 per cent of those ill, compared to 4.2 per cent). The daily routine of 306 pupils was studied for a fortnight, and it transpired that in addition to their two to four hours of extra classwork the language school pupils spent half as much time again as the others on homework, and thus less time in the open air.[90]

The authorities' concern about overloading is evidenced in the gradual cutback of the weekly workload of forms 2 to 9 by two or

three hours over the period 1961 to 1972, first at the partial expense
of manual and socially useful work (after the downfall of
Khrushchev in 1964) and, later, Russian language, and in the recent
abolition of options in these schools, even though such options were
a further vehicle for language study.[91] Pupils who do not make the
grade are transferred to ordinary schools.[92] I am informed that at one
Moscow school unsuitable children are weeded out at the end of the
first year, and this may well be typical. (Transfer in the reverse
direction is officially possible, but seems to be rare).[93] At another
school in 1962 weaker children were helped by eleventh-formers and
the few parents who knew French, and three French circles were
organized for other parents.[94] For, unlike many special schools, it
seems that most of the language schools are day schools, and this
means that parents themselves may feel the daily pressures, though
perhaps not as acutely as in the case of Serezha, quoted earlier, which
involved, among much else, urgent journeys across Moscow and a
midnight visit to a neighbour in quest of drawings of a pie and a
plate.[95]

These, then, are the special language schools. Despite certain
problems, they appear to be efficiently performing their function of
providing the country with young people who possess a fluent
command of a foreign language. As far as one can glean from the
press, their future prospects are not so obviously overshadowed with
misgivings as are those of the special mathematics and physics
boarding schools (FMShs), to be considered in the next chapter.
Language schools are not yet very numerous in relation to the total of
schools, but they have acquired a *locus standi* and they enjoy well-
publicised statutory backing; in general they are no longer regarded
as experimental, and they have not been subjected to exuberant and
embarassing eulogies by the press. They are sufficiently like the mass
schools to avoid problems of upbringing; the presence of younger
children strengthens the collective, and very little criticism of their
pupils on the scores of arrogance and complacency has been noticed.
Some reasons why their atmosphere is *a priori* less rarefied than in
the FMShs must be that recruitment at the tender age of six or seven
cannot possibly be foolproof, their catchment areas are far less
extensive, and there are many more of them. Any brake on their
development, as Noah pointed out in 1966,[96] is due primarily to a
lack of suitably qualified teachers.

It cannot, however, be claimed that they are entirely without their
critics. Specialized schools for the gifted are very occasionally
indicted by social commentators (see chapter 7 below), and although
language schools are seldom cited specifically there are exceptions to
the rule. Thus in 1971 a factory director expressed concern lest these

and other schools inculcated a sense of exclusiveness in the child, and he blamed parental ambitions.[97] V.N. Stoletov, President of the Academy of Pedagogical Sciences, had no compunction about numbering them among experimental schools and called for the experiment to be evaluated; it seems that his basic objection was to what he regarded as a form of social selection reminiscent of bourgeois notions and practices.[98]

Stoletov's call evidently fell on ears that, if not actually deaf, were not particularly open; why this was so will be suggested after the remaining kinds of special schools for clever children have been examined. There is a dilemma facing the language schools, but it is of the long-term future rather than the present. Apart from their educational viability, they were justified to Joan Simon on the grounds that the increasing demand for linguists 'can only be met by concentrating resources, at any rate until the number of qualified language teachers itself increases.[99] What then? Will they merely cease to develop? It is rather difficult to imagine their dispersal. Indeed, there is another view that the schools should be expanded until they can cater for all who wish to enter them, and that only by so doing can the authorities give the lie to the notion that they are special institutions. If this does happen — and it will take a long time because it is not intended to be at the expense of their quality — it is unlikely that they will forfeit their popularity among parents. The question then arises as to the nature of their relationship with, and effect on, the mass schools, and the Stoletovs will doubtless continue to worry about their social implications. For the present, however, the crystal ball remains cloudy.

Notes

1   *Sobranie postanovlenii i rasporyazhenii pravitel'stva SSR*, no. 25, 17 September 1940; German text in Bernhard Schiff, *Entwicklung und Reform des Fremdsprachenunterrichts in der Sowjetunion* (Berlin [West], 1966), 153-154.

2   Berthold C. Friedl, 'Shcherba and the Status of Foreign Languages in the USSR and the USA', *Modern Language Journal*, vol. XLVI, no. 7 (November 1962), 293-295.

3   Schiff, *op. cit.*, 107, citing L.V. Shcherba, *Prepodavanie inostrannykh yazykov v srednei shkole* (M., 1947), 31.

4   Schiff, *op. cit.*, 107-108, citing Shcherba, *op. cit.*, 39.

5   Soviet schools were officially single-sex from 1943-1954; this was effected only in part.

6   O.I. Moskalskaya, 'The Development of Foreign Language Study in the USSR', in Fred Ablin (ed.), *Education in the USSR*, vol. II (New York, 1963), 131. (Translated from *Inostrannye yazyki v shkole*, 1962, no. 1.)

7 M.P. Kashin and E.M. Chekharin (eds.), *Narodnoe obrazovanie v RSFSR* (M., 1970), 258. For excerpts from the RSFSR regulations of 1957, see Schiff, *op. cit.*, 160. Calling for an increase in language schools, the educationist N.K. Goncharov cited not only widening international links but also scientific and technological development ('O perspektivnom plane razvitiya narodnogo obrazovaniya v SSSR na blizhaishie 15-20 let', *Sov. ped.*, 1957, no. 4, 21); according to *Sovetskaya Rossiya*, 27 March 1957, eight further schools were to be opened in the RSFSR. — Prikazy are ministerial orders.

8 *Pravda,* 24 November 1957; 'Prepodavanie vedetsya na inostrannom yazyke', *Uch. gaz.*, 30 December 1958.

9 *Bringing Soviet Schools Still Closer to Life,* Soviet Booklet No. 44 (London, 1958), 12.

10 V. Vaneeva, 'Inostrannye yazyki izuchat' s detstva', *Izvestiya,* 30 November 1958.

11 Z.M. Tsvetkova, 'O povyshenii kachestva prepodavaniya inostrannykh yazykov v shkole i v vuze', *Sov. ped.*, 1958, no. 3, 40.

12 E. Kayukova, 'Na razbege', *Narodnoe obrazovanie,* 1964, no. 6, 54.

13 *Spravochnik partiinogo rabotnika* (M., 1963), 403-408.

14 For balanced comment on the effectiveness of this legislation three years later, see Kayukova, *op. cit.*, 54-55, 58.

15 *Sbornik prikazov i instruktsii Ministerstva prosveshcheniya RSFSR,* 1963, no. 26, 31.

16 Kayukova, *op. cit.*, 55.

17 Information from Mr Peter Frank (University of Essex).

18 I.A. Blokhin, 'Voprosy internatsional'nogo vospitaniya v shkole-internate', in *Iz opyta uchebno-vospitatel'noi raboty shkol-internatov goroda Moskvy* (M., 1960), 26-27.

19 Alexander Mirolyubov, 'The Russian Way: How Successful is it?', *Times Educational Supplement,* 20 February 1970. (Percentages recalculated.) At one Moscow school only 10 per cent were said to make a career in English (Universities of London, Reading and Oxford, *Comparative Education Tour to the USSR* (hereafter *CET*), *Easter 1968,* 30).

20 *Sbornik prikazov . . .,* 1961, no. 29, 12.

21 *Sbornik prikazov . . .,* 1961, no. 38, 17.

22 *Ibid.,* 17-18.

23 Harold J. Noah, *Financing Soviet Schools* (New York, 1966), 34.

24 Kayukova, *op. cit.*, 54.

25 Detlef Glowka, *Schulreform und Gesellschaft in der Sowjetunion 1958-1968* (Stuttgart, 1970), 193, citing *Uch. gaz.*, 25 April 1963.

26 N.K. Goncharov, 'Eshche raz o differentsirovannom obuchenii v starshikh klassakh obshcheobrazovatel'noi shkoly', *Sov. ped.*, 1963, no. 2, 39. This figure cannot be substantiated from other sources.

27 *Sbornik prikazov . . .,* 1963, no. 12, 24.

28 *Educational Planning in the USSR . . . with Observations of an IIEP Mission to the USSR* (Paris, 1968), 249; *CET, 1964,* 27.

29 Mirolyubov, *loc. cit.* In 1969/70, complete secondary day schools

totalled 42,924 (*Narodnoe obrazovanie, nauka i kul'tura v SSSR* (M., 1971), 44). If eight-year schools are included, the proportion is 0.6 per cent. It is rather difficult to express language school totals in percentage terms, since the 1961 decree did not stipulate whether they were to be eight-year or complete secondary schools. Although four of the eleven schools due to be opened in Moscow in September 1961 were of the former kind (Schiff, *op. cit.,* 109), according to earlier and subsequent regulations for the RSFSR (which tends to act as a pace-setter) they were to be of the latter type, but new schools were to be opened with forms 1 to 5 only. However, by the late 1960s they should have mostly built up their senior forms, so that for the recent past it is reasonable to regard them as 10-year schools. — For confirmation of Mirolyubov's figure, see note 41 to chapter 7.

30 In Moscow there were three in the early 1950s (Jennifer Louis, 'Streaming and Selection have their Advocates', *Times Educational Supplement,* 6 March 1970); seven in 1961, with another 11 scheduled for September (Schiff, *op. cit.,* 108); 38 in August 1965 (*Spisok abonentov Moskovskoi gorodskoi telefonnoi seti* (M., 1966), 111-112, with acknowledgements to Mervyn Matthews, whose brilliant idea it was to consult, in a later edition, this unorthodox source; the 1966 edition reflects the position as of 1 August 1965); 68 in 1967/68 (Joan Simon, 'Differentiation of Secondary Education in the USSR', *Forum for the Discussion of New Trends in Education,* vol. 11, no. 3 (Summer 1969), 89); 70 in 1968 (*Spisok abonentov . . .* (M., 1968), 123 ff., cited by Mervyn Matthews, *Class and Soviet in Soviet Russia* (London, 1972), 272-273, and confirmed in *CET, 1968,* 30); 76 in 1970 (*Moskva v tsifrakh* (M., 1972), 125); 77 in 1971 (information from Mr Bryan Woodriff (Kingston Polytechnic)) and also in May 1972 ('Supruga Prezidenta SShA posetila Moskovskuyu shkolu', *Izvestiya,* 24 May 1972); and 83 in 1973/74 (information from Ms Ann Simpson). In Leningrad they numbered 24 in 1966/67; 34 the following school year (Simon, *loc. cit.*), with over 20,000 pupils by December 1968 (N.B. Bushanskaya and N.N. Rundal'tseva, 'Zabolevaemost'' uchashchikhsya shkol s prepodavaniem ryada predmetov na inostrannom yazyke', *Sovetskoe zdravookhranenie,* 1968, no. 12, 37); and 35 in 1971/72 (I. Kossakovsky, 'Est' takaya shkola', *Izvestiya,* 23 March 1972), which now suggests stabilization.

31 Calculated from *Moskva v tsifrakh, loc. cit.,* and *Leningrad i Leningradskaya oblast' v tsifrakh* (L., 1974), 159. For absolute figures see previous note.

32 Schiff, *op. cit.,* 108.

33 Jaan Pennar *et al., Modernization and Diversity in Soviet Education* (New York, 1971), 46.

34 Kashin and Chekharin (eds.), *op. cit.,* 45.

35 Calculated from *Narodnoe khozyaistvo RSFSR v 1968 godu* (M., 1969), 373.

36 *Sbornik prikazov . . .,* 1966, no. 24, 5.

37 *Spisok abonentov . . .* (1966), *loc. cit.;* information from Mr Woodriff.

38   Simon, *loc. cit.*

39   *CET, 1967,* 39.

40   *CET, 1964,* 11. Early in 1963 the RSFSR government set a target for
      the *mass* schools according to which by 1970/71 50 per cent of form 5
      pupils should be studying English, 20 per cent French, 20 per cent
      German, and 10 per cent Spanish and other languages (*Sobranie
      postanovlenii pravitel'stva RSFSR,* 1963, no. 6, 35).

41   I. Tarabrin, 'Druzheskii vizit', *Uch. gaz.,* 4 September 1976.

42   Totals from mass schools from *Narodnoe khozyaistvo SSSR v 1974
      godu* (M., 1975), 678, with allowance for more recent trends.

43   A. Useinov, 'Slishkom medlennyi "razgon" ', *Uch. gaz.,* 8 September
      1973, and follow-up, 17 November 1973.

44   T. Lashkarashvili, 'Neischerpaemyi reserv', *ibid.,* 10 January 1976.

45   'V Ministerstve prosveshcheniya SSSR', *ibid.,* 11 November 1975.
      For an interesting account of a special Russian-language school at
      Tallinn in Estonia — 'it is no coincidence that all our language and
      literature staff teaching in the special classes are communists' (*i.e.*
      party members) — see O. Chelpanova, 'Nash vek — neukrotimoe
      stremlenie', *ibid.,* 27 October 1977.

46   *CET, 1967, loc. cit.*

47   Oskar Anweiler, *Die Sowjetpädagogik in der Welt von heute*
      (Heidelberg, 1968), 107.

48   K. Kostina, 'Papa, mama i osobaya shkola', *Izvestiya,* 24 September
      1965.

49   *Sbornik prikazov . . .,* 1961, no. 38, 18. The 1957 regulations (cited in
      Schiff, *op. cit.,* 160) had also stipulated the head of languages and two
      other teachers. Perhaps the panel had been whittled down in an
      attempt to make it less frightening; but read on.

50   E. Polyakova, 'Bol'shaya Moskva, Medvedkovo', *Novyi mir,* 1967,
      no. 10, 156.

51   *Observations . . .* (see note 28 above), *loc. cit.;* Simon, *loc. cit.;* Louis,
      loc. cit. In 1966 the RSFSR Education Ministry called for the
      regularization of selection procedures *(Sbornik prikazov ...,* 1966, no.
      24, 7-8).

52   *Times Educational Supplement,* 20 February 1970. For similar
      comments see *CET, 1968,* 27. At a Tallinn English school in 1973,
      there were two or three interviews, the criteria being ability to imitate
      sounds, oral facility and powers of concentration (A. Owen and F.R.
      Watson, *Report to the British Council on a Visit to the USSR* (1973),
      62). Earlier, in Riga, there was reported to be an oral examination, but
      only for entrants to forms other than the first, and a fortnight's
      probation in the spring prior to entry (*CET, 1966,* 20, 37). The RSFSR
      regulations stipulated an examination for occasional vacancies in
      these forms (*Sbornik prikazov . . .,* 1961, no. 38, 19).

53   *Ibid.,* 18.

54   Simon, *op. cit.,* 90.

55   Louis, *loc. cit.*

56   Leonid F. Kolesnikov, 'Selective Schools in Russia: How the System

works', *The Times,* 20 September 1975 (letter).

57 Bushanskaya and Rundal'tseva, *loc. cit.*

58 Simon, *op. cit.,* 89.

59 Detlef Glowka, 'Das sowjetische Schulwesen am Beginn einer neuen Etappe?', *Neue Sammlung,* vol. 7, no. 3 (May-June 1967), 219.

60 Owen and Watson, *loc. cit.*

61 Polyakova, *op. cit.,* 155.

62 M. Borodulina, 'Zhazhda znat' yazyki', *Pravda,* 26 October 1966.

63 David Burg, 'Notes on Foreign Language Teaching in the USSR', in George Z.F. Bereday and Jaan Pennar (eds.), *The Politics of Soviet Education* (New York, 1960), 120.

64 Yurii Trifonov, 'Obmen', *Novyi mir,* 1969, no. 12, 57. Emphasis original. I am endebted for this reference to Dr. Marianna Butenschön.

65 Polyakova, *loc. cit.*

66 *CET, 1967,* 40.

67 See note 19.

68 Calculated from *Narodnoe obrazovanie, nauka i kul'tura v SSSR* (M., 1971), 102, 187. Entry to day courses. 35.4 per cent of those completing secondary education of all types (day, evening and correspondence courses) entered *vuzy* of all types (ditto).

69 *CET, 1960,* 26; 'Besuch in der Moskauer Schule Nr. 50', *Sowjetunion heute,* 1 May 1972, 31.

70 Roy Medvedev, *Kniga o sotsialisticheskoi demokratii* (Amsterdam and Paris, 1972), 102-103. I am obliged to my colleague Mr M.J. Berry for this reference.

71 *Sbornik prikazov . . .,* 1961, no. 38, 20.

72 *Ibid.,* pp. 21-24. Yet at a French-language school in Leningrad visited in 1962, the boys had three hours of technical translation compared to one for the girls, who alone did two hours of French shorthand and typing (Yvonne Plaud, 'Notes prises "sur le vif" septembre 1962', *Aspects de l'école soviétique,* 1962, no. 6, 21).

73 'The Curriculum for the Eight-year and Secondary Schools of the RSFSR', *Soviet Education,* vol. II, no. 3 (January 1960), 30-31 (translated from *Narodnoe obrazovanie,* 1959, no. 11).

74 *Uch. gaz.,* 12 August 1969.

75 *Sbornik prikazov . . .,* 1972, no. 11, 2-5.

76 *CET, 1967,* 40.

77 Information from Mr. Woodriff. Kayukova, *loc. cit.,* mentions three groups of 10; thus too the 1972/73 curriculum.

78 Information from Mr Woodriff.

79 Elizabeth Moos, *Soviet Education Today and Tomorrow* (New York, n.d. [?1959]), 45.

80 *Sbornik prikazov . . .,* 1961, no. 38, 19, 21-23; Moskalskaya, *loc. cit.* (two periods per week attributed to engineering). At a Moscow school visited in 1962, attempts were also being made to teach PE in French (Plaud, *op. cit.,* 22).

81 *Times Educational Supplement,* 6 November 1964; 'Improving Soviet

Foreign Language Training', *School and Society*, vol. 93, no. 2259 (1965), 230, quoting *Soviet News*.

82   *Observations . . ., loc. cit.*
83   *CET, 1966,* 37.
84   Owen and Watson, *op. cit.,* 61.
85   *Spravochnik dlya postupayushchikh v vysshie uchebnye zavedeniya SSSR 1969* (M., 1969), 272, 275, 285, 287. Data at 1 January 1969. Other courses appear to have been available in the Ukraine (O.A. Zavadskaya, *Razvitie obshcheobrazovatel'noi shkoly Ukrainy v period stroitel'stva kommunizma (1959-1968 gg.)* (Kiev, 1968), p. 78). At the Lenin Pedagogical Institute in Moscow, some 50 out of the 1966/67 intake of about 225 mathematicians were destined for English-language schools (Bryan Thwaites, 'Mathematical Education in Russian Schools', *Mathematical Gazette,* vol. LII, no. 382 (December 1968), 326).
86   *Sov. ped.,* 1965, no. 7, 29, cited in Schiff, *op. cit.,* 112n.
87   A.A. Luk'yanova, 'Prepodavanie geografii na angliiskom yazyke v spetsshkole', *Geografiya v shkole,* 1972, no. 6, 54-55.
88   Schiff, *op. cit.,* 110.
89   It is noteworthy that in Poland, which has special 4-year secondary schools where most subjects are taught in a foreign language, mathematics is specifically excluded from this practice (W. Jane Bancroft, 'Foreign Language Teaching in Poland', *Modern Language Journal,* vol. LIX, no. 4 (April 1975), 163).
90   Bushanskaya and Rundal'tseva, *op. cit.,* 37-40. Excessive homework was a frequent complaint by the parents of pupils at Special School No. 6, Moscow (Colin Williams, 'Seven Years in Moscow', *Times Educational Supplement,* 8 July 1977).
91   *Sbornik prikazov . . .,* 1961, no. 38, 21-23; 1962, no. 28, 22; 1964, no. 28, 22-23; 1965, no. 20, 26-27; 1966, no. 18, 23-24; 1972, no. 11, 4. The eleventh year, abolished in the RSFSR with effect from 1966/67, appears to have been reintroduced into language schools for a time, partly to relieve overloading (Werner Kienitz *et al., Einheitlichkeit und Differenzierung im Bildungswesen* (Berlin [East], 1971), 319, 325, 386). It has since been discontinued again.
92   Anthony Potts, *Times Educational Supplement,* 20 February 1970. This is also implied in the 1957 regulations quoted by Schiff, *op. cit.,* 160.
93   *CET, 1968,* 28. At School No. 7, Tallinn, however, the few leavers after form 8 are said to be roughly balanced by others transferring in (Owen and Watson, *op. cit.,* 22). See also note 52 above.
94   Plaud, *loc. cit.*
95   Kostina, *loc. cit.*
96   Noah, *op. cit.,* 34-35.
97   G. Kulagin, 'Shkola truda', *Pravda,* 19 June 1971.
98   V.N. Stoletov, in foreword to *Obshchestvo i molodezh'* (M., 2nd edn., 1973), 14. I am obliged for this reference to Murray Yanowitch, *Social and Economic Inequality in the Soviet Union* (New York and

London, 1977), 78.
99   Simon, *op. cit.*, 90.

Chapter 6

Mathematics and Physics Boarding Schools

Early Debates

The notion of specialized schools for the most gifted young people became a major subject of public debate during the weeks before the inauguration of the 1958 reform. The urgency was caused by a proposal to introduce a mandatory two-year work period between school and *vuz;* this raised grave fears as to the academic level and uninterrupted supply of future *vuz* entrants. The discussion got under way that summer,[1] when E.I. Afanasenko, then Minister of Education of the RSFSR, and I.A. Kairov, then President of the Academy of Pedagogical Sciences (APN), presented a draft of the proposed changes at a conference of region-level officials in education, local government and the party.[2] Afanasenko alluded briefly to the possibility of setting up a small number of special schools, in association with *vuzy,* for children specially gifted in mathematics, physics and chemistry, but said nothing about methods of selection. From the outset there was opposition: during preliminary discussion, said the director of education (*zaveduyushchii oblono*) for Leningrad Region, the proposal had not found approval. Both he and the secretary of the Ivanovo Region party committee felt that gifted children should go the same way as their coevals and work in production.[3] Thus already there were objections on grounds of privilege.

Initially, however, supporters of the suggestion seem to have monopolized what limited press coverage there was. The director of education for Smolensk Region saw it in broader terms, including provision for pupils with particular abilities in draughtsmanship and arts subjects,[4] and G.I. Zelenko, director of the Chief Administration of Labour Reserves, saw it in a similar light, giving specialized schools a specific place as one of four means of continuing secondary education on the basis of the eight-year general school.[5] Kairov himself made favourable mention of the idea, though without reference to the humanities,[6] and Khrushchev took it up in his September Memorandum to the Central Committee, justifying it by the argument that continuity was needful for training specialists, but commenting that such schools should be exceptional.[7] Party support ensued from V. Kuroedov, regional committee secretary in Sverdlovsk, on the grounds that such schools were very necessary for the advancement of science. But here, apparently for the first time, explicit reference was made to the existence of a great controversy among teachers and parents; those in favour, though speaking with much force, were in a minority. Kuroedov summed up the plainly ideological objections underpinning the majority view: a privileged position for a particular group of children would inculcate a sense of exclusiveness in them and encourage parental go-getting.[8]

The first eminent advocate of such schools who was prepared to paint a fairly full picture of what he envisaged was Academician N.N. Semenov, the chemist. Of children completing the eight-year school, 5 to 8 per cent, the best of the gifted ones who had evinced a talent for mathematics and science, should be selected for three-year special schools. The age of selection was justified by that at which a proclivity for scientific research appeared, namely from 12 to 16. This could be identified by the pupil's showing an interest in scientific literature and creative experiment. Selection should be the responsibility primarily of the schools' pedagogical councils, but also that of their sponsors and the local Komsomol branches, who should help the children by providing good facilities and observing their progress in study and club activities; no notice should be taken of parental influence or status. To exploit resources of talent, the schools should have residential accommodation for children from rural areas and under-privileged homes. There should be several types: for laboratory assistants in physics, chemistry and biology respectively; for computer personnel; and for draughtsmen and designers. Their functions would be not only to train such personnel but also to prepare some 25 per cent for entry to *vuzy* and research institutions, of which local ones could sponsor the schools. Half of the three-year course should be *beyond* the secondary general education stage, and the schools would be the main source of *vuz* recruitment, providing three-quarters of the intake.[9]

However, a further month was to elapse before the press debate suddenly gained momentum. The signal for this was the publication, on 16 November, of the Theses of the Central Committee and the Council of Ministers on the education reform. The concept of special schools was expressed anew, but more cautiously. 'Thought should be given to the question of establishing special schools for young people with a particular inclination and aptitude for mathematics, physics, chemistry and biology'. Selection would be by special examination and on the recommendation of the pedagogical councils.[10] There is a hint here of doubt and probably controversy in top party and government circles, matching that already noted at regional and local levels. This impression is reinforced by an earlier comment from I. Beloded, the Ukrainian Minister of Education, that such schools should be organized at certain universities *by way of experiment*,[11] and by some discreetly vague comments by Kairov in an article appearing in *Sovetskaya pedagogika* at about the same time: care should be taken over selection and instruction must be linked with socially useful work.[12] The Central Committee Theses were immediately followed by support for Semenov by fellow academicians Zeldovich and Sakharov, who went even further: a highly intensive two-year course would be sufficient, enabling young people to enter *vuzy* at 16 or 17, and thus be well prepared by the time they reached their peak period of creativity, which for theoretical mathematicians and physicists is primarily from 22 to 26. Some of the schools could be within the *vuzy*. The very difficulty of getting in and staying the pace would foil over-ambitious parents.[13] Some mathematicians on the staff of Voronezh University supported the proposal for special schools because of the unsatisfactory level of attainment in mathematics and physics by school leavers.[14]

Yet these were in effect lone voices, to be drowned in a chorus of protests during the five weeks preceding the issue of the decree of 25 December. Possibly the first important objections in the national non-educational press were those advanced in *Izvestiya* by one V. Pugachev, who did not otherwise identify himself but wrote from Nizhneudinsk, Irkutsk Region, He seems to have been an ordinary citizen whom it befell to represent high-level dissent. He opposed the removal of some pupils from others and their being placed in special conditions — a point already familiar and destined to become even more so — and he denied that talent could be easily detected at an early age.[15] This new argument was subsequently taken up and forcefully elaborated by educationists and teachers.[16]

Concurrently with Pugachev's contribution, two eminent members of the APN, the educationist N. Goncharov, a vice-president, and the psychologist A. Leont'ev, a presidium member, in a *Pravda* article advocating differentiated instruction for all, spoke of the psychological harm done by setting apart certain gifted children and making them feel exceptional.[17] Since the mid-1950s the APN had consistently advocated the encouragement of individual talents by restructuring the senior part of the general school to allow for up to three or four alternative courses,[18] and still continued so to do. This third view was never really at the centre of the 1958 debate, nor did it appear in the December legislation; however, it is worth noting as it was to figure prominently in the earlier 1960s, as will be shown hereafter. For the moment its critics seem to have been outnumbered by its supporters,[19] some of whom found special schools for the gifted unnecessary or inappropriate; these were to include such eminent figures as Academicians A.N. Nesmeyanov, President of the USSR Academy of Sciences, and N. Muskhelishvili, President of the Georgian Academy of Sciences and a full member of the USSR Academy.[20]

On 25 November Academician M.A. Lavrent'ev, founder of Akademgorodok, the 'science city' near Novosibirsk, took up the principle theme, stressing that such schools would contradict the basis principle of communist upbringing that there should be no sharp boundary between physical and intellectual labour. Not the singling-out of privileged *Wunderkinder,* but stimulating the broad masses should be the aim, as the main thing in creative activity was hard work and perseverance.[21] A. Aleksandrov, Rector of Leningrad State University (LGU), objected in similar terms, though he would accept a few experimental schools.[22] The Kazakh Minister of Education deemed special schools unnecessary, though the highly gifted should be exempt from the proposed two years in industry before entering *vuzy,*[23] while the educationist N. Levitov flatly denied the possibility of natural gifts in most sciences.[24] Despite Beloded's support, mentioned above, a Ukrainian Ministry of Education report found such schools socially undesirable.[25] Meanwhile there was an apparent upsurge of grassroots opinion, from workers within and outside the teaching profession, against the proposal,[26] showing popular fears of the development of exclusive schools and unacceptable attitudes and suggesting that the turning point in the unseen high-level struggle had come (though *Uchitel'skaya gazeta* of 5 December asserted that the question had yet to be settled). Some correspondents even attacked the existing special schools for the artistically gifted;[27] these, however, most contributors to the debate were prepared to accept.

Confronted by this growing hostility, Academician A.N. Kolmogorov, the distinguished mathematician, had made an apparent last-ditch stand for special schools on 10 December, referring specifically to Khrushchev's comment that they were necessary 'for our state to be able to develop and use the talents innate in the people'. Combining this with a strong plea for boarding facilities to counter the argument that such schools would accentuate urban-rural disparity, Kolmogorov followed Semenov's original line very closely, though he thought that rather more leavers (30-40 per cent instead of 25 per cent) would go on to *vuzy*. The remainder would be able to apply their skills in production: 'a deep knowledge of mathematics, technical drawing, physics, chemistry and biology is necessary for a number of professions which have become mass ones'. Cultivation of potential scientific gifts would go hand in hand with mass training of cadres with a mathematics and physics profile.[28] However, other counsels prevailed, and the decree of 25 December omitted all reference to schools for the gifted, though Rapacz, with foresight, noted that its wording did not render their establishment impossible.[29] Indeed, article 7 stressed the need to ensure that enough secondary school leavers went on to *vuzy* so as to maintain the supply of highly skilled specialists for the economy. Under article 28, experience of work in production was made not mandatory but grounds for priority in respect of *vuz* entry (a quota system was later imposed). This can have only partially allayed the anxieties of the proposal's critics.[30]

But although the decree was silent, the record of the Supreme Soviet session promulgating it contains a few references to the controversy. Kairov made a very brief mention towards the end of his long report: many had been against such schools, but the question merited discussion.[31] Eight speakers, including P.M. Masherov, I.V. Abashidze and A.Ya. Pel'she, found them unnecessary or inadvisable, the first-named considering them incorrect in principle, *i.e.* ideologically.[32] Nevertheless, Abashidze warned against neglecting young talent for fear of isolating the gifted from the collective, for if the school did nothing for such children parents might resort to private coaching with its attendant evils; and Pel'she, a man of some eminence who was to become a member of the Politburo in 1966, advocated special classes, as had been tried out in Latvia.[33] It was thus made fairly clear that the general issue of differentiation in relation to above-average ability had not been put on the index and could well continue, though perhaps in other forms.

Here some comment is due. Schwartz and Keech have used the 1958 reform debate as a case-study of the role of interest groups on decision-making in the USSR.[34] They suggested that Khrushchev's plans to achieve his purposes of inculcating respect in the young for physical labour and eliminating privilege and inequality were substantially modified through the mobilization of occupational groups, such as teachers, educational administrators and scientists, by opponents of the First Secretary at the top of the *apparat*. While their general argument is interesting, their analysis at certain stages does not fit the particular but important issue of special schools for the gifted. They take it as axiomatic that the major proponent of the reform was Khrushchev himself.[35] On this specific matter, however, that is unproven, since it was *totally at variance* with the levelling spirit of the remainder of the First Secretary's proposals. The objection may perhaps be raised that it was most likely an extreme example of Khrushchev's notoriously erratic behaviour. But even then account must still be taken of the high-powered pressure evidenced in print. Furthermore, Schwartz and Keech treat the occupational groups participating in the debate as of one mind, whereas they were not all so. It is convenient to describe those for and against by the terms 'differentiators' and 'egalitarians'. If, as we have seen, the APN President was a cautious differentiator, other leading educationists were either thoroughgoing egalitarians or egalitarian on this particular point, and the top educational bureaucracy in Moscow was neither supported by that of Kazakhstan nor, it seems, by most of the educational rank and file, and the Ukrainian Ministry's view was inconsistent. One regional party committee secretary was a differentiator, another an egalitarian. More strikingly, the Academy of Sciences was openly divided on the issue, with Semenov, Zeldovich, Sakharov and Kolmogorov in favour, Nesmeyanov and Muskhelishvili against but in favour of differentiated mass schools, and Lavrent'ev categorically against; as will be seen, the latter appears to have played a key part also after the debate. It may be conjectured that it was an important section of the influential scientific lobby that induced Khrushchev to adopt the special schools plank of his platform,[36] but that a rift in the Academy developed or materialized which had to be patched up before further attempts could be made to win over the top party leadership. The 1958 debate provides evidence for Skilling's hypothesis of the possible identification, within occupational groups, of strong opinion groups, constellations whose stars are by no means all fixed.[37] Schwartz and Keech make the further point that in the press coverage of the debate as a whole the view of those opposed to the projected changes was clearly a minority one. This is not true of the special schools issue. Here, perhaps, Khrushchev was clearly out on an ideologically dubious limb and it was easier for the majority to have their say. Nevertheless it must not be forgotten that in this matter not even the party spokesmen can all be regarded as root and branch egalitarians.

New Initiatives and Establishment of the Schools

The scientists' heads may have been bloody, but they were not long bowed. All that was necessary was for them to speak with one voice, or at least for dissentients to keep silent. For soon the climate became ripe for renewal of the discussion on differentiation and for a further bid, this time successful, to introduce a very small number of special schools for really promising young mathematicians and scientists. The need for more efficient training of specialists for all branches of the economy seemed all the more urgent when the previously rapid rate of industrial growth, which had lessened in the mid-fifties, showed no signs of resuming. One of the reasons for this was that, since in some ways Soviet technology had learned all it could from the West, further advance was coming to depend more and more on *indigenous* research and innovation.[38] Another reason for the success of the new attempt may well have been that scientists were themselves acquiring greater power; since 1961, when science was promoted in official ideology from being a handmaid of production to a driving productive force, an enhanced status has been accorded to pure research, and scientists have taken over party functionaries' responsibilities in laying down guidelines for its development.[39]

It was Academician Lavrent'ev who in the autumn of 1960 again called for radical changes in the methods and rates of training the rising generation of scientists and engineers. A passion for science and technology must be developed in secondary school, and the *vuzy* should be much more closely involved with the schools to ensure countrywide selection of outstanding pupils. Although Lavrent'ev confined himself to olympiads (see below) as the means to this end, a much louder note of urgency can be detected in this article than in that of 1958.[40] Whatever was happening behind the scenes, over a year elapsed before the next major public pronouncement when Academician Tamm stated categorically that scientific progress could be achieved only by specially gifted people, who must be sought out. Einstein had formulated the theory of relativity at 26; Galois, killed at 21, had already propounded the theory of groups.[41] Tamm was speaking primarily about higher education, but Kolmogorov, with his usual enthusiasm, was quick to back him up and develop this point, while expressing regret at the lack of response to Semenov's earlier proposals. The only test of talent, he said, was the results of active participation in research. This could begin in school clubs, but the work must be creative and sustained. Better still would be schools working to special syllabuses with much increased requirements in mathematics and physics; they might be first set up in large towns, under *vuz* sponsorship and with boarding facilities.[42]

The extent to which the climate had now changed can be surmised from an RSFSR Ministry of Education order of 21 February 1962 requiring mathematics teachers to 'further the development of the individual abilities of pupils showing a particular bent for mathematics',[43] and yet more from the subsequent decree 'On Measures for Further Improving the Selection and Training of Scientific Personnel', which called upon the Ministry of Higher and Specialized Secondary Education (MVSSO) to submit proposals for optimum selection of the most able secondary school pupils for *vuz* study.[44] However, in view of the earlier hostility of Lavrent'ev, the key man at the Siberian Section of the Academy of Sciences, it still comes as a surprise to learn from an *Izvestiya* discussion that it was at the Akademgorodok science centre near Novosibirsk that the first of the specialized schools (*fiziko-matematischeskie shkoly*, FMSh) was to be opened.[45] It must have been sometime during 1961 that Lavrent'ev underwent his conversion. In two subsequent articles he described how the plans outlined in March and April had come to fruition. A mathematics and physics competition by correspondence had been organized throughout Siberia; subsequently a team of 70 scientists had gone into all the regions and territories to make contact with schools and conduct a further round. Some of the winners had entered Novosibirsk State University (NGU), and others would be admitted to the mathematics and physics boarding school which was being set up. He recommended to the Academy that this experimental work of the Siberian Section be extended![46] In January 1963 the school was reported to have opened;[47] flushed with success, Lavrent'ev and his colleagues once again advocated the opening of more such schools under the high-sounding name of Lomonosov Academies.[48]

Contrary, perhaps, to expectations, Novosibirsk was thus the first to blaze the trail, and Moscow, in the persons of Academicians Kolmogorov and Petrovsky, Rector of Moscow State University (MGU), was not slow to follow it. The latter, however, implicitly restrained his impassioned colleague who had called for hundreds of such schools; he advocated a pilot scheme and thought Lavrent'ev's proposed name for them immodest.[49] *Izvestiya* hereupon commended the discussion to the MVSSO, the Academy and the education ministries of the Union republics. Meanwhile, published opposition had been minimal,[50] and on 23 August the USSR Council of Ministers quietly passed a decree legitimating the schools.[51] Even though the attitude of Aleksandrov, Petrovsky's opposite number in Leningrad, had hardened somewhat, during 1963 his university nevertheless saw the emergence of Boarding School No. 45, originally with a chemistry and biology profile but subsequently broadened to include mathematics, physics and geology.[52] The Moscow FMSh (Boarding School No. 18) opened on 2 December 1963 with 199 pupils,[53] and another was organized in Kiev in the same year, by decree of the Ukrainian Council of Ministers on 26 September.[54] These constitute the original group of four FMShs sometimes mentioned collectively in the literature. Since then some nine others have opened; they may not all correspond exactly to the prototype but are evidently similar in many respects.[55] The fewness of these schools can scarcely be over-emphasized; in the 1967/68 school year the ratio of FMSh pupils in the Russian Republic to general school pupils in forms 8 to 10 was one to at least 4,000.[56]

Selection: Policy and Procedures

Against a background of increasing discontent with the quality of mathematics teaching in the upper classes of ordinary schools, the FMShs were thus set up as experimental institutions seeking the best way of training scientific cadres from an early age, recruited from the most promising pupils.[57] Ever since the idea was first mooted in 1958, its proponents had urged that the schools should have residential facilities to accommodate deserving children from rural areas; since their establishment, concern about this function has, if anything, increased. The broad goal of the schools is to develop the creative abilities of the pupils; specifically, the latter are prepared for the mathematics and science faculties of *vuzy;* and a spin-off is anticipated in the form of accumulated experience, utilizable in secondary and higher educational reform.[58]

The greater part of the literature on these schools concerns Novosibirsk, Moscow and, to a lesser extent, Leningrad. The entry procedures are fairly similar but certainly not uniform. The most common method of selection is through the system of mathematics, physics or chemistry olympiads or competitions; details of these must be minimal here as a later chapter will be devoted to the subject. There is an All-Union Olympiad of four rounds, at school, district, region (or equivalent) and republic level, the first two of these being in some instances replaced by a correspondence round. This used to be particularly true of the competition's well-known and somewhat idiosyncratic All-Siberian component, in which the winners of the regional round, numbering between 600 and 700 from up to 12,000 participants,[59] are invited to a summer camp of lectures, practicals and recreational activities on the premises of the Novosibirsk school at Akademgorodok, and are also shown round the research institutes; in the third and last week the final round of the Olympiad is held, and this is simultaneously the entrance examination to the FMSh. In 1967, 200 of the 650 gained admission,[60] the total roll of the school in 1966/67 being over 350.[61] Five years later the success rate was put at about 300 out of 500, with a roll of 503. Unlike the Moscow FMSh, whose pupil complement was 357 in 1965 and 360 in 1972/73, the Novosibirsk school has expanded, though erratically.[62] Its catchment area extends to the Far East and since 1966 has also included the Central Asian republics and Kazakhstan.[63]

As for the All-Union Olympiad, the Moscow FMSh's written examinations (for an example, see Appendix C) are taken in connection with the semi-final round at regional centres within its catchment area. In 1968 this comprised 43 regions and 11 autonomous republics of the RSFSR and also Belorussia.[64] Moscow itself, Leningrad and certain other large university centres had been excluded, as gifted children were already well catered for there.[65] Those who pass undergo oral examinations a few weeks later.[66] A MGU examining board, jointly with representatives of regional education authorities and local *vuzy,* conducts the proceedings and makes recommendations to an admissions committee of the University.[67] The best candidates are admitted direct; about 350 others who show promise are invited to Moscow's own summer school, and of these 160 to 170 fifteen-year-old pupils are finally accepted for form 9 (*i.e.* for a two-year course) and 60 to 70 sixteen-year-olds for form 10 (one year). The latter are late developers who are taught separately from the second year of the two-year intake as they have leeway to make up.[68]

Novosibirsk also has a tenth-year entry; furthermore in 1968, on the suggestion of Academician Belyaev, Rector of NGU, an experimental form 10 was set up for a group of pupils who had evidently not shone in the Olympiad precisely because they came from places with inadequate teaching. All but one of the 26 later entered higher education.[69] The very shortness of these courses highlights their special, intensive *vuz*-preparation function, which is also considered to be 'socially important' from the viewpoint of equal opportunity. However, the admission of pupils from big cities (with good schools) to the one-year tenth-form course is controversial; according to S.I. Literat, formerly deputy director there, the only justification for it is concern lest they leave Siberia.[70]

At Kiev admission to form 8 (14-plus) is the norm, and to forms 9 and 10 the exception.[71] Leningrad and Novosibirsk also take pupils at the age of 14.[72] At Novosibirsk this entry was first organized experimentally in 1966, expressly to augment and improve the intake of pupils from rural areas, but Kolmogorov of Moscow is opposed to enrolment at 14 on the grounds of the transitory nature of many children's apparent abilities and interests at that age, and contends that the dropout rate is high.[73] (The whole question of failure to complete the course will be considered later.) Children in the 14-plus age group were recommended by the schools, which tended to send well-behaved sloggers instead of bright if sometimes lazy pupils, so subsequently scientists from the FMSh have gone out on talent-spotting expeditions.[74] Although most of Kolmogorov's recruits arrive via olympiads, he considers that these do not appeal to all young people, and so pupils recommended by schools and nominated by regional education authorities are allowed to sit the entrance examinations.[75] In addition, both Moscow and Novosibirsk have organized correspondence schools which offer further potential; in 1973 the NGU one catered for 1500 children or more (accounts vary) and it was planned to double or even treble this figure.[76] At the Novosibirsk FMSh some children are even admitted on the direct initiative of their teachers who bring them to the school and ask for them to be tested.[77]

Despite these various ways and means, for several years those in charge of the FMShs did not feel that they were adequately fulfilling their important role of tapping the latent reserves of talent in remote country districts. In 1965, when most of the pupils at the Moscow FMSh were said to come from mathematicians' families,[78] only one in nine and under 20 per cent of those at Akademgorodok were from rural areas.[79] However, the proportion for the 1964/65 *intake* at the Moscow school was better than one in four,[80] and after the 1967 entry about half of the pupils there were said to be from rural areas, small towns or workers' settlements.[81] Nevertheless, in 1968 the Collegium of the RSFSR Ministry of Education still thought there were not enough children of workers and collective farmers in the Republic's three specialized boarding schools.[82] Maintenance fees ought not to have been a major disincentive; they were common to all boarding schools and were not exorbitant.[83] It was claimed that no child had to forego a place at a FMSh by reason of financial hardship since the state would support him.[84] In 1975, 76 out of 550 pupils at Akademgorodok paid no fees, ten orphans received scholarships of between 34 and 44 roubles a month according to performance, and the rest allegedly had merely to pay an income-related charge of up to 10 roubles a month,[85] a trifling sum when the average (non-kolkhoz) family income was around 225 roubles; the scale was subsequently criticized for being out of date.[86]

Literat found the Siberian olympiads imperfect as a net; the maximum number of participants in the correspondence round did not exceed 0.2 per cent of the eligible pupils, and over 70 per cent of such entries were from towns. He blamed this partly on poor publicity but mainly on lack of systematic, scientific work on detecting and developing children's 'innate inclinations'. In 1972 he said that the correspondence round had practically disappeared.[87] By then, however, Kolmogorov was at least able to state that as a rule FMSh pupils came from places where their rapid development would have been extremely difficult or impossible, and this reflected his school's aim of giving equality of opportunity;[88] and Literat felt that the Novosibirsk experiments, including the preparatory eight-form entry and the one-year course for tenth-formers, had helped to solve what he called one of the basic social problems connected with specialized education — ensuring equal opportunities for representatives of different strata of the population.[89] Since 1970 the Faculty of Mathematics and Mechanics at LGU has been organizing summer schools specifically for rural children in the north-west; in 1971, when the exercise was extended to a total of three regional centres, 90 of the 316 participants were admitted to the Leningrad FMSh.[90] As for the sex ratio, there were 38 girls to 319 boys at the Moscow school in 1965, and a similar ratio of one to eight was reported at Novosibirsk in 1972;[91] but according to a later report, based on a spring 1973 visit, it was about one to four (99 girls to 404 boys),[92] which may have indicated a new policy initiative (compare the unusual emphasis on girls' performance in the olympiads at about the same time, described in chapter 11 below). Yet by 1975 it had reverted to one to six.[93] At Kiev, however, girls had constituted some 30 per cent of the roll as early as 1966. [94]

Academic Organization and Atmosphere

Perhaps the most striking feature of the FMShs is their resemblance to the best *vuzy,* both in externals and in atmosphere. They appear to have been deliberately organized so as to form a bridge between secondary and higher education, the abutments projecting well into either side. This is true of syllabuses, framework and methods of instruction, and teaching staff. Even the terms are arranged in two semesters coinciding with those of the *vuzy.* At Novosibirsk the pupils are actually taught within the university and research institutes: in their final year they go into the research laboratories three times a week and also attend seminars.[95] The teaching format for mathematics and the three sciences is one of lectures to all the pupils of a given course-year, followed by work with a full class of 30 if appropriate, but very often by problem-solving or practicals in groups of about 15. The system resembles school only insofar as checks are carried out fairly often.[96] However, the other subjects — and at Novosibirsk and elsewhere, to avoid the fatigue of a double-period lecture, all the subjects for form 8 — are taught as conventional lessons; the ordinary syllabuses are supposed to be followed,[97] but sometimes there have been deviations (see below). At Moscow, Leningrad and Kiev the pupils choose a main subject specialism (mathematics, physics, biology or chemistry) on entry to form 9, but at Novosibirsk this is deferred until halfway through the following year. There it is felt that initial enthusiasms are not always correlated with optimum potential, so that the right choice of specialism can be made only after a lengthy period at the FMSh.[98] As soon as deemed feasible, then, it is determined by assessing the young people's aptitudes whether they should be trained as specialists in a restricted field, as all-rounders or as science administrators.[99] The FMSh curriculum is presented in Table 6.1.

Instruction in the main subjects is two or three times as intensive as in ordinary schools. After a little over a year on home-grown, accelerated versions of school syllabuses in mathematics and physics, *vuz*-level work is begun; attention is paid to higher mathematics and present-day physics and it is claimed that pupils sometimes reach the standard of the third year of a university course.[100] This 'rational intensification' is where the FMShs feel particularly that they have a pioneering role for the betterment of Soviet education generally. The want of suitable textbooks has been remedied from the pens of academicians and others.[101] Bruce Vogeli, a mathematician who has made a special study of mathematics teaching in the USSR, furnishes comparisons of the syllabuses devised and used in the two best-known schools and the official ones employed in ordinary schools specializing in computer programming.[102] That of Moscow is the most theoretical; it contains more analysis and less quantitative methods than that of the latter type of school. The Novosibirsk syllabus occupies a middle position with a greater emphasis on applied mathematics than Moscow,[103] for the Siberian Section of the Academy is much more technologically oriented than its parent body. This explains the paradox that despite its mathematics emphasis the FMSh tries to avoid producing professional mathematicians. As Hugo Portisch saw for himself, 'the intention is to train scientists in all fields who possess a sound knowledge of mathematics, so that they are able to work with electronic computers and make use of mathematics as an auxiliary science'.[104] Thus the physics instruction is not eclipsed by the mathematics; in 1965 the Moscow school was reported to possess equipment such as an audio-frequency oscillator of the latest make and double high-speed oscillographs, which made it superior to some *vuzy,*[105] and a target of twelve specialized laboratories had been set.[106] Originally it was reiterated that *inter alia* the courses provided self-sufficient training for the jobs of laboratory assistants and computer programmers, but

TABLE 6.1 Curriculum for Two-Year Course, Novosibirsk Mathematics and Physics Boarding School, 1968/69

Subjects		Periods per week per form			
		9		10	
		Term 1	Term 2	Term 1	Term 2
Mathematics	Lectures	2	2	2	-
	Problem-solving	6	6	5	6
Physics	Lectures	2	2	2	2
	Problem-solving	5	3	4	4
	Practicals	-	3	3	-
Chemistry	Lectures	-	2	2	-
	Problem-solving	-	2	2	-
Literature		2	2	3	3
History		4	2	2	2
Social Studies		-	-	-	3
Biology	Lectures	-	1	1	-
	Problem-solving	-	2	1	-
Physical Geography		3	-	-	-
Foreign Language		2	2	2	2
Physical Education		2	2	2	2
Photography and Radio Engineering		2	-	-	-
Specialism		-	-	-	5
Total		30	31	31	29
Special Courses and Options		4	4	4	2
Total instruction periods per week		34	35	35	31
Tests, Handing in Assignments, Lab. Work:					
	Physics	0.5	0.5	0.5	0.5
	Chemistry	-	0.5	0.5	-
	History	-	0.5	0.5	-
	Biology	-	0.5	0.5	-
	Physical Geography	0.5	-	-	-
Total		1	2	2	0.5
Method Work and Tutorials		1	1	1	1
Grand total		36	38	38	32.5

Note   For practical work in mathematics, physics, chemistry and biology, and also in foreign language lessons and P.E., the class is divided into two groups.

Source   S.I. Literat, 'Vyyavlyat' i razvivat' sposobnosti', *Sov. ped.*, 1969, no. 4, 83. (Subsequent changes have been insignificant.)

since the partial deposition of polytechnism in 1966 such statements have ceased to be needful.

Apart from the 'rational intensification' of the learning process, the hallmarks of these schools are said to be discernment and creativity.[107] Emphasis is laid on non-standard problems and individual research. At Novosibirsk this is reported and discussed in the pupils' Mathematics Society, which resembles a university seminar. Clubs (*kruzhki*)[108] for subjects like cybernetics and number theory provide research training and help pupils to determine their interests and perhaps their career orientation, as do optional studies.[109] Obviously, the residential setting is conducive to such activities. Institute research workers and university students help both with the clubs and the teaching of the four main subjects. Lectures are delivered by the country's leading scientists, including academicians, *e.g.* Lavrent'ev and Budker at Akademgorodok; nineteen university professors and ten lecturers teach at the Kiev school;[110] in Moscow, Kikoin's lectures on physics, Kolmogorov's on theoretical mathematics and others by senior MGU staff are followed by practice sessions conducted not only by experienced schoolmasters but also by postgraduates and senior undergraduates, many of whom are Kolmogorov's own students. Nowadays former pupils of the FMSh are responsible for over half the mathematics teaching.[111] Kolmogorov himself devotes considerable attention to the school and is chairman of its board of governors (*popechitel'skii sovet*), which in this case is evidently the decision-making body.[112] At Akademgorodok another way in which younger members of the institutes involve themselves in the FMSh is through sponsoring individual pupils, who sometimes work under them later at NGU.[113] This can extend to children who do outstandingly well in olympiads but are too young for the FMSh.[114] The pupils themselves run academic clubs in other local schools,[115] which although primarily an exercise in social responsibility must contribute to their own intellectual development.

The teacher-pupil ratio at the Kiev FMSh in 1966 was reportedly one to four,[116] but one wonders if the notorious pitfall occasioned by Soviet educational statisticians' habit of omitting to distinguish between full- and part-time staff has claimed another victim here. Kolmogorov has stated the Moscow FMSh teacher-pupil ratio to be about 20 'instructors' to a batch of 160;[117] as they usually come in only twice a week this *may* be more like 1:20 in English terms, but the category may not include the lecturers. If these figures were calculated according to normal Soviet practice, the teacher-pupil ratio is surprisingly low, but it evidently does not impair the quality of the specialized teaching. On the other hand, data recently reported from Novosibirsk seem to imply that, given compatibility, Kolmogorov's statement can perhaps be taken at face value. In 1972/73 the Akademgorodok school had 45 staff, and 80 visiting helpers from NGU; of the latter, 30 were mathematicians and represented 10 full-time-equivalent staff.[118] If this can be assumed across the board, the FMSh had a total of over 70 full-time and equivalent staff to its 503 pupils.

Although it is insisted that admission to the FMSh is in itself no guarantee of a *vuz* place and the usual examinations have to be taken, this is clearly no problem to those *'fymyshata'*[119] (the great majority) who survive to the end of the school course. As a Soviet pamphlet remarks with unusual candour: 'Naturally it is easier for the graduates of this school to pass competitive entrance exams at the University than it is for other applicants'.[120] In 1968 the success rate for FMSh applicants to the Mathematics and Mechanics Faculty of MGU was two in three, against one in six from ordinary schools.[121] (The average rate of *vuz* entry for Moscow pupils was reported in 1971 to be 30 per cent of candidates,[122] while the countrywide average was about 25 per cent.) Also in 1968 it was recorded that of the 238 pupils who had so far completed the Kiev FMSh, 192 or over 80 per cent had been admitted to higher education, nearly two-thirds of them to Kiev University.[123] The following year over 40 of the new intake of 250 students in the NGU Mathematics Faculty were from the Akademgorodok school.[124] Because of their exceptional mathematical knowledge, there was a special stream for them.[125] Up to 1970, 1,307 pupils completed the course there; of these 1,236, or 94.5 per cent, went straight on to *vuzy* (including 1,027, or 78.5 per cent, to NGU), and some of the others entered higher education subsequently.[126] A further indicator of the success of the FMSh training is that many of its ex-pupils are doing candidate-level research in their third undergraduate year and some are already publishing.[127]

Problems of the Schools

This hothouse atmosphere has inevitably contributed to a series of problems, academic and moral. The selection procedures are not infallible. By no means all the children are prodigies, and a number of them, especially the older ones from rural areas, have to put in extra work on arrival at the school to fill the gaps in their knowledge.[128] They can thus suffer from overloading, which is reinforced by the psychological pressure of examinations at the end of each term and removal to an ordinary school in the event of failure.[129] At Novosibirsk an average mark of no more than 'satisfactory' over two terms also leads to transfer.[130] In 1965 the dropout rate there was stated to be about 10 per cent,[131] but at Moscow it appears to have been much lower (only four pupils).[132] At Novosibirsk in 1972 it was estimated at 25 per cent, of which about half was due to lack of progress;[133] by 1975, however, it had sunk to some 7 per cent.[134] In both 1966 and 1967 the dropout rate from the preparatory form 8 was nearly 30 per cent, but, by subsequently keeping the less able half of the previous year's intake separate from the new ninth-form entry and giving them special teaching, the staff ensured an impressive increase in the number of former underprivileged country children who ultimately entered *vuzy* (62.1 per cent of the 1967 form 8 entry, against 35.8 per cent of the 1966 entry to that form). This is obviously a matter for much satisfaction,[135] but the price is an increased overall dropout rate, probably comparing badly with Moscow which has eschewed such a policy.

Attempts to lighten the load by reducing requirements in non-specialist subjects conflict with the pedagogical goal of broadening the curriculum, which in this case acquires particular importance precisely because of the narrowness of the specialization. Other ways, however, are being tried: academic tutorials (*konsul'tatsii*) are held for those who desire them,[136] and differentiated tasks are set according to ability,[137] as happens in some ordinary schools. Strenuous efforts are made to safeguard the health of the pupils; at Novosibirsk a 30-period five-day week is worked and a further day devoted to organized games, physical work and excursions, in contrast to the normal Soviet practice of six-day schooling. But this in turn has necessitated intensification of the whole learning process;[138] and the basic 30 periods at the Akademgorodok school do not include optional extras, tests, assignments and tutorials, which, according to its very forthright director interviewed in 1975, brings the working day up to 12 hours: 'Who spends less won't pass'.[139]

The non-specialist subjects are in a difficult position. Leading figures in the FMSh world profess concern for broad education, and this must not necessarily be regarded as inevitable lip-service to the communist principle of all-round development, for Kolmogorov himself is a man of the widest cultural interests who seeks actively to encourage them in his pupils and to foster creativity in all possible ways.[140] Yet a RSFSR Ministry of Education order of 4 July 1966, while praising the academic achievements of the Republic's three schools, castigated them for a cavalier attitude to syllabuses in the non-specialist subjects, especially in Russian and Soviet literature which had been arbitrarily changed, for underestimation of the educational (*vospitatel'nyi*) importance of history and social studies (the ideologically salient subjects), and for unsatisfactory methodological work with staff.[141] In 1968 the Collegia of the same Ministry and of the MVSSO again saw fit to call attention to the impermissible state of the teaching of arts subjects in these schools, the Moscow and Novosibirsk regional education authorities apparently evincing little concern for the selection of skilled teachers.[142] This can do nothing to offset some pupils' dislike of, or even disdain for, such subjects,[143] a phenomenon not unfamiliar to teachers of liberal studies elsewhere.

Although contempt for arts subjects may be manifested only in a minority of the pupils, it seems to be symptomatic of something rather more prevalent: conceited and selfish attitudes. Adumbrated as early as January 1963,[144] they have been the subject of frequent complaints and firm denials. One of the earliest criticisms appeared in 1964 in an article calling upon Komsomol members in the institutes of Akademgorodok to involve themselves more closely in the work of the school. Some of the young people there had begun to give themselves airs: 'it seems to them that they are a cohort of the elect'.[145] A very outspoken article fourteen months later sharply criticized journalists for treating the school as something special; nothing was worse for anything new than to hush up its faults and failings, in this case lack of attention to upbringing.[146] At the Moscow FMSh the authorities were aware of the problem and commented that the lack of pedagogical skills by most of the MGU personnel laid a heavier burden on the tutors (*vospitateli*).[147] In both schools it was hinted that the spirit of collectivism left something to be desired.[148] Those who repudiated such phenomena argued that children who might have been regarded as geniuses in their earlier schools were soon taken down a peg in the society of intellectual equals, hence arrogance was *less* likely to occur in the FMShs,[149] whose ex-pupils were among the most public-minded students at the university.[150] In 1966, however, the RSFSR Minister of Education himself called for improvement in the upbringing work of the FMShs, and eighteen months later the demand was reiterated by the Collegia of both education ministries.[151]

In some cases, unacceptable attitudes must have affected academic performance. In 1965 it was complained that eight of the 29 ex-FMSh pupils who were first-year students in the Mathematics and Mechanics Faculty of NGU had been expelled for under-attainment.[152] In 1966 one of the Novosibirsk school's star pupils failed to obtain admission to the Bauman Higher Technological Institute in Moscow. This caused a minor sensation, and his mathematics teacher came to the capital to argue his case. The debate was in effect between the advocates of imaginative thinking and a creative approach (FMSh) and the proponents of accurate knowledge of basic material, evaluated through examinations (Bauman).[153] Commenting on this, Kolmogorov said that he had repeatedly seen brilliant pupils fail because they had not bothered to do the spadework; as with musicians, talent gave no dispensation from painstaking effort. He was not satisfied with the results of the Moscow FMSh and felt that it needed to improve its own teaching methods.[154] But this was as much a problem of inculcated values as of instruction, as indeed Kolmogorov later acknowledged.[155]

The charge of elitism is often levelled at these institutions by Western critics. In discussing this it is important to remember that within the whole process of Soviet education, according to pedagogical theory, personal achievement cannot ultimately be seen other than in relation to the collective task, to which the individual is bound to contribute to the maximum of his ability. This is reflected in the words of Academician Lavrent'ev who has recently taken up the cudgels in the international arena on behalf of his school. He makes the new point that nowadays with the development of research centres around Moscow and elsewhere in European Russia and the Union republics it has become quite difficult to attract scientists to Siberia, thus it is more important than ever for his branch of the Academy to replenish and revitalise its cadres from its own resources.[156] After a detailed description of the school, Lavrent'ev goes on to face squarely the indictment of elitism. His argument is essentially that there are different kinds of elites; the young people being educated at the FMSh are not a (hereditary) intellectual aristocracy but represent the most talented and dedicated few who will have to undertake the most difficult problems and responsibilities. 'An elite, as we understand it in the Soviet Union, is the ornament of society, its pride, the best part of it'.[157] The critic may feel that Lavrent'ev damages his case by his description of the 'superb hostel', 'more like a hotel' with its self-contained two-room flats, where the pupils live, even though they do have to clean their shared rooms and wash and iron their clothes themselves;[158] but his enthusiasm seems to be running away with him here. The accommodation (with toilet, washbasin and shower for four or five people) may well be generous by normal Soviet residential school standards, but seemed very cramped and sparsely furnished to a Western journalist, who concluded that 'the ascent to the Siberian and Soviet scientific elite goes by way of Sparta'.[159]

Claims (or denials) of elitism in the sense of class privilege demand hard evidence on social composition, *per se* or in relation to pupil progress; this is scanty, but not wholly lacking. In 1966 it was established that the proportion of ex-FMSh entrants to the Mathematics Faculty of NGU in relation to applicants scarcely varied between intelligentsia families (84 per cent) and those of manual workers (82 per cent), whereas, in the case of other pupils, entrants from intelligentsia families (30 per cent of such applicants) fared much better than those from worker families (13 per cent).[160] This was adduced as evidence of the equalizing influence of the FMSh. An extensive discussion in the correspondence columns of *The Times* during 1975 on the subject of selective schools in Russia elicited a long letter from the Novosibirsk City Soviet Executive Committee's vice-chairman responsible for education. Anxious to refute the suggestion that special schools existed to serve a privileged stratum, he presented a breakdown of the social composition of the FMSh. The enrolment figures for children of various occupational groups were then as follows: workers and collective farmers, 254 (43.9 per cent); (white-collar) employees, 162 (28 per cent); technicians and engineers, 105 (18.2 per cent); pensioners, 13 (2.2 per cent); and scientists, 3 (0.5 per cent). Orphans numbered 9 (1.6 per cent) and the unspecified remainder 32 (5.5 per cent).[161] It should be added that, according to the 1970 census, persons engaged in mainly physical work accounted for 72.7 per cent of the USSR's employed population,[162] so that the social composition of the school cannot exactly reflect the wider scene, nor does the letter's author claim this. Neither do the figures reveal the extent of rural representation. Nevertheless the rate of 43.9 per cent for the working and collective farmer classes is impressive enough and a marked improvement on the 16 per cent approximately of 1964/65,[163] and it belies the charge that this school is the preserve of technocrats and in that sense elitist. Anyone who points the finger of suspicion at the 0.5 per cent for children of scientists should note that there are other facilities in Novosibirsk in the shape of non-residential special-profile schools (which form the subject of the next chapter); it appears, for instance, that the former deputy director of the FMSh has moved to such a school, No. 130, which is situated in Akademgorodok and not only has the benefit of the services of the scientists but is an English-language school into the bargain.[164] That the FMSh is out to produce leaders in its field is not in doubt; but the term 'elitist' has been overworked and abused so much as to make it jejune.

Another problem may well be inherent in the peculiar organizational structure of the FMShs. As yet there has, as far as is known, been no systematic Western study of the role of the director or head teacher of the Soviet school, but from reading the education press one feels that, pedagogical councils notwithstanding, his power and authority are not inconsiderable. Latterly they may well have increased.[165] In the FMShs, however, he is eclipsed by the highly eminent scientists actively involved with the schools. His position is symbolized by the IIEP report's erroneous but quite understandable statement that (in 1965) Kolmogorov was director of the Moscow FMSh,[166] whereas it was one P.A. Kuznetsov.[167] Kolmogorov is founder, sponsor, teacher, tutor and, as mentioned above, chairman of the powerful board of governors; in sum, the presiding genius. In his own words: 'I am in charge (*ya rukovozhu*)' of the school.[168] At Akademgorodok the leading figures have been such men as

Academicians Lavrent'ev and Sobolev. In October 1965 it was critically reported that the new director, N.F. Lukanev, was the fourth in three years;[169] a year later he had been replaced by E.I. Bichenkov,[170] subsequently described as a senior research worker at the Institute of Hydrodynamics and the *honorary* director of the school.[171] Whether these rapid changes reflect deliberate policy or a *faute de mieux* situation is not clear; but at worst they must contribute to instability within the school framework, and at best the director must surely query his identity from time to time. In 1966 the RSFSR Minister of Education enjoined the Department of Boarding Schools and Children's Homes to improve the leadership of the FMShs and bade directors take measures to improve the pupil's state of health and study the question of his optimum workload.[172] It would be interesting to know what fruit this bore or could bear, in the given preconditions.

In general, however, those concerned with the FMShs have little compunction about discussing existing shortcomings and are doubtless striving to eliminate them. This is all the more important as they cannot be wholly complacent about the universal acceptability of the schools. Hard evidence of grassroots hostility is extremely scanty, but it is difficult to believe that popular feelings, articulated with such apparent authenticity in 1958, have since undergone diametrical change. The author of an exceptionally frank article cited earlier, said the experiment had fully justified itself; he had 'little sympathy for the man-in-the-street's ill-will towards anything unusual and outstanding'.[173]

It may be conjectured that the schools' major defect of under-valuing pedagogical expertise reflects to some extent impatience with educationists in general. Evidence for this is also fragmentary but there is a suggestion that the APN was split about these schools in their earlier days. In 1958, it will be recalled, the APN's general line had been to back differentiation of the mass school at the senior stage, and thus to deem special schools unnecessary. One eminent member, A.I. Markushevich, a vice-president of the Academy, was reportedly instrumental in setting up the Novosibirsk FMSh along with Lavrent'ev.[174] But just after this Lavrent'ev said that the APN was becoming 'a peculiar barrier' on the road to new ideas.[175] In 1965 A. Arsen'ev of APN, in a cautiously-worded article upholding specialization, stated that some educationists were against it, and he admitted its dangers in terms which could be taken as implicitly critical of FMShs (disregard of upbringing, contempt for non-special subjects, need for special syllabuses common to *all* schools).[176] Other leading figures, *e.g.* El'konin, the psychologist, accepted the specialized schools but regarded them as temporary expedients or 'first aid', to remedy the inadequate performance, in terms of trained output, of the mass schools; ways must be sought to improve the content and methods of instruction for the overwhelming majority of the pupils.[177]

Prospects for Development

Such statements underline the ambiguous position of the FMShs. One must agree with Kaser's surmise that their emergence was less the result of deliberate policy than of personal initiative.[178] The Novosibirsk school was opened months before the USSR Council of Ministers passed the decree forming the legislative basis of the FMShs. Indeed, for the authorities their legitimacy seems to rest on their experimental nature and their tiny number rather than their academic achievement, while for their proponents it is the latter which counts most highly. Yet it is the notion of a small-scale experiment which is more likely to keep the egalitarians at bay, whereas this is less meaningful as a legitimating criterion to the advocates of the schools. For their leading supporters want to develop them. In 1969 Lavrent'ev stated that they were proposing to open more specialized schools at Akademgorodok, first a technical school, and other schools could specialize in biology and agronomy, biology and medicine, and chemistry.[179] However, reports of 1970 speak of the organization of a class in creative technology at the *existing* school.[180] Kolmogorov formerly advocated the rapid expansion of the FMShs and schools for the gifted,[181] but such remarks do not appear in his eight-year review of the Moscow school; while finding 'our experiment' incontestably vindicated by its results, he says: 'Our work, as is generally the case with schools which have similar aspirations, is the subject of much controversy'.[182] In 1976 the controversy was stated to be still unsettled: 'Schools for children who have made great progress in a certain field do exist, but they are so few that they may be called experimental'.[183]

Indeed, the top scientists themselves are still in disagreement about the FMShs. In September 1970 Academician Kapitsa, in a lecture to Hungarian physics teachers, asserted that such schools were even harmful. He referred to the negative effects of selective education on character development, but concentrated on the learning process: if a talented pupil were removed from a school, the collective and the individual suffered, for his classmates were deprived of the benefit of his help and he himself of the stimulus to think a problem right through in order to explain it.[184] These statements caused a stir. When Kolmogorov took public issue with him, on the basis of need and results, Kapitsa shifted his ground, saying that he was not opposed to special schools *per se* but saw their role as model and innovatory; whereas Kolmogorov had said nothing about how his schools (plural!) were affecting the quality of mathematics teaching in ordinary schools.[185] In this connection it should be added that in 1966 the Leningrad FMSh was reported to be accepting children without special abilities as well, since the Leningraders wanted to work out a methodology which could be applied in the mass school.[186] Unfortunately, no further reports of this project have been located.

In 1971 or early 1972 the MVSSO conducted an enquiry into the work of the original four FMShs, taking into account also the achievements of their former pupils. The report concluded that the schools had justified themselves, but wide expansion was inappropriate.[187] The article alluding to this did not spell out any reasons from the report, but made a vague and mildly critical mention of people who talked about 'complexity of organization' and the 'special features of the learning process'. The second point is reminiscent of Kapitsa's strictures; on the first, it appears that it is difficult to find sympathetic, large *vuzy* and suitable staff.[188] Back in 1968 Sokolovsky of Novosibirsk had thought the number of FMShs must increase (as it has done), but not to more than ten or twelve for the time, as the attention each demanded could only be forthcoming in the big science centres.[189] Costs may also be a problem — the IIEP report noted the annual per-pupil cost at Novosibirsk in the mid-sixties as 1,500 to 2,000 roubles, about three times as much as at ordinary boarding schools,[190] the growth of which had been inhibited not least by their expensiveness — but if such is the case it does not appear to be quoted as grounds for suspending development of the special schools. At all events, the climate in 1973 was still such that a strong plea by Academician Belyaev, Rector of NGU, that the proposed 'Legislative Principles on Public Education' should deal with the question of specialized boarding schools at regional centres went unheeded.[191] This extremely important legislation, both in the draft version which had prompted Belyaev's remarks and in the final text, merely mentioned 'schools and classes with intensified theoretical and practical study of individual subjects'.[192]

Successes and Shortcomings

Engendered by economic and consequently political necessity and born of the scientific and technological revolution, with the traditional Russian veneration of science and learning probably an influential if indefinable constant, the specialized mathematics and physics boarding schools have, it would seem, a fine record of scholastic attainment. They have made a pronounced impact on the work of universities and research institutes, quite out of proportion to their tiny number. A major reason for this is that FMSh pupils on entry to *vuzy* already possess certain reserves (*zadel*) of knowledge, facilitating an immediate choice of specialism and purposeful work accordingly. They have also developed the capacity to teach themselves.[193] The schools have also been imitated in other communist countries, for example the GDR, Poland and Cuba.[194] In the West, preoccupation with their allegedly elitist nature has often tended to overshadow examination of their structural and functional characteristics as educational institutions, and to ignore the question as to whether the West might have something to learn from the Soviet example. A notable exception has been Lord Snow, who has consistently advocated their adoption as centres of excellence which have rediscovered the secret of what physicists call 'critical mass' — that the concentration of talent raises its level significantly.[195]

But as well as successes it is useful to consider shortcomings. At least until recently, and apart from the initiatives of Novosibirsk, the FMShs seem to have found some difficulty in fully accomplishing their aim of detecting and fostering talent in pupils from remote country areas. Their main internal problems have included overloading of the pupils, a noticeable imbalance in attitudes towards subjects on the part of teachers and taught alike, and a lack of attention to pedagogical expertise. Chiefly, however, they illustrate that, when heavy emphasis is laid on learning achievement in school, it may be difficult to avoid undervaluing matters of upbringing, and that in certain cases this may have repercussions on academic performance, since upbringing interacts and combines with instruction and learning to form all-round education. Meanwhile the FMShs continue to play their experimental role and to lead their slightly insecure existence; a situation perhaps inevitable in a society which, for all the differentiation that has sometimes emerged in the formal structure of the education system, is steeped in theories of equality. It is this which has contributed to the search for alternative, less extreme forms of encouraging individual interests and promoting special talents: mass schools with a special profile, optional studies, and new kinds of academic extracurricular activities. At the same time, the experience of the FMShs has itself assisted the development of these forms, and indeed that of the new mathematics syllabuses introduced into all schools, as well as authoritative new textbooks and teaching aids.[196]

Notes

1   According to Nicholas DeWitt, *Educational and Professional Employment in the USSR* (Washington, 1961), 18, specialized schools were first mentioned by Khrushchev and others in the spring, but these

references have eluded me. See, however, A. Tikhonov, 'Gotovit' k trudu', *Izvestiya,* 18 June 1958. DeWitt provides a concise introduction to the debate.

2   'Voprosy perestroiki shkoly', *Uch. gaz.,* 14 August 1958; 'Soviet Reform Plan: Special Treatment for Gifted', *Times Educational Supplement,* 5 September 1958.

3   'Po narodnomu obrazovaniyu', *Uch. gaz.,* 14 August 1958.

4   A. Barkalov, 'Izmeneniya neobkhodimy', *Izvestiya,* 23 August 1958.

5   G. Zelenko, 'Gotovit' molodezh' k zhizni, k trudu', *Pravda,* 26 August 1958; *id.,* 'Major Problems of Public Education', *Current Digest of the Soviet Press,* vol. X, no. 35 (1958), 4 (translated from *Komsomol'skaya pravda,* 10 September 1958).

6   I.A. Kairov, 'Nazrevshie voprosy narodnogo obrazovaniya', *Pravda,* 6 September 1958.

7   *Pravda,* 21 September 1958; see also Richard V. Rapacz, 'Polytechnical Education and the New Soviet School Reforms', in George Z.F. Bereday and Jaan Pennar (eds.), *The Politics of Soviet Education* (New York, 1960), 37.

8   V. Kuroedov, 'Obshchenarodnoe delo', *Uch. gaz.,* 9 October 1958.

9   N.N. Semenov, 'Zaglyadyvaya v zavtrashnii den'', *Pravda,* 17 October 1958. This important contribution was first noted by George Z.F. Bereday *et al., The Changing Soviet School* (Boston, 1960), 375-376, q.v. for an extensive paraphrase.

10   *Bringing Soviet Schools Still Closer to Life,* Soviet Booklet No. 44 (London, 1958), 12.

11   I. Beloded, 'Goryachaya podderzhka obshchestvennosti', *Uch. gaz.,* 13 November 1958 (emphasis added).

12   Translated in *Soviet Education,* vol. 1, no. 3 (January 1959), 11.

13   Ya. Zeldovich and A. Sakharov, 'Nuzhny estestvenno-matematicheskie shkoly', *Pravda,* 19 November 1958.

14   'Nuzhny li shkoly dlya odarennykh detei', *Uch. gaz.,* 5 December 1958.

15   V. Pugachev, 'Neobkhodimy li shkoly dlya odarennykh detei?', *Izvestiya,* 21 November 1958.

16   N.A. Menchinskaya, 'Dolg psikhologov', *Uch. gaz.,* 29 November 1958; 'Nuzhny li shkoly dlya odarennykh detei', *ibid.,* 5 December 1958; N. Levitov, 'Razvivat' sposobnosti vsekh detei', *ibid.,* 20 December 1958.

17   N. Goncharov and A. Leont'ev, 'Differentsirovat' obuchenie na vtorom etape srednego obrazovaniya', *Pravda,* 21 November 1958.

18   F. Maksimenko, 'Pora nachat' konkretnyi razgovor', *Uch. gaz.,* 14 April 1956; N.K. Goncharov, 'O vvedenii furkatsii v starshikh klassakh srednei shkoly', *Sov. ped.,* 1958, no. 6, 23-27; Detlef Glowka, *Schulreform und Gesellschaft in der Sowjetunion 1958-1968* (Stuttgart, 1970), 59-61.

19   If one may take as a criterion a comment in *Pravda* of 10 December 1958 about the proportion of letters received.

20   'Vtoroi plenum TsK profsoyuza . . .', *Uch. gaz.,* 13 December 1958;

'Govoryat deputaty . . .', *ibid.,* 20 December 1958.

21 M. Lavrent'ev, 'Nuzhny li spetsial'nye shkoly dlya "osob- odarennykh"?', *Pravda,* 25 November 1958. Also cited by Ber~ *al., op. cit.,* 377.

22 A. Aleksandrov, 'Put' k vysshemu obrazovaniyu', *Izve:* December 1958.

23 A. Sharipov, 'The Main Thing is to Prepare the Youth. Labour', *Soviet Education,* vol. 1, no. 4 (February) (translated from *Sov. ped.,* December 1958).

24 Levitov, *loc. cit.*

25 DeWitt, *loc. cit.*

26 *Ibid.* For other examples, see V. Vasilenko, *Trud,* 22 November; K.I. Oleinik, I.I. Karpov and I. M. Adler; N.F. Markov; N.P. Lagunov; and P.R. Strygina, *Uch. gaz.,* 5 December (in a review of letters for and against, in which the latter were stated to be in the majority, and received over twice as much space); P. Litvinenko, *Pravda,* 13 December (representative, said the editor, of a flood of letters); I. Likhfeld, *ibid.,* 22 December; M. Rylsky and M. Bazhan, *ibid.* A more moderate line was taken by B. Zibel', *Trud,* 13 December, and rare voices in favour were G. Kruglov, *Uch. gaz.,* 27 November; N.D. Popov, *ibid.,* 5 December; and A. Shishov, *Izvestiya,* 19 December. For some of these references I am endebted to Bereday *et al., loc. cit.,* or DeWitt, *loc. cit.*

27 For example, Vasilenko, *loc. cit.*

28 A. Kolmogorov, 'Shkola i podgotovka nauchnykh kadrov', *Trud,* 10 December 1958.

29 Rapacz, *op. cit.,* 39.

30 Although *proizvodstvenniki* (people with production experience) already had priority, the new law caused their numbers to rise drastically, but not necessarily up to the 80 per cent quota. For further data and for the problems thus created at *vuzy,* especially in the sciences, see Yu. A. Zhdanov, 'Nazrevshie problemy universitetskogo obrazovaniya', *Vestnik vysshei shkoly,* 1961, no. 5, 60; G. Vovchenko, 'Na podstupakh k konkursu', *Komsomol'skaya pravda,* 14 May 1963, also quoted in Herbert C. Rudman, *The School and State in the USSR* (New York, 1967), 100-102; and Oskar Anweiler, *Die Sowjetpadägogik in der Welt von heute* (Heidelberg, 1968), 103-104.

31 *Zasedaniya Verkhovnogo Soveta SSSR pyatogo sozyva (vtoraya sessiya). Stenograficheskii otchet* (M., 1959), 255.

32 In 1960 a Soviet psychologist, in conversation with an American colleague, bluntly ascribed the failure of the plan to fears of developing an elite. See Walter R. Reitman, 'Some Soviet Investigations of Thinking, Problem Solving, and Related Areas', in R.A. Bauer (ed.), *Some Views on Soviet Psychology* (Washington, DC, 1962), 50.

33 *Zasedaniya . . .,* 291, 302, 344-345, 386, 410, 421, 446, 468. The stenographic record is sometimes more enlightening than the *Izvestiya* reports.

34   Joel J. Schwartz and William R Keech, 'Group Influence and the
      Policy Process in the Soviet Union', *American Political Science
      Review*, vol. 62 (1968), 840-851.

35   *Ibid.*, 844, 846.

36   Schwartz and Keech stress the likelihood of consultation as a
      preliminary to interest-group influence on policy-making. If in this
      instance the initiative was not Khrushchev's, this would make the
      scientists' role even more ambiguous.

37   H. Gordon Skilling, 'Groups in Soviet Politics: Some Hypotheses', in
      id. and Franklyn Griffiths (eds.), *Interest Groups in Soviet Politics*
      (Princeton, 1971), 24-26, 32.

38   R. Amann, M.J. Berry and R.W. Davies, 'Science and Industry in the
      USSR', in E. Zaleski *et al., Science Policy in the USSR* (Paris, 1969),
      382-383.

39   Helgard Wienert, 'The Organization and Planning of Research in the
      Academy System', in *ibid.,* 202-205.

40   M. Lavrent'ev, 'Molodym — dorogu v nauku!', *Pravda,* 18 October
      1960.

41   I. Tamm, 'Poisk talantov', *Izvestiya,* 3 January 1962.

42   A. Kolmogorov, 'Nauka trebuet goreniya', *ibid.,* 21 February 1962.

43   Quoted in V.A. Krutetsky, 'Matematicheskie sposobnosti i ikh
      razvitie u shkol'nikov', *Sov. ped.,* 1962, no. 9, 111.

44   *Pravda,* 18 May 1962.

45   A. Livanova, 'Razgoraites', iskry talantov', *Izvestiya,* 7 April 1962.
      Lavrent'ev had dropped a strong hint about this in his article, 'Glavnyi
      smysl zhizni', *Pravda,* 18 March 1962. See also M.A. Lavrent'ev *et al.,*
      'V druzhbe s uchenymi', *ibid.,* 18 May 1962.

46   M. Lavrent'ev, 'Kadry — bol'shoi nauke', *Izvestiya,* 18 November
      1962; *id:,* 'Vazhnye problemy organizatsii nauki', *Vestnik Akademii
      nauk SSSR,* 1962, no. 12, 15-18. I am endebted to Glowka (*op. cit.,* 69)
      for the latter reference. (In part it is reproduced verbatim from
      Lavrent'ev's speech at the CC CPSU Plenum, *Pravda,* 23 November
      1962.) For a report of the first summer camp see 'Proekty
      zashchishchayut molodye', *Izvestiya,* 22 August 1962.

47   F. Baturin, 'Integraly v shkol'nykh tetradyakh', *ibid.,* 22 January
      1963. See also P. Rudnev, 'Edinaya dlya vsekh', *ibid.,* 7 February
      1963.

48   M. Lavrent'ev *et al.,* 'Fakel talanta: razvitie matematiki i podgotovka
      kadrov', *ibid.,* 24 March 1963. Another signatory was A. Lyapunov,
      the cybernetician, whom Michael Kaser, 'Salient Features in the
      History of State Boarding Schools', *Annuaire de l'URSS 1968* (Paris,
      1969), 135, credits with the original notion (the attribution being from
      an interview with Lyapunov and others at the school in 1965); Soviet
      writers ascribe it to Lavrent'ev (*e.g.* 'Drug shkoly — uchenyi', *Uch.
      gaz.,* 9 June 1970), but this ignores the pioneering ideas of Semenov
      and Kolmogorov, as well as Lavrent'ev's former opposition.

49   A. Kolmogorov, 'Poisk talanta', *Izvestiya,* 7 April 1963; I. Petrovsky,
      'Uvlechennost', talant, professiya', *ibid.,* 18 May 1963. For a modified

view see B. Konstantinov, 'Talanty vokrug nas', *ibid.*, 14 April 1963.

50   N. Nezhinsky, 'Kvalifikatsiya bortsa i cheloveka', *ibid.*, 11 May 1963; A. Aleksandrov, 'Vospitateli talantov', *ibid.*, 17 May 1963.

51   O.A. Zavadskaya, *Razvitie obshcheobrazovatel'noi shkoly Ukrainy v period stroitel'stva kommunizma (1959-1968 gg.)* (Kiev, 1968), 131; S.I. Literat, *Problemy otbora i obucheniya v spetsializirovannykh fiziko-matematicheskikh shkolakh pri gosuniversitetakh* (Novosibirsk, 1972), 3. (Author's abstract of thesis.)

52   See remarks by V.F. Kovalev on V. Kononykhin, 'Shkola "budushchikh Lomonosovykh",' *Sovetskaya Rossiya,* 9 January 1964; *Molodezh' Estonii,* 3 July 1968, abstracted in *Soviet Studies Information Supplement,* no. 21 (January 1969), 9.

53   M. Potapov and N. Rozov, 'Shkola-internat pri MGU', *Nauka i zhizn',* 1968, no. 4, 70.

54   M. Lavrent'ev and D. Shirkov, 'Yunye matematiki zhdut zadach', *Izvestiya,* 19 March 1964; Zavadskaya, *loc. cit.*

55   The fifth opened in 1964 in Baku, attached to the University of Azerbaidzhan; this was on the initiative of a teacher who had studied the Moscow school and became director of the new one (Georges Cogniot, *Prométhée s'empare du savoir* (Paris, 1967), 196; Kaser, *loc. cit.*). Further schools have been recorded in Minsk and Tiflis (Detlef Glowka, 'Das sowjetische Schulwesen am Beginn einer neuen Etappe?', *Neue Sammlung,* vol. 7, no 3 (May-June 1967), 217), the one at Tiflis following the experience of a special-profile day school there (M.A. Profok'ev (ed.), *Narodnoe obrazovanie v SSSR 1917-1967* (M., 1967), 406); Erevan and Vilnius (Wolfgang Mitter, 'Schule und Bildung in der Sowjetunion in Widerstreit der Meinungen', *Neue Sammlung,* vol. 8, no. 6 (Nov.-Dec. 1968), 558); Riga (*Sovetskaya Estoniya,* 11 August 1968, abstracted in *Soviet Studies Information Supplement,* no. 22 (April 1969), 8); Dushanbe (S.I. Literat, 'Vyyavlyat' i razvivat' sposobnosti', *Sov. ped.,* 1969, no. 4, 77); and Yakutsk, which opened in 1972 ('Universitet dlya starsheklassnikov', *Uch. gaz.,* 7 October 1972). In 1971 one was reportedly being built in Alma-Ata ('Matematicheskii uchebnyi tsentr', *ibid.,* 16 November 1971). — The special school at Gorky, listed by Pennar (Jaan Pennar, 'Five Years after Khrushchev's School Reform', *Comparative Education Review,* vol. 8, no. 1 (June 1964), 74) is almost certainly an *ordinary* school with special teaching, cp. I. Fridlyand, 'Dissertatsiya uchitel'nitsy', *Uch. gaz.,* 29 April 1969.

56   Early in 1968 it was reported that the RSFSR's three schools had a roll of 1,119 ('S kollegii Ministerstva prosveshcheniya RSFSR', *Uch. gaz.,* 27 January 1968). In the same school year there were 2.3 million pupils in the senior forms of day secondary general schools (*Narodnoe khosyaistvo RSFSR v 1968 godu* (M., 1969), 376) and about the same total in form 8; the latter estimate is based on the assumption that the numbers completing rose evenly between 1965 and 1970, as was the case with the USSR, and that the failure rate was about 3 per cent, as in the USSR (*NONK,* 100, 102).

57   'O poryadke priema v fiziko-matematicheskuyu shkolu-internat pri
      Moskovskom gosudarstvennom universitete im. M.V. Lomonosova',
      Sbornik prikazov i instruktsii Ministerstva prosveshcheniya RSFSR,
      1963, no. 43, 27-29.
58   M.A. Lavrent'ev *et al.,* 'V druzhbe s uchenymi', *Pravda,* 18 May 1962;
      Lavrent'ev and Shirkov, *loc. cit.;* A.N. Kolmogorov, 'Fiziko-
      matematicheskaya shkola', *Uch. gaz.,* 11 February 1964; Potapov and
      Rozov, *loc. cit.* For the educational research function of the schools,
      see Yu. Sokolovsky, 'Laboratoriya dal'nego poiska', *Za nauku v
      Sibiri,* 1968, no. 14; abridged German translation in Wolfgang Mitter
      (ed.), *Das sowjetische Schulwesen* (Frankfurt-am-Main, 1970), 137-
      140.
59   Literat, *op. cit.* (1972), 7.
60   *Id., op. cit.* (1969), p. 79. Belyaev (*loc. cit.*) is interesting on how the
      sheep and goats among the *otlichniki* (pupils with excellent school
      grades) are sorted out.
61   Bruce Ramon Vogeli, *Soviet Secondary Schools for the
      Mathematically Talented* (Washington, DC, 1968), 52.
62   A.V. Zosimovsky, 'Interesnyi eksperiment', *Sov. ped.,* 1965, no. 6, 55;
      A. Owen and F.R. Watson, 'The Mathematical Boarding Schools of
      the USSR', *Mathematical Gazette,* vol. LVIII, no. 405 (October
      1974), 191-192. In 1964/65 the Novosibirsk total roll was 607 (Ludwig
      Liegle, *Familienerziehung und sozialer Wandel in der Sowjetunion*
      (Berlin [West], 1970), 132), probably because of the exceptionally high
      intake that year (cp. Table 11.2).
63   Literat, *loc. cit.* (1969).
64   Potapov and Rozov, *loc. cit.;* A.N. Kolmogorov, 'Kak rastyat
      talanty', *Uch. gaz.,* 28 October 1971. The Leningrad school's area
      covers 13 republics and regions in the north-west (I. Kossakovsky,
      'Est' takaya shkola', *Izvestiya,* 23 March 1972); in 1967 its entrance
      examinations comprised mathematics and either physics, chemistry or
      biology, plus interviews (S.I. Kisel'gof and I.A. Urklin, 'Osobennosti
      uchebno-vospitatel'noi raboty v shkole-internate pri LGU', in
      *Vzaimosvyaz' obucheniya, vospitaniya i razvitiya v yunosheskom
      vozraste* (Leningrad, 1967), 40). The Kiev FMSh serves the Ukraine
      and Moldavia.
65   I. Sklyar, 'Akademik v klasse', *Uch. gaz.,* 15 April 1965; Potapov and
      Rozov, *loc. cit.*
66   N. Kolesnikov and M. Potapov, 'O vstupitel'nykh ekzamenakh v
      fiziko-matematicheskuyu shkolu-internat pri MGU', *Nauka i zhizn',*
      1969, no. 1, 110. (One account states that entrants are selected during
      the *final* round — see N. Gorbachev, 'Puteshestvie v zamok logiki',
      Uch. gaz., 12 May 1970.)
67   'O poryadke . . .' (see note 57 above).
68   Kolmogorov, *loc. cit.* (1971). However, he considers it to be a function
      of the *ordinary* school to cater for gifted late developers in general (*id.,*
      'Radost' poznavat' mir', *Pravda,* 1 September 1968, cited at length in
      Wolfgang Mitter, 'Einheitlichkeit und Differenzierung als Problem

der sowjetischen Schulreform', in Oskar Anweiler (ed.), *Bildungsreformen in Osteuropa* (Stuttgart, 1969), 126).

69   Literat, *op. cit.* (1972), 8, 19.
70   *Ibid.*, 26.
71   Zavadskaya, *loc. cit.*
72   Glowka's statement, *loc. cit.* (1967), that children can be accepted from form 5 presumably refers to the establishments at Minsk and/or Tiflis. Kossakovsky, *loc. cit.*, seems to imply that Leningrad does not admit direct to form 10.
73   'A esli eto talant?' (interview with Academician S.T. Belyaev), *Trud*, 10 October 1970; Kolmogorov, *loc. cit.* (1971); Literat, *op. cit.* (1972), 17.
74   Boris Yarantsev, 'Neevklidova pedagogika', *Sem'ya i shkola*, 1967, no. 12, 26.
75   'O poryadke . . .' (see note 57 above); Kolmogorov, *loc. cit.* (1964); Potapov and Rozov, *loc. cit.* Kiev also uses both channels (Zavadskaya, *loc. cit.*), as does Leningrad, which distributes its rules of entry and sample questions to regional education authorities early each year (Kisel'gof and Urklin, *op. cit.*, 39).
76   A. Owen and F.R. Watson, 'Encouraging Young Mathematicians in the USSR', *Bulletin of the IMA*, vol. II (1975), no. 6/7, 134.
77   Literat, *op. cit.* (1969), 80-81.
78   'Mathematics in a Soviet Boarding School', *School and Society*, vol. 93, no. 2261 (1965), 264 (reprinted from *Soviet News*).
79   Literat, *op. cit.* (1969), 79; E. Denis'eva, 'Put' yunykh v nauku', *Pravda*, 14 May 1965.
80   Zosimovsky, *loc. cit.*
81   Potapov and Rozov, *loc. cit.* By then over a third of the Akademgorodok pupils were from rural areas or workers' settlements (calculated from data reproduced in Mitter, *op. cit.* (1969), 129).
82   'S kollegii . . .' (see note 56 above).
83   In the mid-1960s boarding school fees were still charged on a scale between three and 56 roubles per month, related to family size and income, including social services. (The author's colleague Dr. Phillip Hanson considers that for the average (non-kolkhoz) family fees probably amounted. then to about 25 per cent of such income — substantial, but not crippling.) Local soviets were empowered to reduce or waive payments in cases of need.
84   'O poryadke . . .' (see note 57 above); 'Gift for Gifted', *Times Educational Supplement*, 1 November 1963.
85   Dietrich Möller, 'Das Sparta der Wissenschaft', *Der siebente Tag: Wochenendbeilage der Hannoverschen Allgemeinen Zeitung*, 8/9 November 1975 (with thanks to Dr. M. Butenschön).
86   Z. Ibragimova, 'Adres shkoly — Akademgorodok', *Pravda*, 25 March 1976.
87   Literat, *op. cit.* (1969), 79-80; *id., op. cit.* (1972), 22.
88   'Obmen mneniyami s akademikom P.L. Kapitsei', *Voprosy filosofii*, 1972, no. 9, 127; A.N. Kolmogorov, 'Shag v nauku', *Yunyi tekhnik*,

1972, no. 12, 34.

89   Literat, *op. cit.* (1972), 9.

90   V.A. Volkov and Yu. V. Lomakin, 'Letnie matematicheskie shkoly na severo-zapade RSFSR', *Matematika v shkole,* 1972, no. 1, 93.

91   Zosimovsky, *loc. cit.;* Gerald H. Read, 'The Akademgorodok of Novosibirsk', *Intellect,* vol. 101, no. 2343 (October 1972), 56.

92   Owen and Watson, *op. cit.* (1974), 191.

93   Moller, *loc. cit.*

94   Bryan Thwaites, 'Mathematical Education in Russian Schools', *Mathematical Gazette,* vol. 52, no. 382 (December 1968), 324.

95   B. Fomin, 'Doroga v nastoyashchuyu zhizn'', *Nauka i religiya,* 1966, no. 1, 19; Mitter, *op. cit.* (1968), 568.

96   Zosimovsky, *op. cit.,* 47-48; 'Obmen mneniyami . . .' (see note 88 above), 128; Literat, *op. cit.* (1969), 83. In addition to the ordinary school programme, the mathematics syllabus contains material on probability theory, mathematical analysis, analytical geometry, vector algebra, discrete mathematics and number theory. Literat also gives data on the physics course in 'Iz opyta raboty novosibirskoi fiziko-matematicheskoi shkoly', *Fizika v shkole,* 1969, no. 6, 41-42.

97   'O poryadke . . .' (see note 57 above); Zosimovsky, *op. cit.,* 47 note; Zavadskaya, *op. cit.,* 132; Literat, *op. cit.* (1972), 12; Möller, *loc. cit.* (1972).

98   Literat, *loc. cit.* (1972).

99   Mikhail Lavrentiev [Lavrent'ev], 'A School for Young Mathematicians in Siberia', *Prospects,* vol. V (1975), no. 2, 156-157.

100   Baturin, *loc. cit.;* 'Mathematics . . .' (see note 78 above).

101   Vogeli, *op. cit.,* 51-52. Zavadskaya, *loc. cit.,* however, complained of the lack of textbooks and methodological aids at Kiev in 1968. More recently, Owen and Watson, *loc. cit.* (1974), were told that no special textbooks are used at the Siberian school. They provide (193-195) a summary of one by Kolmogorov and associates.

102   Vogeli, *op. cit.,* 50-51, 53.

103   *Ibid.* The IIEP report, however, in *Educational Planning in the USSR . . . with Observations of the IIEP Mission to the USSR* (hereafter *Observations . . .*) (Paris, 1968), 250, stresses the lack of technical applications in the physics and chemistry teaching.

104   Hugo Portisch, *So sah ich Sibirien* (Vienna, 1967), 43. (Since translated as *I saw Siberia.*)

105   Denis'eva, *loc. cit.*

106   Zosimovsky, *op. cit.,* 48.

107   For example, Literat, *loc. cit.* (1969); Zosimovsky, *op. cit.,* 48-49.

108   There were about 30 of them at Literat's school in 1963.

109   Vogeli, *op. cit.,* 53; Literat, 'Vyyavlyat' i razvivat' sposobnosti', *Sov. ped.,* 1969, no. 4, 83.

110   Albert Parry, *The Russian Scientist* (New York, 1973), 165.

111   Zosimovsky, *op. cit.,* 47; I. Kolchina, 'V shkole-internate pri MGU', *Shkola-internat,* 1965, no. 5, 44; Kolmogorov, *loc. cit.* (1971).

112   Zosimovsky, *op. cit.,* 49.

113   Yarantsev, *op. cit.,* 27-28. For the particular role of the Komsomol

here see B. Mokrousov, 'Ne izbrannye, a dostoinye!', *Komsomol'skaya pravda,* 26 August 1964.

114 For an example see Ilya Fonyakov, *Young Scientists' Town* ([M.], n.d. [c. 1963]), 94. The 11-year-old from Sakhalin eventually entered the FMSh and in 1970 won first prize in the All-Union Chemistry Olympiad (V. Sushko and B. Belov, 'Voronezh, itogovyi tur', *Uch. gaz.,* 21 May 1970).

115 Fomin, *op. cit.,* 20.

116 Franklin Parker and Paul Unger (eds.), 'Recent Events in World Education', *Comparative Education Review,* vol. 10, no. 3 (October 1966), 517, citing Henry Chauncey in *Education Teaching Service Developments,* vol. XIII, no. 3 (May 1966).

117 Kolmogorov, *loc. cit.* (1971). The following comparison is based on a notional working week of six days, one of which may well be free.

118 Owen and Watson, *op. cit.* (1974), 190-191.

119 For a translation, we venture 'phys.-kids', though the mathematicians are sacrificed to the analogy.

120 Fonyakov, *loc. cit.*

121 Kolesnikov and Potapov, *loc. cit.* According to Kolmogorov, (*op. cit.* (1972), 35), 80 per cent of FMSh leavers are fully at university entrance level. Two in three go on to MGU or the Moscow Institute of Physics and Technology (B. Bukhovtsev, 'Lektorskaya kontrol'naya', *Yunyi tekhnik,* 1972, no. 12, 36).

122 E. Maksimova, ' "Ogo!" skazali mal'chishki', *Kul'tura i zhizn',* 1971, no. 12, 20.

123 Zavadskaya, *loc. cit.,* from archival sources.

124 *Uch. gaz.,* 5 August 1969. By 1972/73 the proportion had risen to some 25 per cent (Owen and Watson, *op. cit.* (1974), 192). Cp. also Lavrent'ev, *op. cit.* (1975), 163 (mathematics and physics).

125 Fomin, *loc. cit.* According to Owen and Watson, *loc. cit.* (1974), however, they are apparently not exempt from standard course requirements at MGU.

126 Literat, *op. cit.* (1972), 16. He feels (26) that for FMSh pupils, other than those on the one-year course, *vuz* entrance examinations are superfluous. A norm of 80 per cent entering NGU is quoted by Leonid F. Kolesnikov, 'Selective Schools in Russia: How the System works' (letter), *The Times,* 20 September 1975, and by Owen and Watson, *loc. cit.* (1974), who add that about half read mathematics and others physics, economics or geology.

127 M. Lavrent'ev, 'Shkola i poisk prizvaniya', *Trud,* 7 May 1969. The candidate degree approximates to the British Ph.D. Kolmogorov has said that about half of the good research work in mathematics at MGU is by ex-FMSh pupils ('Obmen mneniyami . . .' (see note 88 above), 127).

128 Zosimovsky, *op. cit.,* 54; 'Mathematics . . .' (see note 78 above).

129 Vogeli, *op. cit.,* 52; *Observations . . .* (see note 103 above), 251; Fomin, *loc. cit.*

130 *Ibid.*

131 *Observations . . .*, *loc. cit.*
132 Zosimovsky, *op. cit.*, 55.
133 Literat, *op. cit.* (1972), 16. The other half withdrew for (unspecified) family reasons, *etc.*
134 Möller, *loc. cit.*
135 *Ibid.*, pp. 18-19. An estimate of 20 per cent is reported by Read, *loc. cit.*
136 Kolmogorov, *loc. cit.* (1971); cf. Literat, *op. cit.* (1969), 83 (for all?).
137 Zosimovsky, *op. cit.*, 48.
138 Literat, *op. cit.* (1972), 10-11.
139 Möller, *loc. cit.* See also Ibragimova, *loc. cit.*
140 For example, Zosimovsky, *op. cit.*, 52.
141 'O rabote spetsializirovannykh shkol-internatov fiziko-matematicheskogo i khimiko-biologicheskogo profilei', *Sbornik prikazov i instruktsii Ministerstva prosveshcheniya RSFSR*, 1966, no. 20, 3-6. 'Social studies' (*obshchestvovedenie*) is the compulsory tenth-form course in Marxism and civics. According to Fomin, *loc. cit.*, the special literature syllabus at Novosibirsk had been designed to take account of science fiction, contemporary poetry, etc.
142 'S kollegii . . .' (see note 56 above). Both ministries are involved because, while academic work is the responsibility of the university and consequently the MVSSO, administratively and financially the FMShs are under the aegis of local education authorities. For further comment and criticism see A. Danilov, 'O podgotovke k osushchestvleniyu v RSFSR vseobshchego srednego obrazovaniya molodezhi', *Narodnoe obrazovanie*, 1968, no. 8, 13.
143 Kolchina, *op. cit.*, 44; Yarantsev, *op. cit.*, 28; Kisel'gof and Urklin, *op. cit.*, 47; V. Volkov, 'Doroga v mir iskusstva', *Uch. gaz.*, 18 February 1971. For a flat denial of this see Kossakovsky, *loc. cit.*; according to Denis'eva, *loc. cit.*, such pupils are few. Perhaps the most thoughtful discussion is in E. Goryukhina, 'Zapozdalyi Andrei Bolkonskii', *Molodoi kommunist*, 1973, no. 2, 72-79.
144 P. Rudnev, 'K voprosu o "differentsiatsii obshchego obrazovaniya" v srednei shkole', *Narodnoe obrazovanie*, 1963, no. 1, 20. For more explicit concern, see Genrikh Volkov, 'Chelovek i budushchee nauki', *Novyi mir*, 1965, no. 3, 209.
145 Mokrousov, *loc. cit.*
146 A. Nuikin, 'Na nauku — ravnyais'!', *Komsomol'skaya pravda*, 21 October 1965. See also Kolchina, *loc. cit.*, and P.L. Kapitsa, 'Nekotorye printsipy tvorcheskogo vospitaniya i obrazovaniya sovremennoi molodezhi', *Voprosy filosofii*, 1971, no. 7, 23.
147 Denis'eva, *loc. cit.* The existence of the problem is denied by Zosimovsky, writing a month later! However, he goes on to list some possible shortcomings, *e.g.* social isolation. — This lack of teacher training might also increase the difficulties of the minority of less proficient pupils.
148 See also Literat, *loc. cit.* (1969).
149 Yarantsev, *op. cit.*, 26; Kossakovsky, *loc. cit.* The argument is

reminiscent of Blonsky. See also Ibragimova, *loc. cit.*
150 Fomin, *loc. cit.;* Literat, *op. cit.* (1972), 23-24.
151 'O rabote . . .' (see note 141 above); 'S kollegii . . .' (see note 56 above).
152 Nuikin, *loc. cit.*
153 E. Maksimova, 'Dialog', *Izvestiya,* 20 October 1966.
154 A. Kolmogorov, 'Znaniya, nauki, sposobnosti i konkursnye ekzameny', *Literaturnaya gazeta,* 11 January 1967.
155 *Id.,* 'Matematika na poroge vuza', in *Nauka segodnya* (M., 1969), 244-246.
156 Lavrent'ev, *op. cit.* (1975), 149-150.
157 *Ibid.,* 161.
158 *Ibid.,* 159-160.
159 Möller, *loc. cit.*
160 V.N. Turchenko, *Nauchno-tekhnicheskaya revolyutsiya i revolyutsiya v obrazovanii* (M., 1973), 109.
161 Kolesnikov, *loc. cit.* (percentages ours).
162 *Itogi Vsesoyuznoi perepisi naseleniya 1970 goda,* vol. VI (M., 1973), 6-7.
163 Liegle, *loc. cit.*
164 S. Literat, 'Reservy sposobnostei', *Uch. gaz.,* 30 August 1973; Kolesnikov, *loc. cit.*
165 Since 1966 it has been policy to enhance his decision-making role, and this is reflected in the Secondary School Statute of 1970 (*Uch. gaz.,* 15 September 1970).
166 *Observations . . .* (see note 103 above), 250.
167 Denis'eva, *loc. cit.*
168 'Obmen mneniyami . . .' (see note 88 above), 128.
169 Nuikin, *loc. cit.*
170 Maksimova, *loc. cit.*
171 Yarantsev, *op. cit.,* 27 (emphasis added).
172 'O rabote . . .' (see note 141 above).
173 Nuikin, *loc. cit.*
174 Kaser, *loc. cit.*
175 Lavrent'ev *et al., loc. cit.* (1963). This was in respect of better teacher training and teaching materials, but the authors may also have had special schools in mind as they proceed to advocate them.
176 A. Arsen'ev, 'Ekzameny v shkole, uroki, prognozy', *Trud,* 22 June 1965 (emphasis added).
177 D. El'konin and V. Davydov, 'Na vlastnyi zov vremeni', *Izvestiya,* 13 October 1963.
178 Kaser, *loc. cit.*
179 Lavrent'ev, *loc. cit.* (1969).
180 'Drug shkoly — uchenyi', *Uch. gaz.,* 9 June 1970; 'A esli eto talant?', *Trud,* 11 October 1970. This may have originally been intended as a pilot scheme — see M. Lavrent'ev, 'Molodezh' i nauka', *Izvestiya,* 25 May 1968. By 1972 there were such classes in all three years (Literat, *op. cit.* (1972), 9). Much of the work is extracurricular, at the exceptionally well-equipped local 'Young Technologists' Club' (Owen and Watson, *loc. cit.* (1975)).

181 Kolmogorov, *loc. cit.* (1963); *id., loc. cit.* (1967); *id., op. cit.* (1969), 246.
182 *Id., loc. cit.* (1971).
183 S. Soloveichik, *Soviet Children at School* (M., 1976), 16.
184 Kapitsa, *loc. cit.*
185 'Obmen mneniyami . . .' (see note 88 above), 128-129.
186 Fomin, *loc. cit.*
187 Cited by Kossakovsky, *loc. cit.*
188 *Ibid.* At first sight this seems to conflict with Joan Simon, 'Differentiation of Secondary Education in the USSR', *Forum for the Discussion of New Trends in Education,* vol. 11, no. 3 (Summer 1969), 89, who says that other universities want to start FMShs, but a few schools have opened since she wrote (see note 55 above).
189 'Laboratoriya dal'nego poiska', *Za nauku v Sibiri,* 1968, no. 14, translated 'in Mitter (ed.), *op. cit.,* 138.
190 *Observations* . . . (see note 103 above), 282.
191 S. Belyaev, 'Priglashenie v nauku', *Izvestiya,* 17 April 1973.
192 *Uch. gaz.,* 5 April and 21 July 1973. These are a separate phenomenon, though sometimes confused with the FMShs; see the following chapter.
193 Kolmogorov, *loc. cit.* (1971); Literat, *op. cit.* (1972), 20, 24-25.
194 For the GDR, see Nigel Grant, *Society, School and-Progress in Eastern Europe* (Oxford, 1969), 218-219, and Helmut Brauer and Hans Deubler, 'Studentafeln der Spezialschulen und Spezialklassen für Mathematik in sozialistischen Ländern', *Vergleichende Pädagogik,* 1971, no. 4, 453-454, *q.v.* also for Poland, 455-456. For Cuba, see P. Goncharenko and Ya. Pilipovsky, 'Ostrov svobody: prosveshchenie segodnya', *Uch. gaz.,* 28 March 1972. How far these schools are residential is not clear. For plans to develop boarding education for gifted children in Cuba see Castro's speech in N. Kolesov *et al.,* 'Otkrytie shkoly-internata imeni V.I. Lenina', *Uch. gaz.,* 2 February 1974.
195 C.P. Snow, 'Elitism and Excellence', *The Mathematics Teacher,* vol. LXII, no. 6 (October 1969), 505-509, reprinted from *New Science Teacher,* vol. 12, no. 1 (October 1968).
196 Simon, *op. cit.,* 90; Literat, *op. cit.* (1972), 14, 25, 27; thus realizing, if only in part, the early hopes of Lavrent'ev ('V druzhbe s uchenymi', *Pravda,* 18 May 1962), and to some extent meeting the demands of Kapitsa (see note 82 above). Belyaev stated that in 1966 the Novosibirsk biology syllabus was adopted for all Soviet schools (Read, *loc. cit.*).

Chapter 7

Mass Schools with Special Profile

Early Discussion

The 1958 debate about the desirability of special schools for the highly gifted had been preceded by discussion of an alternative proposal for more effectively furthering individual talents in the service of the economy. In the mid-1950s the Academy of Pedagogical Sciences (APN) drew up a new curriculum for the secondary general school in conformity with the decree of the XIX Party Congress of October 1952 that attention should be paid to polytechnical subjects. This was adopted, but also a proposal was formulated that the senior division of the secondary school should be split into three to provide alternative courses in physics and engineering, biology and agronomy, and social science and arts subjects. This sytem, known as 'furcation' (*furkatsiya*), authoritatively mooted also for the proposed new boarding schools, caused controversy and was resisted by the Moscow regional education authority on the grounds that the general school would thereby be turned into a specialized (technical) school.[1] Nothing daunted, in 1957 the Presidium of the APN convened a conference of educationists, teachers and administrators at which N.K. Goncharov, a vice-president, further canvassed the idea. A.I. Markushevich, the eminent educationist and mathematician, endorsed it on behalf of the Academy.[2] After further deliberation Goncharov read a paper to the APN Presidium expatiating on the proposal and extending the range of specialisms to include a fourth possibility, chemistry (earlier suggested by Professor D.A. Epshtein) and engineering. Schools that had not at least three parallel forms could have one of these branches; otherwise secondary schools with sufficient parallel classes should be set up, which was preferable with regard to equipment and cadres. As Lunacharsky had maintained, the unity of the school certainly did not betoken uniformity; what it meant was equal rights and opportunities for all.[3]

When the controversy about special provision for gifted children was at its height, Goncharov, together with A. Leont'ev, the psychologist, brought this proposal before the general public, now concentrating on the notion of schools with a particular specialism; such differentiation, they claimed, was implicit in the Theses of the Central Committee and Council of Ministers, published five days earlier. They now added a significant point: it could be achieved without singling out children with particular aptitudes and treating them as exceptional.[4] Other educationists rallied in support.[5] Epshtein, a corresponding member of the APN, contended that man's production activity had long been differentiated, general technical subjects did not exist, and the school should combine general and polytechnical education by specializing in the science related to a person's future activity, *e.g.* a school with a chemistry profile should teach chemical engineering and chemical analysis. The APN line was later backed by A.N. Nesmeyanov, the then President of the USSR Academy of Sciences, and N. Muskhelishvili, President of the Georgian Academy.[6]

The educationists' plan was subsequently attacked by the chairman of a regional committee of the education workers' union, mainly on the grounds that it would aggravate urban-rural disparity, since specialized schools would be feasible only in large towns, and that the pupil would have his career choice greatly restricted, insofar as it would in effect have to be made three years earlier and it would be governed by the school curriculum rather than national needs or his own wishes.[7] A. Aleksandrov, Rector of Leningrad University, also objected to differentiated schools on grounds of premature choice; for him, additional, optional studies were the right way ahead, but there might be a case for a small number of schools to train personnel such as laboratory assistants.[8] *Pravda,* however, commented that there had been many letters about Goncharov's and Leont'ev's proposal, mostly in support; the question of creating special schools for the gifted was thereby eliminated.[9] Nevertheless, one is left with the impression that opposition to the notion of special schools, at least in print, took the form of total hostility towards differentiation by ability to a much greater extent that that of advocating alternative means.

The 1958 decree made no mention of differentiated instruction on the lines suggested by Goncharov and Leont'ev, but neither did it rule it out.[10] Three distinct but related tendencies emerged over the next few years, as attempts were made to gear the study of scientific principles more closely and effectively to production training. In practice, 1958 brought considerable diversification, as under polytechnism the eight-year general education course was followed by a variety of modes of labour training, within the school and without. Against this background, the first differentiationist trend was that, despite the general faults and failings of polytechnism, resulting in the retrenchment of 1964 and 1966, several schools, some of them experimental at first, developed high-quality specialisms in areas such as *computer programming*. Secondly, discussion of the ideas put forward by Goncharov and Leont'ev continued, promptly shifting back to Goncharov's original concept of furcation, or differentiation by a series of specialized *subject groupings* coexisting within a given school; despite high-level support, however, this was not to be the party line. Thirdly, and subsequently, the notion of specialized *options* additional to the common course was to gain wide acceptance. In all cases not an elite but the mass of pupils were intended to be catered for. The two latter trends bear witness to a steady move by reformist educational thought towards a more unified school structure than had been canvassed in 1958, either by those who favoured extreme differentiation or indeed by the proponents of polytechnism. It is possible to trace these developments, linking them together at various points.

Computer Programming and Related Areas

In 1959 it was reported that MGU was carrying out special mathematics instruction in several Moscow schools for selected pupils in forms 9 to 11 at a level well beyond the usual syllabus. There were also reports of special courses arranged by engineering institutes.[11] In September 1959, a special class for the training of computer programmers was set up at School No. 425 in the Pervomaisky District of Moscow. Syllabuses were worked out by S.I. Shvartsburd, mathematics teacher at the school, together with experts from the APN Mathematics Section, MGU and the Central Computing Centre of the Academy of Sciences. The results were very encouraging, and the next year two further schools adopted the idea.[12] In 1961 a special-profile school (Secondary School No. 14) was opened in Gorky, originally for forms 9 to 11 (it was joined to an 8-year school in 1966); it developed extended or intensified (*uglublyennyi*) courses in mathematics, computer technology, physics and electronics, staffed mainly by university personnel, and other specialized schools followed.[13] Also in 1961, the Ministry of Education set up a commission to investigate the question of specialized mathematics schools; its proposals were discussed at a conference in November 1962 and its recommendations published and approved in the spring of 1963.[14] As computer technology was one of the areas where the Soviet level of sophistication was well below that of the West, it may be assumed that, along with the expressed aim of producing medium specialists to operate the equipment, there existed the hope that the best pupils would go on to become research workers in computing science. Also, apparently for the first time in a semi-official document, it was stated that such schools would enable pupils interested in mathematics to receive intensified instruction in that subject. As Vogeli rightly points out, recognition of this need represented a departure from former policy with far-reaching implications for Soviet education.[15] It will be recalled that the first of the FMShs, at Novosibirsk, had just opened, which is further evidence of the changing climate.

Furcation: Experiment and Further Debate

In 1959 M.A. Mel'nikov of APN introduced the system of differentiated instruction called 'furcation' into School No. 710, Moscow, otherwise known as the Academy's Laboratory School No. 1. It incorporated 3-year courses in three of the four subject areas previously proposed by Goncharov: physics and engineering, chemistry and engineering, and arts subjects. In the school year 1960/61, biology and engineering was added. At a second experimental centre, School No. 18, Pavlovskii Posad, Moscow Region, special courses were arranged in physics and engineering, natural science and agronomy, and chemistry. The syllabuses penetrated more deeply into certain aspects of the subjects and provided links with vocational training. To give an example, the arts course was a pioneering attempt to organize the training of librarians, office workers, and journalists and editorial staff for factory newspapers. The main subjects were Russian language and literature, history and a foreign language. Not only the syllabuses for these subjects but also the overall curriculum was different: the arts course was the only one to contain Russian language and it had less physics. In addition, certain specialized skills were taught, such as shorthand and proof-reading, and the pupils underwent training in relevant establishments.[16] Mel'nikov later summarized his experience thus: differentiated instruction helped to raise the level of general and polytechnical education, improved vocational training, encouraged the development of firm interests, facilitated a choice of specialism in accordance with interests and inclinations, and provided conditions for spotting capable pupils and organizing systematic work with them.[17]

An extreme version of furcation, proposed in June 1962 for

Akademgorodok by Academician Sobolev on behalf of his colleagues at the Siberian Section of the Academy of Sciences, was for initial division into two or three areas (exact sciences, natural sciences and arts) with effect from form 6 (12-plus), specializing still more narrowly from form 9. If successful it would, he thought, gradually be adopted by most schools.[18] It is assumed that this was too radical, as there have apparently been no more reports of it, but it does show how open the discussion had become.

In July 1962 the majority of the APN leadership, taking their cue like the scientists from the recent call from the CPSU Central Committee and the USSR Council of Ministers for improved selection for *vuzy,* reaffirmed their support of a differentiated curriculum in the upper forms of schools to allow for more profound study of selected subjects, thus providing early training for all sorts of specialists and catering for individual inclinations and abilities.[19] In November, M.N. Skatkin read a paper to the Learned Council of the Institute of General and Polytechnical Education of APN describing embryonic plans for differentiating general education in two branches (natural sciences and humanities) for 400 to 800 hours over the three final years. A little later, the Institute proposed the introduction, after an experimental stage, of four-branch furcation (physics and mathematics, chemistry, biology and general) throughout secondary schools in 1970-72.[20] This led to two fierce attacks on furcation by P. Rudnev, a veteran educator and former colleague of Krupskaya's, mainly because he expected it to be prejudicial to production training, but he also fired off a barrage of other arguments. The differentiators themselves were in disarray, he claimed, for some said its purpose was to satisfy existing abilities, and others considered it was to define them; they were not agreed as to how many branches there should be,[21] and some wanted furcation from form 6. Schools with single-form entry (19 per cent of urban and 72 per cent of rural secondary schools) could not provide a proper choice without costly and complicated mergers. In any case, the development of abilities was not a quantitative problem soluble by increasing the amount of instruction; in the Soviet context it was a question of all-round upbringing and also of greatly improved teaching methods; to assume that abilities were restricted to particular subjects was fatalistic. Increasing the time for some subjects would involve reducing it for others, thus lowering the overall basic level. Production training had, of course, to be differentiated, but that did not mean that general education should be so too. Rudnev's attack was followed by supporting action from R. Medvedev on methodological grounds; criticizing a recent book on Mel'nikov's experiment, he insisted that it lacked a proper scientific basis, was conceptually vague, glossed over problems and thus was inadmissible evidence.[22]

The first of these articles appeared in *Narodnoe obrazovanie,* the leading organ of the RSFSR Ministry of Education, and provoked an equally strongly-worded reply by Goncharov in *Sovetskaya pedagogika,* the organ of APN. Goncharov reasserted Mel'nikov's claims about the general, polytechnical and vocational role of differentiated education; there was no question of circumventing the law on polytechnism in order to train pupils for *vuz* entry, as 'certain leading officials' of the Education Ministry had been alleging. As for small schools, they were bound to go in any case. Lunacharsky had advocated furcation, indeed Marx had said that it was impossible to create anything outstanding unless one restricted oneself to a single sphere of activity, and in an era of rapid technological advance it was even more impossible to master equally the fundamentals of science; thus specialization was essential. Differentiation assisted the development of pupils' powers of thought and independent work habits. Aptitudes differed, and the Communist principle 'from each according to his ability' allowed for this. However, the first eight years should be the same for all, and the children must not be made to feel exceptional, nor must *vuz*-level work be done, lest they be overtaxed.[23] Despite Rudnev's fears, Mel'nikov subsequently reiterated that the prescribed state minimum of general-education knowledge was not impaired.[24]

On 17 April 1963, ten days after the appearance of an article by Kolmogorov expressing strong support of specialized classes,[25] the APN Presidium, having heard a report by its above-mentioned member D.A. Epshtein, chairman of a committee set up to study its work on differentiated instruction, issued a decision on the subject. Differentiation should be based on a well-rounded general education, but instruction should be intensified in one or several subjects to develop special abilities, make general education more thorough, and strengthen its links with production training, technical subjects, both general and specialized, and labour. The Presidium listed three forms of differentiated instruction: (1) scientific and technical fields such as computer mathematics, or electrical and radio engineering; (2) theoretical subject areas (*cf.* Mel'nikov's work) — physics and mathematics, natural sciences, or arts — which as a rule included two or more examples from the first category; and (3) options. The Academy's Institutes of Production Training and of General and Polytechnical Education must speed up their work on curricula and syllabuses for production training, they should experiment on differentiation by options, and the organization of differentiated instruction by subject area was to be tested on a broader basis.[26] In the December issue of the APN journal an editorial again made a case for differentiation by subject area in the senior forms. It now rather grudgingly accepted a small number of special schools, but warned against creating an atmosphere of exclusiveness and a one-sided approach. Rejecting western-style streaming, it called for individualized classroom teaching.[27]

Goncharov had stressed the 'sharp and totally unjustified objections' that differentiated instruction had incurred,[28] and substantial disagreement may indeed be deduced between the Ministry and the majority of the APN leadership. Philip D. Stewart has elaborated on this and much else in an important article appraising the nature and function of interest groups in the Soviet system.[29] Without contesting Stewart's general conclusions — that interest groupings, arising mainly among individuals, formulate proposals, build support for them via the media and urge their adoption by the leadership, and thus can and do exercise influence and share power in policy making — it must be pointed out that the position in 1963-64 regarding differentiation was even more complex than he suggests. To see production education and differentiated education as the two distinct rallying points from which battle was joined, resulting in the victory of the latter side, is a somewhat simplistic view. For the banner of differentiation was raised above concepts as heterogeneous as the groups who sponsored them, and there was a third issue — unified education in the old egalitarian sense — which to a considerable extent the proponents of production education supported along with some of the differentiators. Furthermore, in some degree the advocates of production education actually accepted differentiated instruction.

Thus, as we have seen, the Ministry were opposed to furcation[30] but in favour of schools with a special profile (even the FMShs), the majority of the APN were for various kinds of differentiation but urged caution with special schools, while members of the Academy of Sciences supported special-profile schools and, while broadly backing furcation, held very divergent views as to what form it should take.[31] The arguments used and the apprehensions expressed by Rudnev, when attacking differentiation according to Goncharov, showed the pervasive influence of traditional egalitarian notions; in his reply Goncharov upheld some of these and attacked others, but he did not criticize polytechnical education. Of course, it can be argued that while Khrushchevian polytechnism was law some other issue had to be used as a stalking-horse by its adversaries. But this obscures the fact that there was not *necessarily* any conflict between certain forms of differentiated education (ordinary schools with special profile, options) and production education, as will be seen.

The real argument early in 1963 was between rival concepts of differentiation; after all, production education itself was inherently differentiated. Finally, although hindsight enables us to trace the first stage of the defeat of polytechnism *à la* Khrushchev in the decree of 10 August 1964, inasmuch as it reduced the 3-year senior course to two years, to say that production education was thereby repealed is factually incorrect, as a glance at the text will confirm.[32]

Legislative Solutions

Following the decree of 1964, the Ministry of Education made it clear that the training of computer programmers was to be continued, and exempted these schools from the 4-week reduction in the general-school year.[33] In March 1966, compulsory vocational training in general-education schools was abolished, although the law was less rigorous than this in its wording that such training would be provided 'given the right conditions'. Schools well-organized in this respect were thus enabled to carry on, and did so, betokening a happy marriage between one form of differentiated instruction and production education. Such arrangements included the special-bias schools but were clearly not restricted to them, for as many as one third of secondary schools retained vocational training.[34]

Meanwhile, in October 1964, the 'Commission for the Definition of the Content of Secondary Education' had been set up to reorganize syllabuses and the curriculum in the light of the reduction in the period of secondary education and the recent findings of pedagogical and psychological research.[35] Its third report, issued in November 1966, formed the basis for the decree of 10 November, 'On Measures for Further Improving the Work of the Secondary General-education School'. The question of differentiation had still been controversial,[36] and the decree suggests a compromise. A common 10-year curriculum was to be the norm (11-year in certain republics), but two further forms of differentiation were publicly enshrined in law: 'In order to deepen pupils' knowledge of mathematics and physics, natural sciences and arts subjects, and also to develop their varied interests and abilities, optional studies according to pupil choice are to be introduced in schools with effect from form 7'; and secondly, 'In view of the positive experience accumulated by the schools, it is permitted to have a certain number (*nekotoroe kolichestvo*) of secondary schools and classes with intensive (*uglublyennyi*) theoretical and practical study, in forms 9 and 10 (or 11), of mathematics and computer technology, physics and radio-electronics, chemistry and chemical technology, biology and agrobiology, and arts subjects.[37] There was no mention of furcation,[38] nor of *compulsory-choice* options, a potentially similar structure which the Commission had advocated in an earlier document.

Mass Schools with Special Profile: an Overview

In the remainder of this section an attempt will be made to marshall the available data on the mass schools or classes with special profile, indicate their problems and assess their prospects. Unlike non-specialized secondary schools, which are established by regional executive committees, they are set up by the ministries of education of the republics,[39] so that there is due provision of cadres and a material base. Statistical information is patchy and does not distinguish meaningfully between schools and classes (a special-bias class may be organized in a school with a number of parallel forms). Goncharov, writing in 1963, said there were over 100 schools for computer technicians in the whole country,[40] while in 1971 it was reported that there were 1,804 classes in 536 schools 'with intensified study of certain subjects',[41] mostly, no doubt, for mathematics and the sciences. This represents 1.2 per cent of Soviet complete secondary schools.[42]

Moscow was stated to have nine schools with specialization in production mathematics in September 1963,[43] 21 schools specializing in computer programming in September 1966,[44] and 45 in mathematics and computing in 1967/68.[45] If these categories may be taken as synonymous it is clear that the decree of November 1966 provided a great fillip to the development of such schools. The same source for 1967/68 lists 20 specialist schools for chemistry, 15 for physics and radio-electronics, two for biology and five for language and literature (not foreign language schools, which were listed separately, but presumably the 'arts subjects' schools mentioned in the decree, *cf.* Leningrad below). The total of 87 does not, however, square with that of 75 given for September 1967, nor with that of 72 supplied by a Deputy Minister of Education in 1968.[46] In 1967/68 Leningrad was reported to have ten schools for mathematics and computing, and still ten in 1971/72; six for chemistry in 1967/68, but three in 1971/72; six for physics in 1967/68, seven in 1971/72; two for 'language and literature' in 1967/68[47] and two for 'arts subjects' in 1971/72.[48] Apart from the curious cutback in chemistry schools, their development in Leningrad appears to have become stabilized, and it would be interesting to know how far this is true of the whole country. Early in 1968 the Russian Republic had over 200 specialized schools, including 98 for maths and computer technology, 40 for physics and radio-electronics, and 41 for chemistry and chemical engineering; about one in three was in Moscow.[49] This comprised about 1 per cent of the republic's complete secondary schools.[50] Also at that time 48 specialized schools were located in the Ukraine, with about 3,000 pupils.[51] This represented an estimated 0.7 per cent of the Ukraine's complete secondary schools and an even tinier proportion of her pupils. In the school year 1971/72 there were special classes in nearly 60 schools in Kazakhstan, with 3,500 pupils,[52] representing some 2 per cent of that republic's complete secondary schools.[53] They have been reported in a variety of industrial or academic centres, *e.g.* Riga, Saratov, Gorky, Lugansk, Alma-Ata, Nal'chik, Chelyabinsk, Ufa, Novosibirsk, Irkutsk, Angarsk and Vladivostok. Some are residential. Finally, a substantially different approach to this question is evinced by Estonia, which in 1968 had special classes in 52 of its 139 complete secondary schools.[54]

In 1967 A. Arsen'ev of APN outlined the admissions procedure to special-profile schools and classes. The microdistrict was not taken into account. There were no entrance examinations, and admission was open to any proficient pupil, but when there were more applicants than places priority was given to pupils with higher marks in the special subjects.[55] The IIEP report presents this in a different light: some schools apparently do have an entrance examination (Olympiad winners being exempt) and sometimes only one candidate in five can be accepted.[56] Secondary School No. 7, Tartu, set a written paper, followed if necessary by interviews, after which some 20 out of 30 applicants were admitted to its special class in history and social studies; on the other hand, a Chelyabinsk school specializing in arts subjects, with particular reference to history, had difficulty in finding enough recruits, 'since many parents undervalue education in the humanities'.[57] More recently Arsen'ev stated that pupils are admitted on the basis of an interview and their previous record, and — in certain schools — some written work; they now come primarily from the microdistrict.[58] Successful candidates may already be in the school, or they may be transferred to it at 15-plus.[59] As with the FMShs, boys outnumber girls, though not necessarily to such an extent: girls formed 30 per cent of a special class in Kursk and 29 per cent of the pupil total at School No. 2, Moscow.[60]

There are, of course, special syllabuses for the profiled subjects from form 9 (see appendix D). Vogeli has provided data on the extent of the special-profile instruction of budding computer programmers in comparison with ordinary schools before the 3-year senior secondary course was reduced in 1964. They had 641 hours of physics and electronics against 382 of physics in ordinary schools and 1,550 hours of mathematics (452), *i.e.* more than 2.5 times as much overall.[61] When the timetable was revised, the special-subject teaching in the senior forms was still about twice as much as in ordinary schools.[62] It was to be combined with optional studies and labour training in a 'special cycle'.[63]

After the November 1966 legislation, experimentation continued. Mitter mentions extra science teaching in specialized schools from the seventh or even fifth school year, but gives no further details.[64] According to two East German commentators, special mathematics teaching in the USSR begins in the sixth school year.[65] They quote the instance of Secondary Mathematics School No. 2, Moscow, whose draft curriculum shows some interesting differences from that for ordinary schools (for full details see Table 7.1). The overall number of hours per week for compulsory subjects (24 for forms 1 to 4, 30 for forms 5 to 10) was ostensibly the same, but the individual subject totals varied with effect from the sixth school year or later. More time was devoted not only to mathematics (one hour in form 9, two in form 10) and physics, but also to Russian, art, foreign language (two hours extra in forms 6 and 7, and one hour more in forms 8 and 9) and P.E. (two hours extra, *i.e.* double the usual amount, in forms 6 to 8 and one hour more in form 9). This suggests a forward-looking appreciation of the value of a fluent command of a modern language for advanced work in mathematics and physics, and also an awareness of the need to counteract the possibility of overloading pupils, and thus endangering their health, that goes with an intensive academic course.

Less time, on the other hand, was allocated to literature, history, geography, technical drawing, and music, and even to chemistry and biology, while labour training was discontinued *altogether* after the fifth year. The sixth year saw the introduction of 'optional' extra mathematics, which, with two hours in forms 6 and 7, four in form 8 and six in forms 9 and 10, started a year earlier than ordinary school options, represented a substantial addition to the compulsory course, and, being combined with it, was optional in name only. Evidently, therefore, there must be occasions when Arsenev's statement that the non-profiled subjects are taught in accordance with normal syllabuses[66] should be taken with a pinch of salt, even though cutting the time for study of such subjects is in contravention of the regulations on these schools.[67] But in the Soviet Union as elsewhere all sorts of educational unorthodoxies may be advanced under the blazon of experiment. (The essential proviso is that they do not blatantly deviate from the party line, and it may well be significant that in the early 1970s this particular school was rumoured to be suffering from 'defects of leadership'.).[68] It seems from the IIEP report that such reduction has been rationalized by the claim that it has to be made up by the pupils' personal work, so that the basic compulsory curriculum is allegedly not impaired.[69]

As with the FMShs, sponsorship by *vuzy* or research institutes

TABLE 7.1 Draft Curriculum in a Special-Profile School, 1967/68
(Secondary Mathematics School No. 2, Moscow)

Periods per week per form (showing forms 6 to 10)
only[1])

Subject	6	7	8	9	10
Russian Language	4 (3)[2]	3	2	1	1 (−)
Literature	2	2	3	3 (4)	3
Mathematics[3]	6	6	6	6 (5)	7 (5)
History	2	2	2 (3)	2 (4)	3
Social Studies	−	−	−	1 (−)	1 (2)
Nature Study	−	−	−	−	−
Geography	2 (3)	2	2	2	−
Biology	2	1 (2)	1 (2)	− (1)	2
Physics	1 (2)	2	5 (3)	6/5(4)	6 (5)
Astronomy	1 (−)	−	−	−	− (1)
Technical Drawing	− (1)	− (1)	− (1)	1 (−)	−
Chemistry	−	2	2	2/3(3)	3
Foreign Language[4]	5 (3)	5 (3)	3 (2)	3 (2)	2
Art	1	1 (−)	−	−	−
Music and Singing	− (1)	− (1)	−	−	−
Physical Education	4 (2)	4 (2)	4 (2)	3 (2)	2
Labour Training	− (2)	− (2)	− (2)	− (2)	− (2)
Total periods per week	30	30	30	30	30
Options: Mathematics[3]	2 (−)	2	4	6	6

Notes

1 The periods for forms 1 to 5 are as for ordinary schools.
2 The periods in brackets are those for ordinary schools when differing from this school and do not appear in the original.
3 The mathematics option is integrated with the compulsory subject and thus becomes in effect compulsory.
4 For the foreign language there is a choice between English, French and German.

Source Helmut Brauer and Hans Deubler, 'Stundentafeln der Spezialschulen und Spezialklassen für Mathematik in sozialistischen Ländern', *Vergleichende Pädagogik*, 1971, no. 4, 457-458.

plays an important role in the provision of staff and facilities. Already in September 1963, all the specialized mathematics teaching at Secondary School No. 7, Moscow, was undertaken by part-timers from such establishments, who also ran weekly maths clubs.[70] Secondary Boarding School No. 1, Ufa, is sponsored very actively by the Institute of Aviation there,[71] and Secondary School No. 23, Vladivostok, enjoys the patronage of the State University of the Far East and the Far East Branch of the Siberian Section of the Academy of Sciences.[72] Many other examples could be quoted. One consequence of this seems to have been the emergence of a hierarchy of prestige among schools offering specialized mathematics teaching.

A discussion of upbringing problems involving a minority of FMSh pupils was followed by the comment that the same could be said of the 'extremely small group' of schools with competitive entry to form 9 sponsored by universities, whereas the difficulties experienced by the 'fairly broad network' of schools specializing in computing were largely akin to those of the ordinary schools, which sprung from excessively formalized teaching.[73] Parallel problems and variations in availability suggest parallel (though, given the specialized character of all the mass schools with special profile, in their case certainly far less extreme) differentials in public esteem.

In a number of Siberian schools there have for several years been special mathematics and physics classes linked to the FMSh at Akademgorodok,[74] though they are too remote for the teaching to be done by visiting experts. Here and elsewhere, the burden is borne by ordinary teachers, who altruistically send their star pupils to the FMSh. A 5-year training course with dual specialization in mathematics and computer programming was, however, inaugurated at the Lenin Pedagogical Institute in Moscow,[75] and, if the experience of Chelyabinsk Region is typical, advanced training for serving teachers is provided at institutes of advanced teacher education.[76] To improve the efficiency of such teachers, Academician Lavrent'ev has put forward some revolutionary proposals. The best teachers in specialized schools, judged by their success in discovering and teaching capable children, should receive the title of school professor. 'In every specialized secondary school there should be up to three such posts of professor and reader. Such a teacher should have a minimal load and instruct not only the pupils but also the other teachers. He must have one foot in the school and the other in science and production'.[77] However, nothing more has been heard of this.

Mass Schools with Special Profile: Problems and Prospects

The problems with which the special-profile mass schools (except those for a foreign language) have to contend are somewhat more widely-ranging than those faced by language schools and perhaps more akin to those of the FMShs. They are pedagogical, economic and social. Although it has been claimed that there is no dropping out by those who cannot make the grade,[78] the Ministry circular of 12 July 1967 on the organization of such schools and classes certainly allowed for the transfer of pupils to ordinary classes,[79] and at one school at least they were said to be in constant fear of expulsion, causing the reporter, herself one of the parents concerned, to raise the question of an entrance examination (as this school had none) to make the admission procedure more rigorous.[80] The increased morbidity noticed in respect of language schools also applies to maths and physics schools.[81] The Education Minister of the USSR has criticized a number of these for inadequate teaching of arts subjects, implying that their concept of education was too narrow,[82] and early in 1971 the Collegium of the Ministry, though expressing general approval, found the specialized teaching in some of them too academic and theoretical. The biological sciences and arts subjects were also under-represented as specialisms.[83] A recent commentator bewails the shortage of methodological literature and study aids.[84]

The economic problems affecting the schools are, however, basically external ones. The vast territory of the USSR, its varying demographic patterns, and the often restricted character of local production greatly impeded choice of specialism,[85] and this combined with lack of residential facilities caused children living in many rural areas to become seriously disadvantaged,[86] as the schools had naturally tended to be established in cities where the pre-conditions were more favourable. Within the cities, distribution might be uneven; in 1971 there were four such schools in the Vasileostrov District of Leningrad, where the University and the Leningrad Academy of Sciences are mainly situated, and one each in other districts, but none in the industrial Kirov District.[87] However, the fact that the university quarter was so well supplied may reflect convenience for sponsorship rather than the prestige of the area.

There is no doubt that the mass schools with special bias offer their pupils better opportunities than do ordinary schools. Soviet sources claim that they have superior chances of entering *vuzy*,[88] and the proportion of their leavers who do this has been stated variously to be 70 per cent in Chelyabinsk Region, RSFSR,[89] almost 80 per cent in Kazakhstan and Estonia,[90] 83 per cent at Ufa,[91] and 98 to 99 per cent (this probably refers to Leningrad),[92] while the average for ordinary school leavers is about 25 per cent; in the Faculties of Physics and of Mathematics and Mechanics at Leningrad State University, one-third of the students have attended special schools.[93] Detailed evidence is to hand from a study conducted in 1967 in the Lenin District of Perm'. That year 1,349 pupils completed the eight secondary schools and of them 421 or 32 per cent entered *vuzy*. But, whereas only between 10 per cent and 25 per cent of those leaving the six ordinary schools gained *vuz* entry, the corresponding figures for the English language school and the maths and computing school were 70 per cent and 85 per cent.[94] The minority not admitted to *vuzy* also have advantages. They are naturally better equipped for medium-level training and, although the school-leaving certificate is the same as that issued in ordinary schools, a note is added testifying to the specialized character of the school or class attended and thus indicating the holder's potential to prospective employers.[95]

This important aspect of the special-profile schools clearly creates a social problem. If they are considered to confer better chances, their very existence will encourage go-getting tendencies, at the same time as *intended* elitist functions may be strenuously and quite properly denied; and while supply lags behind demand this will be particularly marked at the point of entry. Thus during 1967, the year of their accelerated development, it was stated categorically that they were not for an elite,[96] but also over-ambitious parents were criticized for turning the pupils' competition into a 'mums' competition' (*'konkurs mam'*) based on the mothers' preconceived ideas instead of what was most appropriate for the children. This regrettable phenomenon was even cited as an argument for psychologically-based tests of ability in some subjects.[97] In one case of a specialized 9th form, which many pupils had entered because it was a *vuz* preparation class rather than on account of its intensified mathematics teaching, only about 33 per cent of the pupils were workers' children, while in the parallel non-specialized form the proportion was nearly 80 per cent and the pupils were resentful and under-motivated.[98] It must have been for such reasons that in 1971 Arsen'ev felt constrained to repudiate allegations that the pupils were selected solely from the intelligentsia.[99] In the mid-1970s, however, a German enquirer was informed at the RSFSR Ministry of Education that 70 per cent of the children at special schools (including presumably, language schools) came from white-collar employees' families;[100] admittedly this social category covers a wide gamut of occupational prestige, but 70 per cent is more than double the share of persons engaged mainly in mental work within the entire population. Speaking of *spetsshkoly,* a recent writer has deplored the fact that sometimes parental vanity comes to be reciprocated in the children themselves, and that too much attention is paid to the acquisition of knowledge, to the detriment of moral education and human relationships.[101] The FMShs had met similar criticism.

Such misgivings must be borne in mind when one seeks to go behind the statistical data quoted earlier and to appraise the factors affecting the schools' development since 1967, which according to a RSFSR government source was the year when they began to be formally established,[102] *i.e.* they were no longer to be regarded as experimental. Their efficiency in providing initial training for future specialists, measured by the yardstick of *vuz* entry, must have already become obvious, and in 1967 Cogniot rightly predicted an increase in their numbers.[103] Kolmogorov, however, qualified a similar prognosis, saying that the specialized schools must remain only a secondary means of satisfying the differentiated interests of senior pupils. He gave two reasons: the economic one of the difficulty of rapidly developing a sufficiently wide network, and the pedagogical one that firm inclinations towards a definite line of future studies are by no means always formed by the age of 15, so that if there were immoderate expansion of such schools pupils might be admitted fortuitously.[104] The great demand for these schools, for whatever reasons, gives credence to this view; in 1966 there were two applicants for every place in the 9th forms of School No. 17 in the Lenin District of Perm', whereas only 65 per cent of the planned intake applied to enter those of ordinary schools.[105] It also indicates that the wide development of the special-profile schools would have led to the intellectual impoverishment of ordinary ones, as may happen with ordinary classes parallel to special ones.[106]

The primary means to satisfy the pupils' varied interests was to be optional studies. M.A. Mel'nikov subsequently explained that his experiments at School No. 710, Moscow, had shown that intensified study of the profiled subjects deepened the pupils' knowledge but did not adequately cater for the wide interests which they developed in the meantime; thus options arose as a complement to the special subjects.[107] So options had an important role in special-bias schools, but, still more significantly, as Kolmogorov stressed, they would be 'available to all pupils in all schools'.[108]

This is surely the key to the legislation of 1966. As two Soviet teachers have said, after echoing Kolmogorov's remarks on the pedagogical limitations of the specialized schools: 'From the first days of the people's power, our school was established as unified for all children. Options are that happy form of instruction which, given syllabuses common to all schools, make possible an individual approach to every pupil'.[109] The above-mentioned economic and pedagogical factors militating against the nationwide expansion of special-profile schools are not in dispute. But it should also be remembered that in some quarters there were psycho-pedagogical denials of innate abilities, which negated the legitimacy of such schools absolutely.[110] These were inextricably linked with a further factor: the deep belief and pride in the unified school, which is found right across the spectrum of Soviet society and causes departures from the principle to be treated with suspicion, articulated especially when evidence arises of unacceptable attitude formation.

In 1963 it was claimed that the mechanical conception of this principle had been spontaneously destroyed by the rise of schools with production training for computer programmers.[111] But, whether mechanically conceived or not, the principle itself is alive and well. In May 1967 the Rector of Leningrad University referred to controversy over the very idea of specialized schools.[112] That certain officials in the RSFSR Ministry of Education had no love for special-profile schools was evidenced in 1967 when a number of them in Perm' were reported to have become ordinary schools again, as the Ministry had not sanctioned their (continued) specialization and had recommended that the intensified study of individual subjects should be effected by means of options.[113] A few months later the USSR Minister of Education, while asserting that on the whole the special-bias schools had justified themselves, reiterated the primacy of optional studies in developing useful interests.[114] In Leningrad it was thought that because of the growth of the latter, the specialized schools in science (and also literature) were no longer so necessary and might be phased out.[115] It certainly seems that public doubts about them have not abated, as there have been references to this in the press; they were particularly noticeable about the time of the XXIV Party Congress (March–April 1971), the Directives of which called for a substantial improvement in out-of-school activities.[116]

What of the future? Two conflicting tendencies can be detected. The special-profile schools were not only legitimated by the decree of 1966, but this has now been reaffirmed in the 'Legislative Principles of the USSR and Union Republics on Public Education' of 1973. The draft (section IV, article 16) stated:

'With the aim of developing the many-sided interests and abilities of pupils and improving careers guidance . . . optional courses according to pupil choice are organized. For the same purpose, schools and classes with intensive theoretical and practical study of individual subjects, different kinds of physical work, art and sport can be organized. Given the conditions, production training may also be provided in the secondary general-education school; in this case the obligatory corpus of general-education knowledge must be common to all schools of general education.'[117]

The final version (article 18) is identical, except for the omission of 'in this case' in the last sentence.[118] If there was any opposition between April and July to this safeguarding of the special-profile schools — as far as the writer knows, none was published in *Uchitel'skaya gazeta* — it had no effect, except perhaps that the need for all specialized schools, not just schools with production training, to cover the common obligatory curriculum was re-emphasized by the deletion of 'in this case'. And although the pace may have greatly slowed down, such schools and classes are continuing to be advocated and occasionally established. In 1970, concerned about the small number of applicants to read mathematics and physics at

Erevan State University, and the fact that Armenia required 700 applied mathematicians but the *vuzy* could only supply forty a year, the Head of the Department of Cybernetics called for specialized mathematics classes in all secondary schools from the sixth year for pupils of proven ability.[119] A leading sociologist commended them, among other forms of specialization and among other reasons, as a means to equalize opportunity for *vuz* entry.[120] A biologist, concerned at the overburdening of her children with school work, leading to negative attitude formation, thought that specialized schools would give their pupils pleasure in learning, equip them for a deliberate choice of career and bring about the demise of cramming for entry to higher education.[121] A specialized mathematics and physics school was subsequently opened at Navoi in Uzbekistan, where the first intake of 100 pupils was selected through olympiads and contests organized by the Kurchatov Institute of Atomic Energy; this school will also give the specialism of computer operator.[122]

However, a few weeks before the draft document was published, there appeared in *Uchitel'skaya gazeta* what can only be described as a swingeing attack on the whole concept of special schools for the gifted, by no less a person than V. Stoletov, President of the APN, whom we encountered earlier. Stoletov's attitude appeared to have hardened greatly since 1966, when, in the wake of the November decree and the context of a call for school-*vuz* links on a massive scale, he had nevertheless referred to FMShs without criticism and indeed with implicit approval.[123] Of course, at that moment criticism of special arrangements was hardly to be expected. But in 1972 he had quietly commented that 'university secondary schools' (to use his term) were not the way to solve the problem of educating the gifted; the whole education system must be improved. Moreover, it was on the educational level of the whole nation that the continued optimum development of the scientific and technological revolution depended.[124]

Stoletov's onslaught of 1973 was not limited to any particular kind of special school, and so is best considered here now that all types of full-time institutions for gifted youngsters have been reviewed. The proponents of a special system, Stoletov said, were anxious about scientific and technological progress; their naïve sincerity was not in question, but that the schools would produce what their devotees and the pupils' parents expected of them was very much in doubt. 'Incomparably more significant is the probability of morally crippled young people coming out of such schools'. The basic aim of the Soviet school should be not a utilitarian one but education (*vospitanie*) of the human personality. Nothing authoritative could be said about the purposeful nurturing of talents, but certainly good socialist breeding (*vospitannost'*) would lead more surely to a thorough degree of training (*obuchennost'*) than the reverse of that process. For pupils capable of working to a more demanding syllabus, Stoletov recommended 'supplementary' schools such as correspondence schools attached to universities and institutes.[125] Whether Stoletov is considered to have changed his mind or to have expressed with increasing forcefulness what had been his genuine view all along is not important; what is noteworthy is that the reassertion of egalitarian principle which we have already discerned is here symbolized at an authoritative level.

As the title of his article implies, Stoletov invited further discussion, but none has been noticed in the paper, except for a brief note of dissent as much as a year later.[126] The conclusion is that, at a time when current provisions were about to be crystallized in an enactment of virtually constitutional significance, further criticism was considered inopportune, and that there was no official desire to make an issue of a subject which, judging by past experience, was potentially explosive and on which in any case broad agreement had formerly been reached. As to the special-profile schools in particular, they had a specific role but a limited one, although in view of the existence of the opposition to them it would be unwise to rule out future changes. In a book on the school of the future published in 1974, the educationist M.N. Skatkin lists the familiar advantages of specialized competitive-entry schools for the gifted, but goes on to refer to the 'unhealthy speculative activity of parents' which is often caused by superior chances of *vuz* entry afforded by such schools. However, if *all* were specialized, pupils could be admitted freely in accordance with their interests; but this is not possible in small towns and settlements with only one or two secondary schools. The whole problem demands further study.[127] Meanwhile since 1967 it has been widely felt that the right way for the school to take necessary account of differentiation is through a system of optional courses. It is to this, the ultimate compromise, that the present study now turns.

Notes

1   F. Maksimenko, 'Pora nachat' konkretnyi razgovor', *Uch. gaz.*, 14 April 1956; N. Petrov, 'Smelee reshat' novye zadachi', *ibid.*, 25 April 1956; *id.*, 'O novoi sisteme obshchestvennogo vospitaniya', *Sov. ped.*, 1956, no. 6, 10-11; I.A. Kairov, 'Osnovnye voprosy organizatsii i soderzhaniya uchebno-vospitatel'noi raboty v shkolakh-internatakh', *ibid.*, 1956, no. 7, 15.

2   N.K. Goncharov, 'O perspektivnom plane razvitiya narodnogo obrazovaniya v SSSR na blizhaishie 15-20 let', *Sov. ped.*, 1957, no. 4, 10-25; cited by Detlef Glowka, *Schulreform und Gesellschaft in der Sowjetunion 1958-1968* (Stuttgart, 1970), 59-61.

3   'O perspektivakh razvitiya narodnogo obrazovaniya v SSSR', *Sov. ped.*, 1957, no. 4, 139 (for Epshtein); N.K. Goncharov, 'O vvedenii furkatsii v starshikh klassakh srednei shkoly', *ibid.*, 1958, no. 6, 23-27. The continuing 5-year debate on furcation was first reported by Oskar Anweiler, 'Diskussion über die Differenzierung der Mittelschule', *Informationsdienst zum Bildungswesen in Osteuropa*, issue no. 7 (1964), 8-16.

4   N. Goncharov and A. Leont'ev, 'Differentsirovat' obuchenie na vrorom etape srednego obrazovaniya', *Pravda*, 21 November 1958.

5   D.A. Epshtein, 'Neobkhodimo differentsirovannoe srednee obrazovanie', *Uch. gaz.*, 29 November 1958; P.A. Shevchenko, 'Uchitelya predlagayut', *ibid.*; N. Levitov, 'Razvivat' sposobnosti vsekh detei', *Uch. gaz.*, 20 December 1958.

6   'Vtoroi plenum TsK profsoyuza . . .', *Uch. gaz.*, 13 December 1958; 'Govoryat deputaty', *Uch. gaz.*, 20 December 1958.

7   I. Ivanenko, 'Shkoly neskol'kikh napravlenii ne nuzhny', *Pravda*, 8 December 1958.

8   A. Aleksandrov, 'Put' k vysshemu obrazovaniyu', *Izvestiya*, 10 December 1958.

9   In connection with letter from I. Teplyakov, 'V podderzhku predlozhenii N. Goncharova i A. Leont'eva', *Pravda*, 10 December 1958.

10   In the Supreme Soviet discussion just one deputy, from Tadzhikistan, expressed support of their proposals, which would raise the effectiveness of secondary education by enabling highly-qualified teachers, who were in short supply, to be concentrated in certain schools. *Zasedaniya Verkhovnogo Soveta SSSR pyatogo sozyva (vtoraya sessiya). Stenograficheskii otchet* (M., 1959), 453.

11   Nicholas DeWitt, *Education and Professional Employment in the USSR* (Washington, DC, 1961), 19.

12   Bruce Ramon Vogeli, *Soviet Schools for the Mathematically Talented* (Washington, DC, 1968), 11, 13.

13   V. Veksler, 'Interes dvizhet delo', *Uch. gaz.*, 30 May 1967; I. Fridlyand, 'Dissertatsiya uchitel'nitsy', *ibid.*, 29 April 1969; 'Doroga v nauku', *ibid.*, 5 June 1969.

14   Vogeli, *op. cit.*, 14.

15   *Ibid.*, 19. The APN has recognized it earlier. See below.

16   M.A. Mel'nikov, 'Opyt differentsirovannogo obucheniya v srednei obshcheobrazovatel'noi shkole', *Sov. ped.*, 1960, no. 8, 34-50; *id.*, 'Opyt differentsirovannogo obucheniya v sovetskoi srednei shkole', *Sov. ped.*, 1962, no. 9, 98-109; P. Rudnev, 'K voprosu o "differentsiatsii obshchego obrazovaniya" v srednei shkole', *Narodnoe obrazovanie*, 1963, no. 1, 15-16; N.K. Goncharov, 'Yeshche raz o differentsirovannom obuchenii v starshikh klassakh obshcheobrazovatel'noi shkoly', *Sov. ped.*, 1963, no. 2, 39-42.

17   M.A. Mel'nikov, 'Differentsirovannoe obuchenie', *Pedagogicheskaya entsiklopediya*, vol. 1 (M., 1964), col. 761.

18   S.L. Sobolev, 'Uchit' myslit'', *Literaturnaya gazeta*, 26 June 1962.

Lavrent'ev had previously called for three-pronged furcation from form 9 ('Glavnyi smysl zhizni', *Pravda,* 18 March 1962).

19   'Podbor i podgotovka nauchnykh kadrov — vazhnaya gosudarstvennaya zadacha', *Sov. ped.,* 1962, no. 7, 2-10. On 'the majority', see Philip D. Stewart, 'Soviet Interest Groups and the Policy Process: the Repeal of Production Education', *World Politics,* vol. 22 (1969-70), 33-34.

20   Rudnev, *op. cit.,* 16.

21   In addition to the above-mentioned, a three-branch division had recently been proposed by N.K. Goncharov ('Ne prosmotret' by Lomonosovykh', *Literaturnaya gazeta,* 11 December 1962). He broadly approved of the schools for computer programmers, but felt they could not cater for the masses. These must surely be the schools described in this connection by Glowka (*op. cit.,* note to 64)'as the elite schools which had arisen in Moscow, Leningrad and Kiev'. The FMShs were not yet in existence, although the Novosibirsk one was about to open.

22   Rudnev, *op. cit.,* 17-22; *id.,* 'Edinaya dlya vsekh', *Izvestiya,* 7 February 1963; R. Medvedev, 'Ob itogakh odnogo nauchnogo eksperimenta', *Narodnoe obrazovanie,* 1963, no. 2, 122-5.

23   N.K. Goncharov, 'Yeshche raz o differentsirovannom obuchenii v starshikh klassakh obshcheobrazovatel' noi shkoly', *Sov. ped.,* 1963, no. 2, 39-50.

24   Mel'nikov, *loc. cit.* (1964).

25   A. Kolmogorov, 'Poisk talanta', *Izvestiya,* 7 April 1963.

26   'O differentsirovannom obuchenii v starshikh klassakh srednei shkoly s proizvodstvennym obucheniem', *Sov. ped.,* 1963, no. 7, 144.

27   'Zakon o shkole v deistvii', *Sov. ped.,* 1963, no. 12, 9-10.

28   Goncharov, *op. cit.,* 42.

29   Stewart, *op. cit.,* 29-50.

30   Detlef Glowka, 'Das sowjetische Schulwesen am Beginn einer neuen Etappe?', *Neue Sammlung,* vol. 7, no. 3 (May-June 1967), 215, says they were non-committal, but if Rudnev and Medvedev are to be taken as spokesmen they can be regarded as hostile. For opposition at regional level, see note 1 above.

31   For further discussion see M. Lavrent'ev *et al.,* 'Fakel talanta', *Izvestiya,* 24 March 1963; A. Aleksandrov, 'Vospitateli talantov', *Izvestiya,* 17 May 1963 (he had been won over since 1958); A.N. Kolmogorov, 'Fiziko-matematicheskaya shkola', *Uch. gaz.,* 11 February 1964.

32   *Spravochnik partiinogo rabotnika,* issue no. 6 (M., 1966), 357-358.

33   Vogeli, *op. cit.,* 33.

34   *Uch. gaz.,* 26 November 1966, cited by Glowka, *op. cit.,* 218.

35   For sources on the work of the Commission, see note 60 to chapter 2.

36   Glowka, *op. cit.,* 210; 'Obshchee sobranie Akademii pedagogicheskikh nauk RSFSR', *Sov. ped.,* 1966, no. 2, 21, 23.

37   *Spravochnik partiinogo rabotnika,* issue no. 7 (M., 1967), 281-282.

38   Despite Prokof'ev's opposition ('Proveryaetsya zhizn'yu', *Pravda,* 12

March 1968) the idea has nevertheless recurred; see M. Lavrent'ev, 'Molodezh' i nauka',*Izvestiya,* 25 May 1968, and M. Rutkevich, 'Kak uravnyat' vozmozhnosti', *Pravda,* 21 June 1969.

39   *Spravochnik . . ., loc. cit.;* 'Sovetskaya shkola na novom etape', *Sov. ped.,* 1967, no. 1, 7.
40   Goncharov, *op. cit.,* 39.
41   A. Arsen'ev, 'Spetsial'nye shkoly. Khorosho ili plokho?', *Trud,* 18 March 1971. This figure can be confirmed independently: in 1970 there were 1,130 language and special-profile schools (*Prepodavanie istorii v shkole,* 1971, no. 2, 4, cited in Oskar Anweiler and Karl-Heinz Ruffmann (eds.), *Kulturpolitik der Sowjetunion* (Stuttgart, 1973), 108), of which over 600 were language schools (Alexander Mirolyubov, 'The Russian Way: How Successful is it?', *Times Educational Supplement,* 20 February 1970).
42   44,226 on 1 September 1970 (*Narodnoe obrazovanie, nauka i kul'tura v SSSR* (M., 1971) — hereafter *NONK* — 44).
43   G. Garrett, 'Visit to a Moscow School, September 1963', *Mathematical Gazette,* vol. 48 (1964), 209.
44   Vogeli, *op. cit.,* 8.
45   Joan Simon, 'Differentiation of Secondary Education in the USSR', *Forum for the Discussion of New Trends in Education,* vol. 11, no. 3 (Summer 1969), 89.
46   A. Orleanskaya, ' "Revolyutsii god pyatidesyatyi" ',, *Uch. gaz.,* 2 September 1967; M.P. Kashin, 'God raboty po vypolneniyu postanovleniya TsK KPSS i Soveta Ministrov SSSR "O merakh dal'neishego uluchsheniya raboty srednei obshcheobrazovatel'noi shkoly" ',*Sov. ped.,* 1968, no. 2, 15, cited in Mervyn Matthews, *Class and Society in Soviet Russia* (London, 1972), 271-272.
47   Simon, *loc. cit.* For data on such a school operating thus in 1968/69, see O.A. Cherepanova, 'Gotovyatsya stat' yazykovedami', *Russkaya rech',* 1969, no. 6, 80-82.
48   I. Kossakovsky, 'Est' takaya shkola', *Izvestiya,* 23 March 1972.
49   Kashin, *loc. cit.* Another source reports 222 such schools in the 1967/68 academic year (mathematics 110, physics and radioelectronics 51, chemistry and chemical engineering 48, biology and agrobiology 2, and humanities 11), rising to 258 in 1968/69 (M.N. Rutkevich and F.R. Filippov, 'Social Sources of Recruitment to the Intelligentsia', in Murray Yanowitch and Wesley A. Fisher (eds.), *Social Stratification and Mobility in the USSR* (New York, 1973), 265).
50   Calculated from *Narodnoe khozyaistvo RSFSR v 1968 godu* (M., 1969), 373.
51   O.A. Zavadskaya, *Razvitie obshcheobrazovatel'noi shkoly Ukrainy v period stroitel'stva kommunizma (1959-1968 gg.),* (Kiev, 1968), 130.
52   'Matematicheskii uchebnyi tsentr', *Uch. gaz.,* 16 November 1971.
53   Deduced from 1970/71 figures in *NONK,* 56.
54   F.M. Eisen, 'Ob osushchestvlenii vseobshchego srednego obrazovaniya v Estonskoi SSR', *Sov. ped.,* 1968, no. 12, 20;

Narodnoe khozyaistvo Estonskoi SSR v 1969 godu (Tallinn, 1970), 270.

55   A. Arsen'ev, 'Uroki po interesam', *Trud,* 16 March 1967. The subsequent circular of the USSR Ministry of Education added that in the latter case candidates were interviewed (*Spravochnik rabotnika narodnogo obrazovaniya* (M., 1973), 122).

56   *Educational Planning in the USSR . . . with Observations of the IIEP Mission to the USSR* (Paris, 1968), 249. (Hereafter *Observations . .*).

57   Khillar Palamets, 'Spetsializirovannyi klass po istorii', *Prepodavanie istorii v shkole,* 1968, no. 5, p. 62; A.I. Aleksandrov, 'Pervyi opyt uglublennoi istoricheskoi podgotovki shkol'nikov', *ibid.,* 1969, no. 3, 65.

58   Arsen'ev, *loc. cit.* (1971).

59   Possibly after a special two-year evening course for pupils in forms 7 and 8 (*CET, 1971,* 60).

60   V.A. Krutetskii [Krutetsky], *The Psychology of Mathematical Abilities in Schoolchildren* (Chicago and London, 1976), 343.

61   Vogeli, *op. cit.,* 29-30.

62   Deduced from *ibid.,* 33-34, and *Observations . . ., loc. cit.*

63   *Spravochnik rabotnika . . ., loc. cit.*

64   Wolfgang Mitter, 'Erziehung in den Vereinigten Staaten und der Sowjetunion', *Bildung und Erziehung,* vol. 20, no. 3 (May-June 1967), 213.

65   Helmut Brauer and Hans Deubler, 'Stundentafeln der Spezialschulen und Spezialklassen für Mathematik in sozialistischen Ländern', *Vergleichende Pädagogik,* 1971, no. 4, 457-458.

66   Arsen'ev, *loc. cit.* (1967).

67   *Sbornik prikazov i instruktsii Ministerstva proshveshcheniya RSFSR,* 1967, no. 26, 16.

68   For the reported outcome of this see Susan Jacoby, *Inside Soviet Schools* (New York, 1975), 197-200, or Hedrick Smith, *The Russians* (London, paperback edn., 1976), 211-212.

69   *Observations . . ., loc. cit.*

70   Garrett, *loc. cit.*

71   F. Kh. Mustafina, *Rastsvet narodnogo obrazovaniya v Bashkirskoi ASSR* (Ufa, 1968), 71, 73.

72   Kashin, *loc. cit.*

73   A.N. Kolmogorov, 'Matematika na poroge vuza', in *Nauka segodnya* (M., 1969), 247.

74   S.I. Literat, 'Vyyavlyat' i razvivat' sposobnosti', *Sov. ped.,* 1969, no. 4, 81. For an account of the exemplary school at Verkhnevilyuisk, see E. Maksimova, ' "Ogo!" skazali mal'chishki', *Kul'tura i zhizn',* 1971, no. 12, 18-20.

75   Vogeli, *op. cit.,* 39, gives the date as 1963, but according to L. Kronrod ('Snachala sleduet podgotovit' uchitelei', *Pravda,* 13 March 1970) the relevant resolution of the RSFSR Ministry Collegium was passed late in 1964.

76   S. Petrushkin, 'Za uglublennye znaniya', *Nar. obr.,* 1975, no. 10, 25.

77   M. Lavrent'ev, 'Shkola i poisk prizvaniya', *Trud,* 7 May 1969.
78   Arsen'ev, *loc. cit.* (1971).
79   *Spravochnik rabotnika . . .,* 123.
80   E. Selivanova, 'Vygonyat ili ostavyat?', *Sovetskaya Rossiya,* 24 November 1966.
81   N. Proferansova, 'Zdorov'e i shkola', *Sov. ped.,* 1972, no. 1, 151.
82   M. Prokof'ev, 'Proveryaetsya zhizn'yu', *Pravda,* 12 March 1968.
83   'V ministerstve prosveshcheniya SSSR', *Uch. gaz.,* 4 February 1971. See also Arsen'ev, *loc. cit.* (1971), and Petrushkin, *loc. cit.*
84   *Ibid.*
85   *Pedagogicheskaya entsiklopediya,* vol. 1 (M., 1964), col. 761.
86   'V ministerstve prosveshcheniya SSSR', *Uch. gaz.,* 4 February 1971; Kossakovsky, *loc. cit..*
87   Arsen'ev, *loc. cit.* (1971).
88   *E.g.,* V. Merlin *et al.,* 'Pust' starsheklassnik sdelaet vybor', *Pravda,* 24 November 1967. I am indebted for this reference to Wolfgang Mitter, 'Schule und Bildung in der Sowjetunion im Widerstreit der Meinungen', *Neue Sammlung,* vol. 8, no. 6, (November-December 1968), 561. See also below.
89   Petrushkin, *loc. cit.*
90   Arsen'ev, *loc. cit.* (1971).
91   Mustafina, *op. cit.,* 71 (*i.e.* 507 of 612).
92   Kossakovsky, *loc. cit.* Similar results have been reported from Tiflis (M.A. Prokof'ev (ed.), *Narodnoe obrazovanie v SSSR 1917-1967* (M., 1967), 406.
93   Kossakovsky, *loc. cit.* It is not certain whether this includes the FMSh.
94   Merlin *et al., loc. cit.*
95   *Observations . . ., loc. cit.*
96   'Sovetskaya shkola na novom etape', *Sov. ped.,* 1967, no. 1, 7.
97   Merlin *et al., loc. cit.* For an example of the unfortunate pedagogical consequences, see Selivanova, *loc. cit.* On these points see also Oskar Anweiler, *Die Sowjetpädagogik in der Welt von heute* (Heidelberg, 1968), 136.
98   T. Yakovleva, '"Vunderkindy" na popechenii', *Komsomol'skaya pravda,* 5 June 1970.
99   Arsen'ev, *loc. cit.* (1971). He mentioned four such schools (three in Estonia and one in Kazakhstan) where the children of workers and/or collective farmers formed a substantial majority.
100 Information from Dr. M. Butenschön.
101 N. Shchurkova, 'Sluchai v desyatom, ili uroki odnogo uroka', *Komsomol'skaya pravda,* 30 January 1973. See also A. Danilov, 'Pervostepennye zadachi novogo uchebnogo goda', *Narodnoe obrazovanie,* 1967, no. 9, 9; G. Kulagin, 'Shkola truda', *Pravda,* 19 June 1971; and Krutetskii, *op. cit.,* 349.
102 M.P. Kashin and E.M. Chekharin (eds.), *Narodnoe obrazovanie v RSFSR* (M., 1970), 99.
103 Georges Cogniot, *Prométhée s'empare du savoir* (Paris, 1967), 197.
104 A.N. Kolmogorov, 'Obnovlenie shkol'nogo kursa matematiki', *Uch.*

gaz., 14 February 1967.

105   Merlin, *et al., loc. cit.*

106   N. Gorbachev, 'Kollegi', *Uch. gaz.,* 6 October 1973.

107   M.A. Mel'nikov, 'O zanyatiyakh po vyboru', *Sov. ped.,* 1967, no. 4, 70-71; W. Kienitz and H. Brauer, 'Das neue System des Wahlunterrichts in der sowjetischen Mittelschule', *Vergleichende Pädagogik,* vol. 3 (1967), 377.

108   Kolmogorov, *loc. cit.* (1967). A firm decision about the primacy of options may have been announced in January 1967, as at the beginning of the year Kolmogorov still seemed to be ascribing the main role in the discovery of talent to specialized schools, though options might help. See his article, 'Znaniya, nauki, sposobnosti i konkursnye ekzameny', *Literaturnaya gazeta,* 11 January 1967.

109   R. Brusnichkina and V. Mislavsky, 'Tramplin dlya poiska', *Komsomol'skaya pravda,* 7 February 1971.

110   *Observations . . .,* 251-252.

111   A. Kolmogorov, 'Poisk talanta', *Izvestiya,* 7 April 1963.

112   K. Kondrat'ev, 'Universitet — shkole', *Izvestiya,* 28 May 1967.

113   Merlin, *et al., loc. cit.*

114   M. Prokof'ev, 'Proveryaetsya zhizn'yu', *Pravda,* 12 March 1968. He also made it clear that he did not favour dividing up the school into separate institutions specializing in different subject areas.

115   Joan Simon, 'Differentiation of Secondary Education in the USSR', *Forum for the Discussion of New Trends in Education,* vol. 11, no. 3 (Summer 1969), 89. But for a contrary expectation see Yakovleva, *loc. cit.*

116   See M. Alekseev, 'Bystrye razumom', *Izvestiya,* 6 February 1971; Arsen'ev, *loc. cit.* (1971); Kulagin, *loc. cit.;* and, for the Directives, *Uch, gaz.,* 14 February and 11 April 1971.

117   *Uch. gaz.,* 5 April 1973.

118   *Uch. gaz.,* 21 July 1973.

119   B. Mkrtchyan, 'Kto stanet fizikom?', *Izvestiya,* 28 August 1970.

120   Rutkevich and Filippov, *loc. cit.*

121   V. Mekhtieva, 'Professiyu — ne po podskazke!', *Literaturnaya gazeta,* 8 March 1972. For more recent support, see V.A. Krutetsky, *Psikhologiya obucheniya i vospitaniya shkol'nikov* (M., 1976), 197; remarks by Kolmogorov in 'Obshchee sobranie APN SSSR', *Sov. ped.,* 1976, no. 3, 150; and by B.E. Paton in 'Peredovoi opyt — v shirokuyu praktiku', *Uch. gaz.,* 2 April 1977.

122   'Put' v matematiku', *Uch. gaz.,* 2 October 1973.

123   V. Stoletov, 'Razmyshleniya o prieme', *Izvestiya,* 29 November 1966.

124   *Id.,* 'Sotsial'naya rol' vysshego obrazovaniya', in *Molodezh' i obrazovanie* (M., 1972), 121.

125   *Id.,* 'Posovetuemsya, tovarishchi!', *Uch. gaz.,* 15 February 1973. He was scarcely less outspoken in his foreword to *Obshchestvo i molodezh'* (M., 2nd edn., 1973), 14-15.

126   'Razryv, kotoryi nuzhno preodolet'', *Uch. gaz.,* 19 February 1974.

127   M.N. Skatkin, *O shkole budushchego* (M., 1974), 39-41. He also

envisages the further development of differentiated teaching. For further evidence and discussion see Murray Yanowitch, *Social and Economic Inequality in the Soviet Union* (London and New York, 1977), 77-79. In the present writer's view, Yanowitch underestimates the constraints on the expansion of specialized schools.

Chapter 8
Optional Studies

The Rise of Optional Studies

If hitherto it has been possible for us to consider special provision for special talent within the limited institutional framework of a variety of specialized schools or classes in a small number of schools, when the spotlight is turned on optional studies this ceases to be the case. For the essence of the concept of options is surely that they are available to all who wish to take advantage of them. It remains to establish whether this is in fact the goal which the authorities have set themselves, and, if so, to estimate how successful they have been in achieving it. As an example of educational innovation it is much more feasible to examine options than the earlier-mentioned channels of fostering talent, since Soviet discussion has been far fuller and apparently uninhibited by ideological embarrassments; one of the fiercest opponents of most forms of differentiation was able to accept them with equanimity.[1]

It has already been noted that, over three and a half years before the decree of 1966 which effectively established options as the main way to deepen knowledge and develop abilities, optional studies were listed by the APN Presidium as one of three possible forms of differentiated instruction. But this was by no means the first time they had been advocated. It may be recalled that as early as December 1958 the Rector of Leningrad University had advocated supplementary, non-compulsory studies in a given specialism as the principal way to prepare young people for higher education,[2] and his was not a lone voice.[3] Indeed, many of the boarding schools set up since 1956, which initially were to some extent vehicles for experiment, had introduced options in foreign languages, cultural and practical subjects, the last-named having been particularly commended earlier by the APN.[4] Unlike that which it replaced, the curriculum for the mass schools published late in 1959 contained two hours a week of optional subjects for forms 9, 10 and 11.[5] But for a MVSSO decision of 1964 to include marks for options examinations in *vuz* entry qualifications,[6] one's impression would be that not much was made of this provision, as seven years later the introduction of options was described as having been done 'experimentally, in certain schools'.[7] The immediate post-Khrushchev period saw much work on defining a new curriculum by the Commission set up for that purpose; its second draft envisaged a great expansion of optional studies — two weekly periods from forms 4 to 7 and four from forms 8 to 10.[8] This represented, among much else, an attempt to lighten the compulsory workload without upsetting subject committees zealous in the defence of their individual interests.[9] However, the provision was still a little too generous and diffuse, and the definitive curriculum heralded by the decree of November 1966 included two hours of options in form 7, four in form 8, and six in forms 9 and 10,[10] thus concentrating the facility in those years when differentiated studies are thought to be most productive.[11] This was to be introduced gradually — for 1967/68 the RSFSR Minister of Education set a target of one hour in form 7, two in 8, and four in 9 and 10[12] — and become fully effective by 1970.

Aims and Scope
As already stated, the aims of options according to the decree of 1966 were twofold: 'to deepen their knowledge of mathematics and physics, natural sciences, and arts subjects, and also to develop their varied interests and abilities'. In an authoritative gloss on this A. Arsen'ev, Deputy Chairman of the Curriculum Commission, said in effect that a basic minimum of all-round education was a necessary precondition for the discovery of talent, but hitherto children displaying well above average success had been neglected and the development of their potentialities impaired. By allocating time for options the new curriculum provided for such development.[13] This was done without overloading the basic syllabuses, indeed these could now be relieved of material necessary only for certain pupils, thus becoming generally more accessible.[14] In achieving these objectives options are claimed to serve several functions: they make school education more versatile, enabling it to respond more fully to scientific, technological and cultural achievement and the local situation, and permitting experiment with new teaching methods and materials, sometimes as a preliminary to their adoption as part of the compulsory course;[15] they develop independent work-habits in the

children, encouraging them to seek out information on their own initiative and thus training them for self-education after leaving school;[16] they improve pupils' labour skills and make them more goal-directed, linking theory organically with practice;[17] and they facilitate the choice of further studies or career, building a bridge between the common basic course and the pupils' future specialism (in forms 7 and 8 they help them to decide whether to stay on in the general-education school or transfer to one of the other two types).[18]

Although developing interests and abilities continues to be the primary goal of optional studies, if there has been a shift of emphasis in their stated aims it has been away from that of deepening knowledge and towards that of occupational guidance — witness the Legislative Principles of 1973[19] — reflecting the Soviet authorities' renewed interest in job orientation in school,[20] with particular regard to young people who are not entering higher education. The school may also have to counteract the advice of uncomprehending and unrealistic parents.[21] Such concerns have been voiced more and more frequently over the last few years, and the school, the influence of which is potentially considerable, is bidden to play an increasingly dynamic role. All the above functions of optional studies, not only the fourth, are means to this end.

In April 1967 a USSR Education Ministry circular established two kinds of options: (1) supplementary materials in parallel with basic compulsory studies, and (2) special courses for detailed treatment of individual sections of the basic studies.[22] (For examples, see Appendix B). The former type was to be taught by the teacher of the corresponding basic course,[23] and syllabuses were to be introduced for all the main subjects. There were to be single-year options in forms 7 and 8, and two-year ones in forms 9 and 10. Courses of the latter type were not intended to be taught in parallel with the compulsory ones, nor necessarily by the same teachers.[24] Examples quoted among many others were, for mathematics, problems of linear programming (forms 9 and 10), and, for history, history of international relations and the foreign policy of the USSR (form 10). In the upper forms two of the options hours could be devoted to practical labour training, and in this case they should be coordinated with the options course proper, *e.g.* practical horticulture with plant physiology.[25] They were mostly of more than one year's duration. The future development of a third type, not directly linked with the basic subjects, was envisaged in fields such as logic, psychology and mineralogy,[26] a further way in which options may be seen as a testing-ground for curriculum innovation.

The issue of such instructions resulted in a flurry of activity, especially on the part of schools and local education authorities, in propagandising this form of instruction among the children and their parents, which was all the more commendable in that detailed syllabuses did not reach the schools until some weeks after the start of the autumn term.[27] Even then they were promptly criticized for being insufficiently thought out,[28] and vague about the pupils' individual work; some syllabuses were overfull in regard to the time available.[29] They were, however, recommendations only, and with the agreement of the pedagogical council (a kind of expanded staff meeting), the teacher could make changes on condition that their general character was retained. In some cases this proviso was interpreted very liberally; at an All-Union conference on the problems of options teaching in June 1968 it was reported that because of the inadequacy of official syllabuses 60 per cent of the options groups in Leningrad were working in accordance with programmes drawn up by local academics and teachers. The first of the types established by the Ministry, the supplementary materials, was by far and away the most popular, accounting for 95 per cent of all such groups in the USSR.[30] This was officially attributed to teachers being unprepared for 'special courses', the second type; but Mitter points out that the supplementary materials anticipated the new syllabuses, thus creating an attractive opportunity for a trial run. In mathematics at least, these had served their purpose by 1976, the new syllabuses having been completely introduced, and were being replaced by a new course entitled 'Selected Problems in Mathematics'.[31] ('New syllabuses' means the compulsory ones.)

The question of qualified personnel was, of course, fundamental to the whole project. Whereas in 1967 all but three of the 523 people running options in Kherson Region, Ukraine, were teachers,[32] Secondary School No. 14, Gorky, was in a privileged position, drawing on specialists from the university,[33] and there were 200 scientists conducting options in Leningrad schools in 1968/69.[34] In 1972, however, Kolmogorov commented that optional studies had again become mainly the responsibility of the teachers.[35] Other schools were able to utilize parental expertise. But already in August 1967 the fear was expressed that options were being introduced without the necessary conditions for them, notably the availability of skilled instruction. Some directors' main concern was to even out the teaching load, whatever the ability of the teacher with a light timetable.[36] Other directors took the view that their teachers were already overloaded with existing commitments.[37] A mathematics lecturer pointed out that two hours of options were more labour-consuming than ten lessons.[38] Despite this the pay was considerably lower; in Moldavia in 1967 it was 80 k. per hour, on a par with extracurricular work.[39] Similar complaints came from Baku and

Moscow a year later, but it was suggested that the rates could be increased if schools pooled pupil numbers and resources.[40] It was also reported that some teachers felt that options might be a passing craze (having lived, perhaps, through the rise and fall of polytechnism) and wondered whether they were worth the effort.[41] A number of them had methodological problems, finding the seminar style unfamiliar.[42]

However, defeatist views were not allowed to prevail. On the credit side it was claimed that options had a stimulating effect on the teacher, improving both his subject knowledge and his teaching skill,[43] and centrally a determined effort was made to further this by provision of special training for serving teachers and students, as enjoined by the April circular. In the summer of 1967 the Moscow City Institute of Advanced Teacher Training had already responded to the call. In February 1968 a Deputy Minister of Education of the RSFSR reiterated the need for summer courses and urged the pedagogical and methodological journals to play their part.[44] The Pro-rector of the Lenin Pedagogical Institute in Moscow said that other pedagogical institutes should also help with in-sevice training and consultancy, and called for a coordinated plan of assistance to local education authorities.[45] In the light of experience the RSFSR Education Ministry came to feel that academics willing to help with options were best deployed not in the classrooms but in training the teachers,[46] though increasingly the plea has been for more such assistance to the schools. In 1970 there was still not enough advanced training to satisfy the USSR Ministry; as a rule there was none at all at district level, and at best there were seminar and consultations in regional centres, and then not in every discipline.[47] In 1972 it was a major problem in Tadzhikistan.[48] However, if the experience of Chelyabinsk Region is anything to go by, consultations in towns and districts for teachers starting work are now becoming available at least in some areas.[49]

As for students in training, Kolmogorov felt that optional studies should be an especially rewarding field for them during teaching practice, long as they were in up-to-date knowledge but short in pedagogy.[50] The Lenin Pedagogical Institute set up several special courses, including an options method course paying attention to requirements peculiar to such studies, *e.g.* how to conduct seminars and quide independent work from primary sources.[51] An *Uchitel'-skaya gazeta* editorial of 19 August 1971, following the Second All-Union Conference on Options Teaching, exhorted more institutes to do this, and such work has expanded. A very interesting development has been the setting up of options in pedagogy in certain schools, but this was not confined to pupils considering teaching as a career.[52]

Three of the research institutes of the APN have worked on the subject matter and content of options, their scope and structure, their relationship to compulsory subjects and extracurricular activities and the methodology of teaching them.[53] Particular attention is devoted to current scientific problems and to occupational guidance. 'The subject matter must . . . develop scientific concepts; it must demonstrate to pupils how scientific research is conducted'. It is important to determine the links between pupils' learning interests and their career interests. The APN has called for greater coordination of research work, feeling that its own institutes lack adequate links with the Union republics.[54]

The Nature of Choice

What of pupils themselves? In the spring of 1967 Detlef Glowka posed some significant questions: what sort of pupils would take part (perhaps, mainly above-average ones), to what extent, and how far participation would really be optional.[55] In other words, how far was this type of differentiation to resemble the more drastic forms that had preceded it? The Curriculum Commission had originally favoured compulsory-choice options.[56] The USSR Ministry of Education, however, took the opposite view in its April circular; 'Under no circumstances should pupils be compelled to study optional disciplines. Pupils who experience difficulties in studying the basic subjects . . . should be treated with particular circumspection'. If the course was over-subscribed, priority would be given to pupils who had shown greater application and interest in this and related subjects.[57] Two East German educationists put it less euphemistically when they said that in such circumstances higher marks in the corresponding subjects were relevant.[58] Thus, although all pupils had the right to choose, the more able ones appeared to be the primary target. Nevertheless, a minimum enrolment requirement of 12 to 15 members[59] — later quoted as 15[60] — caused some directors to involve pupils who were not really interested or who were unable to cope. This led a ministerial spokesman to state categorically that options, with their high theoretical level, were not meant for all pupils but for those who had really shown definite abilities.[61] At the All-Union Conference of June 1968 Arsen'ev spoke of options in the same breath as intensified courses, declaring not for the first time that they were intended mainly to develop the interests and abilities of pupils who displayed above-average interest and proficiency in a given subject.[62] However, 'infringement of the voluntary principle' by school heads continued to occur.[63] In 1975 the minimum enrolment was lowered to ten, which should help to solve the problem.[64]

Apart from this, it is clear that some teachers were loth to accept official statements about what sort of pupils were eligible for options. This was not true of School No. 56 at Kishinev, where options were timetabled at the start of the day and non-participants, 'the weak pupils as a rule', were to use the time for homework and come in for third period.[65] But other teachers definitely felt that options had a role for the weaker brethren. Indeed, a member of the APN expressed the view that they should be used to arouse the interest of such pupils, stimulating their cognitive activity,[66] and at School No. 710, Moscow, one of the APN experimental schools, weak pupils have reportedly been helped thereby to develop abilities.[67] Some people think that an option consisting of interesting talks and visits will broaden backward pupils' outlook and perhaps inspire them to show initiative; some have certainly gained confidence.[68] Others apparently feel that weak pupils already receive enough attention.[69] Most seem to favour the voluntary principle, but as recently as 1971 it was again proposed, both authoritatively and at grassroots level, that options should literally be for all, on a compulsory-choice basis, once a sufficiently wide range becomes available.[70] Although the voluntary basis is now being officially reasserted, utterance of such opinions once more bears witness to the vigour of the 'unified' tradition even in this, the most accessible form of differentiation, and also to the freedom of debate which Soviet education currently enjoys.

This is not to deny that sometimes practical reasons may have contributed to the call for compulsory-choice options. If enrolment is insufficient, either the courses do not run or else they are taught voluntarily and without payment.[72] The numbers problem led to reiteration of the suggestion in the April 1967 circular that neighbouring schools should join forces, although here village schools are at a disadvantage.[73] Enrolment is supposed to involve obligatory attendance, with permission to drop out only at the end of the school year,[74] but sometimes this appears to be impossible to enforce, and the courses have to be discontinued at the behest of the financial authorities,[75] or die a natural death. One report claims that options in aesthetics are vulnerable to the pressures of examination requirements for other subjects.[76] The RSFSR Ministry of Education had ordered marks to be entered in the school-leaving certificate,[77] and some teachers have reiterated this and called for attendance to be recorded there too,[78] but practice evidently varies widely; others, including a USSR Ministry official, have more recently criticized the practice of giving marks for options.[79] An alternative suggestion is to rescue options from their customary

Cinderella-like niche at the end of the day, when everybody is tired
and counter-attractions in the shape of clubs and other activities are
in progress.[80] But the 1975 Statute on Optional Studies lays down
that they must be held either before or after lessons.[81]

Debate on Functions

The lack of overall agreement as to what pupils options should
cater for has led to certain criticism about alleged misinterpretations
of the concept, which have occasionally been stoutly defended.
Optional studies have sometimes been used for remedial purposes,
although the Curriculum Commission had warned against this.[82]
Using the time for extra work with laggards is not what they were
intended for.[83] The arguments expressed against this official view
have already been mentioned. More common and understandably
more controversial was the phenomenon that since options courses
nearly always took the form of 'supplementary materials' parallel to
main syllabuses, they sometimes turned into cramming sessions for
vuz entry; this was officially deplored.[84] The director of a special-
profile school at Gorky which had managed to avoid this claimed
that his pupils were not attracted by utilitarianism but by really
unselfish interest.[85] When *vuz* admissions requirements came to the
fore, options might degenerate into boring extra lessons,[86] taught
without adequate linking of theory and practice.[87] They might be no
more than sessions for solving examination questions. A
mathematician at the APN laid the blame squarely at the door of the
vuzy, which set problems sometimes far removed from school
mathematics; such problems might not be very many, but their
pejorative influence on the schools' teaching was quite
considerable.[88] However, at a meeting of the Bureau of the APN's
Didactics and Methodology Section it was hinted that the successful
completion of relevant options must inevitably play a role in *vuz*
entry,[89] and various people have expressed their active support of
this, as long as cramming is avoided.[90] As one of them asked, who
should prepare for *vuz* entry, if not the school? A powerful argument
is that it would deal a heavy blow to the 'scourge' of private coaching;
although it was known that the practice was widespread, the
authorities were nevertheless surprised when 90 per cent of the first-
year students at a leading Moscow technological *vuz* said they had
used the services of paid coaches.[91] One reason that options may find
it difficult to survive is the need for coexistence with the special *vuz*
preparation classes attended by 'many pupils (in the towns)'; there
are heavy demands on their time and so they naturally choose the
studies they consider to be of maximum direct use. In 1969 options
were as a rule not included in the regular timetable but, as already

mentioned, held after school, clashing with such preparation classes and also with extra-curricular activities.[92]

The relationship between options and extracurricular activities has sometimes been rather nebulous. In 1967 first the RSFSR Education Minister and then a colleague criticized the use of the options slot for meetings of school orchestras, ballet circles and sports clubs. People forgot, the latter said, that such activities would be kept going anyway — indeed, they were to be expanded by the 1966 decree — whereas options were something new, with special allocations of funds.[93] Circle-like meetings in the name of options were thought to be somewhat frivolous, and ballroom dancing received a special frown.[94] By their nature, certain areas of optional studies (*e.g.* art and drama) lent themselves to very different subjects and treatments, some being much more acceptable than others. Options were intended to be much more precise and highly organized than extracurricular study groups,[95] but were not meant to replace them, although to some extent this did happen. If they were run just like clubs, those young people who were most deeply interested would be put off by their superficiality. Options required serious interest and commitment, whereas extracurricular activities would offer variety, amusement, and the satisfaction of rapid results.[96] Clubs of a more academic kind were intended for 'pupils who for the moment are still insufficiently prepared for extended systematic study', *i.e.* those who would have been out of their depth, but some of whom might graduate to options. They would also help the teachers to prepare themselves for teaching optional studies.[97] Indeed, the syllabuses for some options were based directly on the experience of the clubs.[98] Extracurricular activities had a special, expanding role in areas where there were no options.[99] They should thus be regarded not as overlapping but as supplementary and complementary, linking with options so as to enhance the flexibility of the whole system of catering for varying interests and abilities.

Recent Trends

Optional studies are yet another area where statistical information is too patchy to permit more than a shadowy picture of their development since 1967.[100] By October 1967 options groups existed in 89 per cent of the secondary schools and 93 per cent of the 8-year schools in Rostov Region, RSFSR; in 88 per cent of the secondary but 40 per cent of the 8-year schools in Ryazan' Region; and in under 7 per cent of the 8-year schools in Odessa Region, Ukraine.[101] One explanation offered for this was that some 8-year school directors had thought that options were permitted only in secondary schools.[102] In general the situation was regarded as satisfactory in secondary schools but unsatisfactory in 8-year ones, especially in rural areas. (With lack of parallel classes and facilities, many rural schools are clearly in a difficult position).[103] At the end of the 1967/68 school year, there were options in 86 per cent of the RSFSR's secondary schools and 46.4 per cent of her 8-year ones.[104] Two years later, the only set of figures for the whole country reveals that options were then functioning in nearly all urban secondary schools and 82 per cent of urban 8-year schools, but in rural areas the coverage was poor, especially in 8-year schools, and not specified.[105] Eight-year schools, particularly rural ones, remained the weak point in 1976.[106]

However, data on the availability of options tell us little about the numbers of pupils concerned. In June 1968 options involved 32.2 per cent of all pupils in forms 7 to 10 in the RSFSR,[107] and this figure had risen to 40.8 per cent by October 1969, when the different republics showed widely fluctuating totals, ranging from Latvia's 17.4 per cent and Turkmenia's 19 per cent to Lithuania's 64.5 per cent and Estonia's 76.4 per cent; the average for the whole USSR was 39 per cent.[108] It is very curious that the Baltic republics are so disparate; presumably the figures reflect different policies. By 1973 the proportion of eligible pupils taking options had risen to 54 per cent, involving over 8.5m pupils compared with 5.8m in 1971, and varying from 27 per cent in Tadzhikistan and 29 per cent in Uzbekistan to 68 per cent in the RSFSR and 76 per cent in Estonia.[109] Whether the all-Union average is regard as satisfactory or not must depend on one's stance with respect to the purpose of options. Complaints have occasionally been voiced that they are not yet sufficiently widespread,[110] but late in 1975 the figure of over 56 per cent for Chelyabinsk Region was quoted in a context of satisfaction with good progress made.[111]

There has been a concern to broaden the range of options. In 1967/68 the distribution was felt to be uneven, but by October 1969 some improvement had been achieved. The following data give the proportion of options students by major subject areas, USSR, October 1969 (1967/68 approximations in parentheses): mathematics 24.1 per cent (30-35 per cent), physics 11.1 per cent (15-20 per cent), chemistry 9.1 per cent (9-10 per cent), literature 12.8 per cent (25-30 per cent), Russian language 10.2 per cent (10-15 per cent), labour 5 per cent (2-3 per cent).[112] As these figures suggest, and as statistics for 1973 confirm (mathematics 19.1 per cent, physics 8.9 per cent and chemistry 7.8 per cent, compared to labour training 10.6 per cent), there has been a move towards diversification, with increases in such subjects as labour, biology, geography, foreign languages and miscellaneous minor ones.[113] This trend provides further confirmation that in the schools the options system is no longer generally considered to serve goals which are very predominantly academic, as seemed to be the case in 1967; though retaining these, with clearly articulated vocational and also moral (*vospitatel'nye*) objectives it is now becoming increasingly comprehensive in character.

This may be briefly illustrated. The decree of March 1966, whereby production training in the secondary general-education school was no longer bound to be provided, had in some places the effect of throwing out the baby with the bath water: it was never intended that secondary education should altogether stop concerning itself with vocational training and guidance, yet that is precisely how the law was apt to be interpreted.[114] Where a vacuum had been created, options of a practical character would be a convenient means of filling it. Thus in November 1967 the Collegium of the USSR Ministry of Education expressed alarm at the lack of progress of labour options; these were particularly important for rural schools.[115] By September 1970 the Institute of Labour Instruction and Occupational Guidance of the APN had issued syllabuses for forms 9 and 10 on tractors, combines and other agricultural machines, the principles of agricultural technology, stockbreeding and the mechanization of stock farms.[116] Rural schools are still being exhorted to make greater use of options.[117] Where labour options are well organized they can be extremely successful such as the 'Fundamentals of Television' course at School No. 70, Moscow; 17 of the 21 participants decided to make their careers in radio-electronics.[118] At Novosibirsk a course of a rather different kind, on the scientific organization of labour (NOT), has been designed on an inter-school basis.[119]

Labour training is, of course, inherently valuable as a means of inculcating communist morality, with its stress on joyful, self-disciplined pursuit of the worthwhile common task. All options are supposed to develop a thirst for knowledge. Options of other kinds are important in nurturing further qualities of the New Soviet Man. Such studies in aesthetics may encourage creativity, develop a knowledge of the world's artistic heritage in which the Soviet citizen shares, and propagate the achievements of Soviet culture. After a slow start there are indications of a growth of options in history, a subject which ought to be particularly suitable for training in dialectical thinking and forming patriotic attitudes; such sentiments are reinforced by the optional courses in elementary military training.

The question of elementary military training deserves a closer look both for its content and for its effect on other optional studies. The development of pre-conscription training in schools was envisaged by a law of October 1967, probably on account of worsening relations with China. Soon after it began to be introduced as a school subject. But as well as more obvious matters such as weapon training, the military instructor (*voennyi rukovoditel'* or *voenruk*) had the job of improving the existing means of 'patriotic education' on an extracurricular basis. As part of this, it was announced in September 1969 that the USSR Ministry of Education had drawn up model syllabuses for options in military technical training and civil defence.[120] None of the latter have been seen, but from a handbook of options syllabuses issued by the RSFSR Ministry in 1972 it is clear that the term military technical training is interpreted in a broad and elastic way and should be of great appeal to many a pupil from form 10. The range of 70-period courses includes training as a driver of motor-vehicles and cycles (including the official driving test), helmsman of motor launches, radar station operator, radio telephone operator, electrical engineer, radio engineer and TV engineer, and also for special-profile mathematics schools, computer programmer-operator.[121] Here too there is obviously a potential career orientation function.

It does appear, however, that as a subject elementary military training has contributed to a partial cutback in the periods allocated to optional studies. It will be recalled that the timetable resulting from the reorganization of the mid-sixties contained two periods of options in form 7, four in form 8, and six in forms 9 and 10, in addition to thirty periods of compulsory subjects per week; military training was not specifically mentioned. By 1972 the total compulsory periods had risen to 32 in form 9 and 34 in form 10. In form 9, a period of Russian had been moved to form 10 to make room for an additional period of maths, and there were now two periods of military training. In form 10, there was the period of Russian, another period of maths, and again two periods of military training. Presumably to offset this extra load, and to make the increase more gradual, the number of periods allocated to options in form 8 was reduced to three and in forms 9 and 10 to four.[122] Being held outside normal lesson time, a principle upheld by the 1975 Statute, optional studies are the most natural target for timetable cuts, and if new subjects continue to become obligatory and people with powerful subject interests press for a larger slice of the curricular cake, one should not be too sanguine about the prospects for extensive development of options. In certain of the Union republics they are in any case far less well represented on the timetable than in the RSFSR: in the Ukraine and Belorussia in 1976 they were accorded only one period per week in forms 7 and 8 and two in forms 9 and 10.[123]

Taking Stock

When one attempts to draw up an interim balance sheet, it becomes evident that options have made a unique, innovatory and essentially positive contribution to Soviet education, but that in some respects they pose as many questions as they answer. The information explosion, the enhanced role of scientific theory and the accelerated rate of its application set educationists two substantial problems: how to raise the standard of scientific instruction and how to develop pupils' cognitive activity and independent work habits,[124] their interests and abilities. Beyond a certain level, the concept of identical courses for all was becoming increasingly outmoded. Yet ideological objections reinforced by pedagogical misgivings and economic factors inhibited the wide expansion of educational institutions designed to foster the intellectual abilities of a more or less limited number of individuals. The compromise reached was that for the great majority of young people at general-education schools a common stock of basic knowledge should be supplemented by courses from a range of optional extras. The introduction of an element of pupil choice was something radically new in the Soviet school curriculum. In a sense the pupils themselves may have a role in determining these courses, to the extent that they make their teacher aware of their interests and he is able to act upon this knowledge. It is claimed that options facilitate an individual approach to every pupil,[125] raising interest and encouraging initiative in a way which has fruitful repercussions,both on ordinary lessons within the school,[126] and beyond it in the All-Union Olympiads.[127] They also, to some degree, make possible an individual approach to every school, as school directors enjoy a great deal of latitude in organizing these courses, depending on staff interests, the type of outside expertise available, and the nature of the local economy; they are not compelled to follow the syllabuses approved by the Ministry of Education.[128] True, the Ministry evidently prefers a certain degree of conformity, for homegrown syllabuses, which are recommended primarily for labour training,[129] have to be approved by the local education authorities,[130] and these have sometimes been too hidebound even to permit experimental syllabuses published in *Matematika v shkole (Mathematics in the School)* to be tried out.[131] All in all, however, the existence of local syllabuses provides an interesting corrective to the conventional Western stereotype of the straitjacketed Soviet curriculum.

From the vantage point of the mid-1970s, it seems that a further possible trend in the development of options may be glimpsed. Egalitarian and other pressures having inhibited the growth of schools and even regular classes with a special bias, optional studies are apparently being used here and there as a surrogate device. One Moscow school is considered to have a 'theatre profile'; it offers much sought-after courses in acting and in film and drama appreciation, taught by visiting instructors from the M.S. Shchepkin School of Drama, yet these activities are not part of the regular timetable of a special humanities school but are held after normal hours, and the compulsory curriculum is standard.[132] At the Far East Science Centre of the USSR Academy of Sciences, Vladivostok, they 'dream of' a mathematics and physics boarding school; they have gone as far as possible in that direction by sponsoring an ordinary local boarding school which is now extremely well equipped for options in electronics, solid state physics and other scientific subjects, taught by research workers. Interested parties are urged to discuss the matter.[133] One should not rush to generalize from these stray items; but if we are correct in our belief that the spread of special institutional forms has lately been restricted, it is also reasonable to assume that the powerful interests that generated them, far from being altogether incapacitated, will seek their ends through the channels that remain to them. And if they do not succeed in changing the irrigation system, they can at least make those channels superbly efficient.

Let us return, however, to options *en masse*. There are problems: not just the teething troubles of inadequate skills and facilities and imbalance between subjects. Difficulties in coordinating supplementary-type options with the parallel compulsory studies and sometimes the unwarranted broadening of the latter have been reported.[134] The relative lack of options courses in rural areas is one of the many pointers to the enormous task of evening out inequality between town and country, which in education has been a dominant issue of the 1970s. Disadvantaged country children are subjected to a sort of quite involuntary discrimination, and a vigorous campaign is under way to improve their lot. This problem is being faced, yet there is another which is apparently being avoided. Until recently, one had to go to the East German press to find a discussion or even a mention of it.[135] It is all very well to say that options will not affect educational opportunity since all are guaranteed the basic minimum necessary for *vuz* entry. But *vuz* entry is competitive, and the weaker go to the wall. Some children have demonstrated their ability to select the most relevant courses, and the great preponderance of optional studies of the 'supplementary chapters' type is evidence of this. It has already been mentioned that options have been found to have a positive and reinforcing effect on ordinary lessons. Other children may take options of a less academic kind; others again may take none at all. Is this a latent cause for concern on the part of those who call for compulsory-choice options? Even so, changing 'can' to 'must' will not eliminate the problem but merely alter it. If options are not taken by all, only some will benefit; if they are taken by all, given that they are sufficiently flexible to meet diverse needs, all will benefit, but in respect of career chances some will benefit more. At the moment, the problem looks insoluble, for the argument could easily be extended to include extracurricular activities, which for years were the only legitimate way to cater for special interests and abilities. However, it awaits discussion, and in the present relatively free educational climate this could certainly come about. A starting-point might be a recent reference to the emergence of stratification (*rassloenie*) in the regular class, tending to polarise between those who take options and those who do not.[136] Meanwhile we are left with the thought that the perfect compromise is not only elusive but also illusory.

Notes

1   P. Rudnev, 'K voprosu o "differentsiatsii obshchego obrazovaniya" v srednei shkole', *Narodnoe obrazovanie*, 1963, no. 1, 22.

2   A. Aleksandrov, 'Put' k vysshemu obrazovaniyu', *Izvestiya*, 10 December 1958.

3   Cf. I.V. Abashidze's contribution to the Supreme Soviet debate on the education reform, *Izvestiya*, 25 December 1958. Referring to these discussions, DeWitt pointed out that, being additional to the obligatory norm, the term 'optional subject' betokened something quite different from the American system of electives, which a Soviet visitor had described as anarchy (Nicholas DeWitt, *Education and Professional Employment in the USSR* (Washington, 1961), 19-20).

4   'Novyi etap v razvitii sovetskoi shkoly', *Sov. ped.*, 1956, no. 2, 11; M.A. Mel'nikov, 'Pedagogicheskaya nauka v shestoi pyatiletke', *ibid.*, 1956, no. 3, 7; M.M. Deineko, *40 let narodnogo obrazovaniya v SSSR*, (M., 1957), 166. For a concrete example see A.N. Gorshkova, 'Svyaz' shkoly-internata s zhizn'yu', *Sov. ped.*, 1958, no. 6, 62.

5   'The Curriculum for the Eight-Year and Secondary Schools of the RSFSR', *Soviet Education*, vol. II, no. 3 (January 1960), 30-31, translated from *Narodnoe obrazovanie*, 1959, no. 11; for the previous curriculum see I.A. Kairov *et al.* (eds.), *Pedagogika* (M., 1956), 103, or F.F. Korolev, *Education in the USSR* (London, n.d.), 16.

6   G. Vovchenko, letter in *Pravda*, 24 February 1964.

7   A. Kolmogorov, 'Znaniya, nauki, sposobnosti i konkursnye ekzameny', *Literaturnaya gazeta*, 11 January 1967.

8   Reproduced in Nigel Grant, *Soviet Education* (Harmondsworth, revised edition, 1968), 79.

9   Gerda Achinger, *Die Schulreform in der UdSSR* (Munich, 1973), 76-77.

10   N.P. Kuzin, *et al.*, *Education in the USSR* (Moscow, 1972), 38;

Spravochnik rabotnika narodnogo obrazovaniya (M., 1973), 116 (text of USSR Ministry of Education circular of 8 April 1967).

11 Achinger, *op. cit.*, 87, considers that the postponement of optional studies to form 7 was due to a wish to retain the uniform course as long as possible.

12 'V ministerstve prosveshcheniya RSFSR', *Uch. gaz.*, 13 April 1967.

13 A. Arsen'ev, 'Shkola i sovremennaya nauka', *Uch. gaz.*, 15 December 1966; see also his paper, 'Fakul'tativnye zanyatiya v shkole', *Sov. ped.*, 1968, no. 8, 76-87.

14 A.M. Arsen'ev, 'Osnovnye napravleniya sovershenstvovaniya soderzhaniya obrazovaniya v srednei shkole', *Sov. ped.*, 1967, no. 6, 30; Achinger, *op. cit.*, 89.

15 *Ibid.;* W. Kienitz and H. Brauer, 'Das neue System das Wahlunterrichts in der sowjetischen Mittelschule', *Vergleichende Pädagogik*, vol. 3 (1967), 378-379; Arsen'ev, *op. cit.* (1968), 80; M.P. Kashin, in foreword to V.V. Firsov *et al.*, *Sostoyanie i perspektivy fakul'tativnykh zanyatii po matematike* (M., 1977), 5.

16 'V byuro otdeleniya didaktiki i chastnykh metodik APN SSSR', *Sov. ped.*, 1967, no. 6, 152; Arsen'ev, *op. cit.*, (1967), 30; Kienitz and Brauer, *op. cit.*, 378.

17 *Ibid.;* 'Sovetskaya shkola na novom etape', *Sov. ped.*, 1967, no. 1, 7; 'V byuro . . .', *loc. cit.*

18 Kienitz and Brauer, *loc. cit.;* Arsen'ev, *op. cit.* (1968), 76, 79; Arsen'ev, 'Shkola i sovremennaya nauchno-tekhnicheskaya revolyutsiya', *Sov. ped.*, 1969, no. 1, 18; I.D. Zverev, 'Problemy fakul'tativnykh zanyatii v srednei shkole', *Sov. ped.*, 1971, no. 4, 47.

19 *Uch. gaz.*, 21 July 1973.

20 See also Arsen'ev, *op. cit.* (1969), 23-24, and Willi Kuhrt and Hans Deubler, 'Berufswahlvorbereitung in sozialistischen Ländern', *Vergleichende Pädagogik*, 1973, no. 3, 244-249, who quote instances of special options on the principles of choosing a career.

21 K. Asaturova, 'Problemy fakul'tativnykh zanyatii', *Narodnoe obrazovanie*, 1968, no. 11, 40.

22 Full text in *Spravochnik rabotnika narodnogo obrazovaniya* (M., 1973), 116-121.

23 V. Strezikozin, 'Granitsy i perspektivy', *Uch. gaz.*, 15 August 1967; Kienitz and Brauer, *op. cit.*, 379.

24 *Ibid.*, 380.

25 *Ibid.;* 'V ministerstve prozveshcheniya RSFSR', *Uch. gaz.*, 13 April 1967.

26 Kienitz and Brauer, *loc. cit.* See also M.P. Kashin, 'Ob itogakh perekhoda sovetskoi shkoly na novoe soderzhanie obshchego obrazovaniya', *Sov. ped.*, 1976, no. 3, 29-30.

27 Arsen'ev, *op. cit.* (1968), 81.

28 M.P. Kashin, 'God raboty po vypolneniyu postanovleniya TsK KPSS i Soveta Ministrov SSSR . . .', *Sov. ped.*, 1968, no. 2, 15.

29 Arsen'ev, *op. cit.* (1968), 85; E. Semenov, 'Nuzhno iskat'', *Uch. gaz.*,

19 October 1968. Their impreciseness was later blamed for the untimely demise of some options (Kashin, in Firsov *et al., op. cit.,* 7).

30 Zverev, *op. cit.,* 43.

31 Yu. Ivanov, 'Plyus fakul'tativy', *Uch. gaz.,* 22 December 1970; Wolfgang Mitter, 'Einheitlichkeit und Differenzierung als Problem der sowjetischen Schulreform', in Oskar Anweiler (ed.), *Bildungsreformen in Osteuropa* (Stuttgart, 1969), 119-120; Firsov *et al., op. cit.,* 20, 40.

32 O.A. Zavadskaya, *Razvitie obshcheobrazovatel'noi shkoly Ukrainy v period stroitel'stva kommunizma (1959-1968 gg.),* (Kiev, 1968), 128.

33 V. Veksler, 'Interes dvizhet delo', *Uch. gaz.,* 30 May 1967.

34 Arsen'ev, *op. cit.,* (1969), 29.

35 'Obmen mneniyami s akademikom P.L. Kapitsei', *Voprosy filosofii,* 1972, no. 9, 128.

36 Strezikozin, *loc. cit.;* I. Kagan, 'Otkryt' krasotu!', *Uch. gaz.,* 12 November 1968; I. Ovchinnikova, 'Chas shesto', *Izvestiya,* 7 January 1969.

37 S. Shipovsky, 'Gde, kak i skol'ko', *Uch. gaz.,* 3 October 1968.

38 Semenov, *loc. cit.*

39 T. Galkina and O. Chelpanova, 'Shkol'niki golosuyut "za" ...', *Uch. gaz.,* 16 November 1967

40 Kagan, *loc. cit.;* Ovchinnikova, *loc. cit.*

41 Arsen'ev, *op. cit.* (1969), 20; R. Brusnichkina and V. Mislavsky, 'Tramplin dlya poiska', *Komsomol'skaya pravda,* 7 February 1971.

42 *Ibid.*

43 V. Strezikozin, 'Uspekhi i promakhi', *Uch. gaz.,* 9 May 1968; 'Fakul'tativy', *Uch. gaz.,* 19 August 1971.

44 Kashin, *loc. cit.* (1968).

45 L. Atanasyan, 'Shkol'nyi fakul'tativ i pedinstitut', *Uch. gaz.,* 6 April 1968.

46 Strezikozin, *loc. cit.* (1968).

47 Ivanov, *loc. cit.*

48 Yu. Ivanov, 'Uspekhi i trudnosti fakul'tativa', *Uch. gaz.,* 18 April 1972.

49 S. Petrushkin, 'Za uglublennye znaniya', *Narodnoe obrazovanie,* 1975, no. 10, 24.

50 A.N. Kolmogorov, 'Obnovlenie shkol'nogo kursa matematiki', *Uch. gaz.,* 14 February 1967.

51 Atanasyan, *loc. cit.*

52 V. Uspensky, 'Starsheklassnikam — pedagogicheskie znaniya', *Narodnoe obrazovanie,* 1967, no. 9, 74-77; *id.,* 'Pedagogiku — shkol'nikam', *Sem'ya i shkola,* 1967, no. 7, 28-29.

53 'V prezidiume APN SSSR', *UCH. gaz.,* 8 September 1970; Zverev, *op. cit.,* 43.

54 *Ibid.,* 49. See also the recommendations of the Second All-Union Conference on Options Teaching (June 1971) in O. Grekulova and A. Sudarkina, 'Opyt provedeniya fakul'tativnykh zanyatii', *Sov. ped.,* 1972, no. 1, 158.

55   Detlef Glowka, 'Das sowjetische Schulwesen am Beginn einer neuen Etappe?', *Neue Sammlung,* vol. 7, no. 3 (May-June 1967), 216.
56   'Obshchee sobranie Akademii pedagogicheskikh nauk RSFSR', *Sov. ped.,* 1966, no. 2, 10.
57   *Spravochnik rabotnika narodnogo obrazovaniya,* (M., 1973), 118-119. See also Firsov *et al., op. cit.,* 38.
58   Kienitz and Brauer, *op. cit.,* 381; thus also M.A. Prokof'ev (ed.), *Narodnoe obrazovanie v SSSR 1917-1967* (M., 1967), p.106.
59   Kienitz and Brauer, *loc. cit.*
60   Brusnichkina and Mislavsky, *loc. cit.;* 'Problemy fakul'tativov', *Uch. gaz.,* 30 September 1971.
61   Strezikozin, *loc. cit.* (1967, also 1968). See also A. Danilov, 'Pervostepennye zadachi novogo uchebnogo goda', *Narodnoe obrazovanie,* 1967, no. 9, 9.
62   Arsen'ev, *op. cit.* (1968), 78.
63   Ivanov, *loc. cit.* (1970); Kashin, in Firsov *et al., op. cit.,* 10.
64   'Novoe polozhenie o fakul'tativnykh zanyatiyakh', *Uch. gaz.,* 28 January 1975.
65   Galkina and Chelpanov, *loc. cit.*
66   'V byuro otdeleniya didaktiki i chastnykh metodik APN SSSR', *Sov. ped.,* 1967, no. 6, 153.
67   K. Asaturova, 'Problemy fakul'tativnykh zanyatii', *Narodnoe obrazovanie,* 1968, no. 11, 40. See also O. Rynkov, 'Vykhod est': fakul'tativnye kursy', *Sem'ya i shkola,* 1967, no. 9, 28; this commentator is also concerned about clever children who avoid options to escape the extra work.
68   L. Milyukova, 'Okno v zhizn'', *Uch. gaz.,* 19 May 1973.
69   See the frank but inconclusive Komsomol discussion in Ovchinnikova, *loc. cit.,* and remarks by Arsen'ev, *op. cit.,* (1968), 78.
70   I.D. Zverev, 'Problemy fakul'tativnykh zanyatii v srednei shkole', *Sov. ped.,* 1971, no. 4, 47; 'Problemy fakul'tativov', *Uch. gaz.,* 30 September 1971.
71   'Novoe polozhenie . . .', *loc. cit.*
72   Arsen'ev, *op. cit.* (1968), 82; S. Literat, 'Rezervy sposobnostei', *Uch. gaz.,* 30 August 1973.
73   Brusnichkina and Mislavsky, *loc. cit.;* 'Problemy fakul'tativov', *loc. cit.;* 'Novoe polozhenie . . .', *loc. cit.*
74   'V ministerstve prosveshcheniya RSFSR', *Uch. gaz.,* 13 April 1967.
75   Arsen'ev, *loc. cit.* (1968); D. Disko, 'Fakul'tativy vchera, segodnya, zavtra', *Uch. gaz.,* 18 February 1969; Kagan, *loc. cit.*
76   *Ibid.*
77   'V ministerstve prosveshcheniya RSFSR', *Uch. gaz.,* 13 April 1967; Strezikozin, *loc. cit.* (1967). The USSR Ministry circular had called for entry of a 'record of participation', and this remains its line.
78   'Problemy fakul'tativov', *loc. cit.* — At the APN school options are marked because marks for good work are thought good for morale (Asaturova, *loc. cit.*)
79   Brusnichkina and Mislavsky, *loc. cit.;* Ivanov, *loc. cit.* (1972). Yet in

1969 the USSR Ministry instructed the republic ministries to lay down a procedure for pupil assessment ('V Ministerstve prosveshcheniya SSSR', *Narodnoe obrazovanie*, 1969, no. 2, 122).

80   *Ibid.;* V. Eppel', 'O fakul'tativakh, repetitorakh i abiturientakh', *Uch. gaz.*, 13 May 1969; Ivanov, *loc. cit.* (1970).

81   'Novoe polozhenie . . .,' *loc. cit.*

82   Glowka, *op. cit.*, 214.

83   Strezikozin, *loc. cit.* (1967); Ivanov, *loc. cit.* (1970); 'Fakul'tativy', *Uch. gaz.*, 19 August 1971; Yu. Ivanov and V. Nevsky, 'Shkol'nye fakul'tativy segodnya i zavtra', *Narodnoe obrazovanie*, 1972, no.7, 49.

84   Strezikozin, *loc. cit.* (1967); Kagan, *loc. cit.;* Ovchinnikova, *loc. cit.;* Ivanov and Nevsky, *loc. cit.*

85   V. Veksler, 'Interes dvizhet delo', *Uch. gaz.*, 30 May 1967. The special-profile schools were not in fact meant to have options — cp. Strezikozin, *loc. cit.* (1967).

86   'Fakul'tativy', *loc. cit.*

87   Ivanov, *loc. cit.* (1970); Kashin, in Firsov *et al., op. cit.*, 11; *ibid.*, 33-34.

88   'Vsesoyuznaya konferentsiya "Opyt provedeniya fakul'tativnykh zanyatii po osnovam nauk v srednei shkole"', *Matematika v shkole*, 1972, no. 1, 50; S.I. Shvartsburd and V.V. Firsov, 'O kharakternykh osobennostyakh fakul'tativnykh zanyatii', *Matematika v shkole*, 1972, no. 1, 57-58. See also Firsov *et al., op. cit.*, 34.

89   Kienitz and Brauer, *loc. cit.*

90   Galkina and Chelpanov, *loc. cit.;* Disko, *loc. cit.;* Eppel', *loc. cit.*

91   Eppel', *loc. cit.* During the Supreme Soviet discussion of the 1958 education reform, Deputy I.V. Abashidze had feared that if the general-education school did nothing extra for specially gifted pupils, private initiative would step in (*Zasedaniya Verkhnogo Soveta SSSR pyatogo sozyva (vtoraya sessiya). Stenograficheskii otchet* (M., 1959), 345.)

92   Eppel', *loc. cit.*

93   Strezikozin, *loc. cit.* (1967); Danilov, *loc. cit.*

94   'Fakul'tativy', *loc. cit.*

95   Oskar Anweiler, *Die Sowjetpädagogik in der Welt von heute* (Heidelberg, 1968), 136.

96   Shvartsburd and Firsov, *op. cit.*, 58-59; Firsov *et al., op. cit.*, 36.

97   Strezikozin, *loc. cit.* (1968).

98   Kienitz and Brauer, *op. cit.*, 389.

99   Strezikozin, *loc. cit.* (1968).

100   Interestingly enough, the Second All-Union Conference on Options Teaching of 1971 called upon the Ministry to include such data in school statistics (Grekulova and Sudarkina, *loc. cit.*).

101   Arsen'ev, *op. cit.* (1968), 81.

102   Zavadskaya, *op. cit.*, 129-130.

103   Strezikozin, *loc. cit.* (1967); 'Problemy fakul'tativov', *loc. cit.*

104   Zverev, *op. cit.*, 43, closely corresponding with alternative figures in

Strezikozin, *loc. cit.* (1968).
105 Ivanov, *loc. cit.* (1970).
106 Kashin, in Firsov *et al., op. cit.,* 7.
107 Zverev, *loc. cit.*
108 *Ibid.,* 47. The figure of 59 per cent is an obvious misprint.
109 Kashin, *op. cit.* (1976), 30; *id.,* in Firsov *et al., op. cit.,* 6. Latvia had increased to 40 per cent and Turkmenia 32 per cent, whereas, surprisingly, Lithuania's share had dropped to 46 per cent.
110 Yu. Ivanov, 'Po vyboru shkol'nikov', *Uch. gaz.,* 25 May 1974; and possibly 'Obshchee sobranie APN SSSR', *Sov. ped.,* 1976, no. 3, 151, where 'serious lagging behind' in the Ukraine is reported.
111 Petrushkin, *loc. cit.*
112 Arsen'ev, *op. cit.* (1968), 83-84; Zverev, *op. cit.,* 45.
113 Kashin, in Firsov *et al., op. cit.,* 10.
114 *Id., op. cit.* (1968), 16.
115 'O fakul'tativnykh zanyatiyakh', *Uch. gaz.,* 21 November 1967; cp. Strezikozin, *loc. cit.* (1968), and Arsen'ev, *op. cit.* (1969), 19.
116 'V prezidiume APN SSSR', *Uch. gaz.,* 8 September 1970.
117 Ivanov, *loc. cit.* (1972) — though not to the extent of using the options periods *exclusively* for labour training, as has happened in some places (Kashin, in Firsov *el al., op. cit.,* 11).
118 'Fakul'tativy', *loc. cit.*
119 B. Rusakov, 'Fakul'tativnye zanyatiya po osnovam NOT shkol'nika', *Narodnoe obrazovanie,* 1972, no. 2, 41-43.
120 A. Averin and G. Vokhnyanin, 'Podgotovit' smenu boevuyu', *Uch. gaz.,* 4 September 1969.
121 *Programmy fakul'tativnykh kursov srednei shkoly* (M., 1972), 316-349.
122 *Sbornik prikazov . . .,* 1972, no. 11, 2.
123 Kashin, in Firsov *et al., op. cit.,* 12.
124 Arsen'ev, *op. cit.* (1969), 20.
125 Brusnichkina and Mislavsky, *loc. cit.*
126 Strezikozin, *loc. cit.* (1968).
127 V. Gorelov, 'Razmyshleniya posle olimpiady', *Uch. gaz.,* 13 October 1970.
128 See note 52 above, and 'Fakul'tativy', *loc. cit.* By 1976 over 70 syllabuses has been approved centrally, and nearly as many by the Union republic ministries (Kashin, in Firsov *et al., op. cit.,* 7-8).
129 *Programmy fakul'tativnykh kursov . . .,* 4.
130 Ivanov, *loc. cit.* (1974).
131 Firsov, *et al., op. cit.,* 31.
132 N.G. Kort (interviewed by G. Simanovich), 'Teatral'nyi klass', *Sovetskaya kul'tura,* 26 July 1974.
133 E. Matveeva, 'Talantam nuzhny poklonniki', *Uch. gaz.,* 12 January 1978.
134 M.A. Danilov and M.N. Skatkin (eds.), *Didaktika srednei shkoly: nekotorye problemy sovremennoi didaktiki* (M., 1975), 273.
135 Kienitz and Brauer, *op. cit.,* 382.
136 Danilov and Skatkin, *loc. cit.*

Chapter 9

Differentiation within mass schools

The Problem of Giftedness Again

The impression may well have been given that the arguments raised during discussions on the issue of particular provision for gifted children, whether by means of specialized schools, classes or optional extras, were essentially pragmatic, supported where it was felt necessary by appeals to ideology. Such an impression is a fair one. In the case of specialized schools and classes it appeared sufficient for most participants to assert the existence or non-existence of natural talents or innate abilities,[1] without delving far into the nature of giftedness. This was not because it was a taboo subject — the Khrushchev regime brought a more relaxed atmosphere here as elsewhere — but rather because it was a neglected one and because such special provision was to involve only a tiny proportion of children; in 1962-63 the principle of the unified secondary school for the mass of young people was not in general held to be seriously at risk. In the case of optional studies the problem was not thought to arise. However, although the specialized schools for gifted children at their inception lacked much theoretical underpinning of a psychological kind, they do seem to have stimulated work on the psychology of giftedness,[2] greatly reinforcing a trend observable from the late 1950s, *e.g.* in the research at the Laboratory of the Psychology of Abilities, Moscow Institute of Psychology.[3]

Meanwhile, and subsequently, a separate and, given the history of the Soviet school, sensational concept of differentiation was publicized which if officially adopted would have required the principle to be fundamentally reinterpreted, as it would have affected the broad masses of pupils. This was to differentiate within the class on the basis of ability, and, later, to differentiate between parallel classes on the same basis. It remains a matter of experiment and debate, which more than any other issue has reflected the growing interest in the psychology of giftedness.

First, certain key terms must be defined in accordance with current theory. *Zadatki* (endowments) are 'the innate anatomical and physiological peculiarities of the organism, especially of the nervous system',[4] and *may* thus represent hereditary factors in the intellectual development of the young.[5] Examples of them are 'the innate features of the visual and aural apparatus'.[6] They are considered to vary between individuals, and may themselves develop, so that 'potentialities' may be preferred as a more dynamic rendering. *Zadatki* are the natural prerequisites for, and the organic basis of, *sposobnosti* (abilities), but they do *not* predetermine them. *Sposobnosti* are attributes developing on the basis of endowments as a result of a person's conditions of life and activity, characterized by the complex interplay of environmental (including social) factors and purposeful upbringing. The notion of *deyatelnost'* (activity) is of paramount importance here, being essential for the development of abilities. Instances of abilities are, for the sportsman, speed of motor reactions, for the artist a fine perception of colour, and for the mathematician an *analytical* memory *(i.e.* for types, methods and schemes, rather than for data).[7] All-round development is the well-known goal of socialist society, but levels of ability may differ, for there are many variables in their formation. These include the degree of interest and enthusiasm, the presence of personal qualities such as diligence, concentration, organization, goal-directedness and resilience, and the extent of satisfaction from effort.[8] Thus the activity must be purposeful and systematic. *Odarennost'* (giftedness) has been defined variously as 'an aggregate of inborn inclinations for an activity'[9] and 'a high level of development of abilities'[10] and may be general or specific. *Talant* is sometimes used synonymously with *odarennost'*, or may further emphasize it.

As formerly heredity had ceded pride of place as the main factor in intellectual development to environment, so by 1936 environment had yielded preeminence to upbringing. This led to the common view that all normal people were born with equal capacity for success, and that it was the teacher on whom everything depended;[11] research came to be concentrated on under-achievers. As late as 1958 an educational psychologist maintained that any normal child could become a good chemist, biologist or historian.[12] From about 1959, however, the existence of endowments was reasserted, but psychologists and educationists differed among themselves as to the implications of this for the development of special abilities. The sovereign role of upbringing, as put forward by A.N. Leont'ev, was queried by V.A. Krutetsky, who conceded that *some* inborn preconditions did not determine the content of abilities, but held that others did influence it. This, he felt, was the only explanation for the appearance of abilities before systematic training or in the absence of favourable conditions, and for the phenomenon of sustained and systematic activity without special ability.[13]

Certain educationists and psychologists denied that their science was capable of prognosticating the intellectual development of the child, and some were opposed on principle to differentiated teaching arrangements. V.N. Stoletov, President of the Academy of Pedagogical Sciences, who is a geneticist by training, came out firmly against the possibility of accurate prediction by the science of biology;[14] he has also stated categorically that 'only by giving *all* young people *identical* teaching up to maturity can the problem of abilities and giftedness be objectively solved'.[15] Leont'ev, perhaps the doyen of Soviet educational psychologists, whose views command wide respect, would presumably not deny the need for the teacher to be aware of individual differences, but would not wish to see this institutionalized to the extent of ability grouping. In 1975 he wrote: 'It is obvious to me that if a person had no clearly expressed innate abilities for mathematics, it does not follow that he must be removed from studying it or take a simplified course... Sorting out according to abilities is in my view nothing but an admission by the upbringer of his weakness in the face of a pedagogically neglected pupil...' As to high-ability children, 'at the present time we have no reliable objective criteria for selection at an early age on this basis'.[16] Leont'ev's attitude to the application of his ideas on purposeful upbringing appears to have hardened slightly since 1958 when he argued for furcation (differentiation in the structure of the senior stage of the general school); he has been consistently opposed to special schools, but now he seems to reject any kind of special bias within the mass school other than that afforded by optional studies.[17]

L.V. Zankov and his followers occupy an intermediate position: he attaches weight to endowments and is led positively to favour differentiated teaching methods within the mixed-ability class, but these should be used to achieve the balanced all-round development of all children, not to cultivate special abilities.[18] Thus, although Zankov's theoretical stance is not that of Leont'ev, his aims are not dissimilar. For other psychologists, *e.g.* Krutetsky, who takes a more positive view of 'natural gifts', all-round development means the maximum development of each ability in every pupil, whether 'backward', 'average' or 'capable'.[19] In a recent work he cites with approval Academician A.I. Berg's remarks about the orientation of teaching on the 'average' pupil: in Moscow the average monthly temperature varies from 19°C to -10°C; the average annual temperature is 5°C; but nobody thinks of producing every bit of clothing to accord with the average annual temperature. Yet in teaching, this is considered permissible and even inevitable![20] Krutetsky, however, believes that 'capable' pupils require particular attention. He considers that every normal individual has the prerequisites for developing the abilities necessary for mastery of the school mathematics course, but not for the higher level of abilities essential for scientific creativity and discovery.[21]

An attempt to reconcile the orthodox position with the need for special treatment was made by N.I. Kovantsov, a Kiev University mathematician, who accepted Leont'ev's view that abilities not innate can be acquired through upbringing, but proceeded from this to argue that one should seek the best returns from one's investment of time and effort. True, any child trained in mathematics from an early age could become a good mathematician, but it would cost too much; those with innate abilities must be spotted at the earliest possible age and the appropriate methods applied.[22] To sum up, it can be said that the differentiated approach might be advocated on diverse grounds and for somewhat disparate goals. We turn now to the varied forms that it sometimes took within the ordinary school.

Group Teaching

An eminent exponent of the Krutetsky-type line was the late V.A. Sukhomlinsky, teacher and educationist, who in 1961 praised the work of a mathematics teached in Kazan' who divided her pupils into three categories within the class, 'weak', 'capable' and 'talented', and set them different tasks accordingly, but made them all work very hard; if the weak ones moved to other schools they immediately jumped to the top, while the talented ones did university-level assignments and became the best students at Kazan' University. Sukhomlinsky said he himself had taught Russian literature by this method for fifteen years, but head teachers and education authorities mistrusted the maxim 'from each according to his ability'.[23]

By the middle of the decade differentiated instruction again became a subject of controversy, because of the problem of repeaters;[24] at the end of the 1964/65 school year this was most conspicuous in the middle school (then forms 5 to 8) where such a fate befell some 869,000 children (5 per cent).[25] In February 1965, for example, *Uchitel'skaya gazeta* published a long front-page article explaining how teachers in Kirovograd structured their lessons to take account of differing learning abilities.[26] Prominent among the many other articles which appeared in 1965 were those by V.

Strezikozin, head of the Curriculum and Methods Department of the RSFSR Ministry of Education, and A. Demintsev, director of the Rostov Institute of Advanced Teacher Training.[27] The former advocated the differentiated approach for both below-average and above-average pupils, as long as the common syllabus was safeguarded; the bright children, instead of moving on more rapidly, should therefore study each topic more deeply. For Demintsev, however, this approach was an exceptional measure to be used only in necessary cases and certainly not in every lesson, otherwise it impaired collective labour and led to molly-coddling *(teplichnoe vospitanie)*; he deplored the fact that the idea of supplementary work with backward pupils out of lesson time had lately been under a cloud. This was presumably the corollary of the new interest in talents which characterized the 1960s.

Later, in a balanced and thoughtful summary of the debate, Strezikozin insisted that the proponents of differentiated instruction did not see it in terms of permanent groups. Its aim was 'to make it easier for *everyone* to master the *whole* corpus of knowledge and to open up possibilities for the *maximum satisfaction of the interests* of individual pupils'.[28] Linking thus the two separate goals of differentiated teaching, Strezikozin provides more than a hint of the new liberating spirit at work in the Curriculum Commission which would find expression in the decree of 10 November legitimating specialized schools and classes and reinvigorating optional subjects.[29] Most contributors had said that only independent work should be differentiated, and the methodologist saw this in terms of revision and initial reinforcement; it could be done on the basis either of the degree of autonomy[30] or of the level of difficulty. Assessment was obviously a problem; the idea of not grading differentiated work deserved attention, and there should be no differentiation in tests as the unified requirements of the syllabus were not to be lowered.[31]

The differentiated approach within the class has continued to be advocated by responsible people, but there are problems in securing its adoption. A survey reported in 1968 showed that teachers devoted 58 per cent of lesson time to work with the whole class, geared mainly to the average pupil; 33 per cent to individual work, of which 22 per cent was with 'weak' pupils, 5 per cent with average, and 6 per cent with 'strong' ones;[32] 4 per cent to group work; and 5 per cent was wasted. This showed disparity between work with the full collective and the differentiated approach; too little time was given to group work and there was a widespread and anti-pedagogical opinion that this should be used to equalize children's knowledge, whereas the real aim was to ensure the greatest progress in each child's development.

The writer's message was clear, and he evidently regretted the rarity of this approach.[33] Hostile attitudes apart, differentiated lessons are extremely difficult to organize.[34] Even so, these methods are insufficient for some enthusiasts; a leading Novosibirsk teacher has advocated individual tutorials as well.[35] Another way to individualize teaching is to provide diversified material in textbooks, by including, along with the obligatory material, more difficult sections and problems for those children able to take up the challenge.[36]

Streaming: Controversy and Experiment

But this sort of differentiation was mild and relatively unexceptionable compared to the proposal which overshadowed it in 1967. Four mathematicians, headed by B. Gnedenko of the Ukrainian Academy of Sciences, wrote an article expressing their concern about the low academic level of *vuz* entrants and insisting that pupils had obligations as well as teachers, who were constantly under pressure from local education offices and heads to cook the record books — a symptom of the mental condition called 'percentomania' which requires ever better success rates. They proposed four remedies: removal of inhibitions about awarding 'twos' (unsatisfactory); triple streaming from form 5 (11-plus); entrance examinations to form 9; and wider development of specialized vocational schools.[37]

Critics of these proposals varied according to whether they were basically hostile or strove to find some good in them. Not surprisingly, it was the second suggestion which encountered the greatest opprobrium. Again it was Demintsev who spoke most forcefully, and this time without concession. The mathematicians' plan was tantamount to legalizing backwardness (by accepting 'twos')[38] and introducing a class character into the schools (by streaming), while making entry to form 9 dependent on examination would impair universal secondary education by orienting it exclusively to *vuzy*. Upbringing was ignored. Demintsev did not specifically criticize the proposal to expand vocational schools, but this may be implicit in his comment that the future skilled worker must have a fully-fledged secondary education.[39] The eminent psychologist Zankov felt that streaming hampered the development of slower learners and formed undesirable attitudes;[40] a colleague criticized the schools' preoccupation with *vuz* entry, but at the same time he attacked bureaucratic percentomania.[41] On the last point he was moving to the mathematicians' position, and this was an issue where they received much support; the suggestion about expanding vocational schools and in some cases promoting pupils who had received a 'two' also proved popular.[42] Response to the idea of entrance examinations to form 9 was mixed; but even the teacher who gave that her unqualified support was worried about streamed classes.[43]

Have any of these proposals for change been much translated into practice? Here we shall not go further into the question of promotion from form to form — except to record an experiment in Simferopol' whereby bright children were permitted to *skip* a form[44] —nor into that of vocational schools, which have since received much attention and whose future as one of the means of achieving universal secondary education now seems assured. Other action has been strictly on an experimental basis; it is necessary to stress this, otherwise the mistaken impression may be given of a widespread departure from pedagogical orthodoxy. As early as 1964, senior forms had been differentiated in a few Moscow schools, though retaining the standard syllabus.[45] By the end of 1967 the complaint was voiced that differentiated classes were already appearing in some schools; even worse, the criterion was not abilities but attainment, which was formed by many supplementary factors, such as the culture of the family and material conditions.[46] A school director announced that his school had abandoned a specialized mathematics class because the two classes from which it was formed became impoverished.[47] Yet subsequently it was reported — disapprovingly and with the same caveat — that in September 1969 a similar tenth form had been set up, with the best teachers, in Kuibyshev.[48] In 1969-71 an American journalist heard science teachers referring casually to 'slow' and 'fast' classes in the middle and senior forms, apparently in the context of ordinary schools.[49] A similar phenomenon in Leningrad was commended: nobody transferred from School No. 241 to the ninth forms of specialized ones, for its work was well organized. Two of the four final-year forms were comprised of pupils who had shown their mettle in mathematics and physics, and 72 out of 76 pupils were admitted to *vuzy;* in the other two, acceptances numbered 30. 'Differentiated school instruction on a firm basis of general education solves the problem of selection for institutions of higher education and businesslike liaison with them': such was the author's conclusion.[50]

At the time of writing, Zankov is reported to be supervizing a research project on new teaching methods which emphasize activity, a spirit of inquiry and the ability to observe and to argue a case; the experimental classes have evinced a rate of entry to higher education of about 80 per cent.[51] Knowing Zankov's views, one infers that this is differentiation of another kind, intended to be a restricted means of gathering experience which if successful will later be generalized, disseminated and applied for the benefit of the mass of children. It would be interesting to know more about these thriving guinea-pigs; the report says nothing about how the classes were formed. But the aim is the same: to facilitate learning for everyone. It is certainly not to get four pupils in five into higher education when the *vuzy* can accommodate far fewer and nobody is seriously advocating higher education for the masses.

Egalitarians and Differentiators

Differentiation within the mass school is thus a matter of some complexity. Here again two basic pedagogical positions may be determined, although the people on each side may not always speak with one voice. There are the egalitarians, who wish to eschew distinctions and divisions in education for as long as possible, identifying these with labelling and the emergence of a class character. The fundamentalists among them are sceptical about talents and want an identical instructional diet to be administered; the wisest of them see equality in terms of compensation for disadvantage by levelling up to a common basic standard. Then there are the differentiators, who interpret 'from each according to his ability, to each according to his need' as insisting on maximum individual development and therefore in some cases setting the school's goal beyond or well beyond the basic minimum. If learning is to outpace development, and teaching to precede learning, the differentiators have Vygotsky, as it were, on their side; the egalitarian view contains the unfortunate implication that, within the classroom at any rate, there must come for some individuals a point at which further development is to be discouraged, so that teaching can logically no longer be permitted to lead it on. The differentiators also have as their allies academics and statesmen who associate the cultivation of talents with the economic and political pre-eminence of the country.

It can be said that the egalitarians are essentially collective-oriented, the differentiators individual-oriented. It is true that in Soviet society the individual is held to be subservient to the collective, but the differentiators would argue that only by developing his talents to the full does he make his due contribution to the life of society, and so they too have the greater good in mind. At the same time they cannot deny the objection of the egalitarians that any sort of singling out may induce unacceptable attitudes and perpetuate existing advantages springing from extraneous factors. Those who favour *discreet* differentiation within the class represent what many teachers would probably regard as an enlightened compromise which is everyday practice in a casual, unsystematized way but very difficult and time-consuming to apply rigorously, though 'purpose-built' textbooks would help. For certain children it promotes levelling up, without paying the price of levelling down by default in respect of others. But two problems remain: extrinsic factors cannot be entirely eliminated (nor is it necessarily desirable in every case that they should be, unless intellectual parents are to cease from conversation and throw away their books), and exceptional children towards either end of the intelligence range may suffer deprivation of one kind or another. However, for the mentally handicapped, assessed in accordance with a well-defined system, special schools and other institutions exist; and of the various possibilities (and their limitations) for the unusually bright Soviet child, it remains to review the oldest and most widespread — extracurricular and out-of-school activities.

Notes

1 Some examples *for:* A. Kolmogorov, 'Nauka trebuet goreniya', *Izvestiya,* 21 February 1962, and 'Fiziko-matematicheskaya shkola', *Uch. gaz.,* 11 February 1964; S.I. Literat, 'Vyyavlyat' i razvivat' sposobnosti', *Sov. ped.,* 1969, no. 4, 80. *Against:* I. Ivanenko, 'Shkoly neskol'kikh napravlenii ne nuzhny', *Pravda,* 8 December 1958; P. Rudnev, 'K voprosu o "differentsiatsii obshchego obrazovaniya" v srednei shkole', *Narodnoe obrazovanie,* 1963, no. 1, 19. P.L. Kapitsa, 'Nekotorye printsipy tvorcheskogo vospitaniya i obrazovaniya sovremennoi molodezhi', *Voprosy filosofii,* 1971, no. 7, 22-23, accepts the notion of natural talents but opposes selective schools.

2 For documentation see Detlef Glowka, *Schulreform und Gesellschaft in der Sowjetunion 1958-1968* (Stuttgart, 1970), 143.

3 Reported from a 1960 visit by Walter R. Reitman, 'Some Soviet Investigations of Thinking, Problem Solving, and Related Areas', in R.A. Bauer (ed.), *Some Views on Soviet Psychology* (Washington, D.C., 1962), 48, 50; and described by V.A. Krutetsky; 'Matematicheskie sposobnosti i ikh razvitie u shkol'nikov', *Sov. ped.,* 1962, no. 9, 110-116.

4 *Pedagogicheskaya entsiklopediya,* vol. 2 (M., 1965), col. 62.

5 Yu. A. Samarin, in *ibid.,* vol. 4 (M., 1968), col. 112, says 'Soviet psychologists do not deny the importance of hereditary (*nasledstvennye*) factors, expressed in endowments'. But, for B.N. Teplov, innate does not necessarily mean hereditary; see Ekkehard Eichberg, 'Das Problem der Differenzierung in der sowjetischen allgemeinbildenden Schule', *Die Deutsche Schule,* 1968, no. 5, 340.

6 V. Krutetsky, 'Sposobnosti vashikh detei', *Uch. gaz.,* 4 January 1973.

7 *Ibid.; id., Psikhologiya obucheniya i vospitaniya shkol'nikov* (M., 1976), 200.

8 *Ibid.,* 199; *id., loc. cit.* (1973).

9 *Id., The Psychology of Mathematical Abilities in Schoolchildren* (Chicago and London, 1976), 76. (Russian original, 1968.)

10   *Pedagogicheskaya entsiklopediya,* vol. 3 (M., 1966), col. 186. Another common term is *sklonnost'* (inclination), 'a person's disposition to engage in a specific activity'. It often points to an ability and affects its formation (*ibid.,* col. 858).

11   G.W. Boguslavsky, 'Psychological Research in Soviet Education', *Science,* vol. 125 (1957), 916.

12   N. Levitov, 'Razvivat' sposobnosti vsekh detei', *Uch. gaz.,* 20 December 1958.

13   Krutetsky, *op. cit.* (1976 (1968)), 65-66.

14   V.N. Stoletov, 'Posovetuemsya, tovarishchi!', *Uch. gaz.,* 15 February 1973.

15   *Id.,* in foreword to *Obshchestvo i molodezh'* (M., 2nd edn., 1973), 14. (Emphasis original).

16   A. Leont'ev, 'Pochemu plachet Petya?', *Komsomol'skaya pravda,* 22 August 1975 (with thanks to Dr M. Butenschön). See also A. Vedenov, 'Okonchena shkola . . . a dal'she?', *Literaturnaya gazeta,* 5 December 1967.

17   Leont'ev, *loc. cit.;* cp. note 4 to chapter 7.

18   Eichberg, *op. cit.,* 341; L.N. Zankov, 'Dvoechnik stanovitsya otlichnikom', *Literaturnaya gazeta,* 18 October 1967.

19   Eichberg, *op. cit.,* 340-342; Krutetsky, *op. cit.* (1962), 116 (Krutetsky seems here to be using *vozmozhnosti* synonymously with *zadatki, i.e.* potentialities); *id., op. cit.* (1976 (1968)), 5. For a further criticism of 'anti-pedagogical levelling', see V. Zagvyazinsky, 'O differentsirovannom podkhode', *Narodnoe obrazovanie,* 1968, no. 10, 85.

20   Krutetsky, *op. cit.* (1976), 188.

21   *Id., op. cit.* (1976 (1968)), 63.

22   N.I. Kovantsov, 'Yavlyayutsya li vrozhdennymi matematicheskie sposobnosti?', *Voprosy psikhologii,* 1965, no. 3, 151-152, 154.

23   V. Sukhomlinsky, 'Urgent Problems of the Theory and Practice of Education', *Soviet Education,* vol. IV, no. 7 (May 1962), 6, translated from *Narodnoe obrazovanie,* 1961, no. 10. The Kazan' method was noted in A. Agranovsky, 'Poisk talantov', *Izvestiya,* 11 May 1960, and cited approveingly by Academician Lavrent'ev, 'Molodym — dorogu v nauku!', *Pravda,* 18 October 1960.

24   Eichberg, *op. cit.,* 343.

25   *NONK,* 100. The official average for *all* classes was 4 per cent; by 1970 it had fallen to 3 per cent. (A somewhat more sophisticated index of achievement is the rate of completion of the eight-year course on time — see chapter 2.)

26   A. Khmura, 'Adres opyta — Kirovograd', *Uch. gaz.,* 11 February 1965. The new material was first explained to the whole class, which was then divided into two groups, those who immediately embarked on independent work (I) and those requiring further exposition (II); after a while the latter group was subdivided on the same basis, sub-group IIA joining group I and sub-group IIB receiving yet more explanation. The class was then brought together for 'explanation of

ways of applying theory to practice', after which they carried out practical tasks in three variants according to difficulty. — For a similar account, see A. Makoev, 'Nado, no kak . . .', *Uch. gaz.,* 13 November 1965.

27 V. Strezikozin, 'O nekotorykh voprosakh dal'neishego sovershenstvovaniya uchebnogo protsessa', *Narodnoe obrazovanie,* 1965, no. 7, 12-13; A. Demintsev, 'Esli nado i kogda nado', *Uch. gaz.,* 26 August 1965.

28 V. Strezikozin, 'Nuzhna li differentsiatsiya?', *Uch. gaz.,* 15 January 1966. Emphasis original.

29 Wolfgang Mitter, 'Schule und Bildung in der Sowjetunion im Widerstreit der Meinungen', *Neue Sammlung,* vol. 8, no. 6 (Nov.-Dec. 1968), 562, has pointed out that optional studies represent a separate kind of differentiation, by course content rather than attainment. This is true, and yet even with options, as we have seen, attainment criteria have sometimes been applied.

30 For example, the sequence of operations might or might not be indicated.

31 Strezikozin, *loc. cit.* (1966). Opinions varied on the assessment of routine work, cp. Zagvyazinsky, *op. cit.,* 86-87.

32 'Weak' and 'strong' and the usual terms denoting non-average ability; note that they are not static in their implications. — Awareness of possible dangers is suggested by an injunction to avoid public labelling of the three groups (I. Butuzov, 'Chtoby kazhdyi uchenik byl aktivnym', *Narodnoe obrazovanie,* 1969, no. 11, 53).

33 Zagvyazinsky, *op. cit.,* 85-87.

34 Cp. the elaborate structure described above, note 26. For some of the practical problems, sympathetically treated by advocates of differentiation, see N. Bikbaeva and I. Nikolaev, 'So vsemi vmeste i s kazhdym v otdel'nosti', *Uch. gaz.,* 23 November 1972.

35 S. Literat, 'Rezervy sposobnostei', *Uch. gaz.,* 30 August 1973.

36 M.N. Skatkin, *O shkole budushchego* (M., 1974), 47.

37 B. Gnedenko *et al.,* 'A dvoechnik spokoen . . .', *Literaturnaya gazeta,* 16 August 1967. The ensuing debate was first reported by Mitter, *op. cit.,* 559-563.

38 This had, however, been tried out experimentally, and the experiment approved retrospectively by USSR Ministry of Education *prikaz* of 12 August 1967 (T. Tamarin, 'Byt' ili ne byt' vtorogodnichestvu?', *Izvestiya,* 4 June 1968).

39 A. Demintsev, 'Znaniya — kazhdomu!', *Uch. gaz.,* 19 September 1967. Not until April 1969 was it decreed that vocational schools offering complete secondary education should be developed.

40 Zankov, *loc. cit.*

41 Vedenov, *loc. cit.*

42 The discussion is summarized by T. Snegireva, 'Iz punkta "A" vyshel chelovek . . .', *Literaturnaya gazeta,* 28 February 1968.

43 N. Dolinina, 'Pust' dvoechnik volnuetsya', *Literaturnaya gazeta,* 13 September 1967.

44 *Current Digest of the Soviet Press,* vol. XVII (1965), no. 13, 6-7. The original cannot be located.

45 Universities of London and Oxford, *Comparative Education Tour of the USSR, 1964,* 17, 25-26 (duplicated typescript).

46 E. Vlasova, 'Dvoechkami ne rodyatsya', *Literaturnaya gazeta,* 5 December 1967. The distinction is confused; according to Soviet psychological theory abilities are also affected by external factors.

47 I. Piratinsky, in Snegireva, *loc. cit.* See also Jennifer Louis, 'Streaming and Selection have their Advocates', *Times Educational Supplement,* 6 March 1970.

48 T. Yakovleva, ' "Vunderkindy" na popechenii', *Komsomol'skaya pravda,* 5 June 1970.

49 Susan Jacoby, *Inside Soviet Schools* (New York, 1975), 111.

50 I. Kossakovsky, 'Est' takaya shkola', *Izvestiya,* 23 March 1972.

51 N. Dmitrieva, 'Sovet uchitelei-novatorov', *Uch. gaz.,* 13 April 1976.

Chapter 10
Extracurricular Activities in Academic Subjects

As the traditional means of catering for special talent, extracurricular activities are located at the opposite end of the differentiation spectrum from the mathematics and physics schools for the highly gifted. In that many of them are extramural, they pass beyond the spectrum altogether, but it would be inappropriate to omit them and it is convenient to consider them here. The vigour of the tradition is evidenced by its repeated invocation at various stages of the differentiation debates, sometimes by eminent figures, right down to comparatively recent times.[1] In passing, it should be recalled that the development of particular gifts is just one of the functions of out-of-class activities, their principal aim being to provide further and wider scope for the all-round education of the young Soviet citizen.

Clubs in the Schools
It is well-known that the school is one of several agencies for the fulfilment of this objective,[2] but it is a major one. Subject clubs or circles (*kruzhki*) in the schools have constituted an important means of pursuing special interests, in academic fields among others. The advent of options has caused some confusion and a partial appropriation of their role,[3] creating a need to redefine it: circles of a more academic kind may now be a less demanding alternative to optional studies. However, where options are not yet adequately developed, the subject clubs must retain their old functions, and, except where there is differentiation within the class and in the case of

foreign language work in specialized schools of that profile, they remain the mass school's sole means of encouraging special intellectual abilities in children up to the age of fourteen.

Consequently, their importance is still considerable, and any doubts on this score should be resolved by the fact that the decree of 1966 created the new secondary-school post of organizer of out-of-class and out-of-school activities, with the rank of deputy director; this was reaffirmed by article 47 of the Secondary School Statute of 8 September 1970.[4] Given the personnel to lead them, the only inhibiting factor may be lack of accommodation when the school works on a shift basis; hard information on this point is difficult to come by, but in 1965/66 30 per cent of schoolchildren were attending an afternoon shift and 1 per cent an evening one. The end of the latter was in sight, but not that of the former.[5] Up-to-date information is to hand for certain republics: in 1975 over 80 per cent of pupils were on single-shift studies in Moldavia and 80 per cent in the Mordovian Autonomous Republic, whereas in Azerbaidzhan 72 per cent of schools were working two shifts.[6]

Clubs at Other Institutions

'Palaces and Houses for Pioneers and Schoolchildren' are another important agency for out-of-school activities of all kinds, including those under discussion. Children's sections at Palaces of Culture and clubs under trade union auspices may provide further opportunities. It is reported that at the Pioneer Palaces there are special circles in subjects such as maths, science, astronomy and languages for academically gifted children, with 12 to 15 members, who qualify for acceptance by a good school record. On completing his time in the circle, the child is given a testimonial which is useful when he applies for *vuz* entry.[7]

The institutions where these activities are conducted are developing all over the country, though obviously they are more accessible to town children than country ones and some republics are better provided for than others: to quote an extreme case, in 1970 a Lithuanian child was twice as likely to have access to such an establishment as one in Uzbekistan, even before allowance is made for easier communications in the north-west; to be fair, however, the average Soviet child's chances were much nearer the Lithuanian's. The ratio of Pioneer Palaces and Houses to pupils in the corresponding school years is estimated for the USSR at 1:6481 and for selected republics as follows: Lithuania 1:5338; Ukraine 1:5664; RSFSR 1:6429; Azerbaidzhan 1:8485; Kirgizia 1:9947; Uzbekistan 1:10882. The median for all 15 republics is Georgia with 1:6250.[8] Over the last two decades the construction of these institutions has been pursued with more diligence in Uzbekistan than in most of the other republics, increasing nearly sevenfold, but at over 3 million she has the third largest schoolgoing population in the USSR, and it has more than doubled since 1960/61. So has that of Azerbaidzhan, but here the development of such facilities has been virtually at a standstill since 1960. Thus there are varying reasons for these less favourable figures, but they alike betoken differentiated opportunities for receiving the benefits of high-powered out-of-school instruction under Ministry of Education auspices.

The same applies still more acutely to four of the five other extracurricular agencies for promoting special intellectual talents which appear most often in the literature. They are: clubs attached to *vuzy,* evening schools, summer schools, and the so-called 'Little Academies'; they seem most frequently to cater for mathematicians. Correspondence schools make up the fifth. Prominent among the *vuzy* organizing weekly mathematics clubs and Sunday lectures for young people was Moscow University, which in 1956/57 also opened fifteen circles in secondary schools within the region, their activities culminating in the then Moscow Olympiad.[9] However, by 1970 these circles attached to MGU were reported to have virtually ceased their work,[10] presumably because of the growth of other facilities. A more ambitious project was the Scientific Society of School Students at Chelyabinsk, established in 1963/64 for senior pupils on the joint initiative of the local pedagogical *vuz* and the Pioneer Palace. These, along with the laboratories of a variety of institutes, provided the setting for its activities, which were supervised by over a hundred *vuz* lecturers, and sixteen of the best subject circles in the area's schools were affiliated to it.[11]

Special Evening and Summer Schools

The most important extracurricular development of the sixties was the 'Young People's Mathematics Schools' (*yunosheskie matematicheskie shkoly* or YuMSh). The first were opened in 1959, such as the one at Ivanovo, under the aegis of the local pedagogical institute, with support from MGU and the Lenin Pedagogical Institute. The aims were to introduce pupils to modern mathematics, to develop their ability to cope with difficult and non-standard problems, and to foster interest in such fields as engineering design, electronics and computer technology; the emphasis lay on application.[12] Originally, it appears, recruitment was not intended to be competitive, but the proposed intake of 50 was over-subscribed and so the best were selected on the basis of an interview, their academic record, and a testimonial from their school. At first there were three classes, parallel to forms 9, 10 and 11, each dividing into two groups of six to twelve, meeting twice a week for two to three hours in the evenings.[13] By 1962/63 the YuMSh had a total enrolment of over 100 pupils in 11 groups of five to twenty; the eight first-year groups were comprised of pupils from form 8 to 11. There were two second-year groups and one third-year; new pupils could also be admitted direct to these.[14]

One unsatisfactory feature of the circles had been their fluctuating membership, and apparently attempts had been made to counteract this by choosing particularly interesting but discrete topics;[15] it was evidently hoped that the more highly organized evening schools would permit more systematic work. Thus attendance and hard work were obligatory, indeed applicants had to produce medical certificates to the effect that they were constitutionally able to stand the pace; nevertheless some dropping-out was anticipated, quite correctly, as the above-quoted distribution of year groups indicates.[16] Syllabuses were drawn up by the sponsoring *vuzy*, which also provided the teaching staff. Indeed, the evening school attached to the Herzen Pedagogical Institute in Leningrad was staffed by students and directed by a fourth-year undergraduate.[17] Subsequently Professor E.B. Dynkin set up a 150-pupil school for forms 7 and 8, with three ranks based on achievement: 'guests', 'candidates' and 'pupils'. By 1965 the Young People's Mathematics Schools had over 5,000 students.[18] In general they prepared for *vuz* entry,[19] but A.I. Markushevich, a leading member of the Academy of Pedagogical Sciences, has referred to evening mathematics schools providing a supplementary two-year course for pupils in forms 7 and 8 to help the ablest to transfer to form 9 of a special school.[20] How far the development of the YuMShs has continued is unclear. In 1969 Literat spoke of rapid expansion in recent years,[21] but Vogeli stated that this had been retarded by the growth of the schools with computer programming, and thought a wide increase unlikely.[22]

Special evening schools were set up in several other subjects, though the scientific ones received most publicity. In 1963, for example, it was reported that a School for Young Chemists had been founded at the University of Tiflis, for senior pupils who evinced great abilities in this field.[23] In 1969 a School of Economics for some 200 seniors was opened on student initiative at Novosibirsk, and a high-powered School of Natural Science, specializing in physics and biology as well as mathematics, was established at the I.V. Kurchatov Institute of Atomic Energy in Moscow.[24]

The summer schools for talented children, some of which have already been mentioned in connection with the FMShs, will reappear in the next chapter, devoted to the olympiads to which they are closely linked. For the present it may be noted that they are not merely arenas where olympiad winners aspiring to FMShs pit their skills. Young people selected by local education authorities may also be sent to such camps. In 1971 they were held, among other places, at Pskov, Vologda and Barnaul and in Kamchatka. In the two former cases some participants received recommendations to the mathematics and physics faculties of pedagogical *vuzy*, presumably those at Pskov and Vologda whose staff and students helped to run the summer schools.[25] Here too, it seems, much depends on the presence of higher educational institutions at which social responsibility and self-interest have contracted a fruitful marriage.

'Little Academies'

The third type of extracurricular institution has been the 'Little Academy' (*Malaya akademiya*). This differs from the foregoing in that it covers a wide range of subjects; the one at Ukhta described in 1965 had faculties of architecture and construction, geology and geophysics, 'biogeography', maths and physics, chemistry, medicine, history, foreign languages, literature and journalism. It was for pupils in forms 9 and 10, with competitive entrance examinations. Its director was a schoolgirl, and its activities — lectures, discussions, debates, excursions, research work etc. — were supervised by various specialists on a voluntary basis. It had a 'learned council' of research and production workers, who gave its best graduates recommendations for *vuz* entry.[26]

Other academies were reported at Simferopol', Novosibirsk and Vorkuta. One set up in the Crimea had several branches within the region.[27] Yet another, that of Tadzhikistan, is based on the Pioneer Palace in the capital, Dushanbe, and its proceedings are supervised by *vuz* lecturers and scientists from institutes of the Tadzhik Academy of Sciences.[28] The Little Academy in Minsk caters for some 1,500 children under the leadership of a council consisting of pupils and scientists; its full members are from the eleven specialized schools attached to the Belorussian Republic's Academy of Sciences. Its main aim is 'to develop the creative abilities of gifted children and to provide vocational guidance for them'.[29] The activities of the Moldavian School Academy include an annual correspondence olympiad in mathematics.[30]

Correspondence Schools

The availability of all the latter three types of extracurricular provision is inevitably restricted, depending as it does on the existence of sponsoring institutions prepared to display initiative. To overcome this problem Professor Gel'fand of MGU established in 1964 a 'Republic Mathematics Correspondence School'

(*Respublikanskaya zaochnaya matematicheskaya shkola* or ZMSh),
run by over 150 staff and students at the university. Six thousand
children from all over the RSFSR took the entrance examination,
and 1,429 passed.[31] The school has grown enormously and now
enjoys all-Union status: its full title, of not atypical Soviet sonority, is
the 'USSR Academy of Pedagogical Sciences All-Union
Mathematics Correspondence School attached to Moscow State
University'. By the spring of 1973 it had about 12,000 pupils.[32] In
1975 it had 28 branches and these were said to be increasing yearly. It
caters especially for children at schools remote from regional and
scientific centres; when the entrance papers are marked there is
positive discrimination in favour of those from outlying areas,[33]
and pupils in Moscow, Leningrad and their environs are not
admitted. This school originally took pupils from form 8 for a two-
year course parallel to forms 9 and 10, but from 1972/73 it was
decided to go over to a three-year period of instruction, and now
pupils completing form 7 are eligible.[34]

The prestigious Moscow Institute of Physics and Technology
(MFTI) runs a correspondence school in physics and mathematics;
in 1973/74 along with its Leningrad and Krasnoyarsk branches it
had over 7,000 pupils on its books. That year some 1,700 completed
the course, and of these one in 12 entered the MFTI, forming half its
intake. It runs a ten-day preparatory session for rural candidates
immediately before its entrance examinations.[35] Other mathematics
correspondence schools are reported in Novosibirsk and Kiev.
Novosibirsk University's, founded in 1965, went over to a three-year
course in 1966; the year 1969 saw plans for development here too,
with branches attached to other institutes in regional centres.[36] At the
beginning of the 1970s it catered for some 650 children and 'a few
hundred' teachers;[37] by the spring of 1973, 1,500 pupils were involved
and an increase to 3,000 or even 5,000 was envisaged,[38] the main
problem anticipated here being one of publicity.

Members of a school club can join the correspondence schools *en
bloc* as a 'collective pupil' for two or three years. Under this
arrangement, which in 1973 was scheduled for expansion, the only
admission requirement is a formal application by the club leader,
countersigned by the school director or his deputy. Such a group
receives a monthly package of materials containing explanations of
theoretical problems and questions for solution. It is recommended
that these are worked through in the club; various members then
write their solutions in the same exercise book which is sent to the
ZMSh for marking by the tutors.[39] According to the 1975 statute on
the All-Union ZMSh, teachers supervising these groups are to
receive parity with those teaching optional subjects.[40]

All tuition is free. The programme consists of topics closely linked to key problems in school syllabuses for the compulsory and optional courses, *e.g.* Euclid's algorithm, coordinates and mathematical analysis.[41] On completion of the course, a certificate is awarded. In order to 'increase the authority of the marks displayed' and make them 'more objective', an oral examination is to be instituted,[42] at the end of the course, but it is denied that the school is of a competitive character once the individual has secured entry. Perhaps there are some misgivings about the ZMShs sharing the second-rate reputation of some sectors of correspondence education, but if this is the case it scarcely seems deserved; the high-powered organization meant that in 1971 155 of the 180 students completing the Kiev ZMSh (86 per cent) were able to proceed to higher education, a similar percentage to the previous year.[43] The Rector of the MFTI's correspondence school even gives a figure of 95 per cent.[44]

At Novosibirsk it was envisaged that the correspondence system would provide a further channel of recruitment to special maths and physics boarding schools (FMShs).[45] Although the latter concept finds no place whatsoever in the ideas of the President of the APN, V.N. Stoletov, it is worth recalling that in his recent fierce attack on special provision for the gifted he singled out correspondence schools (instancing the one organized by the MFTI) as *the* way of catering for pupils capable of working to an extended syllabus.[46] Pioneer clubs, circles attached to *vuzy,* young people's evening and summer schools and Little Academies all permit specialized instruction while safeguarding the basic minimum of education for all, as well as keeping the principle of the unified school intact and unalloyed, but for geographical reasons alone it would be a truly Herculean task to make them accessible to all Soviet children, while to make them accessible to all *equally* would surely be a Sisyphean one. Circles in the schools are more feasible, but may tend to be unsystematic and are clearly likely to vary in quality according to the expertise available to lead them. Such problems will probably be aggravated the more dependent schools are upon their own resources. The development of a nationwide series of correspondence schools linked to olympiad competitions will not necessarily remedy this at a stroke, but it will enhance the work of the circles by providing quality, direction and continuity, and it has the merit of being extremely appropriate to Soviet conditions.

Notes

1   *e.g.* 'Shkola dlya "osobo odarennykh" ne nuzhny!', *Pravda,* 13 December 1958; P. Rudnev, 'K. voprosu o "differentsiatsii obshchego obrazovaniya" v srednei shkole', *Narodnoe obrazovanie,* 1963, no. 1,

18; M.A. Lavrent'ev, 'Molodezh' j nauka', *Izvestiya*, 25 May 1968; G. Kulagin, 'Shkola truda', *Pravda*, 19 June 1971; V.N. Stoletov, 'Posovetuemsya, tovarishchi!', *Uch. gaz.*, 15 February 1973.

2   For a detailed account of the various facilities, see Deana Levin, *Leisure and Pleasure of Soviet Children* (London, 1966).

3   See chapter 8 above.

4   *Uch. gaz.*, 15 September 1970.

5   M. Kaser, 'Salient Features in the History of State Boarding Schools', *Annuaire de l'URSS 1968* (Paris, 1969), 135 n.

6   For Moldavia: V. Cheban, 'Rodina stanovitsya bogache i sil'nee', *Uch. gaz.*, 7 January 1975; for Mordovia: 'V Sovete Ministrov RSFSR', *ibid.*, 16 January 1975; for Azerbaidzhan: 'V Tsentral'nom komitete profsoyuza', *ibid.*, 7 October 1975.

7   Billie K. Press, 'Education of the Gifted in the USSR', *Exceptional Children*, vol. 30, no. 6 (February 1963), 242.

8   Calculated from *NONK*, 78-89, 146-147. Figures for forms 5 to 8 inflated by 25 per cent of figures for forms 1 to 4. Participation in activities is not, however, restricted to children of Pioneer age, thus the ratios are of value for comparative purposes rather than as absolutes.

9   A.N. Kolmogorov and I.M. Yaglom, 'Yunosheskie matematicheskie shkoly', *Vestnik vysshei shkoly*, 1959, no. 11, 66; Izaak Wirszup, 'The School Mathematics Circle and Olympiads at Moscow State University', *Mathematics Teacher*, vol. LVI, no. 4 (April 1963), 201.

10   I. Petrakov, 'Sil'neishie i dostoinye', *Uch. gaz.*, 20 August 1970.

11   'Zasedanie Soveta molodykh uchenykh pri TsK VLKSM', *Fizika v shkole*, 1972, no. 2, 110.

12   Kolmogorov and Yaglom, *op. cit.*, 66-67; Bruce Ramon Vogeli, *Soviet Secondary Schools for the Mathematically Talented* (Washington, 1968), 55-56.

13   *Ibid.*

14   S.I. Kukushkin, 'Shkola novogo tipa', *Uchenye zapiski Ivanovskogo gosudarstvennogo pedagogicheskogo instituta*, vol. XXIV (1963), 133.

15   Kolmogorov and Yaglom, *op. cit.*, 67.

16   According to Kukushkin, *loc. cit.*, it was between 50 per cent and 66 per cent over the three years.

17   *Uch. gaz.*, 12 March 1970.

18   Vogeli, *op. cit.*, 59-60.

19   Kukushkin, *op. cit.*, 134.

20   *CET, 1971*, 60.

21   S.I. Literat, 'Vyyavlyat' i razvivat' sposobnosti', *Sov. ped.*, 1969, no. 4, 77.

22   Vogeli, *op. cit.*, 60.

23   'Shkola molodykh darovanii', *Izvestiya*, 13 April 1963.

24   A. Ovchinnikova, 'Izuchayut ekonomiku', *Uch. gaz.*, 5 December 1969; 'Zasedanie Soveta . . .' (see note 11 above), 109.

25   *Ibid.;* V.A. Volkov and Yu. V. Lomakin, 'Letnie matematicheskie shkoly na severo-zapade RSFSR', *Matematika v shkole*, 1972, no. 1,

93.

26   G. Nadezhdin, 'Shkol'naya akademiya', *Izvestiya,* 28 January 1965.
27   O.A. Zavadskaya, *Razvitie obshcheobrazovatel'noi shkoly Ukrainy v period stroitel'stva kommunizma (1959-1968 gg.)* (Kiev, 1968), 134.
28   'Tam, gde rozhdaetsya prizvanie', *Uch. gaz.,* 28 October 1975. Kazakhstan has recently followed suit ('Malaya Akademiya nauk', *ibid.,* 23 November 1976).
29   Igor Osinsky, ' "Malaya" akademiva', *ibid.,* 10 June 1975.
30   V.D. Belousov and Ya. I. Nyagu, 'Moldavskoi Respublikanskoi matematicheskoi olimpiade 15 let', *Matematika v shkole,* 1972, no. 1, 70.
31   Vogeli, *op. cit.,* 60-62. For further data as of 1968 see Anatoly Agranovsky, 'Pered startom', *Izvestiya,* 14 November 1968.
32   A. Owen and F.R. Watson, 'Encouraging Young Mathematicians in the USSR', *Bulletin of the IMA,* vol. 11 (1975), no. 6/7, 134.
33   E. Torpedov, 'Ne sorevnovanie . . . obuchenie!', *Uch. gaz.,* 13 March 1975.
34   N. B. Vasil'ev *et al.,* 'Zaochnaya matematicheskaya shkola ob 'yavlyaet priem uchashchikhsya', *Matematika v shkole,* 1972, no. 1, 60.
35   'Institut pomogaet shkol'niku', *Izvestiya,* 3 June 1975.
36   Literat, *op. cit.,* 80.
37   *Id., Problemy otbora i obucheniya v spetsializirovannykh fiziko-matematicheskikh shkolakh pri gosuniversitetakh* (Novosibirsk, 1972), 24. (Author's abstract of thesis.)
38   Owen and Watson, *loc. cit.*
39   'Novyi priem v ZMSh', *Matematika v shkole,* 1973, no. 1, 95.
40   Torpedov, *loc. cit.*
41   'Novyi priem . . .', *loc. cit.*
42   Torpedov, *loc. cit.*
43   *Istoriya matematicheskogo obrazovaniya v SSSR* (Kiev, 1975), 74. With this rather small output, however, it is possible that the Ukrainians had recruited more rigorously.
44   'Institut pomogaet . . .', *loc. cit.*
45   Literat, *loc. cit.* (1969); Owen and Watson, *loc. cit.*
46   Stoletov, *loc. cit.*

Chapter 11
Olympiads

Origins and Development

In 1960, it will be recalled, Academician M.A. Lavrent'ev, Chairman of the Siberian Section of the USSR Academy of Sciences and founder of the famous science city of Akademgorodok, then under construction, voiced his concern about the supply of cadres of scientists and engineers, especially in the new branches of technology. He criticized the rates of training and stressed that research scientists should develop much closer links with *vuzy* and that the latter should become much more involved with the schools, thus ensuring more effective selection of the best young recruits. A means to this end which Lavrent'ev singled out was all-Union olympiads or academic competitions, with large-scale preparation by correspondence.[1]

Olympiads on an all-Union basis, except by correspondence, were not to start until 1967, but the idea of such intellectual contests was nothing new. The first, in mathematics, had been organized in 1934 by the University of Leningrad,[2] on the initiative of B.N. Delone, a Corresponding Member of the Academy of Sciences, and the second the following year in Moscow.[3] After the war there were ventures in the Union republics: in Moldavia, for example, a mathematics olympiad inaugurated in 1949 by Kishinev University was initiated in other towns and this developed into an all-republic competition in 1957; in 1953 a physics olympiad for the whole republic was instituted in Lithuania.[4] By the time that Lavrent'ev wrote, the olympiads, mostly in mathematics and physics but also in such subjects as astronomy, geography and history, had spread widely in and beyond the USSR, sponsored by local *vuzy,* usually on a two-round basis and with separate competitions for the top three or four classes. They were of proven worth in the selecting of talented young people, but the nature of the questions set varied from one district to another.[5] Their effectiveness would clearly be enhanced if they were expanded and put on a systematic nationwide footing.

Lavrent'ev's article was followed by rapid developments along these lines. In 1961 the First All-Russian Mathematics Olympiad, in which Moscow State University (MGU) played a leading role, attracted hundreds of thousands of participants,[6] including teams from other republics. Subsequently Academician I. Tamm, taking up the theme of the need to identify and exploit youthful talent, called for the extension of the MGU experience in organizing mathematics, physics and chemistry olympiads to other *vuzy* and other subjects.[7] Lavrent'ev himself was instrumental in establishing the First All-Siberian Mathematics and Physics Olympiad in 1962,[8] to which a competition in chemistry was added two years later.[9] Academician Sobolev considered the Siberian Olympiad to be rather different from traditional ones, which were more of a sporting than a scientific character and as a rule only covered the large towns.[10] The year 1963 saw the inception of the All-Russian Physics Olympiad, under the joint auspices of the Moscow Institute of Physics and Technology and the Faculty of Physics at MGU.[11] An All-Union Correspondence Olympiad in mathematics and science was set up, serving also as an alternative to the first two rounds of the All-Russian Olympiad;[12] in the 1966/67 school year the latter was reorganized as the First All-Union Olympiad, held in mathematics, physics and chemistry.[13]

Aims of the Olympiads

The Statute on the All-Russian Mathematics and Physics Olympiad, issued in November 1963 and approved jointly by the Union and RSFSR Ministries of Higher Education, the RSFSR Ministry of Education and the Central Committee of Komsomol, listed the main aims of the competition. It was to increase interest in mathematics and physics among wide circles of pupils, raise the quality of mathematics and physics teaching, serve as the culmination of the work of extracurricular study groups and lecture courses for interested pupils, help young people to choose their specialism, detect the most capable ones and attract them to the leading *vuzy*.[14] In the document the masses were mentioned first and the 'strongest' last, though in the light of contemporary pronouncements there is little doubt as to where priorities then lay; the universities were anxious to find entrants of superior calibre.

Indeed, a report on the First All-Union Olympiad unambiguously ascribes to olympiads the main role in the selection of gifted young people.[15] However, over the next few years what might be termed the more egalitarian functions of these contests were increasingly stressed. As misgivings about the concept of special provision for academically gifted children again surfaced here and there, so did the performance (though seldom the principle) of the olympiads come under closer scrutiny.

The above-mentioned aims had been anticipated, and were to be elaborated, by a goodly number of contributors to the press. Here, in respect of such comment, we shall not distinguish between the major olympiads, since there was no disparity of purpose. Indeed, in many respects they apply also to the multitude of other olympiads. On the question of talent-spotting, career orientation and *vuz* recruitment it was felt, according to Ilya Fonyakov, that the existing system of competitive entrance examinations to higher education did not guarantee that pupils gifted in a given subject would present themselves for examination.[16] At this point, knowing the prestige of higher education and the pressure on places in the USSR, and aware of candidates' propensity to lead with their strongest suit, the reader may well pause in surprise; but Fonyakov goes on to mention late developers and probably also has in mind young people in remote areas. The olympiads were intended to discover these, and most of the really outstanding ones were to be groomed for higher education by advanced training at the specialized boarding schools.

However, the detection of talent was not perceived solely in quantitative terms. It was not just a matter of finding as many clever children as possible; the nature of their cleverness was even more important. To cope with complicated but familiar tasks was not enough. One must go beyond knowledge to reasoning power, and beyond reasoning power to creative ingenuity (*nakhodchivost'*). Inventiveness and innovation require hard logic, but also a certain flair. Problems were therefore to be set which would help to show not only whether a contestant could think logically but also whether he was capable of taking an unorthodox and independent path in his quest for the solution.[17]

The olympiads were also meant to improve teaching standards in the subjects concerned. Academician I.K. Kikoin, the physicist, who had been associated with these competitions since their inception, in an interview mentioned three ways in which this was achieved: weak spots in teaching were pinpointed, teachers were compelled to develop and in the towns where the olympiad was held they were keen to show their schools in the best light. In particular the contests exposed a gap between theory and practice: even the victors felt awkward in the laboratories, were inaccurate and had no feeling for the experiment.[18] Reports on the olympiads tend to be critical of participants' performance in practicals, and sometimes to blame teachers who regard such work as a formality.[19] One commentator, however, sees an improvement which he ascribes to the newly-introduced optional courses and the revitalization of extracurricular work,[20] which itself may be closely geared to preparation for these contests, as will presently be seen. The vastness of pupil involvement in the early stages must have wide-scale repercussions on the teaching; Kikoin thought that pupils might ask for help in solving problems previously set, and their teachers too would need to ponder on them.[21]

In recent years, one gathers, this has been truer than ever. Writing in *Pravda,* two eminent Novosibirsk academics, one much involved with the maths and physics boarding school and the other head of the NGU Department of Education, stressed that the new secondary school syllabuses resulting from the movement to reform the curriculum in the sixties required both a wider and a deeper knowledge of one's subject than the pedagogical institutes had hitherto provided, as well as a basically different approach. Older teachers might be out of touch, and often younger ones were ill-acquainted with scientific developments and incapable of solving olympiad problems. The remedy lay in advanced in-service training and college courses combining subject and method.[22]

To the extent that olympiads induce teachers to update their knowledge and skills, and training institutions respond to pleas to furnish the wherewithal, it is clear that many more children than actually take part in the competitions will enjoy the benefits which thus indirectly accrue. The olympiads themselves, however, not infrequently have a mass role ascribed to them. A commentator on the Fourth All-Russian Olympiad put this point cogently:

> Representatives of educational establishments and science centres who regard the aim of the olympiads solely as the selection of 'talents' for *vuzy* are wrong. Talents must grow. The precondition for this is to inspire the mass of pupils with an interest in study and knowledge and to develop the mathematical abilities of all children.[23]

Another writer was thinking on similar lines when he summarized the purpose of olympiads under two headings: to stimulate pupils showing definite talents and interests, but also to promote the development of cognitive interests in pupils, *especially in those in whom they had not yet been revealed.*[24]

It is not surprising that this equalizing function of the olympiads came to be applied in particular to the perennial problem of the urban-rural gap. At one extreme, they were seen as the means to give all children, irrespective of where they lived, equality of opportunity for selection for, and admission to, the maths and physics boarding school at Akademgorodok,[25] and no doubt to those elsewhere. At the other, they were regarded as a challenge which highlighted the disadvantaged situation of many country children and manifested the need for special measures to enable them to cope with the contest itself,[26] let alone what might lie beyond. In general, it was hoped that the olympiads would be an effective means of starting to bring budding or hidden talents to full flowering, however sequestered the spot where they were discovered. How far the hope was justified will be discussed below.

The Major Olympiads: Organizational Aspects and Procedures

Let us now consider what steps were taken in pursuit of these goals; and we begin not with the olympiads themselves but with the extensive programme of preparatory work to which they were meant to serve as the climax. Far from being isolated one-off entities, they were planned as the culmination of a systematic series of lectures and extracurricular activities in the subject. Together all these events were to form a strong basis for further successful study.[27] Subject circles in schools, at Pioneer Palaces and at higher educational institutions, and such organizations as the Young People's Mathematics Schools and the All-Union Mathematics Correspondence Schools, described in the previous chapter, provide the context of such preparation.

According to the statute of 1963, the former All-Russian Mathematics and Physics Olympiad was to be run by a Central Organizing Committee consisting of representatives of the RSFSR Ministry of Education, the RSFSR and USSR Ministries of Higher Education, the country's leading *vuzy,* the USSR Academy of Sciences and the Central Committee of Komsomol.[28] Although certain eminent scientists had been leading lights in the olympiad movement, hitherto the two latter bodies had not been formally included in the committee; their addition suggests that the contests were now seen to have an increasingly important role both scientifically and politically. Since the Olympiad has been mounted on an all-Union basis, the USSR Ministry of Education has taken over from the RSFSR Ministry; the All-Union Central Council of Railways, which has its own schools, the Academy of Pedagogical Sciences and the 'Znanie' Society are also involved.[29]

The All-Union (formerly All-Russian) Olympiads consist of four rounds. In 1963 the initial round was held in the schools, in January; the teachers set the problems and marked the pupils' work. In maths, all pupils in forms 5 (11-plus entry) and upwards were entitled to take part if they so wished, and, in physics, all in forms 7 (13-plus) and above. Pupils at specialized secondary schools, which train medium technicians, were also eligible to participate,[30] but there is no evidence that they did so very widely. Presumably to encourage schools with inadequate resources and to achieve a degree of homogeneity in standards, All-Union Correspondence Olympiads were established in physics and mathematics, and subsequently in chemistry and biology. These are also open to students at specialized secondary schools, young workers and members of the armed forces.[31] In the autumn the problems are published in the press, and solutions have to be sent to the main universities by the beginning of December.[32]

The second round is for winners of the internal school olympiads. (According to the 1963 statute, victors in the correspondence contests were likewise permitted to take part, but they normally enter at the stage of round three.[33]) Held in February on a district basis, or on a town basis for towns not divided into districts, the second round is administered by a local organizing committee of teachers and representatives of the local education authority, higher and specialized secondary educational institutions, and the Komsomol committee. In normal Soviet fashion, coordination and supervision are effected through the agency of a representative of the similar committee at regional level, which in turn includes a member of the national committee. Such organizations as trades unions and methodological centres are also represented on the regional committees.[34]

The third round, at the level of regions, territories, autonomous republics and cities independent of regional jurisdiction, admits winners both of round two and of correspondence olympiads. Ministry of Railways schools also participate and teams consist of not less than five members.[35] The state pays pupils' expenses, but not, apparently, those of winners of the correspondence contests.[36] To facilitate contact with the grassroots, the RSFSR was divided for Olympiad purposes into three zones, where the management of the arrangements was respectively in the hands of Leningrad, Moscow and Novosibirsk Universities. Academic members of the Central Organizing Committee travel out to the regional centres to assist in the actual conduct of the Olympiads, thus helping to ensure uniform standards. They also use the occasion to give lectures to the pupils.[37] In recent years regional Physics Olympiads have begun to include practicals in some areas.[38] The costs of rounds two and three are met respectively by the district and regional education authorities.[39]

The fourth and final round used to be held in Moscow in late April. In 1965 each region and parallel administrative unit sent a team of nine members (including three for the Chemistry Olympiad), as did the other Union republics. According to the 1963 statute, each team was to be accompanied by a leader (usually a teacher, but sometimes an inspector, methodologist or lecturer) who was a member of the regional committee and had first to present a written report on the third round, with work by the winners appended, otherwise the team would be disqualified.[40]

With the advent of the All-Union Olympiads, the venue came to vary between subjects. The second in the series (1968) was held in Erevan (physics), Vilnius (chemistry) and Leningrad (mathematics). Teams now comprised four contestants per subject and the umbrella had been opened wider to accommodate three (from 1971, two) teams from schools under the authority of the Ministry of Railways, 31 Olympiad winners from six specialized maths and physics boarding schools, and 32 from the First All-Union Olympiad.[41] In 1970 separate teams were also expected from the capitals of the Union republics and also the schools of the Chief Political Directorate of the Soviet Army and Navy.[42] The following year Moscow, Leningrad and the cities where the final round would be held were invited to furnish *two* teams, but overall at this stage the team size was reduced to three.[43] Latterly the whole basis of the final round has been drastically altered, but a consideration of this is best left until a full picture has been drawn and the good points and blemishes of its subject identified.

The questions in round four are set by a 'jury' of scientists from universities and research institutes. The biters may themselves be bitten. In addition to the contest itself, it is customary for a supporting programme of excursions, lectures and question-answer sessions (*konsul'tatsii*) to be arranged, the whole thing taking up to a week. At one of these sessions a young lecturer questioned by form 8 entrants said it was like being in a tigers' cage.[44] On another occasion the academics were floored by several of the questions, since they concerned problems not yet solved by modern science. When the time for the written competitions comes, the pupils sit in one room and their teachers in another, and both are given the problems at the same time. The teachers are often up in arms about the difficulty: 'Do you take them for Mendeleevs?' they ask. Yet they underestimate their pupils, many of whom are clearly quite formidable.[45]

Various ways of organizing the final round have been tried out. In 1968, for the first time, the Mathematics Olympiad was conducted in two stages, problem-solving and then a *viva voce*. Candidates were given five problems and five hours in which to solve them, but each solution had to be defended in personal discussion with members of the jury.[46] The forward-looking Leningrad City Maths Olympiad had had a final oral stage for over ten years.[47] The following year, however, the oral contest was dropped in favour of a second written one, the participants thus having to deal with a total of six problems.[48] In 1970, reportedly to exclude any element of chance, there seems to have been a double written round, consisting of ten problems to be tackled in two 4-hour sessions, for form 10 pupils, while for the others it was voluntary.[49]

The year 1971 saw further innovation in the final mathematics round. Pupils in form 9 were invited to try their intellectual strength at any one of three research problems, in the fields of geometry, functional analysis, or cybernetics. They were not expected to reach a final solution in five hours, but it was felt that modern research would be attractive to them and serve as a complex test of the entire extent of their knowledge. The experiment, it was later claimed, had proved to be fully justified; by finishing time five of the contestants had investigated all three problems approximately to the extent of the knowledge of members of the jury.[50]

In 1968 and 1969 the Physics Olympiad comprised two parts, the first theoretical, with four or five questions, and the second practical, with an oral defence component.[51] The next year the arrangements seem to have been different again, though information is sparse: 'two stages, first a colloquium, after which only 200 out of 680 will be admitted to the second stage'.[52] In 1971 an eliminating theoretical stage (five problems in five hours for forms 9 and 10, four in four in the case of form 8) was followed by a practical session (five hours, one problem and a supplementary one for those who coped with it) for the top 28 per cent, *i.e.* those who had solved no fewer than half the theoretical problems, and finally those who had done well in both rounds were interviewed individually.[53]

The final round of the Chemistry Olympiad also consists of written work followed by practicals. In 1970, for example, the theoretical session was allotted four hours in the case of forms 8 and 9, and five for form 10. Ten problems were set, of varying difficulty. Hardly anyone completed them all, but that did not matter, as quality ranked higher than quantity. This arrangement was subsequently quoted as a model, since each participant could show his abilities more accurately than in the Mathematics Olympiad with its uniformly difficult problems.[54]

All competitors receive a commemorative badge and book presents; the winners are awarded diplomas and special book prizes provided by the Soviet Ministry of Education, the 'Znanie' Society and organizations in the Olympiad towns. The high-powered maths and physics magazine for young people, *Kvant* (see below), has instituted a prize for the best young physicist. Winners from form 10 receive recommendations to a *vuz*;[55] in addition, those who win the top three prizes are exempted from the *vuz* entrance examinations.[56] For years advocates of the Olympiads had been urging that winners should receive priority when applying to *vuzy*, and this should have the support of the law.[57] There was concern that certain meritorious candidates who had distinguished themselves in Olympiads were not securing admission 'because of the stereotyped calculation of marks in all subjects'.[58] Very little had in fact been achieved in this direction; in 1969 it was claimed that it was much more difficult to become an Olympiad prizewinner than to get a gold medal, yet although gold medals secured priority for applicants to higher education, 'recommendations' carried no legal weight.[59] The point was well made: gold medals, which are awarded at the discretion of individual schools to senior pupils with excellent records in work and conduct, had just acquired this enhanced status. Nevertheless, one would be surprised if, other things being equal, *vuz* authorities were not swift to take appropriate action on candidates with Olympiad successes to their credit; indeed, the 1963 statute had mentioned this.[60] Younger stars have a good chance of admission to one of the special boarding schools, and the teachers who have trained the champions are themselves rewarded with diplomas.[61]

Recruitment to the maths and physics boarding schools (FMSh) attached to Novosibirsk State University (NGU) is a major, perhaps the major, objective of the All-Siberian Olympiad. Because of worldwide interest in the establishment and activities of the 'science city' at Akademgorodok, the All-Siberian Olympiad has received almost as much publicity as the All-Union one of which it is now a component; along with similarities it has certain special features and to some extent has pursued its own course.

The All-Siberian Olympiad is intended for all the regions and territories of Siberia and the Far East; since 1966 it has also catered for the Central Asian republics and Kazakhstan. Since its foundation (maths and physics in 1962, chemistry in 1964), it has always consisted of two eliminating rounds followed by a third in the setting of a summer camp. The first is a correspondence round, publicized through the press and by posters, for pupils in forms 6 to 10. The second, part written and part oral, is at regional level, and since the mid-1960s winners of the RSFSR district rounds have also been admitted to it. Representatives of the Siberian Section of the Academy of Sciences travel out in pairs — a mathematician and a physicist — to the regional centres to interview the children and conduct practice sessions, and the best contestants, some 600 of them from forms 7 to 9, are selected for the Academy's summer school at Akademgorodok.[62] The importance attached by the Academy to the competition is manifest in the fact that it meets the children's fares and maintenance for round three; indeed it used to do so for round two as well,[63] but, presumably with the growing institutionalization of the Olympiad, this part of the costs has been taken over by the education authorities.[64]

The young people stay for about a month at a tented lakeside camp with the usual excursions, club activities, sports competitions and singing round the campfire. What is unusual is that they have four hours of lectures and practicals a day as well and are visited by scientists, some extremely distinguished, who give them talks and lead discussions; they also tour the institutes of the Siberian Section. At the end of the stay the third round of the Olympiad is held, again written and oral, and it is from this that the Novosibirsk FMSh recruits into forms 8, 9 or 10 the majority of its pupils, about three in five of the contestants, whilst many of the older ones are admitted on examination to NGU.[65] In 1969 it was said that over half the student intake into that university's physics and mathematics-and-mechanics faculties had been former Olympiad participants.[66] Over 100 NGU students, nearly all of them ex-FMSh pupils, help on a voluntary basis to run the correspondence and regional contests and the same number are involved in organizing the summer school.[67] The top pupils at the camp go on in due course to the finals of the All-Russian Olympiad.[68]

Like the All-Union Olympiad, the All-Siberian competition has its own particular fund of anecdotes. Academician Lavrent'ev tells the delightful story of Boris Tsikanovsky, a boy of about 11 from Sakhalin who came to the summer camp and tackled the papers for the senior forms. While the others were still hard at work, he brought up his paper to the invigilator. ' "What's this?" said the invigilator in surprise. "It's the problems", said the boy, "I've done them". "You? Finished them? Already?" "Yes", said the boy, "I've done them all".' The astonished invigilator told him to go and sit down. Half an hour later the boy was back again with another sheet of paper. ' "And what's this?" asked the invigilator, even more surprised. "This is an alternative way of solving all five problems." ' Such an extraordinary performance called for an extraordinary assessment, and the boy was given 50 marks out of 25.[69] The scientists kept in touch with him and when he was old enough he entered the FMSh and became a distinguished young chemist.[70]

The Major Olympiads: Problems and Criticisms

How many young people take part in the All-Union and All-Siberian Olympiads? Details on the former and its forebears are fragmentary, but they do give an idea of the evolution of the competition from a local into a national event involving hundreds of thousands of participants. (See Table 11.1). The series for the Siberian zone shows signs of stabilization after the admission of district olympiad winners to the regional round in 1965. (See Table 11.2). However, the Siberian table does not reveal the more recent decline in the correspondence round, nor does either table illustrate what percentage of young people in the relevant age-groups are directly involved. Figures for total participants, where available, are unsuitable for use because of the possibility of double or even treble counting. Ideally one would like to base such calculations on an initial round which clearly had an eliminating role and catered for a clearly defined area, without alternative olympiads; such desiderata, however, do not coexist. Even if in desperation one takes the Siberian figure of 12,000 for round two in or about 1972 and correlates it with an estimated total number of pupils in forms 7 to 10 in Siberia and the Far East alone (say 1,700,000), obtaining a result of 0.7 per cent, one still does not know what allowance should have been made for pupils in form 6 and those from other regions of the RSFSR, Kazakhstan and Central Asia.

This brings us nevertheless to the most crucial of a number of problems concerning the major olympiads: they are failing to draw in participants on the massive scale originally envisaged. This may be due to a variety of reasons or a combination of them: inadequate publicity; disparity between the standard of the questions set and the level of teaching in understaffed and poorly equipped schools, especially in rural areas; lack of contact between higher and secondary education; and suspicion on the part of schools. Thus they have been criticized both by those who wish to scour the length and breadth of the land so that no village Lomonosov may go undetected, and by those who placed their hopes in them as an effective means of enhancing the mathematics and science education of all children wherever it might be found wanting.

Of course, as with any project of this organizational magnitude, teething troubles were to be expected. A picture of the scale of the operation and of the concomitant difficulties appeared over the co-signature of Academician Lavrent'ev in 1964 in connection with the Third All-Siberian Olympiad, which, it was claimed, was in danger of being wrecked. At the beginning of February the questions had been distributed to all secondary schools in Siberia and the Far East and to all education offices from regional level downwards.

TABLE 11.1 Selected Moscow, All-Russian and All-Union Olympiads

Date	Description	Subject(s)	Participants in rounds: 1	2	3	4	Total participants
1948a	11th Moscow	M	800		n.a.	n.a.	
1953a	16th Moscow	M	1350	517	n.a.	n.a.	
1956b	19th Moscow	M	1120	478	n.a.	n.a.	
1961c	1st All-Russian	M					25,000-
1963d	3rd All-Russian	M, P				300	
1964e	4th All-Russian	M, P				300+	1,500,000+
1968f	2nd All-Union	M, P, C				1677	
1969g	3rd All-Union	M, P, C				1900±	
1975h	9th All-Union	M, P, C				428*	
1977i	11th All-Union	M, P, C				424*	

Notes:

M	mathematics
P	physics
C	chemistry
n.a.	not applicable
*	on revised basis

Sources:

a B.V. Gnedenko, 'Mathematical Education in the USSR', *American Mathematical Monthly*, vol. 64 (1957), 396.

b D. Panov, 'Science and Socialism', *Current Digest of the Soviet Press*, vol. X (1958), 6 (translated from *Kommunist*, 1958, no. 1); Izaak Wirszup, 'The School Mathematics Circle and Olympiads at Moscow State University', *Mathematics Teacher*, vol. LVI (1963), no. 4, 205.

c G. Vovchenko, 'Zdes' "arifmeticheskii podschet" ne goditsya', *Pravda*, 24 February 1964; but Wirszup (*op. cit.*, 196) gives 'hundreds of thousands'.

d A. Kolmogorov, 'Poisk talanta', *Izvestiya*, 7 April 1963.

e V. Popov, 'Olimpiada smekalistikh', *Pravda*, 18 April 1964; I. Petrakov, 'Olimpiady shkol'nikov', *Narodnoe obrazovanie*, 1965, no. 1, 125.

f 'Vtoraya Vsesoyuznaya olimpiada shkol'nikov', *Narodnoe obrazovanie*, 1969, no. 2, 123.

g 'Kto eti trinadtsat'?', *Uch. gaz.*, 3 April 1969.

h Z. Svirel'shchikova, 'Itogi Vsesoyuznoi olimpiady', *Uch. gaz.*, 22 May 1975.

i V. Gorelov, 'Odinnadtsataya Vsesoyuznaya', *Uch. gaz.*, 16 August 1977.

TABLE 11.2 All-Siberian Olympiads

Date	Description	Subjects	Participants in rounds:			Accepted for FMSh
			1	2	3	
1962	1st	M, P	1,500	600	250	84
1963	2nd	M, P	2,500	1,000	380	218
1964	3rd	M, P, C	5,000[1]	1,500	650	420
1965	4th	M, P, C	7,000	10,000[2]	750	330
1966[3]	5th	M, P, C	6,500	11,000[2]	650	250[4]
1967	6th	M, P, C	6,000	11,000	650	200
1972(?)	11th	M, P, C	n.s.	12,000-	600-700	n.s.

Notes: Total participants nowhere stated.   n.s.   not stated

M   mathematics   P   physics   C   chemistry

Numerical footnotes from original (1962-1967):

1   of which 2500 letters from the European part were forwarded to other FMShs
2   including winners of district olympiads
3   for the Eastern Zone (*i.e.* including Kazakhstan and the Central Asian republics — J.D.)
4   excluding rural recruitment into form 8
     There are variants, but none of much significance except for 1963: Round 1, 1,400 (S. Literat, 'Novosibirskaya matematicheskaya', *Uch. gaz.*, 17 October 1963; A.A. Bers and B.A. Frolov, *Olimpiada — pervyi shag v nauku* (Novosibirsk, 1964), 6); and Round 2,000 (*ibid.*).

Sources: 1962-1967: S.I. Literat, 'Vyyavlyat' i razvivat' sposobnosti', *Sovetskaya pedagogika*, 1969, no. 4, 79. 1972 (?): *Id., Problemy otbora i obucheniya v spetsializirovannykh fiziko-matematicheskikh shkolakh pri gosuniversitetakh* (Novosibirsk, 1972), 7.

Simultaneously they had been sent for publication to regional party and youth papers. These materials went to 2,000 addresses. Now, however, with two weeks to go to the end of round one, hundreds of letters were pouring daily into Akademgorodok asking if the Olympiad was to be held and where the problems could be obtained. Despite telegrams to regional party committee secretaries, newspaper editors and directors of education, in many areas the questions remained unpublished.[71] As Table 11.2 shows, the eventual response was nevertheless well up on the previous year; but the figures are complicated by the introduction of a competition in chemistry, and half the replies appear to have come from European Russia, which the All-Siberian Olympiad was not designed to serve.

Five years later the situation remained problematical. The maximum number of participants in the correspondence round of the All-Siberian Olympiad did not exceed 0.2 per cent of the pupils in forms 6 to 10, and the sources were still felt to be largely untapped.[72] In 1968 only 24 of the 572 finalists (4.2 per cent) in the All-Union Mathematics Olympiad had come from rural areas;[73] for 1969 the respective figures were 85 out of 660 (12.9 per cent),[74] and for 1972, 77 out of 564 (13.7 per cent)[75] — better, but not yet satisfactory. Rural children accounted for 1 per cent of the ordinary prizewinners in 1972 and 4 per cent in 1973, whereas urban pupils (excluding those at FMShs) comprised 77 per cent and 80 per cent respectively.[76] In a newspaper interview Academician Kikoin attributed the imbalance to the standard of teaching and lack of equipment in country schools, and said it was being debated whether every region should be compelled to include one rural child in its team; this would help country children to get much more attention. Also, as olympiad questions and worked solutions were published in journals not always available to children, the USSR Academy of Sciences and the Academy of Pedagogical Sciences planned to produce for them a new physics and maths magazine, *Kvant (Quantum)*, which would keep them up to date.[77] The former proposal was not adopted, but *Kvant* is now a going concern, and important enough for bundles of back numbers to be seen occasionally on the counters of Moscow's second-hand bookshops.

The frequent reluctance of good teachers to go and work in remoter areas meant not only relatively lower standards of compulsory subject teaching but also inadequate regular provision of academic out-of-school activities and optional studies. In 1968 it was claimed that options should have been the answer to the problem, but in many schools they were still not 'held in esteem'.[78] This was not the only reason for their slow growth — often the pupils were too few to form a group. In such circumstances the means of preparing these disadvantaged children were twofold: correspondence schools and summer camps (not the famous ones linked to the final rounds of olympiads, but less sophisticated ones which would train and encourage pupils to take part in the district competitions). Much depended on the initiative and enthusiasm of higher educational institutions and their willingness to work with the schools. An example of what might be done was reported from Perm' Region: the University of Perm' ran a correspondence school for the children of Komi-Permyak National Territory, and for several years summer maths camps had been held for pupils of forms 7 to 10, staffed by teachers, lecturers and students; those involved were convinced that they should be set up for other subjects too.[79] Special in-service training for rural teachers was another suggestion.[80]

In the early days, at least, the olympiad organizers apparently had to contend with suspicions on the part of some schools, and lacked support at the local level. In one instance the director persistently deterred the children from making the trip to compete in round two by threatening to write their names down for truancy. Why? 'Perhaps it was a false idea of responsibility to higher authority', who, he thought, would say, ' "You've let all the talents go out of the district, now you've nobody to blame but yourself." '[81] Too much importance ought not to be attached to this as no other evidence of it has been found, but it has the ring of truth about it; it is perfectly human for teachers to resent their abler children being creamed off (though fear of the local education office in a country where the brain-drain from rural areas contributes to a serious socio-economic problem suggests pressures quite unfamiliar to the English reader.) At the opposite extreme, fame is the spur for certain teachers, whose pursuit of prestige has led to cramming.[82]

As far as the All-Siberian Olympiad is concerned, dissatisfaction has continued to be expressed with the coverage of pupils from villages, workers' settlements and small towns. Table 11.2 shows a decline in the correspondence round from 1965 to 1967, and in 1972 this was described as systematic; in the past few years it had virtually disappeared.[83] No official reasons for this surprising situation have been located, but as the regional round has evidently well exceeded the correspondence round in terms of entrants since 1965 and has retained its popularity, the conclusion is that the latter round has been deemed to present insufficient return on investment and the former has largely taken over its initial eliminating role.

It is only fair to point out that this picture of urban-rural disparity in olympiad participation is not replicated in every Soviet republic. In Azerbaidzhan, at any rate, two in three of the republic's 1972 Maths Olympiad entrants in each of its three rounds were from rural areas, although town and country children in the relevant age-groups at that time must have formed roughly equal proportions. This is impressive. The total number of participants, urban and rural, in round one, 35,000, probably comprised about 13 per cent of young people in the relevant school years.[84] One suspects that these figures are atypically high. Comparable data, however, are not readily available for other republics, although the Moldavians expressed dissatisfaction with their rural coverage in the previous year.[85]

Another kind of inequality is evidenced in the olympiads, but, interestingly, it does not appear to be a burning issue as far as the organizers are concerned, since no discussion has been noticed, and it has been left to American commentators to draw attention to it. The competitions have always attracted far fewer girls than boys. In the 19th Moscow Maths Olympiad of 1956, girls formed only 21 per cent of the entrants to round one, 15 per cent of those to round two, 14 per cent of those who passed, and 20 per cent of those who obtained certificates of merit.[86] More recently, one girl from Tashkent is mentioned among the prizewinners of the 1968 All-Union Maths Olympiad,[87] but there are none among those of the 1970 Maths and Chemistry Olympiads or the 1971 Chemistry Olympiad.[88] A very detailed list of the best individuals in the 1971 Physics Olympiad includes not a single girl among the 25 names.[89] The absence of critical references to this suggests that it has generally been regarded as unexceptional; it would seem to form a silent comment on Soviet sexual stereotyping. This is tantamount to what Krutetsky, the psychologist, means when he attributes girls' frequent lack of interest in mathematics to tradition, upbringing, and the notion of professions as masculine or feminine.[90]

Yet we must not leap to conclusions, for 1972 may have been a modest turning point. In that year girls accounted for 15.8 per cent of the finalists in the All-Union Maths Olympiad and on the evidence of the published lists it is calculated that they comprised about 4 per cent of the prizewinners (1973: likewise 4 per cent). In 1972 the three girl prizewinners also received *special* prizes by virtue of their sex, and in 1973 three such awards were again presented specifically to girls: to the most successful girl from a rural area and to those obtaining the best results or winning an All-Union prize for the third time.[91] True, girls were markedly under-represented, but the special prizes suggest a new awareness. At the 1973 All-Union Physics Olympiad also, a special prize was awarded 'for the best result among the girls'.[92] In a report on the 1975 All-Union Olympiads no fewer than five girls are mentioned for distinguished performances, whereas no boys at all are named except the youngest prizewinners.[93] This even more may betoken a new departure, an effort to boost the role of girls in these contests and encourage others to follow.|

The olympiads have been criticized not only for their failure to draw in generally but also for their failure to select efficiently. This is said to be particularly true of the correspondence (school) round, which is inherently unsystematic, not least because the teachers' notions about their pupils may prevent the most competent from being selected.[94] It was noticed, in connection with the Akademgorodok FMSh entrance examinations, that teachers might sometimes nominate well-disciplined plodders rather than bright but lazy or mischievous children. One can well believe that the idle and naughty may not have received much encouragement to enter the Olympiad competition either, given the importance attached by the Soviet school to hard work and good behaviour.[95] But at the opposite end of the contest errors were also made, which necessitated some pupils' withdrawing from the FMSh, and this too the deputy director attributed to the selection process.[96]

Another problem has been to draw up a satisfactory set of rules for the game and to ensure adherence to them. Amendments to the statute on the All-Union Olympiad and other regulations have been introduced fairly often, and news of this may be slow to percolate to some areas of the vast country. Too few teams or too many members may turn up.[97] But a more searching question is whether or not FMShs should be represented. At the Second All-Union Maths Olympiad (1968) 23 of the 31 FMSh representatives went home with a prize. Far more pupils from these schools, it was said, were worthy to be 'Olympians'; perhaps they should have special competitions, requiring much and large in representation.[98] Perhaps the thought was also present that this would give the rank and file a better chance.[99] A report of the Fifth All-Union Maths Olympiad criticizes this attitude and rejects the proposal[100] and the FMShs continue to send their teams, on the same footing as the regions.[101] FMSh pupils contributed 17 prizewinners (or 22 per cent, from five schools) in 1972, and 15 (16 per cent, from four) in 1973. (Novosibirsk was apparently not represented). This is still considerable, but other urban schools, particularly, no doubt, maths secondary schools in the major cities, provide growing competition.[102]

The content of the olympiads has also been criticized. The All-Union Maths Olympiad of 1970 was alleged to have been too hard, causing diffidence in the pupils and thus being educationally dubious.[103] Although they are supposed to detect imagination and creativity in the young people as well as logical thought, it has been claimed that they do not always fulfil this role. Sometimes they merely check received knowledge (which, as Academician Belyaev has pointed out, is to the particular disadvantage of rural children).[104] There should, then, be greater care in setting the problems, to ensure that they are a test of creative ingenuity. In 1971 it was felt that the Academy of Pedagogical Sciences should do more to help.[105]

It was mentioned above that the Union republics conduct their own olympiads, and send their prizewinners to the all-Union final.[106] Until recent years all regions, territories, autonomous republics, non-regionalized Union republics and the latter's capitals were eligible, along with various other categories, to send a three-man team. Because of the highly diversified administrative structure of the USSR and the great differences in size among the constituent republics, this principle meant, assuming an even distribution of talent across the population, that the two largest republics had an unduly high chance of winning prizes. Of the 500 or so participants from the fifteen republics it is estimated that the RSFSR, with some 70 major administrative units, let alone special provision for Moscow and Leningrad teams, was eligible to send about 225 representatives and the Ukraine some 75. Thus in the final round of the 1971 All-Union Physics Olympiad (see Table 11.3) the RSFSR could have provided up to 45 per cent of the candidates but it was awarded nearly 53 per cent of the diplomas and certificates; the Ukraine could have fielded about 15 per cent of the contestants but it won 23 per cent. Although in the RSFSR's case the share of honours was closely correlated to the estimated percentage of pupils in the relevant forms, and in that sense fair, the Ukraine did disproportionately well. Whether these proportions have been inflated by more effective teaching and superior publicity is uncertain, but quite possible. If we take the two republics which are middle-sized in terms of their schoolgoing population, it appears that Kazakhstan with potentially 11.6 per cent of the contestants won 5.4 per cent of the awards, and the comparable figure for Uzbekistan are some 7 per cent and 3 per cent. The Central Asian republics were certainly likely to be outdone by the Baltic countries with their well-developed academic tradition and 11-year course; the most striking contrast is presented by Turkmenia, which could have provided 3 per cent of the competitors but won no awards at all and obtained a mere three points, and little Estonia with a maximum of 1.2 per cent of the participants, over 3 per cent of the prizes and the top score of 22 points.

Such considerations put flesh on the dry bones of the USSR Ministry of Education announcement about revision of the rules as from 1975.[107] The involvement of teams from all regions in the final round, it said, was not justified by the results: the role of the republic olympiads was demeaned, and the teams proved to be extremely unequal, *e.g.* the physics practicals were usually not completed by more than one in four participants.[108] Doubtless certain republics were likely to be demoralized by the conspicuous insuccess of their ablest 'Olympians' in a wider stadium, and the regional representation meant that large numbers were doomed to disappointment, particularly from the RSFSR.

So it was decided that for the final round the Union republics, Moscow, Leningrad, the Chief Directorate of the Soviet Army and Navy and the Ministry of Railways should each provide one team. These teams were to vary in broad accordance with the number of pupils in the republic: RSFSR, 43; Ukraine, 12; Belorussia, Kazakhstan and Uzbekistan, 6; and the remaining teams, 3. As Table 11.3 shows, the former scheme, whether by accident or design, was already quite fairly geared in percentage terms to pupil numbers in the relevant school years, except that Kazakhstan and Turkmenia were apparently over-represented. In absolute terms, however, the new arrangements promised to be much more satisfactory; nothing had been said about reducing the number of awards, and nominations for the final round would be considerably more selective. Thus pupils who reached the final stage would in general enjoy greater prospects of success, while the increased competition for the honour should add lustre to the previous round. The results of the 1975 All-Union Olympiads vindicated the changes: selection for the final round had been more rigorous, yet 309 out of 428 contestants (in all three subjects) were awarded diplomas and certificates, and hardly any of the work earned zero marks.[109]

Popularity and Prospects

Despite their difficulties and imperfections, some remedied and others not, there seems little doubt that the olympiads have enjoyed much popularity and made a sizeable contribution to the stimulation of children's interest in school subjects. The pseudonymous author of *'The Future is Ours, Comrade'* paints a picture of a local boy making good which is strongly reminiscent of pre-1944 rural England and the vicarious pleasure aroused by a scholarship success. The fact that a 15-year-old lad is in Leningrad taking the Maths Olympiad semi-finals is the talk of the little town, and when he passes, his worker parents are delighted. At supper, his father predicts that if he goes on like this he will study at Moscow University and become a great scientist, ' "and even the members of the Central Committee will talk to you with respect, because I'm sure they know nothing about mathematics'."[110]

Olympiads have proliferated. Although they are mostly in mathematics and the major sciences, they are also held in biology,

TABLE 11.3 The Fifth All-Union Physics Olympiad, Final Round, 1971

Republic	Pupils, forms 8-10 (11), est. (1000's)[1]	%	Max. teams, est.[2]	%[3]	Points[4]	Diplomas (1st, 2nd & 3rd prizes)	Certificates	Total Honours[3]	%[3]	Revised teams, 1975
USSR	9730	100	495	100	-	54	75	129	100	103
RSFSR	4996	51.3	225	45.4	18	26	42	68	52.7	43
Ukraine	1670	17.2	75	15.2	21	19	11	30	23.3	12
Uzbekistan	664	6.8	36	7.3	11	1	3	4	3.1	6
Kazakhstan	603	6.2	57	11.6	7	-	7	7	5.4	6
Belorussia	392	4.0	18	3.7	19	2	4	6	4.7	6
Azerbaidzhan	270	2.8	?29	1.9	11	-	-	-	-	3
Georgia	223	2.3	?12	2.4	19	1	1	2	1.6	3
Kirgizia	152	1.6	9	1.9	5	-	1	1	0.8	3
Moldavia	149	1.5	6	1.2	18	1	-	1	0.8	3
Tadzhikistan	143	1.5	9	1.9	7	-	-	-	-	3
Armenia	136	1.4	6	1.2	18	1	2	3	2.3	3
Lithuania	116	1.2	6	1.2	20	1	1	2	1.6	3
Turkmenia	105	1.1	15	3.0	3	-	-	-	-	3
Latvia	68	0.7	6	1.2	14	1	1	1	0.8	3
Estonia	43	0.4	6	1.2	22	1	3	4	3.1	3

Notes: 1 Figures for forms 9-10 (11) are available; figures for form 8 have been estimated and added. (All relate to day general education schools as it is from these that the Olympiad draws the vast majority of its participants).

2 Including Moscow and Leningrad but excluding FMShs, Ministry of Railways schools, military schools, former prizewinners and host town. Grand total was 540 or 549.

3 Columns do not total 100 due to rounding.

4 Points have not been percentualized as it is not clear on what basis they were awarded.

5 FMSh awards apparently omitted.

Sources: Pupil numbers: *Narodnoe obrazovanie, nauka i kul'tura v SSSR* (M., 1971), 78-88.
Points and honours: S.N. Semin, 'V Vsesoyuznaya olimpiada yunykh fizikov', *Fizika v shkole*, 1971, no. 6, 77.
Teams: 1971: calculated from Z. Svirel'shchikova, 'Pyataya Vsesoyuznaya', *Uch. gaz.*, 13 March1971;1975: *id.*, 'Itogi Vsesoyuznoi olimpiady', *Uch. gaz.*, 22 May 1975.

astronomy, geology and arts subjects. Since 1965, for instance, Moscow University's Department of Structural and Applied Linguistics has been holding olympiads in linguistics and mathematics. Mainly for eighth to tenth formers, it is intended to develop a knowledge of linguistics, specialists in which are increasingly needed for work with computerised information systems, and to spot talent for the Department.[111] The organizers' intensive publicity campaign was much in evidence on Moscow's street hoardings when the author visited the city in November 1974. In 1969 members of the Institute of Geology and Geophysics at the Siberian Section of the Academy of Sciences, with the assistance of Novosibirsk student teachers and their lecturers, organized the first Novosibirsk Geology Olympiad.[112]

They cover a wide range of settings. At one extreme there is the small internal competition arranged by and within a particular school or held jointly with a neighbouring one. The advocacy of such olympiads during the 1960s is one facet of the drive for a less hidebound and more active and creative approach to the curriculum. They were to promote the development of existing or potential creative interests. It was reported in *Sovetskaya pedagogika* that when it was proposed to two senior forms that for their annual extended essay they should choose a research topic which would be written up, opposed and defended, all but three pupils reacted favourably in the form which had been engaged in olympiads; in the other, which had not, only three were in favour.[113]

Then there are all sorts of contests organized by institutes or broadcast on television. Thus, although Irkutsk Region in Eastern Siberia lies within the catchment area of the All-Siberian Olympiad, it has for many years had its own maths olympiad arranged by Irkutsk State University.[114] Such competitions have naturally been welcomed, but they have so mushroomed that fears have occasionally been expressed that the children's time budget will be overloaded,[115] or that lack of coordination between the various organizing groups may result in clashes.[116] Institutes have been accused of localistic tendencies (*mestnichestvo*), being preoccupied with catching goldfish and unconcerned about cooperation with the education authorities.[117]

At the opposite end of the spectrum are the international olympiads. The International Mathematics Olympiad was founded on the initiative of the Rumanian Society of Mathematical and Physical Sciences in 1959, as a contest of prizewinners in the national mathematics olympiads of six communist countries, plus a delegation from the GDR, which started its own olympiad the following year. With the self-assurance of the home team, the

Rumanians won most points and five of the eleven prizes; Hungary came second, with four prizes, and the USSR third.[118] By the time of the Sixth Olympiad (1964) Yugoslavia and Mongolia had been included among the 8-man teams;[119] the following year Finland became the first western country to take part; and in 1967 England, France, Italy and Sweden joined in, England being the only non-communist country to get a first class diploma.[120] Also in 1967 the International Physics Olympiad was established.[121] By 1970 fourteen countries were involved in the Maths Olympiad; the Russians did well, coming equal second with the GDR to the Hungarians. A Soviet commentator pointed out that the two latter teams contained people who had taken part two or three times already and who were two or three years older than participants from elsewhere; nevertheless, the USSR team should be more carefully selected (for their moral fibre, among other things — two of the contestants had played truant).[122] It is interesting that in both 1970 and 1972 five of the eight boys were from the Moscow and Leningrad FMShs; in 1972 the rural origins of two of them were spelt out. The Soviet team came top then[123] and again the next year, when a record 16 countries participated.[124] An International Chemistry Olympiad has also been set up.[125]

The most celebrated contest in arts subjects is the International Russian Language Olympiad. This was first held in August 1972 under the aegis of the International Association of Teachers of Russian Language and Literature (MAPRYAL) in Moscow, the arrangements being made by the MAPRYAL Secretariat jointly with the Scientific Methodological Russian Language Centre of Moscow State University (subsequently enlarged and reorganized as the A.S. Pushkin Russian Language Institute). 75 children from sixteen countries took part.[126] The second competition in this series was held in 1975, again in Moscow, likewise the third in 1978.

Although the olympiad net has never spread wide and deep enough to satsify educationists and scientists, it is certainly not considered suitable for all the fish in the sea. This is not so much a criticism of it as an awareness that complementary devices are required. As early as 1962 B. Gnedenko, a leading mathematician, pointed out that olympiads were not appropriate for children temperamentally like those great scientists who had given of their best by working at their own pace in a calm atmosphere.[127] Academician Kolmogorov echoed these words: some young people admitted to the Moscow FMSh simply did not want to take part in these contests, and in any case success in the FMSh entrance exams was only partially correlated with olympiad success.[128] The President of the Armenian Academy of Sciences felt that sometimes too much attention was paid to olympiads, in that they favoured the quick-witted but were to the disadvantage of pupils who were no good at 'displaying their wares', yet who were nevertheless really gifted.[129] Regrettably, pupils who were not conspicuous for their speed but who analyzed every stage of a problem deeply and critically suffered particularly from the diminution of the one part of the All-Siberian Olympiad where they might shine — the correspondence round.[130]

Strictures of this kind have been hotly contested by Academician Kikoin, a founding father of the olympiads. True, some children could cope with these taks, if not in the stress and strain of the competition, then in the quiet of home. In his opinion, however, they do not make the best scientists. Present-day scientists have to be tough and courageous, and the olympiads, testing not only intellectual abilities but also strength of mind and the ability to agrue a case, demonstrate this essential resilience.[131]

Academician Belyaev, who in 1973 came out in favour of extending specialized boarding schools, put forward an alternative to olympiads as a means of selection for them. The present olympiad system was, in his opinion, a way of testing passively acquired knowledge, and thus, it would seem, inherently unsuitable as an index of creative potential. He called for 'mass creative competitions' all the year round on a project basis, either on recommended topics or on subjects chosen by the pupils themselves. Of course, this raises the problem of supplying schools with the necessary materials.[132] As far as one can tell, Belyaev's views on specialized schooling did not gain a sympathetic hearing in the corridors of political power, and the olympiads have continued to play their multifunctional role more or less unrivalled.

There can be no doubt that the olympiads, especially the All-Union ones and their Siberian component, have made a major contribution to the discovery and canalization of talent into the reservoirs of highly-trained manpower. As teachers have sought to meet the challenge and universities and institutes have helped them in their endeavour, it is logical to suppose that the contests have brought about an improvement in the quality of teaching. This in turn will have had repercussions on the teaching of many more children, in addition to the interest aroused in them directly by the competitions themselves. On the other hand, despite enormous efforts and except in certain places, the hopes of the organizers that the olympiads would be a means of bridging the urban-rural gap by helping to equalize opportunities have been largely disappointed. There is also the view that they do not do justice either to reflective or to creative young people. However, such criticisms are linked to calls for improvement or, less frequently, complementation, and never anything more drastic. Leading scientists, educationists and administrators are anxious to improve the effectiveness of the olympiads, and they aim to achieve this not by revolution but by reform.

Notes

1 M. Lavrent'ev, 'Molodym — dorogu v nauku!', *Pravda*, 18 October 1960.

2 B.V. Gnedenko, 'Mathematical Education in the USSR', *American Mathematical Monthly*, vol. 64 (1957), 395.

3 A. Kolmogorov, 'Poisk talanta', *Izvestiya*, 7 April 1963.

4 V.D. Belousov and Ya. I. Nyagu, 'Moldavskoi Respublikanskoi matematicheskoi olimpiade 15 let', *Matematika v shkole*, 1972, no. 1, 69; I.T. Martishyus, 'Olimpiady yunykh fizikov v Litve', *Fizika v shkole*, 1973, no. 3, 103.

5 Gnedenko, *op. cit.*, 397; R. Creighton Buck, 'A Look at Mathematical Competitions', *American Mathematical Monthly*, vol. 66, no. 3 (March 1959), 206; Izaak Wirszup, 'The School Mathematics Circle and Olympiads at Moscow State University', *Mathematics Teacher*, vol. LVI no. 4 (April 1963), 196.

6 *Ibid.*

7 I. Tamm, 'Poisk talantov', *Izvestiya*, 3 January 1962.

8 M.A. Lavrent'ev, 'Glavnyi smysl zhizni', *Pravda*, 18 March 1962; V. Davydchenkov, 'Olimpiada v zolotoi doline', *Izvestiya*, 11 July 1962.

9 V. Molchanov, 'Yunye matematiki, fiziki, khimiki', *Pravda*, 5 August 1964.

10 S.L. Sobolev, 'Uchit' myslit',' *Literaturnaya gazeta*, 26 June 1962.

11 A. Savin and A. Bazykin, 'Poisk talantov prodolzhaetsya', *Izvestiya*, 29 January 1963.

12 Compare previous reference with 'Vsesoyuznaya zaochnaya olimpiada po matematike, fizike, khimii', *Uch. gaz.*, 22 October 1966; V. Berezin, 'Kak i pochemu pobezhdayut sil'neishie', *ibid.*, 9 May 1967.

14 *Sbornik prikazov i instruktsii Ministerstva prosveshcheniya RSFSR*, 1963, no. 49, 21-26.

15 Berezin, *loc. cit.*

16 Ilya Fonyakov, *Young Scientists' Town* (M., no date), 92.

17 Davydchenkov, *loc. cit;* G. Vokhmyanin, 'Poisk talantov' (interview with Academician I.K. Kikoin), *Uch. gaz.*, 10 April 1969; Ya. Barzdin and V. Kurmaev, 'Ispytanie bez shpargalok', *ibid.*, 8 July 1971; S.N. Semin, 'V Vsesoyuznaya olimpiada yunykh fizikov', *Fizika v shkole*, 1971, no. 6, 73.

18 Vokhmyanin, *loc. cit.*

19 A. Evropin, 'Dorogu — eksperimentu', *Uch. gaz.*, 15 May 1969; V. Sushko and B. Belov, 'Voronezh, itogovyi tur', *ibid.*, 21 May 1970; Z. Svirel'shchikova, 'Itogi Vsesoyuznoi olimpiady', *ibid.*, 22 May 1975.

20 V. Gorelov, 'Razmyshleniya posle olimpiady', *ibid.*, 13 October 1970. For further credit to options, see 'Vtoraya Vsesoyuznaya olimpiada

shkol'nikov', *Narodnoe obrazovanie,* 1969, no. 2, 123.

21   Vokhmyanin, *loc. cit.*
22   A. Lyapunov and Yu. Sokolovsky, 'Zapas uchitel'skikh znanii', *Pravda,* 27 October 1970.
23   I. Petrakov, 'Olimpiady shkol'nikov', *Narodnoe obrazovanie,* 1965, no. 1, 125.
24   A.A. Levin, 'Massovye olimpiady i konkursy kak sredstvo vospitaniya poznavatel'nykh interesov', *Sovetskaya pedagogika,* 1965, no. 3, 56. (Emphasis added.)
25   M. Lavrent'ev and D. Shirkov, 'Yunye matematiki zhdut zadach', *Izvestiya,* 19 March 1964; A.A. Bers and B.A. Frolov, *Olimpiada — pervyi shag v nauku* (M., 1964), 2.
26   T. Belyakova, 'Lager' matematikov', *Uch. gaz.,* 21 July 1970.
27   Wirszup, *loc. cit.*
28   *Sbornik prikazov . . .* (see note 14 above), 21-22.
29   'Kto eti trinadtsat'?', *Uch. gaz.,* 3 April 1969. The 'Znanie' (Knowledge) Society is a nationwide organization for the diffusion of political and scientific information by means of lectures, seminars, publications *etc.*
30   *Sbornik prikazov . . .,* 22.
31   *Ibid.,* 23.
32   Albert Parry, *The Russian Scientist* (New York, 1973), 163-164.
33   'Vsesoyuznaya zaochnaya . . .' (see note 12 above).
34   Z. Svirel'shchikova, 'Gotov'tes' k olimpiade', *Uch. gaz.,* 30 December 1969.
35   Z. Svirel'shchikova, 'Pyataya Vsesoyuznaya', *Uch. gaz.,* 13 March 1971.
36   J. Novak, *'The Future is Ours, Comrade'* (London, 1960), 138; *Sbornik prikazov . . .,* 23.
37   *Ibid.,* 23-24; I. Petrakov and T. Yashkina, 'Nauchnaya olimpiada shkol'nikov', *Narodnoe obrazovanie,* 1965, no. 9, 125.
38   Semin, *op. cit.,* 77.
39   *Sbornik prikazov . . .,* 25.
40   *Ibid.,* 24-25.
41   'Vtoraya Vsesoyuznaya . . . (see note 20 above), 123-124.
42   N. Gorbachev, 'Olimpiada, god 4-i . . .', *Uch. gaz.,* 31 March 1970.
43   Svirel'shchikova, *loc. cit.,* (1971).
44   Sushko and Belov, *loc. cit.*
45   S. Churanov, 'Pust' dazhe ne prizer . . .', *Uch. gaz.,* 15 May 1969. There was added point to the question: the 1969 contest was called the Mendeleev Olympiad, commemorating the centenary of Mendeleev's discovery of the periodic system of elements.
46   N. Ermolaeva and S. Neginsky, 'Usiliyami svoei mysli', *ibid.,* 21 May 1968; 'Vtoraya Vsesoyuznaya . . .', 123.
47   Ermolaeva and Neginsky, *loc. cit.*
48   V. Sedakov, 'Trafaretu — net!', *Uch. gaz.,* 13 May 1969.
49   N. Gorbachev, 'Puteshestvie v zamok logiki', *ibid.,* 12 May 1970.
50   Barzin and Kurmaev, *loc. cit.*

51 'Vtoraya Vsesoyuznaya . . .', *loc. cit.;* Evropin, *loc. cit.*
52 Gorbachev, *loc. cit.* (March 1970).
53 'Turnir lyuboznatel'nykh', *Uch. gaz.,* 20 April 1971; Semin, *op. cit.,* 73.
54 Sushko and Belov, *loc. cit.;* Gorelov, *loc. cit.*
55 Gorbachev, *loc. cit.* (March 1970).
56 'Poisk talantov', *loc. cit.*
57 For an early example see Tamm, *loc. cit.*
58 G. Vovchenko, 'Na podstupakh k konkursu', *Komsomol'skaya pravda,* 14 May 1963.
59 'Poisk talantov', *loc. cit.;* Churanov, *loc. cit.*
60 *Sbornik prikazov . . .,* 25.
61 Wirszup, *op. cit.,* 202; 'Poisk talantov', *loc. cit.;* Evropin, *loc. cit.*
62 S.I. Literat, 'Vyyavlyat' i razvivat' sposobnosti', *Sovetskaya pedagogika,* 1969, no. 4, 78-79; *id., Problemy otbora i obucheniya v spetsializirovannykh fiziko-matematicheskikh shkolakh pri gosuniversitetakh* (Novosibirsk, 1972), 7 (author's abstract of thesis); A. Owen and F.R. Watson, *Report to the British Council on a Visit to the USSR* (unpublished duplicated typescript, 1973), 28.
63 Bers and Frolov, *op. cit.,* 6; 'Invitation to Siberia: Scientific Olympics', *Times Educational Supplement,* 20 August 1965.
64 Mikhail Lavrentiev [Lavrent'ev], 'A School for Young Mathematicians in Siberia', *Prospects,* vol. V (1975), no. 2, 157.
65 Fonyakov, *op. cit.,* 93; Bers and Frolov, *op. cit.,* 12-13, 22; Literat, *loc. cit.* (1969); Owen and Watson, *loc. cit.*
66 Literat, *op. cit.* (1969), 79.
67 *Id., op. cit.* (1972), 24.
68 *Ibid.,* 7; Bers and Frolov, *op. cit.,* 42.
69 Lavrent'ev, *op. cit.* (1975), 154.
70 See note 114 to chapter 6.
71 Lavrent'ev and Shirkov, *loc. cit.*
72 Literat, *op. cit.* (1969), 79.
73 Ermolaeva and Neginsky, *loc. cit.*
74 Sedakov, *loc. cit.*
75 L.M. Pashkova, 'VI Vsesoyuznaya matematicheskaya olimpiada', *Matematika v shkole,* 1972, no. 5, 68.
76 *Ibid.,* 68-70 (derived); *id.,* 'VII Vsesoyuznaya matematicheskaya olimpiada', *Matematika v shkole,* 1973, no. 5, 72-74 (derived).
77 'Poisk talantov', *loc. cit.*
78 Ermolaeva and Neginsky, *loc. cit.*
79 Belyakova, *loc. cit.*
80 Ermolaeva and Neginsky, *loc. cit.*
81 Bers and Frolov, *op. cit.,* 18.
82 Z. Ibragimova, 'Adres shkoly — Akademgorodok', *Pravda,* 25 March 1976.
83 Literat, *op. cit.* (1972), 8, 22. This cannot be reconciled with Lavrent'ev's picture (*op. cit.* (1975), 157) of a vigorous correspondence round (unless action has been taken to revive it).

84   V.V. Popov and S.N. Sadykhov, 'Matematicheskie olimpiady v Azerbaidzhane', *Matematika v shkole*, 1972, no. 5, 75; estimates of total age-groups based on 1970/71 figures in *NONK*, 82-83.
85   Belousov and Nyagu, *op. cit.*, 70.
86   Wirszup, *op. cit.*, 205. For a more recent comment, see Parry, *op. cit.*, 166.
87   Ermolaeva and Neginsky, *loc. cit.*
88   Gorbachev, *loc. cit.* (May 1970); *id.*, 'V besede uchastvuyut dvoe', *Uch. gaz.*, 17 June 1971; Sushko and Belov, *loc. cit.*
89   Semin, *op. cit.*, 75-76.
90   V.A. Krutetskii, *The Psychology of Mathematical Abilities in Schoolchildren* (Chicago and London, 1976), 343.
91   Pashkova, *loc. cit.* (1972; *id., loc. cit.* (1973).
92   'VII Vsesoyuznaya fizicheskaya olimpiada shkol'nikov', *Fizika v shkole*, 1973, no. 4, 109.
93   Z. Svirel'shchikova, 'Itogi Vsesoyuznoi olimpiady', *Uch. gaz.*, 22 May 1975.
94   Literat, *loc. cit.* (1972).
95   This supposition is confirmed by Ibragimova, *loc. cit.*
96   Literat, *op. cit.*, 8.
97   'Vtoraya Vsesoyuznaya . . .', 124; Sedakov, *loc. cit.*
98   Ermolaeva and Neginsky, *loc. cit.*
99   Such seems to have been the thinking of a previous commentator (I. Fridlyand, ' "V vyigryshe vse . . ." ', *Uch. gaz.*, 16 May 1967), who suggested a separate group for youngsters from these schools and 'the so-called maths secondary schools'.
100 Barzdin and Kurmaev, *loc. cit.*
101 'Predmetnye olimpiady: kak ikh provodit'?', *Uch. gaz.*, 31 December 1974.
102 Pashkova, *loc. cit.* (1972); *id., loc. cit.* (1973). Schools in larger cities (criterion: omission of region in the lists) accounted for 68 per cent of prizewinners in 1972 and 76 per cent in 1973 (derived).
103 Gorelov, *loc. cit.* For a similar criticism see Fridlyand, *loc. cit.*
104 Gorbachev, *loc. cit.* (May 1970); Semin, *op. cit.*, 77; S. Belyaev, 'Priglashenie v nauku', *Izvestiya*, 17 April 1973.
105 Semin, *loc. cit.*
106 At least, this was so in theory, but a comment of 1975 that things had much improved, 'with the introduction of the compulsory republican stage' suggests a formerly haphazard situation (Svirel'shchikova, *loc. cit.* (1975)).
107 'Predmetnye olimpiady: kak ikh provodit'?', *Uch. gaz.*, 31 December 1974.
108 *Ibid.* The total of final-round competitors here quoted is 600, but in ten instances over the period 1968 to 1972 the precise figures for the three subjects varied from 539 to 660.
109 Svirel'shchikova, *loc. cit.* (1975). Similarly in 1977 awards went to 326 of the 424 contestants (V. Gorelov, 'Odinnadtsataya Vsesoyuznaya', *Uch. gaz.*, 16 August 1977).

110   Novak, *op. cit.,* 138-139.
111   *200 zadach po yazykovedeniyu i matematike* (M., 1972), 5.
112   'Olimpiada geologov', *Uch. gaz.,* 22 May 1969.
113   Levin, *op. cit.,* 58.
114   I. Stepanov, 'Traditsionnaya matematicheskaya olimpiada', *Narodnoe obrazovanie,* 1965, no. 10, 123.
115   'Poisk talantov', *loc. cit.*
116   Gorelov, *loc. cit.;* 'Otvetstvennost' i delovitost',' *Uch. gaz.,* 29 November 1966.
117   *Ibid.;* B. Porshnev, 'Talant — ne zolotaya rybka', *Izvestiya,* 16 October 1963.
118   Izaak Wirszup, 'The First Two International Mathematical Olympiads for Students of Communist Countries', *American Mathematical Monthly,* vol. 9, no. 2 (February 1962), 150-155.
119   Petrakov, *op. cit.,* 126.
120   E. Morozova and I. Petrakov, 'IX Mezhdunarodnaya matematicheskaya olimpiada shkol'nikov', *Narodnoe obrazovanie,* 1967, no. 12, 120.
121   Deduced from Yu. Yakovlev, 'Yunye rytsari nauki', *Uch. gaz.,* 24 July 1971.
122   I. Petrakov, 'Sil'neishie i dostoinye', *ibid.,* 20 August 1970.
123   V. Skvortsov and I. Petrakov, 'XIV Mezhdunarodnaya', *ibid.,* 22 July 1972. Petrakov was in charge of the Soviet team.
124   I.S. Petrakov and V.A. Skvortsov, 'XV Mezhdunarodnaya matematicheskaya olimpiada', *Matematika v shkole,* 1973, no. 6, 63, 66.
125   *Uch. gaz.,* 18 August 1970.
126   'Mezhdunarodnaya olimpiada shkol'nikov', *ibid.,* 15 August 1972.
127   B. Gnedenko, 'Na urovne XIX veka', *ibid.,* 21 June 1962.
128   A.N. Kolmogorov, 'Fiziko-matematicheskaya shkola', *ibid.,* 11 February 1964.
129   V. Ambartsumyan, 'Nauk vozvyshennye tseli', *Pravda,* 17 August 1967.
130   Literat, *loc. cit.* (1972).
131   I. Kikoin (interviewed by E. Demushkin), 'Talant my ne upustim', *Literaturnaya gazeta,* 13 October 1976, 13.
132   Belyaev, *loc. cit.*

Chapter 12
Conclusions

Over the period 1958-1976 the Soviet secondary general education system acquired an increasingly differentiated structure. The need to compete successfully with the West and to sustain the onward march towards communism in an epoch of unprecedented scientific and technological advance — when nevertheless the salvation of Soviet economic growth from its continuing decline, which lasted until the later sixties, lay in developing homegrown research and innovation — lent urgency to the quest of identifying young talent and the search for more efficient ways of subsequently exploiting it. Some saw precedents in the long-standing selective schools for children possessing a high degree of artistic talent. Attempts in 1958 to introduce special provision for intellectually gifted children succumbed to fears of exclusiveness, though occupational groups were mostly divided on the issue. The early 1960s saw a revival of the idea. In 1961 it was decreed that the experimental schools teaching various subjects through the medium of a foreign language should be rapidly expanded (in order to satisfy the demands of the job market, however, not expressly to develop linguistic gifts). Soon afterwards the first of a new type of school designed to produce top-flight sportsmen was set up. From 1962/63 a tiny number of very high-powered boarding schools (FMShs) were established, attached to *vuzy* and mostly specializing in mathematics and physics with their own curricula and syllabuses, catering for exceptionally bright young people but only partly achieving their aim of discovering and fostering rural talent. With this reservation, they represented a highly efficient conveyor to higher education, but were to some extent marred by a one-sided academic approach and a neglect of character training, and this inhibited their development and encouraged the search for less drastic and restricted forms.

And so, concurrently, debates on how best to reform the curriculum and provide for the *mass* of bright children culminated in the decree of November 1966 legitimating schools and classes with intensified study, some of which had emerged under the polytechnical reform, and enhancing the role of optional subjects. The position of all these was reaffirmed in the Legislative Principles of July 1973. But the special-profile schools also had their critics, speaking in the same tones as those of the FMShs, and options soon established their primacy as the principal means of responding to and encouraging pupils' particular interests and abilities and building up their knowledge on the basis of the common curriculum and syllabuses. Latterly their occupational guidance role has been increasingly emphasized, at the same time as economic factors have again induced an official upgrading of a certain sector of vocational education to one of the roads to complete secondary schooling. Optional studies have encountered organizational problems, like any developing institution, but the crucial question, whether they are for all or only for the more able, remains controversial, and the full implications of either answer have failed to find expression in public debate.

How far can Soviet special schools for high-ability children be regarded as what their critics are pleased to term elitist? Prerequisites for an accurate reply are a definition, some criteria, and rather more data than are currently to hand; but the issue must not be ducked. If by elitist we mean 'pertaining to social (occupational) groups which enjoy high status', we have to consider the degree to which the institutions concerned are accessible, their social composition, and the extent to which they confer advantages. The customary Western view has been that they are almost entirely the preserve of already privileged groups. Such a view seems simplistic to a fault. (This summary is also over-simplified, as summaries must be, and for refinements the reader must refer to the foregoing text.) These schools are not closed institutions but are free and available to all who have the ability to meet their entrance requirements in terms of athletic, artistic or intellectual attainment or promise, irrespective of social background. This is not to deny the fact that in some cases earlier life experiences will have conferred advantages and personal circumstances may continue to confer them; disquiet may be expressed about this and cognizance is sometimes taken of it by positive discrimination and other action.

Data on social composition are hard to come by, which itself may suggest unease, but what is available presents a mixed picture.

Schools for the arts vary widely from one area to another, but it seems certain that many of them, including the extremely prestigious Leningrad Ballet School, contain a high proportion of working-class children. The only special sports school on which we have such information is biassed, though not in any deliberate way, towards manual-worker entry and is likely to be typical, making it very difficult to regard this kind of school as elitist in any conventional sense. Mathematics and physics boarding schools probably have proportionately fewer children of parents engaged mainly in physical work than are found in the population at large, but if Novosibirsk at about 44 per cent is anything like representative these schools cannot possibly be regarded as exclusive to higher-status occupational groups. To this extent the elitist label is totally misleading. On the other hand, although instances to the contrary can be cited, the Russians themselves have said that children from white-collar families predominate in those mass schools and classes which have a special profile, visitors to language schools have often received the same impression, these two types of school together comprise the great majority of special schools, and the wide range of the white-collar category does not invalidate the conclusion that ambitious parents have latched upon an educational provision which all the evidence suggests came into being for purely utilitarian reasons.

All these schools furnish superior career opportunities, though again the special sports schools are somewhat anomalous because of ideological objections to the notion of sport as a profession. The visual and performing arts provide occupations which offer high prestige if not high remuneration. Mathematics and physics boarding schools and mass schools with a special senior-stage profile give very favourable chances of entry to higher education, and those provided by language schools are not far behind. It will be recalled that the pupils of language schools are probably about three times as likely to enter *vuzy* as those at ordinary schools, that those at other special-profile schools are three or four times as likely to do so, and FMSh pupils — four times or more (*i.e.* up to 100 per cent *vuz* entry). It should not, however, be concluded from this that special schools have a virtual monopoly of superior opportunities; olympiads with provision for direct entry to *vuzy,* correspondence schools and certain kinds of optional studies are but three examples of further ladders to success. To sum up, it may be said that schools for talented children offer them considerable career advantages, but such benefits are not restricted to young people already in superior social circumstances at the time of entry, nor are these schools by any means the only paths to excellence open to the Soviet child.

It seems reasonable to postulate two contrasting Soviet

perspectives on secondary general education, and for a common reference point or basis of comparison one may take the standard course curriculum (Figure 1). The egalitarian perspective takes as axiomatic the unified mass school with its standard course and common syllabuses for all pupils, except for different native languages and local production conditions; but it does not require all children to be treated in exactly the same way. It does not deny the need to cultivate special interests and abilities, since Marxism calls for the development of man to his full potential, but this must be attempted outside the standard course, and until the advent of options it was strictly the function of extracurricular activities and out-of-school organizations. In theory, and to a lesser extent in practice, the availability of such facilities was wide, and new, up-to-date ones have been devised in the light of present-day requirements.

In the case of the differentiationist perspective, the school is

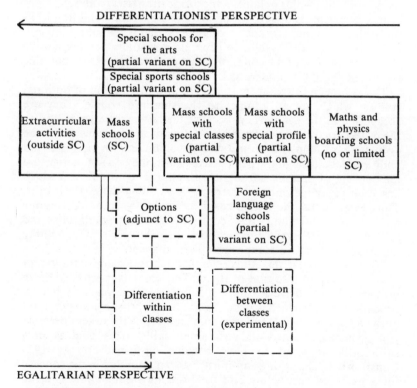

Fig. 1. *Differentiation in Soviet secondary general education*
The boxes with continuous borders represent relevant components of the education system; those with broken borders, actual or possible forms of differentiation within the mass school. SC signifies the standard course curriculum.

regarded as considerably more versatile, flexibility in provision for special abilities and in response to particular economic needs being achieved by schools of different types or possessing one or more specialisms. Thus the maths and physics boarding schools have predominantly their own courses, and the foreign-language and other special-profile schools and classes present partial variants on the standard course. Their advocates would wish them to be available to all young people who could benefit from them, but in practice their development has been severely restricted; the diagram should not be allowed to cloak the fact that at the beginning of the 1970s the four boxes on the right represented only about 2.7 per cent of all complete secondary general-education schools. If the scope of our calculations is broadened to include special schools for sport and the arts — but not those colleges (*uchilishcha*) of music, drama and the fine arts which both pertain to a separate sector of education and recruit only at 15-plus or later — the proportion rises to about 2.9 per cent. The existence of special schools for high-ability children is, in the author's opinion, on such a small scale that it cannot reasonably be claimed that the system has lost its essentially comprehensive character. In view of the common belief to the contrary, perhaps this statement should be underlined.

The two perspectives meet in the compromise notion of optional studies, which are an adjunct to the standard course. They are acceptable to the egalitarians because the latter is preserved and to the differentiators because they indeed provide a framework for the deepening of knowledge and the development of interests and abilities. Yet although the perspectives meet, they do not merge, and the concept of options is fraught with internal contradiction which has been regulated only by restraint in pursuing the analysis of it. Thus, even though the system has succeeded in institutionalizing one means of controlling the conflict between egalitarian and differentiationist forces in education, the pressures remain and the search for integrative compromise is permanent.

More than once in this study reference has been made to the vigour of the egalitarian tradition of the unified secondary school, shown primarily in the drive for implementation of ten years of general education for all, which is regarded as an indispensable concomitant of the advance towards full communism despite the urgent need for young people trained in vocational skills. This goal is now sufficiently achieved to have become enshrined in the 1977 Constitution. The egalitarian spirit is also manifested in the concern for a balanced curriculum and for bringing rural standards up to urban ones, for an education in which as much heed should be taken of upbringing as of instruction, and which ought not to be furnished by various ostensibly parallel institutions conferring by their very nature unequal opportunities, and therefore, though quite inadvertently, encouraging private aspirations. Egalitarian vigour is displayed not least in the fact that people of this persuasion are contesting the official line as to who shall participate in options, and that, despite all the debates since 1956, over 97 per cent of complete secondary schools are still essentially of the traditional type.

But at the same time the small proportion of differentiated schools and the considerable opposition to their expansion must not cause one to underestimate the resilience of that trend, which itself has been able to muster no small degree of ideological backing in terms of outstripping the USSR's rivals and contributing in specific ways to the building of communism; thus it shares the concern about eliminating urban-rural disparities. Its strength is manifest not only in its facility, when impeded, for finding new forms (though not without the same old problems), with limited though initially increasing support from the educational policy makers, but also in the fact of its infiltration into the other camp. It is absolutely no surprise that differentiation between classes should have been rejected, but it is remarkable that it should ever have been publicly mooted and that it should continue experimentally. Differentiation *within* the class, however, is now actively encouraged, provided that it is discreet, and increasingly the teacher is exhorted to make a creative, individual approach to each pupil and encourage him to be imaginative and creative in turn. The call thus to differentiate may so far be more honoured in the breach than the observance, as to apply it thoroughly requires much time and expertise, and it must be admitted that there is no consensus as to its goals, which for some educationists are, paradoxically, egalitarian. However, it seems to be widely felt, other than by a few diehards, that it is good in itself, and various structures exist through which it can be implemented. It remains to be seen whether this potentially radical trend will go so far that pressures are exerted to devise new ways of regulating it.

Appendices

A. Mathematics syllabus for the senior forms of the Soviet secondary general school, 1971/72.

B. Mathematics options syllabuses for the senior forms of the Soviet secondary general school, 1972.

Commentary on Appendices A and B.

C. Mathematics entrance examination to the Mathematics and Physics Boarding School at Moscow State University, 1967.

D. Outline history syllabus for the senior forms of the Soviet secondary general school with specialized classes in arts subjects, 1968/69.

MATHEMATICS SYLLABUS FOR THE SENIOR FORMS OF THE SOVIET SECONDARY GENERAL SCHOOL, 1971/72

FORM 9

(6 hours per week, totalling 210 hours)

ALGEBRA AND ELEMENTARY FUNCTIONS
(4 hours per week, totalling 140 hours)

Linear equations and inequalities (24 hours)
Linear equations in one unknown.
Numerical inequalities. Properties of inequalities and their application to demonstrating inequalities and solving linear inequalities. Examples leading to a system of inequalities. Sytems of two simultaneous linear equations in two unknowns, their study and geometric interpretation.

Real numbers. Quadratic equations (30 hours)
Measurement of intervals. The concept of an irrational number. The theorem 'There exists no rational number whose square is 2'. The geometric representation of real numbers. The concept of operations on real numbers. Quadratic equations, their study and the geometric interpretation of their solution. The solution of quadratic equations and simultaneous quadratic equations. The solution of quadratic inequalities.
Examples of solving irrational equations.

Rational exponents. Step functions (30 hours)
Index rules for powers whose exponent is a natural number. Powers with arbitrary integral exponent. The functions $y = x^n$ for n = 1, 2, 3, -1, -2, and their roots. The arithmetical significance of an nth root.
Powers with fractional exponents. The properties of powers with fractional exponents and their applications to operations on irrational expressions.
The functions $y = x^r$ $(x \times 0)$ for r = ½, ⅓

Trigonometric functions (40 hours)
The concept of vector; addition and subtraction of vectors.
The projection of a vector on to a plane; the coordinates of a vector in space.
Radian measurement of arcs and angles.
The definition of the trigonometric functions of any angle.
Variation of trigonometric functions.
Graphs of trigonometric functions.
Algebraic relations between the trigonometric functions of the same

argument.

Formulae for evaluating trigonometric functions. Inverse trigonometric functions; notation: arc sin x, arc cos x, arc tan x, arc cot x.

The proof of standard identities and the solution of equations.

Progressions (10 hours)

Arithmetical and geometrical progressions. Formulae for the general term and for the sum of the first n terms of these progressions.

The sum of an infinite geometric progression whose common ratio is less than one, and its application to identify the periodic decimal fractions as precisely the ordinary fractions.

Revision (6 hours)

GEOMETRY
(2 hours per week, totalling 70 hours)

Plane geometry

Numerical sequences (12 hours)

Numerical sequences. The general term of a numerical sequence. The concept of the limit of a numerical sequence. The existence of a limit of a monotone bounded sequence (without proofs). Theorems of limits of sums, products and quotients (without proof).

The application of limits to the computation of the length of the circumference and the area of a circle.

Solid geometry

Basic concepts of solid geometry. Parallelism in space (30 hours)

Definitions, axioms and theorems in mathematics. Axioms of solid geometry and their consequences.

The intersection of two straight lines. Corresponding angles. Angles between intersecting straight lines. Parallelism of a line and a plane. Parallelism of planes.

Basic properties of parallel projections (without proof) and their application to the representation of 3-dimensional figures.

Very simple problems on construction in 3 dimensions.

Perpendicularity in space. Dihedral and polyhedral angles (16 hours)

The definition of a perpendicular to a plane. The test for perpendicularity of a line and a plane. The construction of a plane perpendicular to a given line, and of a line perpendicular to a given plane. Perpendicular and inclined planes. The theorem on three mutually perpendicular lines. The angle between a straight line and a plane.

Dihedral angles. The relationship between linear and dihedral angles. The definition of, and test for, perpendicularity of two planes. The intersection properties of lines and planes perpendicular to a given plane. The definition of a polyhedral angle. The property of face angles of a trihedral angle. The sum of face angles of a convex polyhedral angle.

Plane trigonometry
Solving triangles (12 hours)
The sine rule. The cosine rule. Computing the area of a triangle; Heron's formula. The solution of triangles.

Problem-solving and revision (10 hours)

FORM 10
(6 hours per week, totalling 210 hours)

ALGEBRA AND ELEMENTARY FUNCTIONS
(4 hours per week, totalling 140 hours)

Revision (16 hours)

Trigonometry: addition formulae and their consequences (30 hours)
Trigonometric functions of the sum and difference of arguments.
Double and half angle formulae. The expression of the sum and difference of trigonometric functions as a product of trigonometric functions; and conversely.
The proof of identities, and their use in the solution of equations.

Exponential and logarithmic functions (38 hours)
The concept of a power with an irrational exponent. The exponential function, its basic properties and graphical representation.
The logarithm of a number to a given base. The logarithmic function, its basic properties and graphical representation.
The logarithm of products, quotients, powers and roots. Applying the logarithm function and the antilogarithm to algebraic expressions.
Logarithms to base 10. The rationale behind operations on the slide rule.
Tables of logarithms and trigonometric functions, and their construction.
Examples of computations with the use of tables.
Solving equations involving exponents and logarithms.

Generalization of the concept of function (20 hours)
The general concept of function. The notation for functional dependence and its use: f(x), f(a), f(x+a), etc.
The increase and decrease of a function. Maxima and minima.
Even and odd functions, periodic functions, and properties of their graphs.
Inverse functions and properties of their graphs.
Review of properties and graphs of elementary functions already studied.

Generalization of the concept of number. Complex numbers (16 hours)
Formulation of the problem of extending the number concept. Natural

numbers; the concept of mathematical induction. Integers, rational numbers, real numbers.

Complex numbers and their geometrical interpretation. Operations on complex numbers.

The application of complex numbers to the solution of polynomial equations of the third and fourth degree.

Problem-solving and revision of the 'Algebra and elementary functions, course (20 hours)

GEOMETRY
(2 hours per week, totalling 70 hours)

Solid geometry
Polyhedra (28 hours)
Prisms. Parallelepipeds. The pyramid (full and truncated).
The properties of the sides and diagonals of a parallelepiped.
The properties of parallel sections of a pyramid.
The lateral surface of a prism. The lateral surface of a rectilinear pyramid (full and truncated).
Basic assumptions about volumes. The unit of volume. The volume of a parallelepiped and a prism.
The volume of a pyramid (full and truncated).
The concept of a rectilinear polyhedron.

Solids with curved surfaces (24 hours)
The surface of a cylinder. Surfaces of revolution. The right circular cylinder, its unfolding and surface area. The conic surface. The right circular cone (full and truncated) and its unfolding. The lateral surface of a cone (full and truncated).
The volume of a cylinder and a cone (full and truncated).
The spherical surface and the solid sphere. The intersection of a plane and a sphere. A plane as tangent to a sphere. The surface area of a sphere and of its parts. The volume of a solid sphere and of its parts.

Revision and problem-solving (18 hours)
(**Source:** *Programmy srednei shkoly na 1971/72 uchebnyi god. Matematika* (M., 1971)).

APPENDIX B

MATHEMATICS OPTIONS SYLLABUSES FOR THE SENIOR FORMS OF THE SOVIET SECONDARY SCHOOL, 1972

SUPPLEMENTARY CHAPTERS AND PROBLEMS IN MATHEMATICS[1]

FORM 9

(70 hours)

1. *Sets and operations on them* (10 hours)[2]
The set of solutions of an equation and an inequality in one and two unknowns. The set of solutions of systems of equations and inequalities. Sets and elements (general concepts). The union and intersection of sets. The complement of a set. Notations for operations on sets.

2. *The derivative* (40 hours)
The limit of a function, continuity. The derivative.
The derivative of a sum, product, quotient, x^n for any integer n; the derivative of an inverse function.
Increasing and decreasing functions, maxima and minima.
Study of quadratic polynomials. The application of a derivative in geometry (the tangent) and physics (acceleration, velocity).

3. *Topics according to teacher's choice* (10 hours)[3]
(a) Natural numbers and the principle of mathematical induction.
Divisibility, factorization into simple factors. Systems of notation.
The principle of mathematical induction. Problem-solving demonstrated by the method of mathematical induction.
(b) Numerical methods for solving equations.
The method of iteration. The method of tangents. The location of roots of

. . . .

Translator's note
Bibliographies appended in the original are omitted here.

Notes from original
1 Studies may be conducted in accordance with these syllabuses until the introduction of the new syllabus for the basic course.
2 This topic is not studied in form 9 if it has been studied in a form 8 option.
3 Instead of the given topic, the teacher may, at his discretion, examine with the pupils one of topics 2-4, 6, and 7 from the form 8 syllabus.

equations to a given degree of accuracy.
(c) Geometric transformations.
Motion (axes and centres of symmetry, parallel translations, rotation).
Projection mapping onto a plane. The concept of a group of mappings.

4. *Problem-solving in accordance with the basic course* (10 hours)

FORM 10
(70 hours)

1. *The integral* (12 hours)
The primitive of a function. The definite integral and its application to determining the area under a curve. Newton-Leibnitz formula. Applications in geometry and mechanics.
Note: The above topic may be presented to pupils who have previously studied the derivative. If that topic has not been studied, it is advisable to compile a syllabus for form 10 from the topics for forms 9 and 10 which includes the derivative.
 The above topic may be studied at the beginning of the year, and the topic 'Algebraic equations of any degree' at the end of the year in parallel with study of the topic 'Complex numbers' in the compulsory syllabus.

2. *Principles of the theory of probability with elements of combinatorial analysis* (18 hours)
The concept of probability.
The calculation of probability as relative frequency.
Independent tests. Bernouille's scheme. Pascal's triangle.
Formulae:

$$\binom{n}{m} = \binom{m-n}{m}; \ \binom{n+1}{m+1} = \binom{n}{m} + \binom{n+1}{m}; \ \binom{0}{n} + \binom{1}{n} + \ldots + \binom{n}{n} = 2^n$$

Newton's binomial theorem.

3. *Algebraic equations of any degree* (8 hours)
Divisibility of polynomials, Bezou's[?] theorem, theorem of the existence of a root (without proof). Factorization of a polynomial into linear factors. Forming equations and systems of equations (problem-solving).

4. *Topics according to teacher's choice* (10 hours)
(a) Information on electronic computing machines (10 hours).
Decimal, binary and octal systems of calculation. The binary system of calculation as-the arithmetical basis of the computer. The conversion of integral numbers and fractions from the binary system to the decimal and conversely (examples). Binary arithmetic. Binary addition on a binary summator.
Basic computer principles. (memory, arithmetic system, system of operation, input and output).

The address principle of working of the computer. Instructions in the three-address machine (code of operation, address). The concept of a program. Arithmetic operations. The composition of formulae in accordance with instructions. The representation of an instruction in the machine. The encoding of a program for computing the value of a quadratic trinomial or a program for solving a system of equations. Examples: programs for computing the value of a quadratic polynomial, a program for solving a system of two linear equations in two unknowns.

(b) Supplementary problems in the theory of probability (10 hours).
Expected value. Standard deviation and the law of large numbers (proof in form of Chebyshev's theorem). Problem-solving.

(c) Computer practical (with use of slide rule, tables and adding machine) (10 hours).
Approximations. Methods of calculation (composition of formulae and calculation tables, checking calculations).
Linear interpolation.

(d) Final review of geometry course (10 hours).
The concept of non-Euclidean geometries and of the axiomatic method in geometry.
As a variant for the presentation, selected theorems of geometry of the sphere, with proofs, and a talk by the teacher on Lobachevsky geometry and other systems of geometry are suggested.

5. *Problem-solving in accordance with the basic course* (22 hours)
Particular attention is devoted to problems of solid geometry designed to develop spatial concepts.

SPECIAL COURSES
FORMS 9-10

Numerical methods
(70 hours)

Introduction
The optional course 'Numerical methods' is recommended for study in forms 9-10. Its aim is to acquaint pupils with the modern calculation system (generally accepted methods of computation, rules of checking and rounding-off of results, numerical methods of solving equations and systems of linear equations, approximate computation of integrals). Content of a computational nature from the general mathematics course is generalized and systematized in this course.

The following syllabus may be fully implemented in tenth forms with parallel study of the course 'Supplementary chapters and problems in mathematics', in which differentiation will be examined. The topic 'The integral' may be studied in conjunction with topic 7 in the course 'Numerical methods', with a corresponding increase in the time for the study of this topic. In the ninth forms topic 5 ('Functional scales') can be omitted, since it is advisable for the study of this topic to be underpinned by a knowledge of properties of logarithms and the exponential function. In other respects the syllabus coincides with the syllabuses for the main and optional ('Supplementary chapters') courses in mathematics for form 9.

If the course in numerical methods is underpinned only by the main mathematics course, the Newton-Raphson method and the combined method of approximate solution of equations should be omitted from topic 3 and the use of difference tables for finding derivatives from topic 6. The content of topic 7 (including Simpson's rule) may be limited to approximate computation of areas. In connection with topics 3 and 7, one may speak of very simple concepts of analysis (the differential and the integral, the connection between them) by way of review.

Topics 2, 5, 6 and 7 are independent of each other and in accordance with the concrete conditions of his work the teacher may rearrange them and even omit some of them at his discretion.

Syllabus
1. *Approximations* (12 hours)
Natural and standard (fixed and floating point) forms of notation of approximations. Operations on approximations written in natural and standard forms. The calculation of errors in arithmetical operations. Rules for rounding off.
Methods of carrying out calculations: composition of formulae, constructing a calculation table, checking calculations. Examples of calculations according to a given formula.

2. *System of linear equations* (10 hours)
2 by 2 and 3 by 3 determinants. Cramer's rule. The solution of systems of linear equations by Gauss's method, with check on calculations.

3. *Approximate solution of equations* (14 hours)
The graphical solution of equations. Finding roots. The method of chords. The Newton-Raphson method. The combined method.
Examples of solving equations using successive approximations.

4. *Tables of functions* (6 hours)
The use of tables as a further means of computation. Linear interpolation.

5. *Functional scales* (8 hours)
Examples of functional scales (scales of the slide rule) and functional networks (logarithmic and semi-logarithmic networks).
Use of functional scales and networks for computing.

6. *Interpolation* (14 hours)
General statement of the problem of interpolating. Parabolic interpolation by Atkin's method. Examples of parabolic interpolation by a table with a large increment. The concept of inverse interpolation.

Tabular differences and their use for checking calculations and finding approximate values of derivatives.

7. *Approximate calculation of definite integrals* (6 hours)
The calculation of definite integrals by the method of rectangles and trapezia. The application of Simpson's rule.
Note: Parallel to the study of the basic rules of approximate calculations, pupils receive a certain amount of practice in 'manual calculation'. Study is accompanied by practical activities in one of a number of keyboard calculators (8-10 hours), designed to give pupils an idea of the essence of the methods of approximate calculations under consideration.

Programming
(70 hours)

Introduction
The present course is recommended for study in form 9. The study of the material of this optional course is based on a knowledge of mathematics and physics up to the level of the eight-year school.
The aims of the course include familiarizing pupils with the fundamentals of programming and the working principles of computers.
The course content comprises branches of programming which include general school material not connected with the specific features of particular types of computer.
Pupils develop the skill of reducing the solution of any problem to a sequence of elementary arithmetical and logical operations. This sequence is known as an algorithm.
Instruction in programming is conducted in useful notation (in algebraic symbols familiar to pupils), not in machine coding.

Syllabus
1. *Arithmetical principles of programming* (10 hours)
Positional systems of calculation. Writing numbers in binary and octal systems. Natural and standard (with fixed and floating point) forms of notation of numbers. Mixed (binary-decimal and binary-octal) systems of converting numbers from the decimal system to the binary and the inverse operation.

2. *Basic principles of the electronic calculator* (6 hours)
The memory store. Elementary operation and instruction. The number of addresses of the machine. The instruction in the three-address machine.

3. *Methods of programming* (14 hours)
The representation of numbers and instructions in the memory store. Arithmetical operations. Writing out a formula in accordance with instructions. Instructions for transfer of control. Branch programs. Arithmetic and iterated cycles (without variable instructions). Address modification. Cycles with address modification. The restoration of variable

instructions. Binary cycles.

4. *Structure of the program* (10 hours)
The operation of absolute transfer of control with resetting. Blocks. Sub-routines. The library of standard sub-routines. Block programming.

5. *System of instructions and special features of programming on a specific machine* (10 hours)

6. *Concept of automatization of programming* (6 hours)

7. *Examples of programming of methods of approximate calculations* (14 hours)
Programming calculations by the method of chords and tangents. The program for iteration. Programming of the trapezium formula and Simpson's rule.

Note: (1) In the absence of the 'Numerical methods' course, topic 7 is to be omitted.

(2) If both courses are taught, it is desirable for the first four topics in the 'Numerical methods' course to be worked through before the 'Programming' course, and for topic 7 in the 'Programming' course to be studied simultaneously with topics 4, 6 and 7 in the 'Numerical methods' course.

(Source: *Programmy fakul'tativnykh kursov srednei shkoly* (M., 1972), 47-55).

COMMENTARY ON APPENDICES A AND B
The syllabuses were circulated to a number of workers in mathematics education and comments were invited in respect of their content, general approach, interrelationship, and compatibility with English school syllabuses. The four respondents included a secondary school teacher, a university faculty of education lecturer in curriculum and method, a university lecturer in pure mathematics with an active interest in postgraduate maths education and in-service teaching, and a postgraduate student working on Soviet mathematics education. The writer is not a mathematician himself and is therefore particularly grateful for their assistance.

Preliminary considerations
It was agreed that there were very real problems in attempting to gauge the standard of teaching and learning in any subject from an examination of syllabuses, for the obvious reason of the possible existence of a discrepancy between theory and practice. The extent of the gap between the ideal and the real was difficult to measure anywhere, but especially so in the Soviet Union, where there might well be ideological constraints about admitting its existence. The serious teacher shortage alone, however, would seem to cast doubt upon the effective implementation of the syllabuses throughout Soviet schools, and there was a continuing, though apparently lessening, problem of repeaters and dropouts. It was conceded that the expected standard might well be more apparent from examination questions, but these were not available to the writer. Secondly, comparisons with English syllabuses were somewhat difficult because English sixth-formers and Soviet sixth-form-equivalent pupils were in several ways in substantially different situations. The English child would in most cases have entered primary education in the term when he reached the age of 5, secondary at the age of 11, and the first-year sixth at 16-plus. The Soviet child would have begun the primary stage at 7 (though with a much greater likelihood of systematic pre-school education before that), the secondary at 10, and form 9 (the first year of the senior stage) at 15-plus. He would have been far more likely — at a rate of 2 in 3 — to enter the nearest Soviet counterpart to a full-time sixth-form course, but his spread of subjects would be much wider than in the case of his English opposite number. Then there was the whole question of labour as a prominent official Soviet value, with its panoply of incentives and deterrents. It might nevertheless be hypothesized from this that, since Soviet children were younger, represented a much broader band of ability, had had a shorter school course and were specializing to a far lesser extent (if at all) at this stage, their syllabus would be less demanding than the English one. Any specialization would be limited to taking options and possibly labour training in the same field.

Thirdly, for maximum reliability one ought not to compare syllabuses in isolation from the rest of the course. Fourthly, England had no such thing as a sole, nationally prescribed syllabus, so there was no undisputed model to set against the Soviet one. To these might be added a final point — a reminder that by 1976 the Soviet school mathematics syllabuses had all been modernized, so that any inclination to assess the unreformed 1971/72 ones for up-to-dateness could be misleading and should therefore be resisted. In any case, the Russians might have other ideas about what constituted modernity. (These latest syllabuses were not obtainable by the writer and would in any event defeat the object of facilitating comparison with the contemporary options syllabuses and that of locating the comparison within the period under review.) It would be more fruitful to assess for difference of approach. Despite these caveats, however, a number of interesting points emerged from the exercise.

Compulsory syllabuses

The supposition that the syllabus would prove to be less extensive and demanding than in England was found to be generally true, but the position was not entirely clear cut, and in view of the much wider range of ability the conceptual demands of the form 10 syllabus were nevertheless felt to be remarkably high. With respect to the form 9 syllabus, much of the algebra would be included in an English O-level syllabus; irrational numbers would also appear there, albeit without rigorous treatment, and most of the trigonometry would figure in many such syllabuses. The quadratic equation, however, was a notable inclusion, and arithmetical and geometric progression would be first-year sixth work in England, though occurring in additional mathematics at O-level for abler pupils. The form 9 geometry syllabus was more difficult to compare: the plane geometry and trigonometry ranged from English fourth-form level (solving triangles) to well into the sixth-form course (limits, though this topic might appear informally prior to O-level). Solid geometry was unlikely to figure prominently in an English syllabus, though some was found in traditional O-level work. The form 10 algebra course was overall more akin to English sixth-form work, though more restricted in scope. One consultant, who felt that by reason of the pupils' age this year should more properly be compared with the *first*-year sixth, noted the absence of the binomial theorem, parametric equations, matrices, integral calculus and simple mechanics. Solid geometry continued to be unfamiliarly conspicuous.

There was, however, a danger of missing the wood for the trees when breaking down syllabuses into their individual components. In an appraisal of the global intentions of the syllabus designers the geometry was considered to be of outstanding interest. The central object of the Soviet geometry course was evidently 3-dimensional geometry and the plane geometry was merely a tool for the analysis of it. Avoiding the artificiality of the study of plane geometry in isolation, this principle led one commentator to describe the geometry syllabus as 'totally and irreconcilably different' from those pertaining to English schools and to hail the Soviet approach as the 'only obvious' one.

Options syllabuses

It has been shown that options were essentially a device to cater for particular abilities and to allow pupils to follow individual interests in a more or less formal setting without prejudice to the common core curriculum taken by all those pupils who had embarked upon the senior stage of the school course, and that they were nearly all of two kinds, *supplementary* to the compulsory course and *special courses*. Their additional functions included career guidance and serving as a testing ground for material which might later be introduced into the compulsory syllabuses (see the final paragraph below). Hence the 'new mathematics' and mathematical applications might both be expected to figure more prominently here than in the contemporary compulsory syllabuses reviewed above.

Both in form 9 and the form 10 syllabuses for the *supplementary chapters and problems* evinced a mixture of topics which in England would be found partly at O-level and partly at A-level. With regard to form 9, many modern O-level syllabuses would include sets, the derivative (also traditional) and geometric transformations, and numerical methods would appear in a few. Mathematical induction, however, would occur only at A-level, and then not in all syllabuses. As to form 10, integration appeared in many traditional O-level syllabuses. Elementary probability figured in O-level additional mathematics and also, though not to the same extent as in the Russian syllabus, in some modern courses for O-level mathematics; probability might appear at A-level, but especially in a statistics option. Some work on polynomials occurred in most A-level syllabuses. Computing straddled both stages in that elementary ideas would occur at O-level and the more advanced ones in an A-level computer studies option. Non-Euclidean geometries, however would rarely be found, even at A-level; their inclusion might well be regarded as the most interesting feature of this course.

The *special courses* would have their counterparts as the A-level options set up by some examination boards in this country. They appeared to be quite demanding. The inclusion of work on the principles of the electronic calculator was said to be something our courses could usefully emulate.

An authoritative report on the progress of the Soviet curriculum reform provides clear evidence of the role of optional studies in modernizing the content of the compulsory courses.[1] Topics absent from the 1971/72 general syllabuses but occurring in the *supplementary chapters and problems* option which have now found a place in the basic courses include the derivative, mathematical induction, mapping of space (including axial and central symmetry) and the integral (application of the concept to deduce formulae for the volume of spatial figures).

Note
1 M.P. Kashin, 'Ob itogakh perekhoda sovetskoi shkoly na novoe soderzhanie obshchego obrazovaniya', *Sov. ped.,* 1976, no. 3, 27-28.

APPENDIX C

MATHEMATICS ENTRANCE EXAMINATION TO THE MATHEMATICS AND PHYSICS BOARDING SCHOOL AT MOSCOW STATE UNIVERSITY, 1967

I. *For pupils completing form 8, entry to two-year course*

1. Solve the system of equations

$$\begin{cases} \dfrac{9x^2}{x^2 + x + y} + \dfrac{x^2 + x + y}{x^2} = 10, \\[2mm] y^2 - 2x^2 + 16x^3 = 0. \end{cases}$$

2. Let ABCD be a trapezium with AB parallel to CD, AB = a and BC = b, a > b. A line is drawn through the intersection of the diagonals of ABCD parallel to AB. Find its length.

3. Find all the integral values of n, when $\dfrac{n^2 + 1}{n + 2}$ is an integer.

II. *For pupils completing form 9, entry to one-year course*

1. Prove that there exist no natural number which after crossing out the first digit on the left is reduced by a factor of 35.

2. An arc AB subtends an angle of 60° at the centre of a circle. On the arc AB an arbitrary point C is chosen and segments CA and CB are constructed. Prove that the segments joining the centres of the opposite sides of the quadrilateral OBCA are mutually perpendicular.

3. With what values of k has the following system of equations positive solutions, i.e. a positive solution is of the form $(x_1 ..., x_k)$ where $x_1 ..., x_k$ are positive numbers?

$$x_1 + x_2 + \ldots + x_k = 3$$
$$\frac{1}{x_1} + \frac{1}{x_2} + \ldots + \frac{1}{x_k} = 3$$

Find these solutions.

Translator's note

Question I.2 has been completely reformulated in accordance with English usage.

(**Source:** M. Potapov and N. Rozov, 'Shkola-internat pri MGU', *Nauka i zhizn'*, 1968, no. 4, 71).

Comment

In the consultant's opinion, the questions were well-chosen and required certain (possibly subconscious) perspectives which one would like all mathematics and physics students to have. The standard was not impossibly high but would stretch many teachers. Because of this the problems were of a kind that few English pupils ever tackled, and so most present-day 15-year-olds would be unlikely to know how to start (except perhaps in the case of I.3). But in places maintaining the academic grammar-school tradition one might find clusters of pupils who would cope fairly well.

Further note
For an additional example (form 8, 1970), see A. Owen and F.R. Watson, 'The Mathematical Boarding Schools of the USSR', *Mathematical Gazette*, vol. LVIII, no. 405 (October 1974), 195.

APPENDIX D

OUTLINE HISTORY SYLLABUS FOR THE SENIOR FORMS OF THE SOVIET SECONDARY GENERAL SCHOOL WITH SPECIALIZED CLASSES IN ARTS SUBJECTS, 1968/69

Translator's note
The specialized classes have 6 additional hours per week (4 from options and 2 from labour training). One of these hours is devoted to Russian language and stylistics, one to extension of the literature course, and four to history.

FORM 9
(150 hours)
1. Revision of principal problems in the form 7 and form 8 course in the history of the USSR (23 hours)
2. Broadening and deepening of the form 9 history syllabus:
   (a) study and analysis of supplementary factual material; use of memoir literature and documents; conduct of seminars at which pupils give papers (60 hours);
   (b) study of works of Marx, Engels and Lenin on topics directly connected with material in the syllabus and topics affording pupils a more profound understanding of the historical process (20 hours)
3. Study of artistic historical literature (20 hours)
4. Course of local history (*istoricheskoe kraevedenie*) with practical work in the school museum and regional museum (20 hours)
5. Spare (7 hours)

FORM 10
(150 hours)
1. Broadening and deepening certain topics in the 'Social Studies' course (35 hours)
2. Ditto, 'Contemporary History' (10 hours)
3. Ditto, 'History of the USSR' (10 hours)
4. Work on summarizing writings of Lenin (*The Immediate Tasks of Soviet Power*, sections from *What is to be Done?*, *The Development of Capitalism in Russia*, etc.) (10 hours)
5. Revision of problems in the history of the USSR from ancient times to the socialist epoch (20 hours)
6. Practical work in bibliography and local studies in the regional public library and regional records office (40 hours)
7. Study of monographs on the history of the USSR, modern and contemporary history (20 hours)
8. Spare (5 hours)

Example

Five supplementary hours on the topic 'The Franco-Prussian War and the Paris Commune' (allotted five hours in the form 9 modern history course — *trans.*) were used for more detailed exposition of the material by the teacher, involving excerpts from memoir and artistic historical literature, and also, to a greater extent, the observations of Karl Marx on this event. A total of two extra hours went to this. In addition the pupils prepared papers on Russian and Polish revolutionaries — E. Dmitrieva, A. Korvin-Krukovskaya and Ya. Dombrovsky — who took part in the events. A whole lesson was devoted to this. Before revision of the entire topic, the pupils spent two hours in class making a synopsis of V.I. Lenin's *In Memory of the Commune*.

(**Source:** A.I. Aleksandrov, 'Pervyi opyt uglublennoi istoricheskoi podgotovki shkol'nikov (O rabote spetsializirovannykh klassov srednei shkoly No. 10 g. Chelyabinska)', *Prepodavanie istorii v shkole,* 1969, no. 3, 60, 61).

Bibliography

I. **BOOKS AND PAMPHLETS**
  . 1.   **General Works**
      A.   Soviet
      B.   Western

    2.   **Works on education**
      A.   Soviet and East European
      B.   Western

    Note: Where country of origin and country of publication do not coincide, works are listed in accordance with the latter criterion.

II. **ARTICLES IN BOOKS AND JOURNALS**
    A.   Soviet and East European
    B.   Western

    Note: Where country of origin and country of publication do not coincide, articles are listed in accordance with the latter criterion; the provenance of translated articles is added where possible.

III. **OTHER SERIALS**
    A.   Soviet newspapers
    B.   Other Soviet serials
    C.   Western serials

I. BOOKS AND PAMPHLETS
1. **General Works**

A. **Soviet** (M. signifies Moscow and L., Leningrad)

Itogi Vsesoyuznoi perepisi naseleniya 1959 goda RSFSR (M., 1963).
Itogi Vsesoyuznoi perepisi naseleniya 1970 goda, vols. VI (M., 1973) and VII (M., 1974).
Leningrad i Leningradskaya oblast' v tsifrakh (L., 1974).
Moskva v tsifrakh (M., 1972).
Narodnoe khozyaistvo Estonskoi SSR v 1969 godu (Tallinn, 1970).
Narodnoe khozyaistvo RSFSR v 1968 godu (M., 1969).
Narodnoe khozyaistvo SSSR v 1974 godu (M., 1975).
Spisok abonentov Moskovskoi gorodskoi telefonnoi seti (M., 1966 and 1968).
Zasedaniya Verkhovnogo Soveta SSSR pyatogo sozyva (vtoraya sessiya). Stenograficheskii otchet (M., 1959).

B. **Western**

ANWEILER, Oskar and RUFFMANN, Karl-Heinz (eds.), *Kulturpolitik der Sowjetunion* (Stuttgart, 1973).
KASSOF, Allen (ed.), *Prospects for Soviet Society* (London, 1968).
KATZ, Zev, *Patterns of Social Mobility in the USSR* (Cambridge, Mass., 1973).
MADISON, Bernice Q., *Social Welfare in the Soviet Union* (Stanford, 1968).
MATTHEWS, Mervyn, *Class and Society in Soviet Russia* (London, 1972).
NOVAK, J., *'The Future is Ours, Comrade',* (London, 1960).
PARRY, Albert, *The Russian Scientist* (New York, 1973).
PORTISCH, Hugo, *So sah ich Sibirien* (Vienna, 1967).
RAHMANI, Levy, *Soviet Psychology: Philosophical, Theoretical and Experimental Issues* (New York, 1973).
RIORDAN, James, *Sport in Soviet Society* (Cambridge, 1977).
SKILLING, H. Gordon, and GRIFFITHS, Franklyn (eds.), *Interest Groups in Soviet Politics* (Princeton, 1971).
SMITH, Hedrick, *The Russians* (London, paperback edn., 1976).
YANOWITCH, Murray, *Social and Economic Inequality in the Soviet Union* (New York and London, 1977).
ZALESKI, E., *et al., Science Policy in the USSR* (Paris, 1969).

2. **Works on education**

A. **Soviet and East European**

BERS, A.A., and FROLOV, B.A., *Olimpiada — pervyi shag v nauku* (M., 1964).
CHEPELEV, V.I. (ed.,), *Public Education in the Ukrainian SSR* (Kiev,

1970).
DANILOV, M.A., and SKATKIN, M.N. (eds.), *Didaktika srednei shkoly: nekotorye problemy sovremennoi didaktiki* (M., 1975).
DEINEKO, M.M., *40 let narodnogo obrazovaniya v SSSR* (M., 1957.
200 [Dvesti] zadach po yazykovedeniyu i matematike (M., 1972).
Educational Planning in the USSR, with Observations of an I.I.E.P. Mission to the USSR (Paris, 1968) (a joint Soviet-Western production under OECD auspices).
FIRSOV, V.V., *et al.*, *Sostoyanie i perspektivy fakul'tativnykh zanyatii po matematike* (M., 1977).
FONYAKOV, Ilya, *Young Scientists' Town* ([M.,] n.d. [c. 1963]).
Istoriya matematicheskogo obrazovaniya v SSSR (Kiev, 1975).
Iz opyta uchebno-vospitatel'noi raboty shkol-internatov goroda Moskvy (M., 1960).
KAIROV, I.A., *et al.*, (eds.), *Pedagogika* (M., 1956).
KASHIN, M.P., and CHEKHARIN, E.M. (eds.), *Narodnoe obrazovanie v RSFSR* (M., 1970).
KIENITZ, Werner, *et al.*, *Einheitlichkeit und Differenzierung im Bildungswesen* (Berlin [East], 1971).
KRUTETSKY, V.A., *Psikhologiya obucheniya i vospitaniya skhol'nikov* (M., 1976).
KUZIN, N.P., *et al.*, *Education in the USSR* (M., 1972).
LEITES, N.S., *Umstvennye sposobnosti i vozrast* (M., 1971).
LITERAT, S.I., *Problemy otbora i obucheniya v spetsializirovannykh fiziko-matematicheskikh shkolakh pri gosuniversitetakh* (Novosibirsk, 1972). (Author's abstract of thesis).
A.V. Lunacharskii o narodnom obrazovanii (M., 1958).
MARX/ENGELS, *Über Erziehung und Bildung* (Berlin [East], 1971).
MUSTAFINA, F. Kh., *Rastsvet narodnogo obrazovaniya v Bashkirskoi ASSR* (Ufa, 1968).
Narodnoe obrazovanie, nauka i kul'tura v SSSR. Statisticheskii sbornik. (M., 1971 and 1977).
Narodnoe obrazovanie v SSSR. Obshcheobrazovatel'naya shkola. Sbornik dokumentov 1917-1973 gg. (M., 1974).
Obshchestvo i molodezh' (M., 2nd edn., 1973).
Pedagogicheskaya entsiklopediya, vol. 1 (M., 1964), vol. 2 (M., 1965), vol. 3 (M., 1966), and vol. 4 (M., 1968).
Programmy fakul'tativnykh kursov srednei shkoly (M., 1972).
PROKOF'EV, M.A. (ed.), *Narodnoe obrazovanie v SSSR 1917-1967* (M., 1967).
SKATKIN, M.N., *O shkole budushchego* (M., 1974).
SOLOVEICHIK, S., *Soviet Children at School* (M., 1976).
Spravochnik dlya postupayushchikh v vysshie uchebnye zavedeniya SSSR 1969 (M., 1969).
Spravochnik rabotnika narodnogo obrazovaniya (M., 1973).
TURCHENKO, V.N., *Nauchno-tekhnicheskaya revolyutsiya i revolyutsiya v obrazovanii* (M., 1973).
VASIL'EVA, E.K., *Sotsial'no-professional'nyi uroven' gorodskoi molodezhi* (L., 1973).

ZAVADSKAYA, O.A., *Razvitie obshcheobrazovatel'noi shkoly Ukrainy v period stroitel'stva kommunizma (1958-1968 gg.)* (Kiev, 1968).
ZHAMIN, V.A., *Optimizatsiya razmeshcheniya seti obshcheobrazovatel'-nykh shkol* (M., 1975).

B. Western

ACHINGER, Gerda, *Die Schulreform in der UdSSR* (Munich, 1973).
ANWEILER, Oskar, *Geschichte der Schule und Pädagogik in Russland vom Ende des Zarenreiches bis zum Beginn der Stalin-Ära* (Berlin [West], 1964).
ANWEILER, Oskar, *Die Sowjetpädagogik in der Welt von heute* (Heidelberg, 1968).
BAUER, Raymond A. *The New Man in Soviet Psychology* (New York, 1952).
BEREDAY, George Z.F., *et al., The Changing Soviet School* (Boston, 1960).
BEREDAY, George Z.F., and PENNAR, Jaan (eds.), *The Politics of Soviet Education* (New York, 1960).
Bringing Soviet Schools still Closer to Life, Soviet Booklet No. 44 (London, 1958).
BRYCE, Mayo, *Fine Arts Education in the Soviet Union* (Washington, D.C., 1963).
COGNIOT, Georges, *Prométhée s'empare du savoir* (Paris, 1967).
DEWITT, Nicholas, *Education and Professional Employment in the USSR* (Washington, D.C., 1961).
EICHBERG, Ekkehard, *Vorschulerziehung in der Sowjetunion* (Düsseldorf, 1974).
FITZPATRICK, Sheila, *The Commissariat of Enlightenment* (Cambridge, 1970).
GLOWKA, Detlef, *Schulreform und Gesellschaft in der Sowjetunion 1958-1968* (Stuttgart, 1970).
GRANT, Nigel, *Soviet Education* (London, 1st edn., 1964; Harmondsworth, 2nd edn., 1968 and 3rd edn., 1972).
GRANT, Nigel, *Society, Schools and Progress in Eastern Europe* (Oxford, 1969).
JACOBY, Susan, *Inside Soviet Schools* (New York, 1975).
KING, Edmund J. (ed.), *Communist Education* (London, 1963).
KOROLEV, F.F., *Education in the USSR* (London, n.d. [?1958]).
KRUTETSKII, V.A., *The Psychology of Mathematical Abilities in Schoolchildren* (Chicago and London, 1976).
LEVIN, Deana, *Leisure and Pleasure of Soviet Children* (London, 1966).
LIEGLE, Ludwig, *Familienerziehung und sozialer Wandel in der Sowjetunion* (Berlin [West], 1970). Translated as *The Family's Role in Soviet Education* (New York, 1975).
MITTER, Wolfgang, and NOVIKOV, Leonid, *Sekundarabschlüsse mit Hochschulreife im internationalen Vergleich* Weinheim and Basel, 1976).
MOOS, Elizabeth, *Soviet Education Today and Tomorrow* (New York, n.d. [?1959]).
MORTON, Miriam, *The Arts and the Soviet Child* (New York and London,

1972).

MORTON, Miriam, *The Making of Champions* (New York, 1974).

NOAH, Harold J., *Financing Soviet Schools* (New York, 1966).

OWEN, A., and WATSON, F.R., *Report to the British Council on a Visit to the USSR* (unpublished duplicated typescript, 1973).

PENNAR, Jaan, *et al.*, *Modernization and Diversity in Soviet Education* (New York, 1971).

RIORDAN, James, *Sport and Physical Education in the Soviet Union* (London, 1975).

ROSEN, Seymour M., *Education and Modernization in the USSR* (Reading, Mass., 1971).

RUDMAN, Herbert C., *The School and State in the USSR* (New York, 1967).

SCHIFF, Bernhard, *Entwicklung und Reform des Fremdsprachenunterrichts in der Sowjetunion* (Berlin [West], 1966).

SIMON, Brian and Joan (eds.), *Educational Psychology in the USSR* (London, 1963).

Sports Council (Olive W. Newson), *USSR Physical Education and Sport Study Tour . . .* (London, 1975).

Sports Council for Northern Ireland, *Physical Education and Sport in the Soviet Union: Report of a Study Tour* (Belfast, 1975).

TOMIAK, J.J., *The Soviet Union*. World Education Series (Newton Abbot, 1972).

Universities of London, Reading and Oxford, *Comparative Education Tour to the USSR* (London, 1960, 1964, 1966, 1967, 1968, 1971). (Unpublished duplicated typescript at Institute of Education Library, University of London).

VOGELI, Bruce Ramon, *Soviet Secondary Schools for the Mathematically Talented* (Washington, D.C., 1968).

VOLPICELLI, Luigi, *L'évolution de la pédagogie soviétique* (Neuchâtel, 1954).

II.   ARTICLES IN BOOKS AND JOURNALS

A.   Soviet and East European

ALEKSANDROV, A.I., 'Pervyi opyt uglublennoi istoricheskoi podgotovki shkol'nikov', *Prepodavanie istorii v shkole*, 1969, no. 3, 59-65.

AL'TSHULLER, R., and BAZHANOVA, E., 'Fakul'tativam nuzhna pomoshch'', *Narodnoe obrazovanie*, 1971, no. 8, 87-88.

ANTROPOVA, M.V., and MARKOSYAN, A.A., 'O rezhime dnya i nagruzke uchashchikhsya', *Sovetskaya pedagogika*, 1966, no. 10, 42-59.

ARSEN'EV, A.M., 'Fakul'tativnye zanyatiya v shkole', *Sovetskaya pedagogika*, 1968, no. 8, 76-87.

ARSEN'EV, A.M., 'Osnovnye napravleniya sovershenstvovaniya soderzhaniya obrazovaniya v srednei shkole', *Sovetskaya pedagogika*, 1967, no. 6, 28-38.

ARSEN'EV, A.M., 'Shkola i sovremennaya nauchno-teckhnicheskaya

revolyutsiya', *Sovetskaya pedagogika,* 1969, no. 1, 16-29.
ASATUROVA, K., 'Problemy fakul'tativnykh zanyatii', *Narodnoe obrazovanie,* 1968, no. 11, 37-40.
BELOUSOV, V.D. and NYAGU, Ya. I., 'Moldavskoi Respublikanskoi matematicheskoi olimpiade 15 let', *Matematika v shkole,* 1972, no. 1, 69-70.
BERDICHEVSKY, Yu. I., and MEFODOVSKY, V.E., 'Poka edinstvennaya', *Fizicheskaya kul'tura v shkole,* 1969, no. 7, 15-16.
BLONSKY, P., 'Vospitanie odarennykh detei', in *Pedagogicheskaya entsiklopediya,* vol. 2 (M., 1928), cols. 423-428.
BRAUER, Helmut, and DEUBLER, Hans, 'Stundentafeln der Spezialschulen und Spezialklassen für Mathematik in sozialistischen Ländern', *Vergleichende Pädagogik,* 1971, no. 4, 448-460.
BUKHOVTSEV, B., 'Lektorskaya kontrol'naya', *Yunyi tekhnik,* 1972, no. 12, 34-36.
BUSHANSKAYA, N.B., and RUNDAL'TSEVA, N.N., 'Zabolevaemost' uchashchikhsya shkol s prepodavaniem ryada predmetov na inostrannom yazyke', *Sovetskoe zdravookhranenie,* 1968, no. 12, 37-40.
BUTUZOV, I., 'Chtoby kazhdyi uchenik byl aktivnym', *Narodnoe obrazovanie,* 1969, no. 11, 52-55.
CHEREPANOVA, O.A., 'Gotovyatsya stat' yazykovedami', *Russkaya rech',* 1969, no. 6, 80-82.
DANILOV, A., 'O podgotovke k osushchestvleniyu v RSFSR vseobshchego srednego obrazovaniya molodezhi', *Narodnoe obrazovanie,* 1968, no. 8, 7-16.
DANILOV, A., 'Pervostepennye zadachi novogo uchebnogo goda', *Narodnoe obrazovanie,* 1967, no. 9, 6-11.
EISEN, F.M., 'Ob osushchestvlenii vseobshchego srednego obrazovaniya v Estonskoi SSR', *Sovetskaya pedagogika,* 1968, no. 12, 17-27.
FOMIN, B., 'Doroga v nastoyashchuyu zhizn', *Nauka i religiya,* 1966, no. 1, 19-20.
GAEVSKAYA, K.A., 'Uchilishcha iskusstv v SSSR', in *Pedagogicheskaya entsiklopediya,* vol. 4 (M., 1968), cols. 438-440.
GAL'TSOV, S.S., and TYUL'PANOV, S.I., 'Podgotovitel'nye otdeleniya, komplektovanie i metodika', *Vestnik vysshei shkoly,* 1971, no. 3, 81-83.
GONCHAROV, N.K., 'O perspektivnom plane razvitiya narodnogo obrazovaniya v SSSR na blizhaishie 15-20 let', *Sovetskaya pedagogika,* 1957, no. 4, 10-25.
GONCHAROV, N.K., 'O vvedenii furkatsii v starshikh klassakh srednei shkoly', *Sovetskaya pedagogika,* 1958, no. 6, 12-37.
GONCHAROV, N.K., 'Yeshche raz o differentsirovannom obuchenii v starshikh klassakh obshcheobrazovatel'noi shkoly', *Sovetskaya pedagogika,* 1963, no. 2, 39-50.
GORSHKOVA, A.N., 'Svyaz' shkoly-internata s zhizn'yu', *Sovetskaya pedagogika,* 1958, no. 6, 62-69.
GORYUKHINA, E., 'Zapozdalyi Andrei Bolkonskii', *Molodoi kommunist,* 1973, no. 2, 72-79.
GREKULOVA, O., and SUDARKHINA, Z., 'Opyt provedeniya

fakul'tativnykh zanyatii', *Sovetskaya pedagogika,* 1972, no. 1, 156-158.
GUROV, Lev, 'Shkola, gde rozhdayutsya muzy', *Kul'tura i zhizn',* 1972, no. 4, 26-27.
IVANOV, Yu., and NEVSKY, V., 'Shkol'nye fakul'tativy segodnya i zavtra', *Narodnoe obrazovanie,* 1972, no. 7, 48-50.
KAIROV, I.A., 'Osnovnye voprosy organizatsii i soderzhaniya uchebno-vospitatel'noi raboty v shkolakh-internatakh', *Sovetskaya pedagogika,* 1956, no. 7, 3-16.
KAPITSA, P.L., 'Nekotorye printsipy tvorcheskogo vospitaniya i obrazovaniya sovremennoi molodezhi', *Voprosy filosofii,* 1971, no. 7, 18-24.
KASHIN, M.P., 'God raboty po vypolneniyu postanovleniya TsK KPSS i Soveta Ministrov SSR "O merakh dal'neishego uluchsheniya raboty srednei obshcheobrazovatel'noi shkoly" '. *Sovetskaya pedagogika,* 1968, no. 2, 9-20.
KASHIN, M.P., 'Ob itogakh perekhoda sovetskoi shkoly na novoe soderzhanie obshchego obrazovaniya', *Sovetskaya pedagogika,* 1976, no. 3, 24-32.
KAYUKOVA, E., 'Na razbege', *Narodnoe obrazovanie,* 1964, no. 6, 54-58.
KIENITZ, W., and BRAUER, H., 'Das neue System des Wahlunterrichts in der sowjetischen Mittelschule', *Vergleichende Pädagogik,* vol. 3 (1967), 377-385.
KISEL'GOF, S.I., and URKLIN, I.A., 'Osobennosti uchebno-vospitatel'noi raboty v shkole-internate pri LGU', in *Vzaimosvyaz' obucheniya, vospitaniya i razvitiya v yunosheskom vozraste* (L., 1967), 39-47.
KOLCHINA, I., 'V shkole-internate pri MGU', *Shkola-internat,* 1965, no. 5, 43-45.
KOLESNIKOV, N., and POTAPOV, M., 'O vstupitel'nykh ekzamenakh v fiziko-matematicheskuyu shkolu-internat pri MGU', *Nauka i zhizn,* 1969, no. 1, 110-114.
KOLMOGOROV, A.N., 'Matematika na poroge vuza', in *Nauka segodnya* (M., 1969), 242-248.
KOLMOGOROV, A.N., 'Shag v nauku', *Yunyi tekhnik,* 1972, no. 12, 34-35.
KOLMOGOROV, A.N., and YAGLOM, I.M., 'Yunoshekie matematicheskie shkoly', *Vestnik vysshei shkoly,* 1959, no. 11, 66-69.
KOVANTSOV, N.I., 'Yavlyayutsya li vrozhdennymi matematicheskie sposobnosti?', *Voprosy psikhologii,* 1965, no. 3, 150-155.
KRUPSKAYA, N.K., 'Znat' osobennosti kazhdogo raiona', in *id., Pedagogicheskie sochineniya,* vol. 8 (M., 1960), 289-298.
KRUTETSKY, V.A., 'Matematicheskie sposobnosti i ikh razvitie u shkol'nikov', *Sovetskaya pedagogika,* 1962, no. 9, 110-116.
KUHRT, Willi, and DEUBLER, Hans. 'Berufswahlvorbereitung in sozialistischen Landern', *Vergleichende Padagogik,* 1973, no. 3, 242-265.
KUKUSHKIN, S.I., 'Shkola novogo tipa', *Uchenye zapiski Ivanovskogo gosudars vennogo pedagogicheskogo instituta,* vol. XXIV (1963), 129-136.
LAVRENT'EV, M., 'Vazhnye problemy organizatsii nauki', *Vestnik*

Akademii nauk SSSR, 1962, no. 12, 15-18.

LAVRENYUK, B., 'Shkola Bol'shogo Baleta', *Sovetskaya zhenshchina,* 1972, no. 1, 29-31.

LEVIN, A.A., 'Massovye olimpiady i konkursy kak sredstvo vospitaniya poznavatel'nykh interesov', *Sovetskaya pedagogika,* 1965, no. 3, 56-60.

LITERAT, S.I., 'Iz opyta raboty novosibirskoi fiziko-matematicheskoi shkoly', *Fizika v shkole,* 1969, no. 6, 41-42.

LITERAT, S.I., 'Vyyavlyat' i razvivat' sposobnosti', *Sovetskaya pedagogika,* 1969, no. 4, 77-84.

LUK'YANOVA, A.A., 'Prepodavanie geografii na angliiskom yazyke v spetsshkole', *Geografiya v shkole,* 1972, no. 6, 54-55.

MAKSIMOVA, E., ' "Ogo!" skazali mal'chishki', *Kul'tura i zhizn'',* 1971, no. 12, 18-20.

MARTISHYUS, I.T., 'Olimpiady yunykh fizikov v Litve', *Fizika v shkole,* 1973, no. 3, 103-104.

MEDVEDEV, R., 'Ob itogakh odnogo nauchnogo eksperimenta', *Narodnoe obrazovanie,* 1963, no. 2, 122-125.

MEL'NIKOV, M.A., 'Differentsirovannoe obuchenie', in *Pedagogicheskaya entsiklopediya,* vol. 1 (M., 1964), cols. 760-761.

MEL'NIKOV, M.A., 'Opyt differentsirovannogo obucheniya v sovetskoi srednei shkole', *Sovetskaya pedagogika,* 1962, no. 9, 98-109.

MEL'NIKOV, M.A., 'Opyt differentsirovannogo obucheniya v srednei obshcheobrazovatel'noi shkole', *Sovetskaya pedagogika,* 1960, no. 8, 34-50.

MEL'NIKOV, M.A., 'Pedagogicheskaya nauka v shestoi pyatiletke', *Sovetskaya pedagogika,* 1956, no. 3, 3-14.

MOROZOVA, E., and PETRAKOV, I., 'IX Mezhdunarodnaya matematicheskaya olimpiada shkol'nikov', *Narodnoe obrazovanie,* 1967, no. 12, 120.

NIKOLAEV, A.A., 'Muzykal'noe obrazovanie', in *Pedagogicheskaya entsiklopediya,* vol. 2 (M., 1965), cols. 890-891.

NIKOLAEV, A.A., and SUKHANOV, V.V., 'Muzykal'noe obrazovanie', in *Bol'shaya sovetskaya entsiklopediya,* vol. 17 (M., 1974), 95-96.

'Novyi etap v razvitii sovetskoi shkoly', *Sovetskaya pedagogika,* 1956, no. 2, 3-14.

'Novyi priem v ZMSh', *Matematika v shkole,* 1973, no. 1, 95.

'O differentsirovannom obuchenii v starshikh klassakh srednei shkoly s proizvodstvennym obucheniem', *Sovetskaya pedagogika,* 1963, no. 7, 144.

'O perspektivakh razvitiya narodnogo obrazovaniya v SSSR', *Sovetskaya pedagogika,* 1957, no. 4, 138-142.

'Obmen mneniyami s akademikom P.L. Kapitsei', *Voprosy filosofii,* 1972, no. 9, 126-130.

'Obshchee sobranie Akademii pedagogicheskikh nauk RSFSR', *Sovetskaya pedagogika,* 1966, no. 2, 8-29.

'Obshchee sobranie APN SSSR', *Sovetskaya pedagogika,* 1976, no. 3, 149-152.

PALAMETS, Khillar, 'Spetsializirovannyi klass po istorii', *Prepodavanie istorii v shkole,* 1968, no. 5, 60-62.

PASHKOVA, L.M., 'VI Vsesoyuznaya matematicheskaya olimpiada', *Matematika v shkole,* 1972, no. 5, 68-70.

PASHKOVA, L.M., 'VII Vsesoyuznaya matematicheskaya olimpiada', *Matematika v shkole,* 1973, no. 5, 72-74.

PETRAKOV, I., 'Olimpiady shkol'nikov', *Narodnoe obrazovanie,* 1965, no. 1, 125.

PETRAKOV, I., and YASHKINA, T., 'Nauchnaya olimpiada shkol'nikov', *Narodnoe obrazovanie,* 1965, no. 9, 125-126.

PETRAKOV, I.S., and SKVORTSOV, V.A., 'XV Mezhdunarodnaya matematicheskaya olimpiada', *Matematika v shkole,* 1973, no. 6, 63-69.

PETROV, N., 'O novoi sisteme obshchestvennogo vospitaniya', *Sovetskaya pedagogika,* 1956, no. 6, 3-12.

PETRUSHKIN, S., 'Za uglublennye znaniya', *Narodnoe obrazovanie,* 1975, no. 10, 24-25.

'Podbor i podgotovka nauchnykh kadrov — vazhnaya gosudarstvennaya zadacha', *Sovetskaya pedagogika,* 1962, no. 7, 3-10.

POLYAKOVA, E., 'Bol'shaya Moskva, Medvedkovo', *Novyi mir,* 1967, no. 10, 135-154.

POPOV, V.D., 'Nekotorye sotsiolo-pedagogicheskie problemy vtorogodnichestva i otseva', in GUROVA, R.G. (ed.), *Sotsiologicheskie problemy obrazovaniya i vospitaniya* (M., 1973), 22-37.

POPOV, V.V., and SADYKHOV, S.N., 'Matematicheskie olimpiady v Azerbaidzhane', *Matematika v shkole,* 1972, no. 5, 75.

POTAPOV, M., and ROZOV, N., 'Shkola-internat pri MGU', *Nauka i zhizn',* 1968, no. 4, 69-71.

RUDNEV, P., 'K voprosu o "differentsiatsii obshchego obrazovaniya" v srednei shkole', *Narodnoe obrazovanie,* 1963, no. 1, 12-22.

RUSAKOV, B., 'Fakul'tativnye zanyatiya po osnovam NOT shkol'nika', *Narodnoe obrazovanie,* 1972, no. 2, 41-43.

RUTKEVICH, M.N., 'Sotsial'nye istochniki vosproizvodstva sovetskoi intelligentsii', *Voprosy filosofii,* 1967, no. 6, 15-23.

'VII [Sed'maya] Vsesoyuznaya fizicheskaya olimpiada shkol'nikov', *Fizika v shkole,* 1973, no. 4, 108-111.

SEMIN, S.N., 'V Vsesoyuznaya olimpiada yunykh fizikov', *Fizika v shkole,* 1971, no. 6, 72-77.

SHVARTSBURD, S.I., and FIRSOV, V.V., 'O kharakternykh osobennostyakh fakul'tativnykh zanyatii', *Matematika v shkole,* 1972, no. 1, 55-59.

'Sovetskaya shkola na novom etape', *Sovetskaya pedagogika,* 1967, no. 1, 3-13.

SOYA, N., 'Khudozhestvennaya shkola-internat', *Sem'ya i shkola,* 1958, no. 3, 33.

STREZIKOZIN, V., 'O nekotorykh voprosakh dal'neishego sovershenstvovaniya uchebnogo protsessa', *Narodnoe obrazovanie,* 1965, no. 7, 8-15.

TRIFONOV, Yurii, 'Obmen', *Novyi mir,* 1969, no. 12, 29-65.

TSVETKOVA, Z.M., 'O povyshenii kachestva prepodavaniya inostrannykh yazykov v shkole i v vuze', *Sovetskaya pedagogika*, 1958, no. 3, 35-42.

USPENSKY, V., 'Starsheklassnikam — pedagogicheskie znaniya', *Narodnoe obrazovanie*, 1967, no. 9, 74-77.

'V byuro otdeleniya didaktiki i chastnykh metodik APN SSSR', *Sovetskaya pedagogika*, 1967, no. 6, 152-154.

'V Ministerstve prosveshcheniya SSSR', *Narodnoe obrazovanie*, 1969, no. 2, 122-123.

VASIL'EV, N.B., *et al.*, 'Zaochnaya matematicheskaya shkola ob"yavlyaet priem uchashchikhsya', *Matematika v shkole*, 1972, no. 1, 60-61.

VOLKOV, Genrikh, 'Chelovek i budushchee nauki', *Novyi mir*, 1965, no. 3, 194-212.

VOLKOV, V.A., and LOMAKIN, Yu. V., 'Letnie matematicheskie shkoly na severo-zapade RSFSR', *Matematika v shkole*, 1972, no. 1, 93.

'Vsesoyuznaya konferentsiya "Opyt provedeniya fakul'tativnykh zanyatii po osnovam nauk v srednei shkole"', *Matematika v shkole*, 1972, no. 1, 49-55.

'Vtoraya Vsesoyuznaya olimpiada shkol'nikov', *Narodnoe obrazovanie*, 1969, no. 2 123-124.

YARANTSEV, Boris, 'Neevklidova pedagogika', *Sem'ya i shkola*, 1967, no. 12, 26-28.

ZAGVYAZINSKY, V., 'O differentsirovannom podkhode', *Narodnoe obrazovanie*, 1968, no. 10, 85-87.

'Zakon o shkole v deistvii', *Sovetskaya pedagogika*, 1963, no. 12, 9-10.

'Zasedanie Soveta molodykh uchenykh pri TsK VLKSM', *Fizika v shkole*, 1972, no. 2, 109-110.

ZEMTSOV, L.G., 'Nekotorye sotsial'nye aspekty vseobshchego srednego obrazovaniya', in GUROVA, R.G. (ed.), *Sotsiologicheskie problemy obrazovaniya i vospitaniya* (M., 1973), 6-22.

ZHDANOV, Yu. A., 'Nazrevshie problemy universitetskogo obrazovaniya', *Vestnik vysshei shkoly*, 1961, no. 5, 59-63.

ZOSIMOVSKY, A.V., 'Interesnyi eksperiment', *Sovetskaya pedagogika*, 1965, no. 6, 46-56.

ZVEREV, I.D., 'Problemy fakul'tativnykh zanyatii v srednei shkole', *Sovetskaya pedagogika*, 1971, no. 4, 43-49.

ZYUBIN, L.M., 'Psikhologicheskii aspekt problemy perevospitaniya pedagogicheski zapushchennykh detei i nesovershennoletnykh pravonarushitelei', *Voprosy psikhologii*, 1969, no. 3, 132-143.

B.   Western

ANWEILER, Oskar, 'Diskussion über die Differenzierung der Mittelschule', *Informationsdienst zum Bildungswesen in Osteuropa*, issue no. 7 (1964), 8-16.

ANWEILER, Oskar, 'Educational Policy and Social Structure in the Soviet Union', in MEISSNER, Boris (ed.), *Social Change in the Soviet Union* (Notre Dame and London, 1972), 173-210.

AVIS, George, 'The Sociology of Soviet Higher Education: a Review of Recent Empirical Research', in HARASYMIW, Bohdan (ed.), *Education and the Mass Media in the Soviet Union and Eastern Europe* (New York, 1976), 39-64.

BOGUSLAVSKY, G.W., 'Psychological Research in Soviet Education', *Science,* vol. 125 (1957), 915-918.

BUCK, R. Creighton, 'A Look at Mathematical Competitions', *American Mathematical Monthly,* vol. 66, no. 3 (March 1959), 201-212.

BUTENSCHÖN, Marianna, 'Aber manche sind gleicher', *Die Zeit,* 1976, no. 36, 52.

CAREY, David W., 'Developments in Soviet Education', in *Soviet Economic Prospects for the Seventies* (Washington, D.C., 1973), 594-636.

'The Curriculum for the Eight-year and Secondary Schools of the RSFSR', *Soviet Education,* vol. II, no. 3 (January 1960), 30-31 (translated from *Narodnoe obrazovanie,* 1959, no. 11).

DUNSTAN, John, 'Curriculum Change and the Soviet School', *Journal of Curriculum Studies,* vol. 9, no. 2 (November 1977), 111-123.

DUNSTAN, John, 'An Educational Experiment: Soviet Mathematics and Physics Boarding Schools', *Soviet Studies,* vol. XXVII, no. 4 (October 1975), 545-573.

DZERZHINSKY, I., 'Let us Talk about our Union', *Current Digest of the Soviet Press,* vol. VIII, no. 12 (1956), 35-36 (translated from *Sovetskaya muzyka,* 1955, no. 10).

EICHBERG, Ekkehard, 'Das Problem der Differenzierung in der sowjetischen allgemeinbildenden Schule', *Die Deutsche Schule,* 1968, no. 5, 337-344.

FITZPATRICK, Sheila, 'Cultural Revolution in Russia 1928-1932', *Journal of Contemporary History,* vol. 9, no. 1 (January 1974), 33-52.

FRIEDL, Berthold C., 'Shcherba and the Status of Foreign Languages in the USSR and the USA', *Modern Language Journal,* vol. XLVI, no. 7 (November 1962), 292-298.

GARRETT, G., 'Visit to a Moscow School, September 1963', *Mathematical Gazette,* vol. 48 (1964), 209-211.

GLOWKA, Detlef, 'Das sowjetische Schulwesen am Beginn einer neuen Etappe?', *Neue Sammlung,* vol. 7, no. 3 (May-June 1967), 203-222.

GLOWKA, Detlef, 'Das Verhältnis zwischen Wissenschaft und Curriculumreform in der UdSSR', *Bildung und Erziehung,* vol. 24, no. 5 (September-October 1971), 474-484.

GNEDENKO, B.V., 'Mathematical Education in the USSR', *American Mathematical Monthly,* vol. 64 (1957), 369-408.

GREENBERG, Pearl, 'Art Education in Russia', *School Arts,* vol. 57, no. 10 (June 1958), 9-12.

'Improving Soviet Foreign Language Training', *School and Society,* vol. 93, no. 2259 (1965), 230.

INKELES, Alex, 'Social Stratification and Mobility in the Soviet Union', in BENDIX, Reinhard, and LIPSET, Seymour Martin (eds.), *Class, Status and Power* (London, 2nd edn., 1967), 516-526.

KAIROV, I.A., 'Basic Questions relating to School Reorganization', *Soviet Education*, vol. 1, no. 3 (January 1959), 5-12 (translated from *Sovetskaya pedagogika*, 1958, no. 11).

KASER, M., 'Salient Features in the History of State Boarding Schools', *Annuaire de l'URSS 1968* (Paris, 1969), 131-139.

LANE, David, 'The Impact of Revolution: the Case of Selection of Students for Higher Education in Soviet Russia', *Sociology*, vol. 7 (1973), 241-252.

LAVRENTIEV, Mikhail [Lavrent'ev], 'A School for Young Mathematicians in Siberia', *Prospects*, vol. 5 (1975), no. 2, 147-164.

'Mathematics in a Soviet Boarding School', *School and Society*, vol. 93, no. 2261 (1965), 263-264.

MILLER, Russell, 'From Russia with Laughs', *Radio Times*, 21 December 1974-3 January 1975, 108.

MITTER, Wolfgang, 'Einheitlichkeit und Differenzierung als Problem der sowjetischen Schulreform', in ANWEILER, Oskar (ed.), *Bildungsreformen in Osteuropa* (Stuttgart, 1969), 108-140.

MITTER, Wolfgang, 'Erziehung in den Vereinigten Staaten und der Sowjetunion', *Bildung und Erziehung*, vol. 20, no. 3 (May-June, 1967), 205-222.

MITTER, Wolfgang, 'Schule und Bildung in der Sowjetunion im Widerstreit der Meinungen', *Neue Sammlung*, vol. 8, no. 6 (November-December 1968), 557-569.

MÖLLER, Dietrich, 'Das Sparta der Wissenschaft', *Der siebente Tag: Wochenendbeilage der Hannoverschen Allgemeinen Zeitung*, 8/9 November 1975.

MOSKALSKAYA, O.I., 'The Development of Foreign Language Study in the USSR', in ABLIN, Fred (ed.), *Education in the USSR*, vol. II (New York, 1963), 129-135 (translated from *Inostrannye yazyki v shkole*, 1962, no. 1).

'Observations of an IIEP Mission to the USSR' — see *Educational Planning* . . . in the previous section.

OWEN, A., and WATSON, F.R., 'The Mathematical Boarding Schools of the USSR', *Mathematical Gazette*, vol. LVIII, no. 405 (October 1974), 188-195.

OWEN, A., and WATSON, F.R., 'Encouraging Young Mathematicians in the USSR', *Bulletin of the IMA*, vol. II, no. 6/7, (June/July 1975), 133-137.

PARKER, Franklin, and UNGER, Paul (eds.), 'Recent Events in World Education', *Comparative Education Review*, vol. 10, no. 3 (October 1966), 514-524.

PENNAR, Jaan, 'Five Years after Khrushchev's School Reforms', *Comparative Education Review*, vol. 8, no. 1 (June 1964), 73-77.

PLAUD, Yvonne, 'Notes prises "sur le vif", septembre 1962', *Aspects de l'école soviétique*, 1962, no. 6, 21-23.

PRESS, Billie K., 'Education of the Gifted in the USSR', *Exceptional Children*, vol. 30, no. 6 (February 1963), 241-244.

READ, Gerald H., 'The Akademgorodok of Novosibirsk', *Intellect*, vol. 101, no. 2343 (October 1972), 54-56.

REITMAN, Walter R., 'Some Soviet Investigations of Thinking, Problem Solving, and Related Areas', in BAUER, R.A. (ed.), *Some Views on Soviet Psychology* (Washington, D.C., 1962), 29-61.

RUTKEVICH, M.N., and FILIPPOV, F.R., 'Social Sources of Recruitment to the Intelligentsia', in YANOWITCH, Murray, and FISHER, Wesley A. (eds.), *Social Stratification and Mobility in the USSR* (New York, 1973), 241-274 (translated from *Sotsial'nye peremeshcheniya* (M., 1970)).

SCHWARTZ, Joel J., and KEECH,William R., 'Group Influence and the Policy Process in the Soviet Union', *American Political Science Review,* vol. 62 (1968), 840-851.

SHARIPOV, A., 'The Main Thing is to Prepare the Youth for Productive Labour', *Soviet Education,* vol. 1, no. 4 (February 1959), 32-34 (translated from *Sovetskaya pedagogika,* 1958, no. 12).

SIMON, Joan, 'Differentiation of Secondary Education in the USSR', *Forum for the Discussion of New Trends in Education,* vol. 11, no. 3 (Summer 1969), 87-90.

SNOW, C.P., 'Elitism and Excellence', *Mathematics Teacher,* vol. LXII, no. 6 (October 1969), 505-509 (reprinted from *New Science Teacher,* vol. 12, no. 1 (October 1968)).

SOKOLOVSKY, Yu.,'Ein Laboratorium umfangreichen Forschens', in MITTER, Wolfgang (ed.),*Das sowjetische Schulwesen* (Frankfurt-am-Main, 1970), 137-140 (abridged and translated from *Za nauku v Sibiri,* 1968, no. 14).

STEWART, Philip D., 'Soviet Interest Groups and the Policy Process: the Repeal of Production Education', *World Politics,* vol. 22 (1969-70), 29-50.

SUKHOMLINSKY, V., 'Urgent Problems of the Theory and Practice of Education', *Soviet Education,* vol. IV, no. 7 (May 1962), 3-12 (translated from *Narodnoe obrazovanie,* 1961, no. 10).

SZIANAWSKI, Ignacy, 'Die vierte Schulreform in der UdSSR', *Bildung und Erziehung,* vol. 22, no. 4 (July-August 1969), 253-264.

THWAITES, Bryan, 'Mathematical Education in Russian Schools', *Mathematical Gazette,* vol. LII, no. 382 (December 1968), 319-327.

WIRSZUP, Izaak, 'The First Two International Mathematical Olympiads for Students of Communist Countries', *American Mathematical Monthly,* vol. 9, no. 2 (February 1962), 150-155.

WIRSZUP, Izaak, 'The School Mathematics Circle and Olympiads at Moscow State University', *Mathematics Teacher,* vol. LVI, no. 4 (April 1963), 194-210.

III.   OTHER SERIALS

(full citations in the notes; the more important titles bear an asterisk)

A.   **Soviet newspapers**

Izvestiya*
Kazakhstanskaya pravda

Komsomol'skaya pravda
Literaturnaya gazeta
Moskovskii komsomolets
Pravda*
Sovetskaya kul'tura
Sovetskaya Rossiya
Sovetskii sport
Trud
Uchitel'skaya gazeta*

B.   **Other Soviet serials**

Sbornik prikazov i instruktsii Ministerstva prosveshcheniya RSFSR*
Spravochnik partiinogo rabotnika

C.   **Western serials**

Morning Star
The Times
Times Educational Supplement*

Glossary
of terms not defined in text or notes

Academy of Pedagogical Sciences Leading educational research organization. Founded 1943. In 1966 became all-Union institution with enhanced coordinating role.

Academy of Sciences USSR's highest research institution ('sciences' means fields of academic study). Founded in 1724. Also coordinates activities of Union republic academies of sciences (these exist in all republics except RSFSR and Moldavia).

APN *(Akademiya pedagogicheskikh nauk) see* Academy of Pedagogical Sciences.

Collective Peer-group, normally with additional implications of solidarity.

Collegium High-level consultative body established in a ministry to advise on policy.

Complete secondary school Secondary general school, with entry at 7-plus, providing whole basic compulsory course (ten years except in Baltic republics, where it is eleven years).

Eight-year school *see* Incomplete secondary school

FZU *(shkola fabrichno-zavodskogo uchenichestva) see* Industrial apprentice school.

Incomplete secondary school Secondary general school, with entry at 7-plus, providing primary (3-year) and middle (5-year) stages of basic compulsory course. These stages covered four and three years respectively in the 1950s and four each in the 1960s.

Industrial apprentice school Vocational school, also with general subject teaching, first set up in 1920 with 14-plus entry and 4-year course (shortened in 1926 to 2-3 years).

Komsomol (also **VLKSM**) Young Communist League: organization for young people of 14-15 to 26-27. Branch may be formed in any educational institution or place of employment where there are at least three members.

New Soviet Person (or **Man**) Model citizen: politically active, collectively minded, zealous for socialist internationalism, atheistic, hard-working, cheerful and healthy. From later 1930s, traits of purposefulness and self-discipline increasingly emphasized and patriotism added, along with epithet Soviet.

Octobrists Informal organization for children of primary age (7 to 9-10). Divided into 'stars' *(zvezdochki)* of four to six members. Attached to Pioneer brigades *(see* Pioneers).

Pedagogical institute Higher education establishment concerned with the greater part of teacher training.

Pioneers Mass organization for children and young people aged 10-15. Largest unit is 'brigade' *(druzhina)*, identified with school and divided into 'detachments' *(otryady)* of ten or more members. Detachment, usually coinciding with school class, is in turn divided into 'links' *(zven'ya)* of five to ten pupils. Pioneer organization may also function at children's place of residence.

RSFSR Russian Soviet Federative Socialist Republic. Largest of the 15 'Union republics' constituting the USSR.

Ten-year school *see* Complete secondary school.

Index